Penguin Handbooks
The Penguin Book of the Motorcycle

Geoff Francis was born in Droitwich, near Worcester, in 1949. He owned his first bike at the age of eleven and learnt to ride it on the farm where he was brought up. He has been a motorcycle enthusiast ever since and worked for several companies before setting up his own motorcycle repair business in Cardiff. His hobbies include oil painting and off-road motorcycling with his dirt bike. He has also completed a season's production racing on a 750 cc. Triumph bike, but found that the ground is much harder than the human body when the two are brought together at speed and now prefers the role of spectator.

Paul Frost was educated at Sheffield Polytechnic and University College, Cardiff, where he obtained an M.Sc. in Industrial Relations in 1978. He has carried out research on several projects in this field and is the co-author of a number of publications, including *The British Manager in Profile* (1981) and *Managers in Focus* (1982). From 1981 to 1983 he was a lecturer in Industrial Relations at Brighton Polytechnic. After a time as U.K. Director of AFS International Programmes he has now returned to Brighton Polytechnic.

D1331455

Geoff Francis and Paul Frost

THE PENGUIN BOOK OF THE
Motorcycle

A GUIDE TO MAINTENANCE
AND PROBLEM SOLVING

PENGUIN BOOKS

Penguin Books Ltd, Harmondsworth, Middlesex, England
Viking Penguin Inc., 40 West 23rd Street, New York, New York 10010, U.S.A.
Penguin Books Australia Ltd, Ringwood, Victoria, Australia
Penguin Books Canada Ltd, 2801 John Street, Markham, Ontario, Canada L3R 1B4
Penguin Books (N.Z.) Ltd, 182–190 Wairau Road, Auckland 10, New Zealand

Published in Penguin Books 1985

Typeset, printed and bound in Great Britain by
Hazell Watson & Viney Limited,
Member of the BPCC Group,
Aylesbury, Bucks
Set in 9pt Helvetica

Thanks, Steve

Thanks, Fabienne, for introducing me to motorcycles

P.F.

Thanks, Jan, for being there and being patient

G.F.

CONTENTS

INTRODUCTION 9

1 ENGINES: THE BASIC DIFFERENCES 11

2 MAINTENANCE AND SERVICING 22

3 SOLVING ENGINE PROBLEMS 87

4 ENGINE FAILURE PROBLEMS 90

5 ENGINE PERFORMANCE PROBLEMS 146

6 ELECTRICAL PROBLEMS 199

7 TIPS AND TRICKS 229

GLOSSARY OF MOTORCYCLING TERMS 273

USEFUL ADDRESSES 286

YOUR BIKE'S SPECIFICATIONS 295

INDEX 299

INTRODUCTION

This book deals with the repair and maintenance of motorcycles – not a new idea you might think, and to some extent you'd be right. What is new, however, is the way we have gone about dealing with the issues involved. It begins with what you can reasonably be expected to know of the situation – the symptoms accompanying the problem – and leads you through a series of possible causes and solutions to the actual source of the problem, enabling you to repair it simply, effectively and, perhaps most importantly, cheaply.

The book is designed for the riders of all motorcycles, regardless of the motorcycle's make, size or engine design, or the rider's prior motorcycling experiences, mechanical skill or knowledge.

As the popularity of motorcycling continues its revival, and as workshop charges move higher and higher, the number of motorcyclists *wanting* to maintain and repair their own motorcycles is growing. Unfortunately, however, despite the long-standing tradition of motorcyclists doing their own work, increases in motorcycle sophistication and complexity are now causing many riders to be apprehensive about such tasks.

The situation is not made any easier by the insistence of manufacturers and dealers that you take even the simplest of jobs to them – for obvious reasons – and by the fact that many of the repair manuals currently available are somewhat incomprehensible.

It is clear that a book specifically designed to provide an effective yet simple method of fault diagnosis and solution is needed by both the old and the new motorcycling fraternity. This book sets out to fulfil that need.

The modern motorcycle is already a complex piece of engineering, and consequently no one book can hope to cover the precise detail of all the work likely to be required by the enormous range of new and used motorcycles on the roads today. This book, therefore, is not designed to replace the repair manuals currently available, but to complement them and to compensate for their shortcomings.

The first chapter 'Engines: the Basic Differences', provides a brief explanation of the two types of engine commonly used in motorcycles, their different operational cycles and their various characteristics. Chapter 2 sets out to describe the items in the typical service schedule you should follow if you are to maintain your motorcycle and keep it in a satisfactory operating condition.

The procedures for resolving engine problems – both failure and performance problems – and electrical faults are covered in Chapters 3–6.

In the final chapter a series of hints and tips are gathered together, under three principal headings: (1) *maintenance and repair*; (2) *engine efficiency*;

and (3) *motorcyling in general*. Within these sections they are listed alphabetically – so as to pass on to you some of the 'tricks of the trade' that are regularly used in motorcycle workshops throughout the country.

After a glossary of motorcycling terms we have provided several pages titled 'Your Bike's Specifications'. The idea here is that you can gather together the information most frequently needed to maintain or repair a motorcycle (which is normally scattered through the workshop manual) on one page.

The two key ways of using this book are: (1) to satisfy your general interest in motorcycles and their operation by reading it from cover to cover; and (2) to use it as a reference book which can be opened at the appropriate page to help you solve a problem or carry out regular maintenance.

The information on how to use each chapter is set out in its own introduction, when necessary.

Finally, as a word of caution, motorcycles can be dangerous. Many accidents occur through incorrect maintenance and repair, so take your time and be thorough. Double-check each stage as you go along. Although we hope your motorcycling days will be trouble-free, if they are not we feel confident that the solution will be in this book.

Remember: if you look after your motorcycle, it will look after you.

Happy motorcycling
G.F. and P.F.

CHAPTER ONE
ENGINES: THE BASIC DIFFERENCES

Outwardly there are substantial differences in the engines used to power modern motorcycles. From one to six cylinders are used to create engine capacities which range from 50 cc. to 1,300 cc. The configurations of these cylinders are numerous: singles, parallel twins, flat twins, in-line V-twins and transverse V-twins, and in-line three-, four- or six-cylinder engines. They can all be seen on our roads, and some of these may be either liquid-cooled or air-cooled.

Despite these differences, however, the basic components of an engine – the piston, cylinder, connecting rods, crankshaft and crankcases – although now combined in a far more sophisticated manner remain the same. Moreover, except for the rotary engine, every internal combustion engine uses these fundamental components, and does so in basically the same way (Figure 1): petrol vapour is compressed by a piston at the top of a closed cylinder, at a predetermined and critical point a spark occurs to ignite the mixture, and the force of the explosion propels the piston downwards. Because the piston is connected to the crankshaft by a connecting rod, the shaft rotates and provides the basic motion to drive the motorcycle (Figures 2–5). Heavy flywheels then continue the movement of the crankshaft – which pushes the piston back up the cylinder, expelling the waste gases.

However, because there are basically two methods of expelling these waste gases and drawing in fresh mixture, engines are described as being two-strokes or four-strokes. Understanding this distinction will make any regular maintenance or problem solving so much easier. Let us be clear at the outset then: the 'two' and the 'four' describe the number of times the piston moves up or down the cylinder during one operating cycle, not the number of cylinders – nor any other feature of the motorcycle's design. In principle you can have two-stroke or four-stroke engines with any

piston rising; spark occurs

combustion begins

combustion continues rapidly

combustion complete, forcing the piston back down

fuel/air mixture

mixture burning

Figure 1 Normal combustion

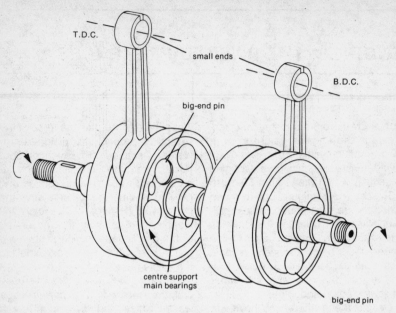

Figure 2 A twin-cylinder crankshaft; 180° apposed

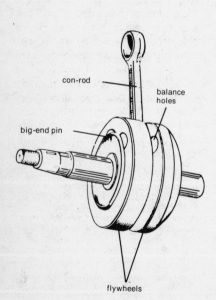

Figure 3a A single-cylinder crankshaft

number of cylinders. (Although to date, whereas four-strokes have used up to six, two-strokes have not commonly used more than three cylinders; the exceptions to this are the four-cylinder two-strokes used in the 500 cc. Grand Prix racing machines and a 125 cc. five-cylinder which was also developed only for racing.) One stroke is a complete movement of the piston from the top of the cylinder, known to mechanics as top dead centre (T.D.C.), to the bottom, known as bottom dead centre (B.D.C.). The key difference between the two types of engine is that the two-stroke fires *every two strokes* of the piston (or if you prefer, *every time* the piston is at the top of the cylinder) and the four-stroke only fires *every four strokes* of the piston (or if you prefer, *every other time* the piston is at the top of the cylinder).

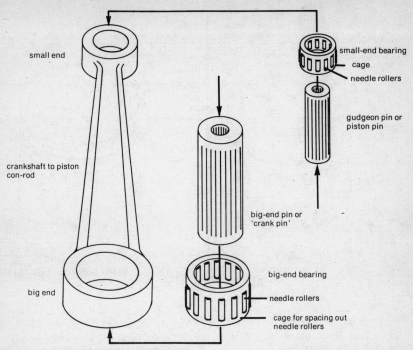

small end

crankshaft to piston
con-rod

big end

small-end bearing

cage

needle rollers

gudgeon pin or
piston pin

big-end pin or
'crank pin'

big-end bearing

needle rollers

cage for spacing out
needle rollers

Figure 3b Big ends and small ends

Figure 4 'Shell' or 'plain' bearing crankshaft layout (single cylinder)

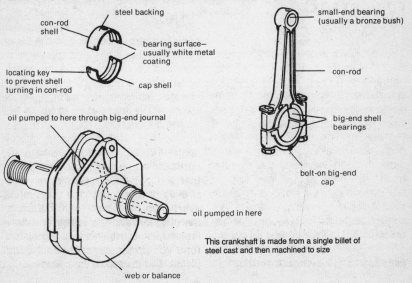

steel backing

con-rod
shell

bearing surface—
usually white metal
coating

locating key
to prevent shell
turning in con-rod

cap shell

small-end bearing
(usually a bronze bush)

con-rod

big-end shell
bearings

oil pumped to here through big-end journal

bolt-on big-end
cap

oil pumped in here

This crankshaft is made from a single billet of
steel cast and then machined to size

web or balance

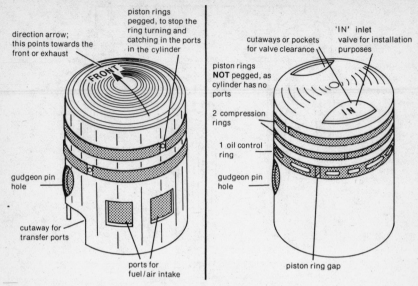

Figure 5 left: *two-stroke piston;* right: *four-stroke piston*

Let's look in a little more detail at how each type operates.

FOUR-STROKE

OPERATIONAL CYCLE

The operational cycle of the four-stroke is carried out in four distinct operations (Figure 6): (1) inlet (or induction); (2) compression; (3) combustion (or power); and (4) exhaust. Each occurs on a separate stroke of the piston. The expulsion of waste gases and intake of fresh mixture is done through valves in the cylinder head. The head is equipped with an inlet and an exhaust valve, each being mechanically opened and closed in a sequence determined by the position of the piston in the operational cycle.

If we begin by assuming that the piston is at T.D.C., ready to begin its induction stroke, we can follow a cycle through from start to finish.

1. INLET (OR INDUCTION) STROKE

The first stroke begins with the piston at T.D.C., the inlet valve open and the exhaust valve closed. As the crankshaft turns, the piston is drawn down by the connecting rod, reducing the air pressure in the cylinder to below that in the atmosphere.

Because of this drop in internal pressure, air is drawn through the carburettor (where it is mixed with petrol) and via the open inlet valve into the combustion chamber. This intake of mixture continues until the piston reaches B.D.C., when the inlet valve is closed. In short, the induction stroke involves the piston moving from T.D.C. to B.D.C. with the inlet valve open.

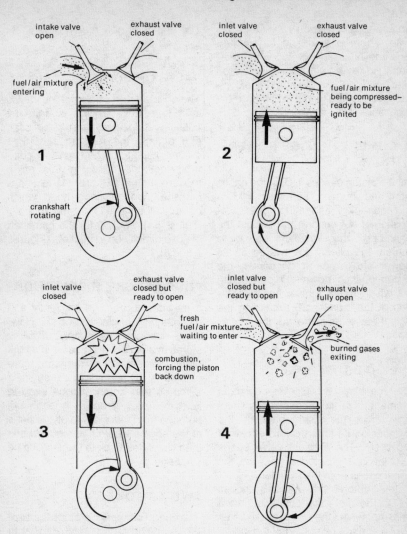

intake valve open

exhaust valve closed

fuel/air mixture entering

crankshaft rotating

1

inlet valve closed

exhaust valve closed

fuel/air mixture being compressed— ready to be ignited

2

inlet valve closed

exhaust valve closed but ready to open

combustion, forcing the piston back down

3

inlet valve closed but ready to open

fresh fuel/air mixture waiting to enter

exhaust valve fully open

burned gases exiting

4

Figure 6 Four-stroke cycle

2. COMPRESSION STROKE

With the crankshaft continuing its momentum, the piston now begins its first upward stroke of the cycle, and with both valves now closed the combustion chamber is sealed.

As a result the petrol/air mixture, trapped between the piston crown and the cylinder head, will be compressed to about one tenth its original volume by the time the piston reaches T.D.C. (Exactly how much the volume is compressed will be determined by the engine's compression ratio, and this differs from one engine to another. See the Glossary for more information.) However, just before the piston reaches T.D.C. on this stroke the compressed mixture is ignited by an electrical spark from the spark plug.

3. COMBUSTION (OR POWER) STROKE

As the piston passes T.D.C. the gases from the burning petrol/air mixture expand rapidly, and (although its combustion is not uniform throughout the chamber) the resultant pressure thrusts the piston downwards on its power stroke. As it descends, the piston pushes down the connecting rod which in turn accelerates the rotation of the crankshaft, producing the actual power and drive for the motorcycle.

4. EXHAUST STROKE

On reaching B.D.C. the spinning momentum of the crankshaft flywheel now forces the piston back up the cylinder on its final upward stroke of the cycle. The exhaust valve opens and the rising piston expels the hot spent gases from the cylinder.

Just before the piston reaches T.D.C. the inlet valve opens and, for a brief moment at the end of the exhaust stroke and the beginning of the induction stroke, both valves are open at the same time. This momentary opening of both valves is called valve 'overlap' and allows the exiting exhaust gases to be flushed out by the incoming fresh mixture of petrol and air. Then, as the piston reaches T.D.C., the exhaust valve closes, and a cycle of operations has been completed.

The engine is now ready to begin its cycle again.

VALVE OPERATION

The opening and closing of the valves in a four-stroke engine is done by pushing them away from their seat, and against the resistance of their retaining springs. The two most common methods of doing this on a modern motorcycle are: (1) to use a camshaft, in the cylinder head, which operates the valves by using 'rockers' (Figure 8a); and (2) for the camshaft to push directly on to buckets (Figures 7 and 8b).

FOUR-STROKE LUBRICATION

If they are to perform efficiently and smoothly, all engines need oil. However, although the supply of oil is stored in a variety of places – in a tank under the seat, in the frame, or, more commonly these days, in the engine's sump so that it can also be used to lubricate the gearbox – it is always pumped from this store to all the parts of the engine where it is required and then circulated back to the store to be used again.

TWO-STROKE

The operational principles of the two-stroke engine are entirely different to those of the four-stroke. The complete operational cycle is carried out in only two strokes of the piston instead of four, hence the name, giving the engine a power stroke on *each* revolution of the crankshaft rather than every *other* revolution.

Moreover, when compared to the complexities – especially the mech-

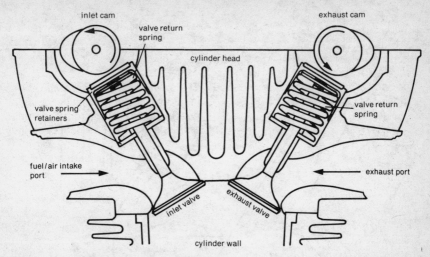

inlet cam

exhaust cam

valve return spring

cylinder head

valve spring retainers

valve return spring

fuel / air intake port

exhaust port

inlet valve

exhaust valve

cylinder wall

Figure 7 Four-stroke valve arrangement

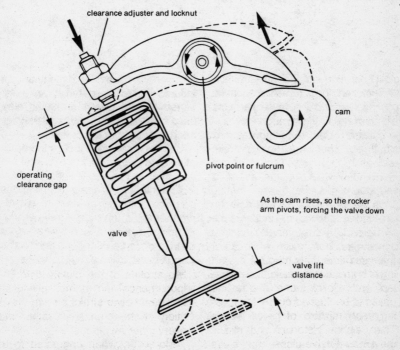

clearance adjuster and locknut

cam

operating clearance gap

pivot point or fulcrum

As the cam rises, so the rocker arm pivots, forcing the valve down

valve

valve lift distance

Figure 8a Rocker-arm layout

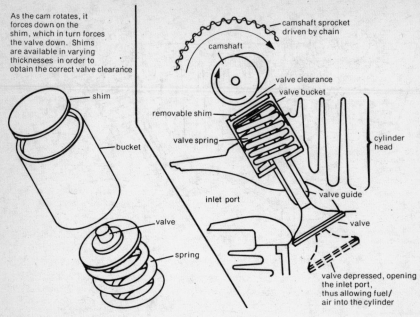

As the cam rotates, it forces down on the shim, which in turn forces the valve down. Shims are available in varying thicknesses in order to obtain the correct valve clearance

shim

bucket

valve

spring

camshaft sprocket driven by chain

camshaft

valve clearance

valve bucket

removable shim

valve spring

cylinder head

inlet port

valve guide

valve

valve

valve depressed, opening the inlet port, thus allowing fuel/ air into the cylinder

Figure 8b Rocker-arm layout

anical operation – of the four-stroke, a two-stroke engine is remarkably subtle in conception and simple in operation. Instead of breathing through valves in the cylinder head, requiring complex actuating mechanisms, the two-stroke breathes through holes (ports) cut into the cylinder wall, and the piston is used to form a sliding valve – that is, as the piston moves up and down in the cylinder, it covers or uncovers the various ports and so inhales mixture and expels spent gases, while either compressing a fresh charge or powering the crankshaft. Indeed, the operational cycle of the two-stroke engine does involve different operations taking place simultaneously: while one stroke combines the power stroke in the cylinder with a compression stroke in the crankcase, the other stroke combines a compression stroke in the

cylinder with what is essentially an induction stroke in the crankcase. Moreover, the power stroke is also used to exhaust old gases and transfer fresh charge from the crankcase.

It will help you to visualize the operational sequence of the two-stroke if you refer to Figures 9 and 10, which indicate the positions of the various ports cut into the cylinder of a two-stroke engine. Highest in the cylinder is the exhaust port, then a little further down are the transfer ports and finally, lowest in the cylinder, is the inlet port.

If we begin by assuming that the piston is at T.D.C. we can look in more detail at the two-stroke's operational cycle.

FIRST STROKE

With the piston approaching T.D.C.

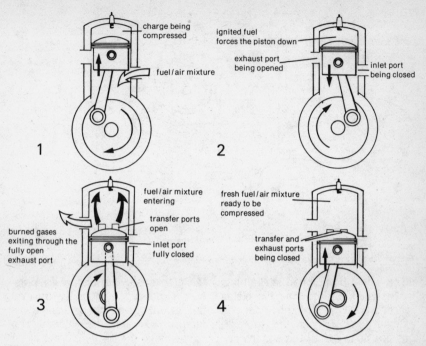

charge being compressed

fuel/air mixture

1

ignited fuel forces the piston down

exhaust port being opened

inlet port being closed

2

fuel/air mixture entering

transfer ports open

inlet port fully closed

burned gases exiting through the fully open exhaust port

3

fresh fuel/air mixture ready to be compressed

transfer and exhaust ports being closed

4

Figure 9 Two-stroke cycle

the previous mixture is now com- pressed at the top of the combustion chamber and ready to be ignited by the spark plug. When ignited, the gases from the burning mixture expand and force the piston down the cylinder, transmitting power to the crankshaft and the motorcycle.

Almost immediately after the piston begins to descend, its lower edge closes the inlet port, trapping a charge of fresh vaporized mixture (which was drawn into the crankcase by the pis- ton's preceding upward stroke) in the crankcase.

As the still expanding gases con- tinue to force the piston downwards, its underside now begins to compress the trapped mixture. Towards the end of this down-stroke the top of the piston uncovers the exhaust port and

the hot gases, under pressure in the cylinder, rush out through the open vent. Only a split-second later the still descending piston uncovers the vent of (usually) two passages running from the upper part of the cylinder to the crankcase. These are known as the transfer ports. Because it is still being compressed the fresh mixture, until now trapped in the crankcase, is forced up the transfer port and into the cylinder.

At the cylinder end these ports are angled towards each other so that the two streams of vapour collide on enter- ing and are deflected upwards and away from the (still open) exhaust port. This is important because the exhaust port, being the first to open, has to be the last to close, and if the transferred vapour mixture were not diverted, too

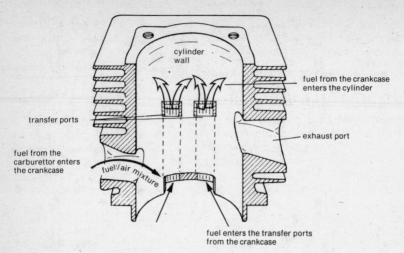

Figure 10 *Port arrangement: two-stroke engine*

much would be pumped straight into the exhaust. By the time the piston reaches B.D.C. both the transfer and exhaust ports are open, the old waste gas has been exhausted and the cylinder is full of fresh mixture.

SECOND STROKE

Having been given added momentum by the piston being thrust down on its power stroke, and because of the inertia from the heavy flywheel, the crankshaft continues revolving and now starts to push the piston back up the cylinder. As the piston rises, its upper edge first covers the transfer ports, and then the exhaust port. Immediately these ports are closed the ascending piston begans to compress the vaporized mixture now trapped in the combustion chamber.

On approaching T.D.C. the piston's lower portion uncovers the inlet port (which is vented into the crankcase). Because the piston's movement upwards has increased the volume of the crankcase, the internal air pressure is reduced. Immediately the inlet port is uncovered, therefore, the difference between the internal and atmospheric pressures causes air to be drawn through the carburettor (where again, as with the four-stroke, it becomes mixed with petrol) and into the crankcase, below the piston.

Just before the piston reaches T.D.C. the compressed mixture above the piston is ignited by a spark from the spark plug. This fractionally premature ignition allows the mixture to start burning while still being compressed, and so extracts the maximum efficiency from the engine. With that, the two-stroke has completed its operational cycle and is set to start all over again.

Because fresh charge is pumped from the crankcase it is very important that the casing is absolutely airtight. Although this is not hard to achieve with modern sealants, it does have implications for lubrication. It would be almost impossible to keep the crankcase airtight if a four-stroke supply/scavenge type lubrication system – with pipes, pumps and so on – were used.

TWO-STROKE LUBRICATION

Fortunately all the parts requiring oil – the big end, the crankshaft main bearings, the cylinder walls and the piston – in a two-stroke engine are passed by the vaporized petrol/air mixture as it travels from the carburettor to the combustion chamber. The problem of lubrication is easily solved, therefore, by adding oil to that mixture. The oil can either be added directly into the petrol, while it is in the tank, or it can be stored in a special tank (often found under the seat), correct proportions being automatically fed into the petrol/air mixture by an oil pump.

THE CHARACTERISTICS OF THE DIFFERENT ENGINES

It is difficult to say that one type of engine is better than another, as both have their own particular characteristics – whether these are advantages or disadvantages depends on the type of motorcycle in which you put the engine, and on what you want to do with it.

FOUR-STROKES

Four-strokes are perhaps best known for their great pulling power at very low revs, but they often have a respectable spread of power over a wide r.p.m. range and are increasingly able to combine this with good rates of acceleration – especially if one considers the abilities of multi-cylinder four-stroke engines. Also, because the four-stroke's method of operation is relatively sophisticated, it is much less prone to plug fouling and engine seizure. The mechanisms required to operate these sophisticated valve systems are sometimes very complex, and it is largely because of this that four-strokes are frequently more expensive to produce and maintain.

TWO-STROKES

A two-stroke, on the other hand, gives its best power at high revs, where you often get a definite power surge. At the same time the lack of any valves and valve gear means that the engine itself can be smaller and lighter. Its mechanical simplicity also makes it more easy to modify. However, you do need to mix oil with the petrol to lubricate the engine, and this does lead to the spark plug becoming dirty and fouled much more easily.

Finally, you may have noticed the difference in the sound of these engines – if you haven't, listen carefully next time you have the opportunity. Basically, the difference occurs because the two-stroke fires *every time* the crankshaft rotates, whereas the four-stroke only fires *every other* rotation. This means that at 5,000 r.p.m., for example, the sound of 5,000 explosions can be heard in a two-stroke and only 2,500 in a four-stroke, and that makes quite a difference when you listen to the pitch of their engine noise.

CHAPTER TWO
MAINTENANCE AND SERVICING

If you stop and think about it for a moment, you'll realize that regular maintenance is important not because the books and manuals say it is, but for several good reasons.

Firstly, it will increase your motorcycle's dependability. There is an old adage which says, 'If it works, leave it alone.' This may be wise for television sets, but motorcycles need continual maintenance and adjustment. When the tachometer says 6,000 r.p.m. it means just that – the engine is turning over 6,000 times every minute. Every time you use the clutch the cable stretches a little. Mechanical parts wear and will fail (often at the worst possible moment) without your attention.

Secondly, it will save you money. The inspections and adjustments involved in servicing will give you the opportunity to detect and remedy any faults before they have time to develop. Often, the minor problems you find during routine maintenance are simple and relatively inexpensive to correct; undetected, however, they may develop into more major – and for that you can read more expensive – problems requiring the help of a professional. Prevention, though, is only part of the value in major servicing: proper attention on a regular basis will also extend the operating life of your motorcycle and enhance its second-hand retail value. In brief, then, regular servicing will save you money and other kinds of pain in the long run.

Thirdly, it will ensure that you always get optimum performance from your motorcycle and, most important of all, that it is safe to ride. By the time you have been through the full service schedule, and often long before that, you will know your motorcycle so well that if any problems do arise which may reduce its performance or become a potential safety hazard, you will be able to diagnose and solve them with far less difficulty.

Finally, it will help your motorcycle pass any government test of roadworthiness. In an increasing number of countries motorcycles are required to be periodically checked by a government-approved test centre. In the U.K. any motorcycle which has been registered for three years or more must have an M.O.T. certificate of roadworthiness (M.O.T. stands for Ministry of Transport, the old name for the government department now called the Department of Transport) – it is illegal to ride without one. Although regular maintenance cannot guarantee that your motorcycle will be automatically issued with a certificate it is the best form of insurance you can have against it failing.

In our view, then, regularly servicing your motorcycle is important for many reasons, and it is irrelevant whether you ride a moped or a superbike – the principles involved are the same whatever the engine's type or cubic capacity. Certainly you should not make the mistake of thinking that because a motorcycle is small in terms of capacity and power it will not need to follow the same type of maintenance schedule as other, larger-capacity motorcycles – it will! Moreover, although two-strokes are simple in principle they still need careful maintenance, and in some areas (particularly in making adjustments) this can be critical. On the other hand, the extra complications of the valve gear and oil-recirculating systems in a four-stroke do not automatically mean that they are more difficult to maintain. As we have tried to demonstrate throughout the maintenance schedules below, motorcycles have their own peculiarities and similarities.

In recent years modern motorcycles have become more and more complex, and many amateurs now feel daunted by the prospect of even simple maintenance tasks. The secret – no matter what machine you are working on – is to take your time and try to be as logical as possible. Be systematic – work out a method of approach and stick to it. Beginning work on one part of the bike and then moving quickly to another greatly increases the chances of you missing something, and it will be this very item that lets you down on the road, making the whole idea a waste of time. Really, there is little reason for even the most mechanically inexperienced to be unsuccessful: if they approach servicing calmly and methodically.

The only time you should not attempt a task is if you know you don't have the equipment or knowledge to do the job safely. Special equipment such as a multi-meter, dial gauge or vacuum gauge may be necessary to complete a task, and attempting the job without it may simply make matters worse. If you don't have the tools, and

you can't borrow them, you will have to take your motorcycle to your local workshop or dealer and get them to do that task for you. If you can do it, servicing and maintaining your own motorcycle is both fun and satisfying.

Unfortunately, however, you can't just service the bike when you feel like it; routine maintenance should be exactly what it says: a regular and ongoing process from the moment the motorcycle is first used. As those of you lucky enough to have owned a brand-new motorcycle will know, during the 'running-in' period it is vital that you observe all the limitations on the engine and cycle speeds, and most people do this. It is no less important, however, that you continue to check and maintain a motorcycle regularly once this period is over.

Service intervals are usually based on a system of elapsed time or distance. Generally speaking, the checks should be carried out after the motorcycle has covered a specified number of miles, although with some items, or if the motorcycle is not used regularly, it may become necessary to service on an elapsed-time rather than an elapsed-miles basis. In brief, then, maintenance should be undertaken on a mileage or calendar basis, depending on which comes sooner.

Although we suggest that you stick as close as possible to the mileage and dates under which the tasks are grouped, they are only meant to be a guide to your maintenance. As your motorcycle gets older – both in terms of miles and years – or if you continually use it in adverse conditions, or if your riding style puts additional strain on some components, such as the brakes, then it is advisable to reduce the mileage and/or time between each series of checks. One thing is for sure

– there is certainly no time in the life of a motorcycle when a routine item can be ignored. Indeed we suggest that you get into the habit of walking around your motorcycle before each ride and checking some of the more obviously essential items: lights, brakes, horn, steering, etc. Not only will this allow you to detect any defective part, but it is, of course, an essential safety precaution whose importance you should not underestimate.

When it actually comes to doing the job, although the tools supplied with a motorcycle are often adequate, it is better to build up a set of your own – perhaps of better quality. The number of tools you require clearly depends on the amount of work you intend to do. However, whatever tasks you do intend to try – even if you feel capable of tackling them all – don't rush out and buy every workshop-listed tool: many of them are only used in workshops to speed up the job of professional mechanics, and you will be able to cope quite easily without them. Take your time; perhaps purchase tools more or less as you need them: that way you can be selective and shop around for the best buys at the time (see 'Tools', pp. 270–71, for more information).

Most motorcycles have special design characteristics (even quirks) peculia to that manufacturer or type of motorcycle – to be unaware of these when servicing is taking a chance. In all aspects of servicing you must use your common sense, but it is also essential that you read the relevant manual before you begin. This will give you some idea of what you should and should not expect to find, and what the specifications are for your motorcycle: the various oil and fluid capacities,

torque settings for nuts and bolts, clearances for piston rings and valves, and the contact breaker and spark plug gaps. All these should be indicated either in your owner's handbook or workshop manual. Being well acquainted with your bike's idiosyncrasies may save you a lot of trouble and avoid dangerous mechanical failures on the road.

Basically there are three sources from which you can obtain the specific data you will need for servicing your motorcycle.

1. The owner's handbook. Although some owner's handbooks are quite detailed, generally they are very basic, restricting themselves to such things as recommended tyre pressures and other specifications, the location of key items and how to start, run, operate and stop the motorcycle. Unfortunately, moreover, because most, if not all, are produced by the manufacturers they continually refer you to the dealer network for tasks which are well within your ability. It should be said, however, that there is an enormous variation in the issues and material these handbooks seek to cover. With your particular motorcycle you may or may not be lucky.

2. The service manual. Although generally available, the service manual is basically designed for the professional mechanic. They are supplied by the manufacturers to dealers, much like the specialized tools required by a particular motorcycle. Giving full information on dismantling, inspection and reassembly these manuals are perhaps the most comprehensive – if not the most comprehensible. Being designed for the professional equipped with a full set of factory tools, they require not only some in-depth

study, but also some degree of experience and ability.

3. Independently produced workshop manuals. These manuals are basically written for the motorcyclist who does not have access to factory tools or the experience and ability of professional mechanics. They set out to provide the owner with a guide to his motorcycle, but to do so with much simpler texts and the extensive use of photographs and diagrams. Although they do have several shortcomings they are certainly better for the non-professional than the service manual. They are also much cheaper.

Figure 11 shows the almost universal motorcycle layout and marks some of the more important parts. You should use this sketch and your owner's handbook or workshop manual to study your own motorcycle and find out exactly where these key items are located.

Below are the various maintenance tasks we recommend you should carry out over a two-year cycle and the elapsed time or mileage when you should attend to them. As we have stressed above, there is no time when any item or group of items can be overlooked. So, for example, when you have to do the three-monthly service you must not neglect the monthly, weekly or daily checks – they too need to be completed.

Finally, unless it is otherwise stated, you can take it that the machine should be thoroughly cool before you begin servicing the engine.

DAILY CHECKS

	Page
1. Handlebar movement	27
2. Any security locks are removed	27
3. Handlebar controls	27

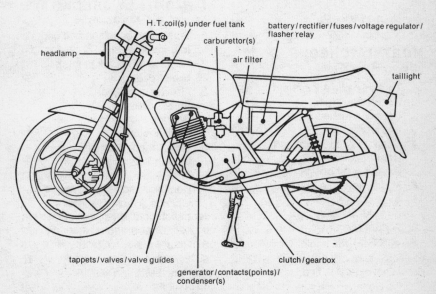

H.T.coil(s) under fuel tank

carburettor(s)

battery / rectifier / fuses / voltage regulator / flasher relay

headlamp

air filter

taillight

tappets / valves / valve guides

generator / contacts(points) / condenser(s)

clutch / gearbox

Figure 11 General layout of components

4. Rearview mirrors 27
5. Speedometer 27
6. Brakes 28
7. Petrol 28
8. Horn 29
9. Lights 29

WEEKLY CHECKS
(or every 100–150 miles)

1. Final-drive chain:
   lubrication and tension 30
2. Tyre pressures and tread
   wear 35
3. Spoke tension 37
4. Battery condition 38
5. Oil levels 39
6. Liquid-cooling system: top
   up 39
7. Crankcase leaks:
   two-strokes only 40
8. Lights 40
9. The seat 41
10. The centre stand and side
    stand 41
11. Nothing is loose 41

MONTHLY CHECKS
(or every 500–600 miles)

1. Throttle cable adjustment 41
2. Clutch adjustment 42
3. Control cable condition
   and lubrication 42
4. Spark plug condition and gap:
   two-strokes only 44
5. Brake pad/shoe wear 48
6. Hydraulic-brake lines 52
7. Air pressure in
   air forks (if fitted) 52
8. Footrest security 52
9. Steering lock 52

THREE-MONTHLY CHECKS
(or every 1,500–2,000 miles)

1. Change the engine oil
   and clean the oil filter 52
2. Final-drive chain condition 54
3. Oil pump adjustment:
   two-strokes only 58
4. Contact-breaker (points)
   condition and gap 60
5. Ignition timing 62
6. Decarbonize the cylinder and
   exhaust system:
   two-strokes only 63
7. External condition
   and security of the
   exhaust system 66
8. Air-filter condition 66
9. Camshaft chain adjustment:
   four-strokes only 67
10. Engine securely mounted 68
11. Crankcase breather tubes:
    four-strokes only 68

SIX-MONTHLY CHECKS
(or every 3,000–4,000 miles)

1. Spark plug condition and gap:
   four-strokes only 68
2. Replace the spark plug(s):
   two-strokes only 68
3. Air-filter condition:
   four-strokes only 69
4. Change the engine
   oil filter element 69
5. Valve (tappet) adjustment:
   four-strokes only 69
6. Fuel system 71
7. Condition, adjustment and, if
   you ride a multi-cylinder
   motorcycle, synchronization
   of the carburettor(s) 72
8. Rear-suspension units 75
9. Swinging-arm movement 76
10. Nuts, bolts and screws
    all tight 76
11. Frame condition 76

12. Cooling system:
radiator condition 76

YEARLY CHECKS
(or every 8,000–10,000 miles)

1. Clean and adjust both front
and rear brakes 77
2. Rear-brake pedal:
position adjustment 78
3 Change the brake fluid in a
hydraulic system 78
4. Steering-head bearings 79
5. Condition and adjustment of
front and rear wheel
bearings 80
6. Front and rear wheel spindles
clean and well greased 80
7. Wheels balanced 81
8. Change the front-fork oil .. 82
9. Replace paper-type air
filters 83
10. Fuses and the fuse box 83
11. Lubricate the final-drive
assembly of shaft-drive
motorcycles 83

TWO-YEARLY CHECKS
(or every 15,000–16,000 miles)

1. Remove and clean oil
pump strainer 84
2. Change the oil in a shaft-
driven final-drive assembly 84
3. Change the coolant in
a liquid-cooled engine 84

MAINTENANCE
OF MOTORCYCLES USED
OFF THE ROAD   85–6

DAILY – OR BEFORE
EACH TIME YOU RIDE
Before you set off check the following:

1. HANDLEBAR MOVEMENT

Make sure the handlebars turn fully to the left and to the right. This will not only ensure that there are no steering problems but will also prevent you forgetting to remove the steering lock before you ride away.

2. ANY SECURITY LOCKS ARE REMOVED

Ensure that you remove any security device you may have attached to the wheels. Failure to do so may quite easily damage your wheel or spokes as you set off.

3. HANDLEBAR CONTROLS

Check the position of the handlebars and the controls and ensure that they are securely fastened in a comfortable position. You should also ensure that the handlebar grips are tight on the handlebar and will not move or rotate in any way. If a grip, or a section of it, is loose you should remove and refit it before you set off. (See 'Refitting grips', p. 239.)

4. REARVIEW MIRRORS

Make sure that the mirrors are positioned correctly and that the locknuts are fully secure.

5. SPEEDOMETER

Exceeding the speed limit is an offence, and so is having a defective speedometer. You must ensure that you always have a working speedometer. While the motorcycle is still at the kerb you can visually check the cable connection, top and bottom, and then immediately you set off you should visually check that the speedometer is operating. Obviously it will not be possible for you to assess the accuracy of any reading, but once set it is rare for a speedometer's accuracy to vary. If there are any problems they are more likely to result in complete failure rather than inaccuracy.

6. BRAKES

Check and, if necessary, adjust both front and rear brakes. If your motorcycle is fitted with hydraulic brakes visually check the level of brake fluid in the master cylinders (Figure 12). The fluid level must be between the maximum and minimum lines marked on the cylinder body: top up with the correct fluid if it isn't (the correct fluid for your motorcycle will be indicated in your owner's handbook or workshop manual). Most cylinders are made from a white or clear plastic which allows you to check the level from the outside. If yours are not, move the

handlebars into a position where the master cylinder is as near horizontal (level) as possible, *before* you remove the cap. This should prevent any spillage. Brake fluid, remember, is a very good paint remover. If you find that the fluid level in either cylinder is excessively low, it may be that the pads are worn or, as is more likely on a daily inspection, that the fluid system has sprung a leak. Any sign of brake fluid leaking must be investigated and rectified before you drive the motorcycle. (If necessary, see 'Brakes', pp. 231–4.)

7. PETROL

Always ensure you have sufficient fuel and, if necessary, fill up as soon as possible. Indeed, it is advisable always to keep a close check on the petrol level. Firstly, because running out of petrol is no fun at all, especially as it always seems to happen at the worst possible time and place. But secondly because if you do run out of petrol any

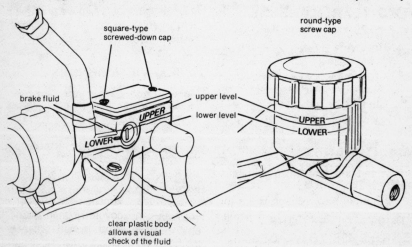

Figure 12 Brake master cylinder fluid levels

particles of rust or dirt in the bottom of the tank may be drawn into the petrol filter (possibly causing a blockage) or, more seriously, they may find their way into the carburettor. If that does happen you will ultimately have to spend time dismantling and cleaning the jets and float bowl. (For carburettor care and problems, see pp. 72–5.)

Basically, there are two ways you can monitor the amount of petrol you have. The first is simply to make a visual check in the tank. Another way, however, and this is much more useful if you are on a long run, is to calculate how many miles per gallon you get from your motorcycle in your normal daily riding and multiply this by the capacity of the petrol tank (this will be indicated in your owner's handbook or workshop manual) to ascertain the number of miles you can travel on a full tank of petrol. Then, if you can fill up the tank and set the tripometer to zero each time you need petrol, the number of miles you have travelled will tell you at a glance about how many miles' worth of petrol are left in the tank, allowing you time to find a petrol station before the level becomes too low.

To measure how many miles per gallon your motorcycle is travelling:

1. Fill up the tank and note the mileage figure (or set the tripometer to zero).

2. Ride your motorcycle in the normal way until you need to fill up again.

3. Fill the tank to the same level as before and note how much petrol this takes.

4. Note the new mileage figure (or the figure registered on the tripometer).

5. Divide the number of gallons you used into the number of miles you travelled; the result will be how many miles you travelled on each gallon.

A final word on petrol: many modern motorcycles prefer to run on three- or four-star – premium petrol. If the grade of petrol required by your motorcycle isn't specified in your handbook or manual, the compression ratio, which certainly should be indicated, can be used as a rule of thumb. If your motorcycle has a compression ratio of over 8·5:1 you need to use a premium petrol (see 'Petrol: Five tips on how to save petrol', pp. 263–4).

8. HORN

It is an offence to ride a motorcycle without an effective horn. After you have started your motorcycle, check that the horn is in working order.

9. LIGHTS

Headlamp

Check that the two beams are working correctly. An accurate headlamp check can be made only by a beam-setter, but you should ensure (especially if you are planning to ride in darkness) that the beam is not obviously deflected up, down or to either side, and that it is securely fastened in that position.

Finally, ensure that the lens is not covered in mud or dirt of any kind and that nothing will obscure the beam. (If necessary, see 'Headlight failure', pp. 215–16.)

Rearlamp

Ensure that the lamp is operating correctly and is not covered in mud, dirt or anything else which would prevent another motorist clearly seeing it. (If necessary, see 'Taillight failure', p. 216.)

Indicators

Check that each indicator operates correctly and that, when indicating left, only the two on the left side flash, and that only the two on the right side flash when you indicate a right turn. (If necessary, see 'Indicator problems', pp. 218–23.)

Stoplamp

Apply the front and rear brakes independently and check that the stoplamp is lighting and extinguishing at the correct moment. You must pay particular attention to this if you have adjusted either of the brakes. (If necessary, see remedy 7.4.3, pp. 210–11.)

WEEKLY CHECKS
(or every 100–150 miles)

First complete all the daily checks and then attend to the following:

1. FINAL-DRIVE CHAIN: LUBRICATION AND TENSION

Ensure that the chain is correctly adjusted and well lubricated.

Chain care is one of the most important items in your weekly check list. Its condition is crucial if your motorcycle is to operate efficiently. In transmitting the power developed in the engine to the rear wheel, the chain is continuously under a great deal of stress. At best, neglect will result in a substantial reduction of power and accelerated chain and sprocket wear. In the extreme, serious neglect may result in the chain failing at high speed, the consequences of which can be both expensive – especially if the chain smashes through the crankcase and causes internal engine damage – and,

more importantly, *dangerous* if it locks the rear wheel.

It only takes a few seconds to assess whether the chain needs your attention and, if it is required, less than five minutes to adjust and lubricate it. Despite this, however, chain care is still possibly one of the most neglected of routine tasks – it should be one of the most regular.

Adjustment

It is always better to adjust the chain before you lubricate it: firstly, because it is far easier to assess wear and tension accurately if it is not covered in grease; and, secondly, because it prevents your hands or tools getting covered in sticky grease.

On a weekly basis adjustment consists of (1) checking for chain and sprocket wear, and (2) checking the chain's tension.

Chain and sprocket wear

The chain: If the chain stretches more than 2 or 3 per cent it is worn out. A quick and easy test you can use to check this is to pull the chain away

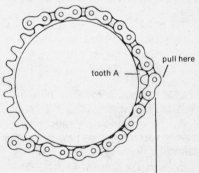

when the chain can be raised off the sprocket, showing more than half of sprocket tooth A, it is high time the chain is renewed

Figure 13 Test for chain wear at the drive sprocket

from the rear sprocket; if you can see more than half the tooth, the chain is worn out and must be replaced (Figure 13).

The sprocket: If a chain is neglected the sprockets will always suffer. However, worn sprockets will also accelerate chain wear, which will increase sprocket wear, and so on. The two effects are cumulative. So, while checking the chain take a good look at the teeth on both the rear-wheel and gearbox sprockets. If they are worn down, cracked or chipped they need replacing (Figure 14).

longer but also gives a smoother, more controlled ride. The correct place to measure the tension of a chain is at a point midway between the two sprockets on the bottom run when the chain is in its tightest position.

Before you make any adjustments, it is important that you raise the rear wheel, using either the centre stand or some form of prop (old bottle crates are very good for this, although you should be careful lest the manufacturers think you stole them), and observe the chain while rotating the rear wheel. In doing so you will see

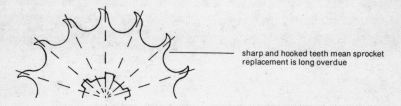

sharp and hooked teeth mean sprocket replacement is long overdue

When a chain has been neglected, the sprockets always suffer, so when replacing a worn chain, take a good look at the teeth

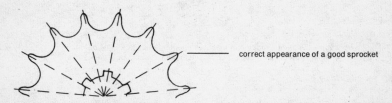

correct appearance of a good sprocket

Figure 14 Final-drive sprockets

Your owner's handbook or workshop manual should instruct you on how to replace the sprockets on your particular motorcycle.

Chain tension

As a chain is used it slowly stretches and becomes slack. It is essential that this slackness is taken up regularly. A correctly adjusted chain not only lasts

that the chain is tighter in some positions than others: this is due to uneven chain and sprocket wear. Any checks or adjustment must be made with the chain in its tightest position.

Although it differs from one motorcycle to another, most chains will be at the correct tension when the maximum vertical movement at the midpoint is about ¾ in. (20 mm.). See

Figure 15. Basically this is achieved by moving the rear wheel back and forth to tighten or loosen the chain as necessary. The precise maximum movement for correct chain tension, and the procedure to achieve it on your motorcycle, will be indicated in your owner's handbook or workshop manual.

An overtight chain, however, is just as bad as one that is too loose. The tension puts additional strain on the wheel bearings, causing them to fail prematurely, and may even result in the chain breaking at the first bump you go over.

two to achieve the correct tension, our advice can only be: *do not* do it! Using a chain which is worn to that extent (and hence substantially weakened) can only do more damage to the sprockets and risks doing far more damage to your motorcycle. Removing chain links is a false and potentially very costly economy. When a chain is worn out, treat your motorcycle to a new one.

Before leaving the chain you should also always ensure that the spring link (if fitted) is located securely.

Having adjusted the chain (which will have involved moving the rear

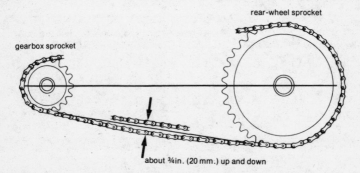

rear-wheel sprocket

gearbox sprocket

about ¾in. (20 mm.) up and down

Before any adjustment is made, check the chain for tight spots by revolving
the wheel. Any adjustment must be made while the chain is at its tightest position

Figure 15 Final-drive chain

Moreover, a chain that seems perfectly adjusted unladen may become overtight when you are mounted. Beware of overtightening in these circumstances and, after making an unladen adjustment, check the tension with weight on the seat. If the chain has worn so much that the correct tension cannot be achieved using the adjustment mechanism, it must be replaced. Although it is suggested by some that you should remove a link or

wheel) on motorcycles with mechanically operated brakes, be sure to check the rear brake adjustment and, of course, don't forget to readjust the stoplamp switch. Both these operations should be described in your owner's handbook or workshop manual.

If you have moved the rear wheel, you must also ensure that the wheels are still aligned correctly. Wheel alignment is controlled by the same nuts and bolts you loosened to adjust the chain tension. Usually, the chain tension adjusters have wheel alignment notches cut into them which have to be matched against the alignment marks on the swinging arm. When turning the adjusters be sure to turn them both by the same amount. If you do move one more than the other, the wheel's alignment will be affected.

A rough check for this can be made by depressing the top run of the chain with your finger or a convenient tool to remove any slack. If the wheel is out of alignment, the chain will have snake-like curves along its length (Figure 16), whereas if the wheel is

cated check can be made by placing a long straight edge (a plank of wood, a board or a pole of some sort – anything which is straight and long enough will suffice) alongside the front and rear wheels (Figure 17). On wheels of equal width that are correctly aligned the straight edge will touch the rims of both wheels at two points. However, if, when running your straight edge down the right-hand side, it touches at two points on the front wheel and at only the front of the rear wheel (Figure 18), the right-hand-side rear-wheel adjuster is further back than that on the left-hand side. The reverse would be true if the straight

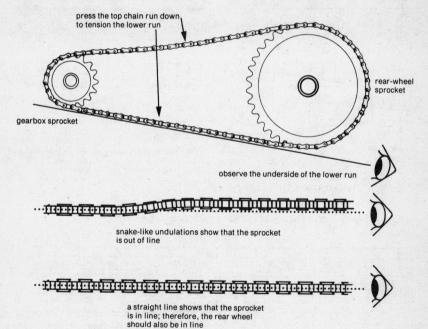

press the top chain run down to tension the lower run

gearbox sprocket

rear-wheel sprocket

observe the underside of the lower run

snake-like undulations show that the sprocket is out of line

a straight line shows that the sprocket is in line; therefore, the rear wheel should also be in line

Figure 16 Quick check of wheel alignment

correctly aligned the chain will run straight from the rear sprocket to the gearbox sprocket. A more sophisti-

edge touched at two points on the front wheel and only at the rear of the back wheel. If the rear wheel is wider than the front wheel (a situation which is increasingly common), you should ensure that the gap at each side of the front wheel is equal (see Figure 18).

lubrication is one of the best forms of protection you can provide. As a simple rule: if the chain looks dry and/or rusty, it needs lubricating. How-

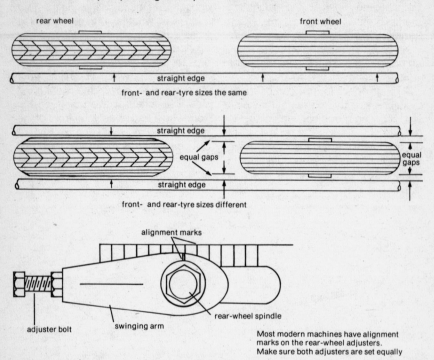

Figure 17 Wheel alignment using straight edges

Figure 18 Wheel alignment, showing rear wheel out of alignment

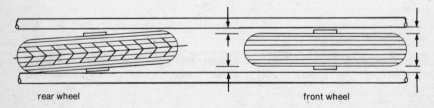

Lubrication
The life of your chain will be greatly increased simply by protecting it, and

ever, although it is not possible to over-lubricate a chain, if you do overdo it you will be wasting lubricant and therefore money. A check once a week under normal circumstances is quite sufficient. Whenever you do lubricate the chain, however, it is essential that you do not get carried away and spray the rear tyre: this is, to say the least, very dangerous!

To do the job correctly it is essential that the lubricant penetrates the spaces between the sideplates, pins, rollers and bushings. These are the surfaces that are in constant contact with each other. Running the oilcan over a dry chain will certainly make it look better but will do little to protect it. A 'spray-on' lubricating grease is far more likely to reach all the important areas, especially if you direct the nozzle carefully between the plates. The modern aerosol cans also have the advantage of being far quicker and cleaner to use.

If a 'spray-on' lubricant is not available, as a temporary measure you can use engine oil from your oil tank or engine casing – and that is certainly much better than nothing at all. However, because this oil does not have the 'sticking power' of today's lubricants, you do need to inspect the chain far more frequently. Also, unlike the more modern lubricants which form a protective barrier around the chain, oil is easily contaminated with the dirt and metal particles it rapidly picks up: increased chain wear is again the likely result.

Some motorcycles are fitted with automatic chain oilers which constantly drip engine oil into the chain. Although these are of some value they are no substitute for your own personal attention. If your motorcycle does have an automatic oiler the oil level should be checked and replenished, if necessary, each week.

Finally, on some motorcycles the chain is almost entirely enclosed. Unfortunately, this often presents motorcyclists with an excuse for neglecting the chain altogether. The metal (or plastic) protective housing is designed to prevent the wet and dirt from the road reaching the chain, and to some extent they do this quite well. Unfortunately, however, dry dirt which does find its way inside gets stuck there and does damage over and over again, steadily getting worse as it builds up. If it is left unattended, enclosure can therefore actually reduce the life of your chain. An enclosed chain should be checked and lubricated just as often as an uncovered one.

2. TYRE PRESSURES AND TREAD WEAR

Make sure that the tyres are at the correct pressure (Figure 19) and inspect them for excessive wear or damage.

The importance of good tyres to the motorcyclist can never be overstated. As the only point of contact between your machine and a hard road they need to be checked and serviced regularly. The compressed air within the tyres carries the entire weight of the motorcycle and you. The sudden failure of a tyre is not only frightening but extremely dangerous. It is essential that tyres are always kept in good order.

Tyre pressures

It is most important that you only check the air pressure when a tyre is cold. Riding the motorcycle causes the tyre to generate internal heat which results in the air pressure increasing – some-

rim

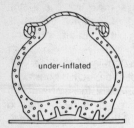 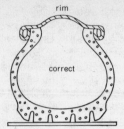 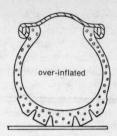

under-inflated   correct   over-inflated

Figure 19 Correct tyre inflation

times by as much as 8 p.s.i. This build-up of pressure within the tyre is normal and should never be bled off. Reducing the air pressure in warm or hot tyres will only cause increased flex in the tyre wall, a build-up of additional heat and a particularly dangerous condition within the tyre itself.

Incorrect tyre pressure will cause your machine to handle poorly (as little as 2 p.s.i. may alter a machine's handling characteristics) and the tyres to wear unevenly. So be sure you use an accurate pressure gauge whenever you check them.

1. *Over-inflation*. If a tyre appears to be wearing more rapidly in the middle of the tread, it is over-inflated. Over-inflating the tyre means that only the area in the centre of the tread is in contact with the road and thus it wears much faster. Exceptions to this general rule are the rear tyres of high-performance bikes: they tend to wear through in the middle of the tread even when they are correctly inflated. There is also a much greater danger, in this situation, of 'casing fracture' and 'tread cutting'.

2. *Under-inflation*. If a tyre appears to be wearing more rapidly on the edges, it is under-inflated. On tyres that are under-inflated the centre of the tread tends to arch up from the road, leaving only the two edges in contact. Because of this, wear is then concentrated on the two outside edges of the tread. Under-inflation also has the most adverse effects on handling and absorbs more power.

3. *Correct inflation*. By spreading the load evenly over the entire treaded area the correct air pressure ensures maximum mileage, cushioning, stability and road holding. It is only at the correct pressure that the tyre's designed contour is maintained while you ride. The correct air pressures for the tyres on your motorcycle will be indicated in your owner's handbook or workshop manual.

Incidentally, as we advised in the introduction, writing the correct tyre pressures in 'Your Bike's Specifications' at the end of this book will save you carrying more than one book around.

Having checked and, if necessary, reinflated the tyre there are three other things you need to do.

1. Check that the valve is not leaking. To do this either spit on it or wipe a film of soapy water across the top of the valve hole. If the valve is not leaking, the film will remain intact. If it bubbles, you have got a leaking valve. However, if it is leaking this does not always mean that the core is defective – it may just be a particle of dust in the seal. To check which it is, press in the

valve pin and let a jet of air escape. Again use soapy water to recheck the valve. If it was dirt, the air jet should have dislodged it; if the film still bubbles, unfortunately you will have to fit a new valve core.

2. Don't forget to refit the valve dust cap. Although it is small the dust cap does give an added safety feature. If the valve fails, the dust cap is there to prevent the tyre deflating in one gush of air. It is important that this cap is screwed on tight and that it makes a good seal with the rim of the valve.

3. Finally, ensure that the valve locking ring is securely fastened. On some motorcycles the inner tubes do tend to creep around the wheel rim. If the valve nut is not secure, the valve may be pulled out and the tyre would deflate as though punctured.

Tyre condition

When checking the condition of your tyres you should:

1. Ensure that the tyres have sufficient tread. Although the legal minimum is 1 mm. of tread it is inadvisable to travel any real distance on tyres with less than 2 mm.

2. Make sure that the tread is not beginning to wear unevenly. As we saw earlier, excessive wear in the middle or on the two sides means that the tyre pressures are wrong; excessive wear on only one side means that the wheel is incorrectly aligned or that it is out of balance.

3. Look out for any splits, rips, cuts, cracks or bubbles in the sidewalls. Any damage to the sidewall is extremely dangerous and the only real solution is to replace the tyre.

4. Inspect the area where the tyre bead meets the wheel rim for any signs of rust. Any brown or orange marks here are likely to be the result of corrosion on an exposed bead wire. Although this does not pose an immediate problem, it is something you should monitor closely. Indeed, if the bead wire were to rust through, the tyre might force itself off the wheel rim at that point.

5. Ensure that there are no stones trapped in the tread grooves. These should be prised out immediately before they damage the rubber.

6. Look generally for any other damage to the walls and the tread of the tyre.

Neglecting any of the above six points may create a serious hazard on your motorcycle, as well as making you liable for prosecution.

3. SPOKE TENSION

If your motorcycle is fitted with spokes ensure that none of them are broken, bent, rusting or loose.

To test whether any of them are loose, simply press two of them together at a point just below where they cross. There should be a slight spring, but nothing more. If any are loose, use a spoke tensioner to take up any slack immediately – loose spokes will cause your wheel to run out of true, and as more and more become loose the wheel will be weakened. When you are tightening them, however, be careful not to puncture the inner tube. If a spoke is very loose, and needs a lot of slack taking up, the safest way is to remove the tyre, inner tube and rim tape (see 'Tyre removal', pp. 245–50). That way there is no danger to the inner tube and you can file down any spoke end sticking up too high. The most you can safely do without removing the tyre is about one full turn; more than that would be unwise. Some experienced ears can tell if a spoke is loose simply by tapping it with a tool and listening to the note. A spoke at the correct tension will ring, whereas a loose spoke will make a rather dull thud. However, until you are sufficiently experienced at using this method it is advisable physically to check the tension with your hand.

4. BATTERY CONDITION

When servicing your battery you should:

1. Wipe the battery casing with a damp rag and check that it is not cracked. If you do discover any splits or cracks in the casing pour out the fluid, remove the battery's innards and wash the outside of the casing around the crack. When it's dry gently use a hot iron to seal the crack, and cover the repair with a good coating of Araldite. This will make a good and permanent seal.

2. Check the level of fluid (known as electrolyte) in the battery's cells (Figure 20), and top up with distilled water if necessary. You will find that most batteries these days have a recommended electrolyte level marked on the side of the casing, which you can see through. Always ensure that the electrolyte is between these maximum and minimum lines. If you overfill it, the loss of electrolyte that is likely to result will lead to reduced battery performance, shortened life and excessive corrosion. On the other hand, if you allow the electrolyte level to fall below the level of the plates, any portion of the plates exposed to the air will be permanently damaged. Once again this will result in reduced battery performance and a shortened life.

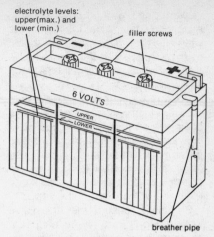

Figure 20 Battery levels

If distilled water is unavailable, melted ice from your fridge or freezer will do just as well, and in some parts of the country even tap water is acceptable. However, unless you are 100 per cent certain of the type of water in your area it is inadvisable to risk it: stick to ice water or genuine distilled water.

3. Test the state of the battery's charge and recharge it if it is holding less than half the recommended output. To measure the electrical charge you can either use a battery charger, on which you can read off the degree of charge on the gauge provided, or you can use a hydrometer to measure the specific gravity of the distilled water surrounding the plates in each cell. A normal, fully charged motorcycle battery should have a specific gravity of $1 \cdot 260 - 1 \cdot 280$.

4. Inspect and clean the battery terminals. If there are any signs of corrosion, they should be removed immediately. Surprisingly, pouring a small amount of boiling water over a terminal will often help remove built-

up corrosion. You can then either rub the terminal with a wire brush or scrape it with a knife, and then (in both cases) rub it over with emery paper to remove any final signs. Terminals that are corroded have a high electrical resistance and so give the impression that the battery is flat when you need to use it.

5. Inspect and clean the contact surfaces of the battery leads. Again, if they are corroded use a wire brush, or a knife, and emery paper to clean them.

6. Coat the terminals and leads with Vaseline and remake the terminal connections. Also ensure that the earth lead is securely fastened to the frame.

7. Check that the battery vent pipe is clear, especially at the bottom end, and has a smooth path as it runs through the frame.

5. OIL LEVELS

Engine oil not only reduces the friction which causes engine wear, but also keeps the engine clean and cool, and assists in cold starting. It is essential, then, that the correct levels are always maintained. Failure to do so may lead to engine seizure – potentially a very expensive problem. (See 'Engine seizure', pp. 252–5).

Four-strokes

Check the level of engine oil held in the oil store (this will be in either the sump, the frame or a reservoir under the seat) using the dipstick, where provided. You should ensure that the oil level is between the maximum and minimum marks on the dipstick. Do not be tempted to overfill this tank in the belief that you can leave it longer before you check again: it may result in excessive oil pressure and expensive damage to the engine oil seals. On four-strokes that do not have a separate oil tank the filler hole and dipstick (if provided) are on the left- or right-hand side of the engine itself.

Two-strokes

On most motorcycles with two-stroke engines there are two stores of oil, and you must check them both: the gearbox oil and (on machines with an auto-lube pump) the store of two-stroke oil for mixture with the petrol. Replenish them when necessary with the correct grade of oil. Using the wrong grade of oil in the gearbox, for example, can cause clutch drag, so see your owner's handbook or workshop manual first.

Access to the gearbox oil is (usually) via a plug screwed into the gearbox housing, whereas the oil tank for the two-stroke oil is (usually) located under the seat or behind the side panel.

Apart from this weekly check you should also check the two-stroke oil level each time you purchase petrol. Letting this supply run too low could allow air into the oil line, effectively cutting off the supply. (See 'Auto-lube systems . . .: Air locks', p. 231.)

On many motorcycles at least one, and sometimes both, these levels can be observed through a 'window'. The location of these oil tanks and the existence of an observation window should be indicated in your owner's handbook or workshop manual.

6. LIQUID-COOLING SYSTEM: TOP UP

While the engine is running and at the normal operating temperature check that the level of coolant in the tank is satisfactory. If necessary, replenish the coolant up to the 'full' mark. For most liquid-cooled motorcycle engines the coolant is made up of 50 per cent distilled water and 50 per cent anti-freeze, with an ethylene glycol base.

IMPORTANT: Do not remove the radiator cap when the engine is hot. The rapid reduction in internal pressure will cause the coolant to boil and possibly to spurt out of the filler hole in a scalding fountain.

It is a good idea to make up a supply of coolant mixture in advance. This can then be used to replenish the system whenever necessary. You should never allow the proportion of anti-freeze in the tank to fall below 40 per cent (if this were to happen the anti-corrosion characteristics of the coolant mixture would be reduced to an unacceptable level and internal corrosion would go unchecked). Ideally you should also use distilled water in the cooling system as this too helps reduce corrosion and prevent 'furring up'. Tap water, however, can be used with little disadvantage, especially if you know it to be soft.

If your engine is constructed of aluminium you must ensure that the anti-freeze you use is acceptable to that type of engine.

7. CRANKCASE LEAKS: TWO-STROKES ONLY

Inspect the engine casing for signs of leakage from any part of the crankcase.

In Chapter 1 we saw the importance of a gas-tight crankcase. This is necessary, you will remember, because the petrol mixture has to be compressed in the crankcase to force it up the transfer port.

Air leaks in the crankcase usually show themselves as an oily film around the area of the leak, as the petrol mixture escapes, and can be clearly identified only if the engine is clean – another important reason why your engine should be regularly cleaned!

Leaks most commonly occur: (1) where there is a loose drain plug on the underside of the crankcase; (2) at the cylinder joint; and (3) at the crankcase seals. All these should be regularly inspected. Although the loose drain plug can easily be tightened, leaking cylinder gaskets and crankcase seals must be replaced. Moreover, if you need to split the crankcase for any reason neither of these seals should be reused – they should always be replaced with new ones before you rebuild the engine. Also, these components don't last for ever so you should be prepared to replace them sooner or later. You will need to take great care when replacing the seals; if you fit them the wrong way round you will get virtually no seal at all. Check with your owner's handbook or workshop manual and pay close attention to the fitting instructions. If there are any leaks in the crankcase the loss of pressure will result in starting difficulties and reduced performance.

8. LIGHTS

Good lights are essential for safe riding at night and in poor visibility. When servicing the headlamp, rearlamp, stoplamp and indicators, in addition to the daily checks you should also attend to the following each week:

1. Ensure that none of the bundles of wiring behind the headlamp are trapped and that there are no abrasions at the point where they all enter the headlamp shell.

2. Check that there is no damage to the lens, and that the reflector at the rear of the lamp has not begun to discolour. Any discoloration will reduce the power and concentration of the beam of light emitted. If either the lens or the reflector are damaged they should be replaced.

3. Remove the lens and check that there is no water trapped in the lamp body. If there is, remove it and dry out the inside with a clean, dry cloth. Also, inspect the gasket and, if necessary, replace it. It is important that the lamp is kept completely waterproof.

4. Frequently rearlamps, stoplamps and indicators are flexibly mounted on a rubber base. If any equipment on your motorcycle is mounted in this way, make sure that the rubber is in good condition.

5. Inspect the rearlamp and indicator lens for any sign of colour fading. If these coloured lenses do begin to fade they should be replaced.

9. THE SEAT

Ensure that the hinges (if fitted) are secure and that the seat lock is operating correctly. Make sure that both are well lubricated.

10. THE CENTRE STAND AND SIDE STAND

Inspect and lubricate (with multi-purpose or graphite grease) the stand pivot bolts, and check the legs for cracks or bends. Inspect and grease the stand returning springs. It is important that the stand on a motorcycle is in good order, especially on the larger and heavier motorcycles.

11. NOTHING IS LOOSE

Finally, on your weekly checks make sure that no nuts, bolts or screws have worked loose, and double-check that every nut and bolt which is supposed to have a split pin or spring clip actually still has one.

Note: Although a spring clip can be reused, once a split pin has been used it really should be thrown away. Although you can often straighten it, doing so will weaken it and create a safety hazard you can so easily (and cheaply) avoid.

MONTHLY CHECKS
(or every 500–600 miles)

Complete all the daily and weekly checks and then attend to the following:

1. THROTTLE CABLE ADJUSTMENT

Ensure that the throttle cable is correctly adjusted, with the required amount of free play. As cables get older they stretch, and any slack which does develop must be taken up. Normally there are two points of adjustment: one on the top of the carburettor and one as the cable enters the throttle twist grip. To obtain the appropriate degree of free play you should:

1. Start the engine.

2. Turn the twist grip adjuster until only a little free play can be felt when you operate the throttle.

Making this adjustment with the engine running enables you to detect if too much play is taken out of the cable: the engine revs will increase, and the adjustment can be slackened off accordingly.

3. When you are satisfied that there is not too much slackness at the twist grip, leave the engine running and move the handlebars, first, fully to the left and then, fully to the right. If the engine speed picks up on either or both locks, the cable must be slackened or re-routed until the revs remain the same during all movements of the handlebars.

4. Be sure to tighten the adjuster locknut after making any adjustments.

Your owner's handbook or workshop manual will indicate if there is to be a specific amount of free play and, if so, how much it should be.

2. CLUTCH ADJUSTMENT

Ensure that the clutch is correctly adjusted and that there is the correct amount of free play in the clutch-actuating mechanism.

As indicated in Figure 21, the extent of free play is measured by the distance between the edge of the lever and the lever mounting fixed to the handlebars.

The exact distance for the clutch on your motorcycle will be indicated in your owner's handbook or workshop manual, but on average it should be about 1/8 in. (3 mm.).

To achieve this there are three separate adjustment points. The first two change the relative lengths of the cable and its sheathing, and are on the lever itself and on the outside of the clutch housing. The third involves varying the throw of the actual operating mechanism in the transmission, inside the clutch housing.

Minor adjustments can be made by screwing the upper adjuster in or out until the correct free play is achieved. No tools are necessary and you can make any adjustments by using the knurled screw and locknut on the clutch lever mount. If the maximum adjustment at the upper point is insufficient, larger adjustments can be made at the point where the cable enters the clutch housing. In brief, then, of the adjusters outside, the lower adjuster should be used for coarse adjustments and the upper adjuster for making finer adjustments to the clutch's operation.

If no further adjustment is possible in the cable, and you still don't have the required free play, the third adjustment mechanism inside the clutch housing should be used. However, for specific details on making adjustments at this point you should refer to your owner's handbook or workshop manual.

3. CONTROL CABLE CONDITION AND LUBRICATION

In servicing the control cables you need to:

1. Check that the cable sleeves and the waterproof outer skin on the brake, clutch, choke (if fitted), tachometer and speedometer cables are undamaged. To prevent any water entering a cable sleeve, which would quickly cause the cable itself to rust, any cracks or splits should be covered with insulating tape immediately. It is also

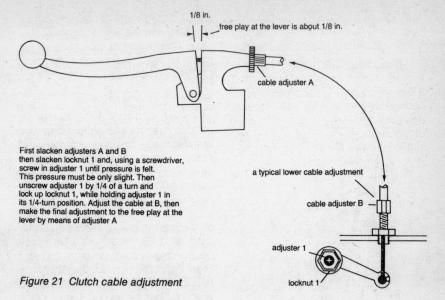

First slacken adjusters A and B
then slacken locknut 1 and, using a screwdriver,
screw in adjuster 1 until pressure is felt.
This pressure must be only slight. Then
unscrew adjuster 1 by 1/4 of a turn and
lock up locknut 1, while holding adjuster 1 in
its 1/4-turn position. Adjust the cable at B, then
make the final adjustment to the free play at the
lever by means of adjuster A

Figure 21 Clutch cable adjustment

a good idea to wrap any mid-way adjusters with insulating tape, and to put a blob of grease on the cable ends, both of which should prevent water finding its way in.

2. Ensure that all the cables are firmly attached at both ends and that they run in a smooth curve from top to bottom.

3. Inspect all exposed cables for fraying or any other damage and lubricate any which look dry.

To lubricate *instrument* cables:

1. Unscrew the security nut and withdraw the drive.

2. While leaving the outer sleeve still attached at the bottom, pull out the complete inner cable.

3. Lubricate the cable with grease and *not* oil. If oil were to be used, the rotating cable would form a pump action and force the oil up into the instrument head, ultimately causing irreparable damage. Moreover, it is inadvisable to grease the top 3–6 ins.

of the cable, in order to avoid contaminating the instruments.

4. Replace the greased cable in the sleeve and reattach it to the instrument head.

To lubricate *clutch*, *brake* and *choke* (if fitted) cables:

1. Detach the cable from the lever and wipe off any dirt or old grease around the nipple.

2. Half fill either a small plastic bag or a party balloon with oil.

3. Insert the end of the cable in the neck of the balloon or bag and secure it to the cable with an elastic band or insulating tape (Figure 22).

4. Squeeze the balloon *gently* and the oil will be forced into the cable.

This is certainly the most effective and efficient way to lubricate the inside of cables and it requires only two items, which should be readily available.

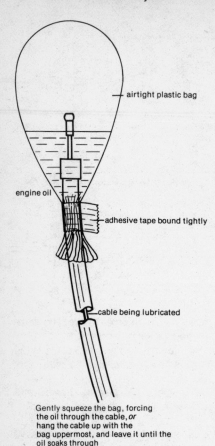

airtight plastic bag

engine oil

adhesive tape bound tightly

cable being lubricated

Gently squeeze the bag, forcing
the oil through the cable, or
hang the cable up with the
bag uppermost, and leave it until the
oil soaks through

Figure 22 Lubricating control cables

4. SPARK PLUG CONDITION AND GAP: TWO-STROKES ONLY

Although the servicing procedure for spark plugs in two- and four-stroke engines is the same, the differences in their operational cycles mean that the plugs in a two-stroke have to be serviced far more frequently. When servicing spark plugs you should inspect the electrodes: ensure that they are in good condition and that the gap between them is correct. Before you can inspect the firing end of a plug, however, the plug has to be removed from the cylinder, and this can sometimes be a problem.

Removing the spark plug

To prevent dirt, or anything else, falling into the cylinder you should clean the area around the base of the plug before you unscrew it. Removing the plug(s) with the engine still warm makes unscrewing a little easier, because the head will have expanded slightly. It also reduces the risk of you damaging the plug threads. If you do have difficulty removing a plug, spray penetrating oil on to the base and wait twenty minutes or so for the oil to work in. Lightly tapping the cylinder head with a rubber mallet sometimes helps here too: the vibrations help the penetrating oil to work through between the threads. Make sure you only tap lightly though, and that it is with a rubber mallet. You must be very careful not to break or crack any of the cooling fins.

Plug condition

Once you have removed the spark plug even the briefest examination of the firing tip will tell you a great deal about the state of the engine in which it has been running (Figure 23). Potential performance problems and premature engine failure can easily be detected, and hence avoided, if you are aware of what caused a particular spark plug condition and how that situation can be rectified.

Normal

If the engine, ignition and carburettor are operating satisfactorily, electrodes will have light brown or greyish

| correct: light brown appearance: very little carbon build-up | over-rich, black, sooty deposits all over the electrodes and insulator | poor engine: a black oily appearance says much about a worn engine |

| simply worn out: badly eroded electrodes indicate that it is time for renewal– this condition wastes fuel and makes the ignition system work overtime | melted electrodes and or a blistered insulator, greyish white in colour– this situation indicates poor ignition timing; or insufficient fuel/air, causing overheating | heavy carbon build-up, yellowish-white in colour, excessive burning of oil with the normal fuel/air mixture –a poor oil control ring or a worn valve guide may be the culprit |

Figure 23 Spark plug conditions

deposits, a very small build-up of carbon and there will have been no abnormal gap wear. Operating under normal conditions the gap between the electrodes should increase by little more than 0·001 in. every 1,000 miles – although, because a two-stroke does fire twice as often as a four-stroke, the gap in a two-stroke engine may open up a little further in that distance.

Oil fouled

In this case the plug will have a black insulator tip, a layer of carbon over the plug nose and a damp oily film over the firing tip. The electrodes themselves, however, will not be excessively worn. A plug in this condition indicates that:

1. The oil pump setting is incorrect.
2. On pre-mix models the petrol/oil ratio is incorrect. Your owner's handbook or workshop manual will indicate the exact proportions required.
3. There is an over-rich fuel/air mixture.
4. You are using the wrong type of oil or oil additive.
5. The air filter is clogged.
6. The ignition system is weak.
7. The idle speed is excessive.
8. Incorrect spark plugs are fitted, that is, they are too cold (see pp. 48 and 265).
9. The exhaust is blocked.
10. There is poor cylinder compression.

In this condition a plug can be cleaned up and refitted but you must correct the problem which caused the plug to be coated in oil. As a temporary solution, try running a hotter plug in the affected cylinder – it may be of help.

Carbon fouled

A carbon-fouled plug will have soft, dry, sooty deposits of carbon on the core nose which allows the spark energy to run to earth. This not only wastes petrol, but also makes the engine run too cool for maximum efficiency and tends to remove the oil from the cylinder bores. The result is that the piston rings and bore both wear more rapidly. Most frequently this situation is attributable to an over-rich mixture, but it may also be caused by:

1. Weak ignition.
2. Retarded ignition timing.
3. Low compression.
4. Heavy deposits of carbon in the combustion chamber.
5. An incorrect grade of oil in a two-stroke.
6. Poor ring control.
7. An incorrectly adjusted auto-lube injection pump.
8. The engine overheating.
9. A clogged air filter.
10. A faulty choke mechanism.

Although a plug in this condition can be cleaned and refitted, once again the condition which caused the carbon deposits must be corrected.

Burned electrodes

Light grey or mid-white chalk deposits on the nose tip, and burned electrodes, indicate that the plug is overheating and burning itself out prematurely. The most likely cause of this condition is that a spark plug from the incorrect heat range is being used, that is, the plug is too hot for the temperatures generated in the engine's combustion chamber. If you are using the correct grade plug other possible causes are:

1. A lean fuel mixture or fuel of insufficient octane rating.
2. Fuel starvation.
3. Over-advanced ignition timing.
4. Air leaks at the carburettor or manifold, possibly the result of loose carburettor mountings.
5. Engine overloading or lugging.
6. Incorrect carburettor jetting.

As with the other plug conditions above, you must discover the source of the problem whose symptoms are shown up on the spark plug's electrodes before you can safely put your bike back on the road. Unfortunately, in this condition there is nothing you can do to salvage the plug – the only solution is to replace it. Check your owner's handbook or workshop manual to ensure you purchase the correct plug grade.

Melted electrodes

If the electrodes are severely melted it is almost certain that sustained pre-ignition (pinking) is the cause (see pp. 252 and 261). Occasionally it may also be because a plug of the wrong heat range (too hot) is being used. However, it is advisable with a plug (or plugs) in this condition to check: (1) the manifold connections; (2) the carburettor mounting; (3) the ignition timing – it may be over-advanced; and (4) the fuel grade (octane rating too low).

Lead fouled

Far less common than the others, lead fouling gives the plug tip a greenish or dark grey tint, and is usually associated with misfiring. The basic cause is that you are using petrol with an octane rating that is too high for your engine. You get no extra performance from high octane petrol – it just costs more.

Worn out

Even in an engine which is running perfectly, spark plugs do wear out.

Because of the corrosive gases formed during combustion and the high voltage of the spark the electrodes are steadily eroded. Characteristically, on worn plugs the edges of the electrodes become rounded and the earth electrode begins to thin. When it gets to this condition the spark plug's voltage requirement increases, often to more than the ignition system can supply. If the plug has no other symptoms of trouble, you can be confident your engine is in good order and simply replace the worn plug with one of the same range.

Plug cleaning

Clearly the most important part of the plug to be cleaned is the firing tip – the electrodes. Having decided that it is worth cleaning a plug you can either take it to your local garage and have it sand blasted, or you can do it yourself. You will need: (1) either a soft wire brush or a stiff-bristled brush, to remove the bulk of the deposits; (2) a piece of emery cloth to remove any final traces of oil or carbon; (3) a small file to square off the earth electrode, etc.; and (4) a clean dry cloth or a soft brush to clean away metallic particles that may be left.

When you have finished, the electrodes should be clean and sharp, without rounding on the edges.

Immersing the plug overnight in ordinary household vinegar (a weak acid) often helps soften hard carbon deposits, which can then easily be scraped away with a wooden toothpick.

A part of the plug which is often neglected when it comes to cleaning is the (white) conductive material at the top. A surface film gathers on this material which can easily lead to leakage of electrical current. The most effective way to remove this film is to use a clean rag and methylated spirits. A dry rag alone won't remove the film and using petrol would only leave another film. Once wiped on, the meths will evaporate, leaving the material perfectly clean. Indeed it is often best to leave this last item of cleaning until just before you are ready to replace the plug. Be careful not to leave oily fingermarks on the white material after you have screwed it into the cylinder head.

Setting the gap

After cleaning the plug you must ensure that the gap is set to the manufacturer's specifications for your motorcycle. To reset the gap, the earth electrode has to be bent either towards the centre or away from it. Briefly, to narrow the gap, gently tap the earth electrode with any small, flat tool, checking after each tap with the correct feeler gauge until you achieve a close fit. When you think it is right do a final check with the next highest feeler, which should not enter. To widen the gap you can either ease the electrode away with the blade of a small screwdriver or grip it with a pair of pliers and gently pull it away. Always raise the electrode so that the gap is just a little wider than the required setting and then tap it into the exact position, checking regularly with the feeler gauge.

Gapping tools are available to lever the earth electrode into position. However, these are an unnecessary expense and may in inexperienced hands even lead to cracking of the insulator nose. Careful tapping or prising is perfectly satisfactory. What is important is that the gap is reset to the manufacturer's specifications for your motorcycle; this will be indicated in your owner's handbook or workshop manual.

Replacing the spark plug

If it is necessary to fit a new plug be sure that you refit one of the correct grade. Fitting the wrong plug always invites trouble and in a high-performance two-stroke engine may have catastrophic results. As will be seen in Chapter 7, in extreme cases the heat generated may even burn the piston crown.

When possible stick to the recommended plug. If that plug is unavailable always consult your local dealer or workshop for an acceptable alternative for your motorcycle. Certainly don't try experimenting with plugs across the heat range – this can only cause trouble. There is some scope for variation but, basically, which plug you choose should be determined by the type of riding you do. If you do a lot of motorway riding and very little in towns or traffic you may need a colder plug (and that would be only one grade cooler, or possibly two). On the other hand, if most of your mileage is done in city streets and heavy traffic, with only the occasional motorway cruise, you may need a hotter plug (again only one or possibly two grades hotter – no more). It would be unwise to widen your choice much beyond this general rule of thumb, especially when a two-stroke engine is involved.

When fitting a new plug do not assume that because it is new the gap is correct. It doesn't take much to disturb the gap – especially in transit from manufacturer to retailer. Always check the gap on *any* plug before you fit it.

When it does come to installing a plug make it hand-tight first and only use the plug spanner to turn it an additional ¼ to ⅓ of a turn. This is sufficient to seal the washer without crushing it. Flattening the washer by screwing the plug down as tight as possible won't necessarily make a very good seal. Indeed, over-tightening the plug may cause the plug to become distorted. If this does happen air leaks can develop quite easily.

Finally, when servicing the spark plugs *never* apply grease or oil to the threads in the hope that it will be easier to remove next time. This is simply not the case. Indeed, the opposite is true: far from making them easier to remove the oil or grease will turn to carbon under heat and virtually 'weld' the two threads together. If possible *always* fit spark plugs with the threads *dry*. If you do have problems removing the plug, try rubbing a soft pencil lead or graphite powder over the threads. The graphite should make it easier next time.

5. BRAKE PAD/SHOE WEAR

Ensure that there is sufficient friction material on the brake pads or shoes. The rate at which your brakes wear will depend on: (1) the climatic conditions under which they operate; (2) your riding style; and (3) the weight your motorcycle has to carry. Because of these variants the rate of wear is not a constant and hence it is very difficult to advise on a specific time interval or number of miles when the brakes should be inspected.

However, because it is unsafe to ride a motorcycle with less than 1·5 mm. of friction material on the pad or shoe, a monthly inspection should enable you to monitor and service the brakes satisfactorily, without being unnecessarily time-wasting.

Brake pads (on disc brakes)

Checking for wear

Fortunately, inspecting the brake pads on many modern motorcycles is made easy: firstly, because most pads today have a red warning line marked on them, indicating when they need to be replaced; and, secondly, because almost all calipers have a small hole or window set into the top. To check the extent of pad wear, therefore, you simply have to remove a cover to the hole or peer through the window and see how far from the red line the disc is. If the line on only *one* of the pads has touched or is about to touch the disc, it's time *both* pads were replaced. If your pads don't have this mark, or if you don't remember if they had one originally, or now suspect that they have been worn away, the only way to be sure is to measure the amount of frictional material left on the metal baseplate.

If there is sufficient material you have no need to worry – being hydraulically operated, disc brakes never require adjustment: simply ensure that the fluid in the master cylinder reservoir is replenished when necessary. Doing this ensures that, as the material on the pad wears down, the fluid automatically establishes the correct amount of free play in the lever or pedal.

The only time you do need to tinker with disc brakes is if replacement pads are necessary. Never replace just one pad from a pair. Indeed, unless you have a problem with one side of the caliper, each pad should have worn equally. Normally brake pads are supplied in pairs and that is how they should be replaced – even if one side still has more than the minimum requirement. More importantly you should take steps to correct the situation, which is likely to be a problem in the caliper piston or pistons.

Brake shoes (on drum brakes)

Checking for wear

Most modern drum brake mechanisms have a wear indicator built into the actuating arm and the backplate. If the arrow on the actuating arm lines up with a mark cast into the backplate when you apply the brake fully, the shoes need replacing (Figure 24). On the other hand, if the arrow indicates that the linings still have sufficient friction material they may only require adjusting.

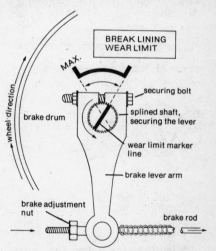

Although the lever arm can be repositioned on the spline to make brake adjustments, the marker on the shaft must not exceed 'max.' when the brake is applied

Figure 24 Brake-lining wear limit

To establish if the brakes do need adjusting you should: (1) raise the wheel and spin it to check that it rotates freely; (2) operate the brake lever or pedal and observe how far it travels before the shoes contact the drum. On the front brake this distance is measured between the lever and the handlebar stock, and on the rear brake by how far the pedal has to be depressed (Figures 25 and 26).

If the lever or pedal moves more than the specified distance, the brakes need to be readjusted to take up the slack caused by worn shoes or stretched cables.

ters, one on the handlebar lever and one on the brake plate (and in fact most modern motorcycles with drum brakes are set up like this), you should:

1. Loosen the locking ring and screw the lever adjuster fully into the lever stock.

2. Loosen the locknut on the lower adjuster and screw the adjuster outwards, taking up the excess slack.

3. When the free play at the lever is

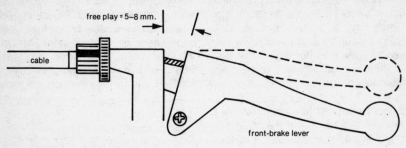

Figure 25 Front-brake adjustment

Figure 26 Rear-brake adjustment

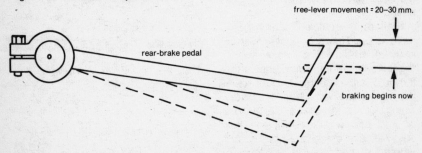

Adjusting drum brakes

All the adjustments made to drum brakes are based on the principle of varying the effective length of the operating mechanism, whether that is a rod or a cable.

The front brake

To achieve the correct adjustment on brake cables which have two adjus-

about correct tighten the lower locknut to secure that adjuster. The precise free-play distance will be indicated in your owner's handbook or workshop manual.

4. Use the adjuster at the lever end to make any fine adjustments once you have made a short test run. Indeed, because of the position of the upper adjuster it is possible to make minor adjustments during the test run

– although before making any such adjustments you should take great care that the road ahead is clear. Ideally you should make these test runs in a large open space, such as a car park.

Twin-leading-shoe brakes (Figure 27)

On twin-leading link brakes each shoe has to be adjusted separately. To do this you should:

1. Loosen off the linking rod.
2. Use the cable adjusters in the normal way to achieve the required amount of free play at the lever.
3. Tighten the linking-rod adjuster until the shoes begin to bind on the drum.
4. Once the shoes do bind, the adjuster nut should be backed off by between 1 and 1½ turns so that the drum rotates freely again.
5. Tighten the locknut on the rod to secure the new setting.

It should be noted, however, that operations 1 to 5 need only be done after a new pair of shoes is fitted; otherwise, normal cable adjustment can be used as shoe wear should be equal. ·

To readjust rear brakes

Rear brakes are operated either by cables (where the adjustment procedure is similar to that on the front brake) or more commonly by rods. The rod runs from the brake pedal to the actuating arm, where a threaded portion passes through a clevis pin secured on the other end by a click adjuster. Being spring loaded the nut locks itself against the clevis pin every half-turn.

With the rear wheel off the ground and spinning freely you can take up the excess play in the pedal with half-turns (inwards) of the adjusting nut. Immediately you hear the brake shoe rubbing on the drum, turn the adjusting nut back one half-turn and check the

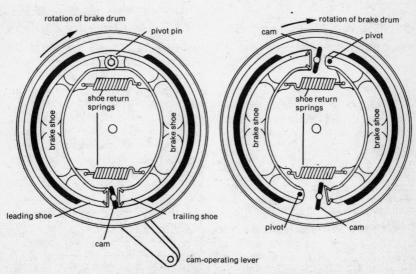

Figure 27 left: *single-leading brake layout;* right: *twin-leading brake layout*

play at the pedal. If the brake appears too fierce – and drum brakes are renowned for locking – you should back off the adjusting nut until you are satisfied. Finally, having adjusted the brakes you should ensure that the respective stoplight switches are also adjusted to come on the instant the brake shoe or pad makes contact and the motorcycle begins to slow down (Figure 28). The correct procedure for this adjustment on your motorcycle will be indicated in your owner's handbook or workshop manual.

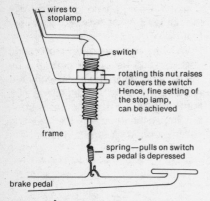

wires to stoplamp

switch

rotating this nut raises or lowers the switch Hence, fine setting of the stop lamp, can be achieved

frame

spring—pulls on switch as pedal is depressed

brake pedal

Figure 28 Stoplamp switch layout

6. HYDRAULIC-BRAKE LINES

The operation of your brakes depends on the security of the pipes (known as 'brake lines' or 'hoses') containing the fluid, so it is important that you:

1. Examine all hose connections and ensure that they are tight. Any damp patches around a connection are a tell-tale sign of fluid leakage and the joint should be sealed immediately.

2. Check the lines themselves for cracking, cuts or abrasions – which do occur despite their armoured construction. Any lines which are defective in this way should be replaced.

7. AIR PRESSURE IN AIR FORKS (IF FITTED)

Ensure that the air in front forks is at the recommended pressure for the riding you intend to do.

8. FOOTREST SECURITY

Make sure that the front and rear footrest bolts are securely hinged and replace any damaged rubber.

9. STEERING LOCK

Ensure that the steering lock is in full working order and lubricate it with a few drops of oil if necessary.

THREE-MONTHLY CHECKS
(or every 1,500–2,000 miles)

Complete all the daily, weekly and monthly checks and then attend to the following.

1. CHANGE THE ENGINE OIL AND CLEAN THE OIL FILTER

Changing the oil is perhaps the single most important maintenance item. Regular oil changes ensure that internal engine wear is kept to a minimum, and as a result the working life of your engine is significantly extended.

Normally, the smaller the sump on your motorcycle, the more frequently you will have to change the oil. If your motorcycle is relatively small, and therefore likely to have a small sump, you should think about an oil change every 1,500 miles. On the other hand, if you have one of the larger motorcycles, an oil change every 2,000 to 2,500 miles will be sufficient. Although continually changing your engine oil too early (that is, if there is still some useful life left in the oil) is an expensive business, it is certainly better to be too early than too late. Circulating through the engine, oil becomes contaminated with dirt, condensation and the products of combustion. Steadily the oil not only becomes thinner, providing less effective protection to the metal, but some of the contaminants it picks up react with oil and produce acids. The more vulnerable metal is then attacked by these acids, resulting in premature wear.

It should be pointed out, however, that there are a few exceptions to these general mileage rules: for example, the Honda CX 500 can travel over 7,000 miles between oil changes. Your owner's handbook will give you the exact mileage or time interval at which the oil in your particular motorcycle should be changed.

The simplest way to change the oil in your engine is to:

1. Ride the motorcycle until the engine is warm – this will allow the oil to flow far more freely.

2. Place a flat pan under the engine, then remove the oil drain plug from the underside and allow all the oil to drain out.

3. Some motorcycles also have a reserve of engine oil in a tank (often at one side of the bike) and this too should be drained. To do this, simply remove the oil tank drain plug on the underside. Before removing the plug, however, be sure you have a funnel and a receptacle correctly placed.

4. Remove the oil filter. If it is a strainer it needs to be cleaned with petrol or solvent and left to dry thoroughly. If, on the other hand, it is a paper-leaf-type filter it should be changed every other oil change (Figure 29).

Attempting to save money by trying to clean these paper filters is a waste of time and it will certainly increase the wear on your engine because of its inability to do its job correctly.

5. Replace the oil filter and the drain plug(s), and refill with fresh oil. The grade and amount of oil you require will be indicated in the owner's handbook or workshop manual.

In between oil changes it is very important that you maintain the correct oil level. If your motorcycle is fitted with a dipstick always keep it between the marks indicated (see 'Daily checks').

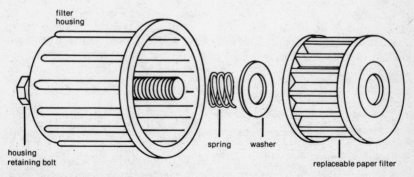

filter housing

housing retaining bolt

spring   washer

replaceable paper filter

Figure 29 Oil-filter arrangement

2. FINAL-DRIVE CHAIN CONDITION

Every three months or 1,500 miles, whichever is the sooner, chain maintenance needs to be far more rigorous than the simple servicing you do each week. The chain should now be removed, thoroughly cleaned, checked for wear, lubricated and replaced. Unfortunately there are no short cuts to this, and it is a dirty job.

There are two types of chain, those which are continuous – usually found on the larger motorcycle of, say, over 60 b.h.p. – and those which are connected by a split link – generally fitted to smaller motorcycles. In terms of the time taken to remove and replace these chains the difference is quite significant.

Removing the chain

1. If it is continuous the chain can only be removed by punching out a link, using a chain breaker. However, although not having a 'split link', many continuous chains are fitted with a special joining link (or soft link) which is relatively easy to split. Usually this link is recognizable by a paint mark or because it is finished in light metal. Having split a chain in this way you can either fit a conventional split link on reassembly – satisfactory for motorcycles of up to 60 b.h.p. – or rivet a new link into place, but this is a job for a professional mechanic.

2. If the chain has a split link, removal and replacement are much simpler. The first thing to do is to remove the spring circlip from the pins – a pair of pliers and/or a medium-sized screwdriver should do the job – and pull off the sideplate. The two pins and the other sideplate (or backplate) can now be pushed out. However, to make refitting the chain much easier use an old chain as a 'pull-through'. Firstly, using the split link, hook an old chain to the end of the existing one. Secondly, steadily draw out the existing, dirty chain and feed in the old one. Finally, when the existing one is out and the old one in place, disconnect the two chains and leave the old one on the motorcycle. You can use this later to pull in the now clean or replacement chain. It is much easier to clean and examine a chain once it has been removed.

Chain cleaning

To clean the chain soak it in a tin of petrol, paraffin or, if you wish, the special chain-cleaning solvents now available. Petrol or paraffin, however, are cheaper and in our opinion more effective. While the chain is soaking either shake the tin occasionally or use an old paint brush to remove all the greasy dirt. When you're sure it is clean hang the chain up to dry, and wipe it down with a clean, dry and non-fluffy rag. You must leave the chain until it is absolutely dry, especially in the areas you can't see – between the rollers. And here is a disadvantage to using paraffin: although it will do the cleaning job just as well as petrol it does contain a greater proportion of water, which takes much longer to dry out, and you cannot rush it. If you were to grease the chain while it was still wet inside the moisture would be trapped and soon begin to rust the rollers.

If you can afford it, one way around this is to have two chains. That way you would always have one ready to replace a dirty chain immediately. Moreover, you would also have plenty of time to clean, dry, inspect and lubricate the spare/dirty chain before you needed it again.

Chain wear

Each time you clean the chain you should inspect the plates and rollers for cracks and test it for wear. Although a loose chain will still transmit the power of the engine to the rear wheel you must resist any temptation to run as many miles out of it as you possibly can. The chain is made of very hard metal – much harder then the sprockets, for example – and if you do try to save money by delaying replacement you will probably end up seriously damaging the sprockets, and so being forced to spend even more money.

Before you can accurately assess the extent of any wear the chain must be clean and dry, so it is always best to make these checks between cleaning and lubricating. Detecting chain wear is not a difficult job and there are several ways to do it.

1. *The 'sticking links' test*. To test if any of the links are sticking, coil the chain by letting it fold under its own weight. If any links do appear sticky you should investigate why and, if possible, correct the problem. If this cannot be done, for any reason, the chain should be replaced.

2. *The chain length test*. Wear in the rollers, bushings and pins creates a slack in the chain which allows it to stretch. To observe just how worn these parts are:

(a) Lay the chain out flat and straight.

(b) Secure one end of the chain by securing/nailing the last link to the surface underneath.

(c) Push the chain towards the secured end as far as it will go without kinking, and mark the length.

(d) Stretch the chain out, away from the secured point, as far as it will go, and mark this point.

(e) Measure the distance between the two marks: this is the amount of stretch in the chain (Figure 30). If the stretch is more than 2 per cent of the original length, or more than ¼ in. for every foot of chain, it should be replaced (there are several other rules of thumb which people use, but by and large they will come to very similar conclusions about when a chain needs to be changed). For example, if your chain's original length was 60 ins. and it now measures 62 ins., it should be replaced. The table below indicates

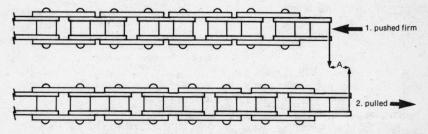

With the chain laid flat on the floor, push, as in (1), until the chain is at its shortest, then pull, as in (2), and the difference, A, is the amount of stretch

Figure 30 Chain wear

the exact lengths at which chains of various original lengths should be replaced.

It should be noted that we recommend, in the strongest possible terms, that you do *not* remove any links to enable you to achieve the correct tension on refitting.

3. *The 'arc (or bow)' tests*. Three other tests are commonly used to determine if the bushings, pins and sideplates are excessively worn. In all of them the minute extra clearances caused by wear are shown by the amount the chain will bend sideways. You can either:

(a) Hold each end of the chain with the sideplates facing upwards (on its edges, you might like to think of it) and get a friend to measure the bow, or sag (Figure 31).

Original chain length in inches	Length at which it will have stretched by 2 per cent, or by approx. ¼ in. in every foot, and therefore will need to be changed*
55	56 ·1
56	57 ·1
57	58 ·1
58	59 ·2
59	60 ·2
60	61 ·2
61	62 ·2
62	63 ·3
63	64 ·3
64	65 ·3
65	66 ·3

* These figures have been calculated on the basis of 2 per cent stretch being the maximum acceptable, and have been rounded off to the closest ⅒ in.

So, for example, if your chain was originally 58 ins. long and it now measures 59·2 ins. (or more), you should replace it.

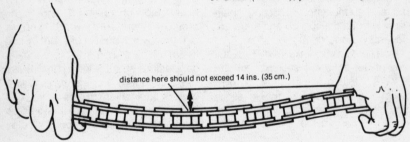

distance here should not exceed 14 ins. (35 cm.)

Figure 31 Chain wear check

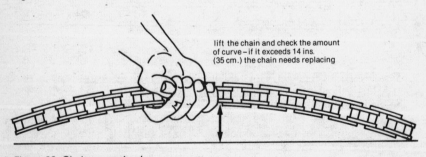

lift the chain and check the amount of curve – if it exceeds 14 ins. (35 cm.) the chain needs replacing

Figure 32 Chain wear check

(b) Hold the chain in the centre, again with the sideplates upwards, and let the ends drop to form an arc. Once again, with a friend, measure the size of the arc (Figure 32).

(c) Lay the chain out in a straight line with the side-plates vertical. Now bend the chain sideways away from that straight line and measure how far off the straight line it will bend (Figure 33).

In all three of these tests, and the choice of which you use is yours, the maximum movement possible in a final-drive chain is about 14 ins. (35 cm.), and your chain should be replaced if it bends or arcs by more than that. If the movement measures less than 14 ins., however, the chain should be good for a few more miles, and so can be lubricated and replaced.

phide – or 'moly' to its friends. As well as providing an excellent protective layer all over the chain, 'moly' is also perhaps the most efficient repellent of dirt and water. Moreover, unlike grease 'moly' is not sticky and, as we mentioned in the weekly checks, any lubricant which allows particles of dirt to stick to it, and eventually reach the bearing surfaces, will result in the chain wearing out even more quickly.

Normally you will purchase this grease already in a 'bath tin', but you should make sure there is plenty of room inside the tin to coil the chain on top of the solid grease. Before you do that, however, bend a piece of long wire through the end link; this will make lifting the hot chain from the boiling grease quite a lot easier.

Now, with the clean chain resting on

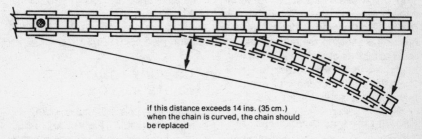

lay the chain out on a flat surface and fix it down here, using a nail or something similar

if this distance exceeds 14 ins. (35 cm.) when the chain is curved, the chain should be replaced

Figure 33 Chain wear check

Chain lubrication

Probably the most effective method of chain lubrication, in terms of protecting the chain and therefore increasing its life, is the grease bath. The special grease used in these baths contains, amongst other things, an old friend of the motorcyclist: molybdenum disul-

the grease, simply heat the whole thing on the cooker – or perhaps a camping stove, if the kitchen is off-limits for motorcycle maintenance – and leave it there until it begins to boil. If the lubricant is to do its job correctly it must penetrate between the rollers, pins and sideplates, and not simply coat the outside. Agitating the chain while it is in the boiling grease will help. After the chain has been in the *boiling* grease for a few minutes pull it out and hang it up to dry. Grease will drip from the bottom of the chain so be careful where you put it. Ideally you should hang it over the grease tin itself – to save you wasting any – but if this is not possible don't forget to place something under the bottom end to catch the grease – this prevents you having a pool of grease to clear up later.

Although this is rather a long and somewhat unpleasant job it does give a much greater degree of protection, from both wear and dirt, than any canned lubricant.

Just a final word on chains with sealed rollers. These superchains, designed for superbikes, can cost a super price – but in our experience they do last significantly longer than ordinary chains. Each individual roller has a small neoprene O-ring on either side which seals in a supply of lubricant. However, constantly using these chains with the outside dry will quickly cause the seals to fail and hence the roller to lose its oil supply. It is still very important, therefore, to keep the drive chain thoroughly lubricated – even the newer, super 'sealed roller' chains.

Refitting the final-drive chain

To refit the clean, lubricated chain simply hook it on to the end of the old chain you left over the gearbox sprocket and use that to pull the clean one into position. If you then place both ends of the chain together on the rear sprocket, the teeth will hold the ends together while you insert the connecting link from the back side. Then fit the other sideplate and secure

it with the spring circlip. When positioning the circlip be sure its closed end is facing the direction it will travel in. On the top run, for example, the closed end should be pointing towards the front wheel (Figure 34). On the

spring clip on the upper run of the chain faces towards the engine

Figure 34 Spring clip

other hand, riveting a new link into place on a continuous chain is a job which should be left to a professional.

If you didn't leave an old chain on the motorcycle try laying the end of the clean chain over the gearbox sprocket and pushing down on the kickstart, with the gears engaged. As the sprocket turns it will pull the chain with it and you can steadily feed in the rest of the chain.

Finally, once the chain has been connected make the necessary adjustments to achieve the correct tension (see pp. 31–4).

3. OIL PUMP ADJUSTMENT: TWO-STROKES ONLY

Ensure that the auto-lube pump is correctly adjusted (Figure 35). Two-stroke engines, you will remember, require oil to be mixed with the petrol and air, to lubricate the crankcase, piston and cylinder (see p. 21). However, if the engine is to operate correctly, just the right amount of oil must be supplied: too little will lead to engine seizure, whereas too much will cause plug fouling and excessive carbon build-up on the piston crown and cylinder head. Although some two-strokes (usually competition motorcycles) require you to pre-mix the petrol and oil, the remainder rely on an automatic pump to supply the right amount at the right time. The adjustment of this pump, therefore, is very important. Like all other cables, the oil pump cable will almost certainly stretch over time, and as it does so the pump settings will become incorrect. You need to take up any slack which develops in the cable and ensure that the two guide marks are in line at the appropriate time. A cable adjuster, often on the outside of the casing and operating in a similar way to the second clutch adjuster (see page 42), is fitted. Your owner's handbook or workshop manual will indicate the correct settings for your motorcycle and should point out any idiosyncrasy of which you may need to be aware.

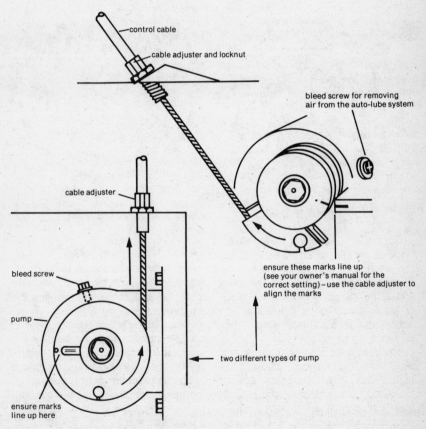

control cable

cable adjuster and locknut

bleed screw for removing air from the auto-lube system

cable adjuster

bleed screw

pump

ensure these marks line up (see your owner's manual for the correct setting) – use the cable adjuster to align the marks

two different types of pump

ensure marks line up here

Figure 35 Two-stroke oil pump layouts

4. CONTACT-BREAKER (POINTS) CONDITION AND GAP

Ensure that the points are in good condition and, if necessary, adjust the gap between them.

Although an increasing number of modern motorcycles are being fitted with 'pointless' electronic ignitions, the majority of motorcyles do still rely on a contact breaker to trigger the spark (Figures 36 and 37).

condition and always open by a precise amount.

Points condition

To inspect the points, lift open the gap by moving the arm as far as possible against the resistance of its retaining spring. Their surfaces should be clean – free from dirt or oil – and smooth – without high spots or pits.

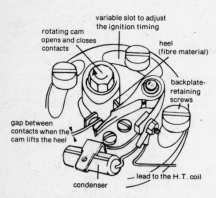

Figure 36 Contact-breaker layout

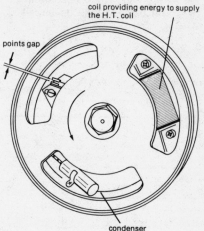

Figure 37 Flywheel/magneto ignition system

Normally, whereas two-stroke engines are fitted with one set of points for each cylinder, four-strokes are often arranged so that two cylinders share the same set of points. Your owner's handbook will indicate the way in which the points on your motorcycle are arranged.

The points are a mechanical device which 'break' the electrical flow to the high-tension coil (hence their correct name: contact breakers) so that each time the points are open a spark occurs at the spark plug. It is because of their role – interrupting electrical flow – that they need to be in good

Oil and dirt on the surfaces

Oily or dirty point surfaces will certainly result in poor performance and are quite capable of even preventing the engine from starting.

Although the points are supposed to operate inside a sealed space it is not unusual for various seals or engine gaskets to leak, allowing oil and/or dirt to contaminate the points; even when the seals are sound, simple condensation or moisture in the air can affect points operation.

To clean oily or dirty points:

1. Either spray the points with a

grease remover and clean them by pulling a dry cloth through the open points or pull a clean cloth soaked in methylated spirits through them.

2. Insert a piece of white paper and rotate the engine until the points close on the paper.

3. Pull the paper backwards and forwards through the closed points until no new marks appear.

4. Make a final inspection to check that there are no traces of oil, dirt or cleaning fluid remaining.

Indeed, once any oil or dirt has been removed it is also much easier to check that the surfaces have neither pits nor high spots.

Pitted surfaces

The heavy electrical charge and continued sparking that are normal in the use of a motorcycle cause the surface of the points to become steadily burned and pitted. Frequently, while one point surface develops a small crater the other surface develops a matching high spot. This condition indicates that arcing is taking place between the points, causing material from one surface to be removed and deposited on the other. This is normally due to incorrect condenser capacity, and you should take steps to correct the problem immediately.

As for the points themselves, the surface with the high spot could be 'dressed', but there is little you can do about the pitted surface and this blemish will undoubtedly continue to affect your engine's performance. The simplest and most efficient way to achieve the best performance is to replace the points. If you decide they are not too bad – perhaps you caught the development in the early stages – and can be cleaned up, lightly stroke a point file across them to remove the blemishes. Don't forget to clean away particles which result from filing as these will only aggravate the arcing and burning. Undoubtedly, however, if the points surfaces are not smooth the best thing to do is to replace them – they don't cost too much and are vital to good performance. Indeed, you would be surprised just how much difference good points can make to your engine's performance.

Points gap

Points cannot be expected to remain in good condition for ever – in normal operation they open and close several thousand times a minute and even though the contact surfaces are made of a tungsten compound they do wear.

The gap between the points is critical in determining the engine's performance; it is essential therefore that you make adjustments to the gap whenever necessary. Indeed, in the extreme case worn points may lead to engine overheating and ultimately serious damage.

The average gap required between the points, when fully open, is 0·014 ins. (0·35 mm.), or about the thickness of the card used for cigarette packets (see pp. 47–8). Your owner's handbook or workshop manual will indicate the exact setting for your motorcycle.

To check the points gap you should:

1. Rotate the crankshaft until the points are fully open: If you remove the spark plug from the cylinder, engage a gear and rotate the rear wheel, you will see the cam lobe rotate and the points open. The points are fully open when the heel of the moving point is on the very peak of the cam.

2. Insert the correct feeler gauge to

determine if any adjustment is necessary: if the points gap is correct you should feel a slight frictional drag as you move the feeler backwards and forwards in the gap. If, on the other hand, there is any slack between the feeler and the points, the gap needs to be narrower or, if the gap is opened up as you force in the feeler, the gap needs to be widened. Occasionally, newly fitted points do tend to close up a little after a few miles.

3. To adjust the gap, loosen the locknut or screw just enough to allow the point assembly base to move against slight resistance and insert the correct feeler.

4. Using a screwdriver blade in the slot and fulcrum provided, lever the baseplate to a position where there is just a light frictional drag (as in item 2) between the feeler and the points.

5. When the gap is correct retighten the locknut or screw. It is important to make sure that the baseplate does not move as you do this.

6. Make a final check of the gap with the correct feeler and feel for friction. You may also wish to double-check by inserting a feeler of the narrowest dimension of the range given, which should be too loose, and by inserting a feeler of the widest dimension given, which shouldn't enter at all. If this is the case you can be confident the gap is satisfactory.

Points mechanism lubrication

Although the surfaces of the points themselves need to be kept free from oil or grease, the rotating cam and the other moving pieces of the mechanism do need a little lubrication. Clearly, however, any lubrication here must be minimal. One drop of oil to each moving-arm post and a blob of grease, half the size of a matchstick head, spread around the cam are sufficient. Some mechanisms do have a small felt pad built into the mechanism, which acts as an oil store giving constant lubrication where necessary. Only a few small drops of oil, however, should be used to replenish this supply. At no time should it be so wet that oil drips off.

5. IGNITION TIMING

Correctly timed ignition is essential for complete combustion in all cylinders. As such it is one of the most important factors in obtaining efficient, economical engine performance.

If the timing is 'advanced', the spark will occur before the piston reaches the correct position, that is, a point fractionally before T.D.C., and if the timing is 'retarded', the spark will occur after the piston has reached this position.

Basically there are two methods of adjusting the ignition timing: strobe timing and static timing.

Strobe timing

With this method a special timing light is connected into the high-tension circuit and the timing light is actuated by the ignition system itself, ensuring the light flashes each time the engine fires.

To set timing using a strobe:

1. Wire the light into the circuit and point it at the mark provided on the engine's crankshaft. The mark will appear to become static because of the strobe effect of the light.

2. Ensure that the strobe static mark is lined up next to the fixed mark

provided on the casing. The timing is correct when the two marks are in line.

3. If the marks do not appear in line you will need to move the points around the cam until they do.

In practice a dial gauge should be used to check the accuracy of the existing mark, but then a strobe should be used to complete the job.

Static ignition timing

This method involves setting the points' opening position with the engine fixed in the correct position.

Using a dial gauge screwed into the spark plug hole, set the piston to the predetermined position. The exact location will vary from one motorcycle to another, but normally will be at 2–3 mm before top dead centre.

On the whole, however, ignition timing is best left to the professional as the cost of having it checked will be considerably less than the cost of any repairs that may be necessary after you have incorrectly set the timing.

6. DECARBONIZE THE CYLINDER AND EXHAUST SYSTEM: TWO-STROKES ONLY

Because they are required to burn oil in a petrol/air mixture, two-stroke engines are particularly susceptible to carbon deposits forming on the piston crown, inside the cylinder head and ports, and in the exhaust system, especially in the silencer.

Carbon deposits in the combustion chamber and around the ports, particularly the exhaust ports, will increase the compression ratio, resulting in over-heating, pre-ignition and therefore possibly engine damage.

This carbon build-up will certainly reduce the engine's overall performance and cause it to consume more fuel than necessary.

It is essential, therefore, that this carbon is periodically removed. Fortunately, not having the valves or valve gear of a four-stroke simplifies matters considerably, and decoking a two-stroke can take very little time indeed.

Decoking the exhaust

Before you begin to attack the carbon remove the exhaust system from the motorcycle and separate the silencer from the remainder of the pipe. Then (Figure 38):

1. If they are detachable, remove the baffles from inside the silencer casing. If the build-up of carbon within the silencer, and particularly around the joints, makes this difficult, heat them first as this should help.

2. Soak both items in a good degreasing solvent to remove the wet, sticky oil you'll find inside, and allow them both to dry.

3. Use a stiff wire brush and/or a blunt blade (a broken hacksaw blade works well here) to remove any hard deposits from both components. You can also try using a nail or screwdriver to poke all the baffle holes clear if the brush or blade fail.

4. If there are some really stubborn deposits which refuse to be removed, try soaking them in caustic soda to burn the carbon off. However, it will also burn your skin or clothes if it happens to get on them; it is essential that you take great care with this substance. It's useful to wear protective clothing (that is, rubber gloves) and to have a bucket of clean water ready – just in case!

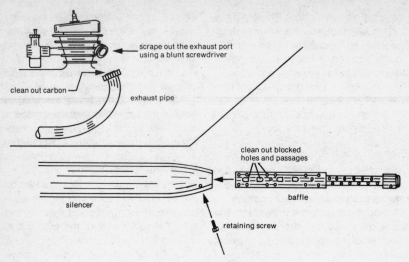

scrape out the exhaust port
using a blunt screwdriver

clean out carbon

exhaust pipe

clean out blocked
holes and passages

silencer

baffle

retaining screw

Figure 38 *Decarbonizing a two-stroke silencer and exhaust port*

To mix a solution of caustic soda you should add the soda to hot water (never add water to soda) and keep doing so until your solution will dissolve no more crystals.

If you have a container large enough, place the silencer casing and the baffle in the solution so that they are both completely covered. If you don't have such a container, block the smaller end of the silencer with putty, clay or earth, etc., and pour in the liquid. To soak the baffle you can now either pour more of the solution into a separate container and immerse the baffle in it, or simply slip the baffle into the silencer casing and leave them both to soak for twenty-four hours, and this will remove or at least loosen even the hardest carbon.

5. Rinse both items in clean water, let them dry thoroughly, and reassemble them.

6. If the baffles are not detachable, getting them thoroughly clean may be a little more difficult. Certainly one point in your favour is that modern two-stroke oils often tend to leave the silencer full of wet oil rather than hard carbon. If you find yours is in this condition, a strong solution of household detergent will probably do the trick.

On the other hand, if there are signs of stubborn carbon deposits, soaking in a solution of caustic soda may be necessary to remove them.

7. Finally, use a length of barbed wire or something similar – perhaps a piece of coat hanger wire with a hook at the end – to clean the remaining curved sections of the exhaust pipe itself.

WARNING: Caustic soda will not only dissolve oil, carbon, and your skin and clothes, it will also *completely* dissolve any alloy engine components. If you put a piston in a strong solution to dissolve carbon on the crown, for

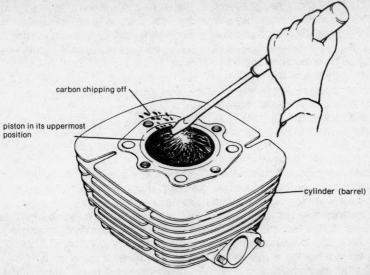

carbon chipping off

piston in its uppermost position

cylinder (barrel)

Take care not to scratch the piston surface and be sure to blow away all loose particles of carbon before refitting the cylinder head

Figure 39 Decarbonizing the piston crown

example, and if the solution is strong enough and you leave it for some time, you may return to find that only the piston rings, circlips and gudgeon pin are left.

Decoking the cylinder

When decoking the cylinder you need to:

1. Remove the cylinder head. Although the head is normally retained by four studs and nuts (which also hold the barrel), it is important that you use the correct procedure as outlined in your owner's handbook or workshop manual. Certainly, before you do begin it is important to ensure that the engine is thoroughly cool. Dismantling the cylinder head and barrel while they are warm will lead to the head becoming warped. Moreover, when removing the head and barrel never twist: it is imperative that you always give a straight pull.

2. Use a scraper made of wood to remove the carbon deposits from inside the head and the piston crown. It may be a good idea to clean the crown while the barrel is in place as this will hold the piston firm while you work on it. If the wooden scraper fails to remove the more stubborn deposits, you can try using a soft metal spoon or the rounded end of a hacksaw blade. If nothing else is available, an old blunt screwdriver may do – but take great care not to scratch the surface. Any scratches in the soft alloy head will cause carbon build-up to be more rapid next time because it will have a 'key' to stick to (Figure 39).

3. Polish the cylinder head and piston crown with wire wool or saucepan cleaning pads to remove any final

traces of carbon, and lightly polish the metal. Indeed, perfectionists may also use a fine metal polish on these surfaces.

4. Scrape off any carbon which has gathered inside the cylinder and around the ports – especially the exhaust port – with a wooden scraper or hacksaw blade, but again be very careful not to mark the metal's finish. Within the barrel the exhaust port is the prime collector of carbon and its diameter may be seriously diminished by the carbon build-up. Indeed, carbon build-up in this region is one of the most common reasons for engine power loss. If the scrapers fail to remove the harder deposits, you may need to consider using a wire wheel attached to an electric drill.

5. If necessary, again use the wire wool to remove all final traces of carbon, and polish the metal surfaces.

6. If you wish to do a thorough job, you should also remove the piston rings and clean the inside of the grooves. This is a very important job as they do tend to get gummed up with oil. Although a special tool is available to do this, it is considerably cheaper, and just as effective, to use a broken piston ring stuck into a piece of wood. If you do decide to do this final task – and it is advisable, if you want to do a good job – make sure not to leave any deposits in the grooves. Any dirt in the grooves will prevent the new rings seating correctly and therefore make the new rings a tight fit in the cylinder, which will lead to overheating, and ultimately the piston will seize in the cylinder.

7. Finally, when refitting the barrel, piston and cylinder head follow the instructions provided in your owner's handbook or workshop manual to ensure that all the joints form a good gas-tight seal. Any air leaks around these joints will have serious effects on your motorcycle's performance.

7. EXTERNAL CONDITION AND SECURITY OF THE EXHAUST SYSTEM

It is important that you attend to the following:

1. Ensure that all the nuts, bolts or screws holding the exhaust system are secure.

2. Inspect all the joints in the exhaust system from the cylinder head to the silencer for any signs of 'blowing' past slack joints or failed seals.

3. Examine the entire length of the system for any cracks or holes in the pipes.

The simplest way to check items (2) and (3) is to have the engine running while you carry out the inspections. That way you actually see any gases which are escaping or being 'blown out'.

If you do detect any signs of blowing within the system you should take steps to remedy the situation as soon as possible. Not only will it lead to occasional, yet persistent backfiring as you throttle down, but it will also make the mixture lean and reduce the motorcycle's performance.

4. If the silencer has holes on the underside for water to escape, ensure that they are clear.

8. AIR-FILTER CONDITION

Ensure that the air filter is clean and in good condition.

If this filter becomes clogged or damaged, the mixture being burned in the cylinder will be over-rich, that is, there will be a higher proportion of petrol to air than is required for maximum efficiency. The result will be a significant loss of power, increased petrol consumption, fouled spark plugs and a smoky exhaust.

For access to the air filter on your motorcycle you must refer to your owner's handbook or workshop manual. This source will also tell you which type of air filter is fitted to your engine – it is essential you know this, for each type requires a different method of cleaning.

1. *Paper filters*. If your engine is fitted with a paper air filter there is little you can do to clean it, save tapping it to remove the excess dust and using high-pressure air, from the inside outwards, to dislodge the dirt. If a pressure hose is unavailable you can try using a foot pump, but the effect will naturally be substantially reduced. Clearly, the methods for cleaning are far from satisfactory, and paper elements need replacing far more frequently than any others.

2. *Foam filters*. Increasingly these days, engines are being fitted with a washable air filter made from polyurethane foam. Cleaning is far simpler and far more effective than on the paper types: simply wash the filter in petrol or a grease-removing solvent (or even soapy water if the filter is not too dirty) and let it dry thoroughly. When it is completely dry apply a light but thorough coating of engine oil, squeeze out any excess oil and refit.

If either of these filters – paper or foam – becomes punctured, torn, soaked (in the case of paper) or simply so clogged that the dirt cannot be removed, it must be replaced.

3. *Metal or cloth filters*. These filters are far more rarely used than either paper or foam, the metal-mesh ones being rapidly replaced by the new foam filters are now only found on old motorcycles, and the cloth filter's popularity is being confined to the performance enthusiast (because of its excellent filtration with minimal air flow restriction).

Metal filters can quickly be cleaned by soaking them in a cleaning solvent and allowing them to dry. Cloth filters, on the other hand, are sprayed with a special oil before they are fitted which retains the dirt particles. When the dirt on the surface becomes too thick you merely tap or brush off the excess. Indeed it is suggested that you need only wash a cloth element when it becomes *extremely* dirty.

Whatever filter you have, however, when you are replacing it be sure that it is securely in place. It is essential that no dirt can possibly leak past its edges.

Finally, under no circumstances should you consider running the engine with the air filter removed: doing so risks overheating the engine and damaging the cylinder and piston(s).

9. CAMSHAFT CHAIN ADJUSTMENT: FOUR-STROKES ONLY

Make sure that the camshaft chain is correctly adjusted.

On more modern motorcycles the push-rod system of opening and closing the valves used on old four-stroke engines has been replaced by the 'overhead camshaft' powered from the crankshaft by means of a chain, the 'camshaft chain'. Although this system does have the advantages of absorbing considerably less energy than the push-rods and lightening the stress placed on the working parts, both of which make it more reliable, it does have the disadvantage of requiring more frequent servicing. It is important that the chain is kept in good condition and at the correct tension. Because of this, periodic checks on chain wear and tension must be carried out. A well-maintained chain, however, should last over 10,000 miles.

Unfortunately, the location of this chain (and in some cases chains) is far from universal, and different motorcycles do demand different procedures. For specific instructions on how to adjust the camshaft chain in your machine either refer to your owner's handbook or, if you are in any doubt (and it can be a tricky procedure), see your local workshop/dealer.

10. ENGINE SECURELY MOUNTED

Ensure that the engine mounts are secure and that all the engine-mounting bolts are firmly fastened.

11. CRANKCASE BREATHER TUBES: FOUR-STROKES ONLY

Ensure that the tubes which allow the crankcase to breathe are not blocked by sludge or any other deposits. Use a small pointed implement to clear them if anything is restricting the passage of air.

SIX-MONTHLY CHECKS
(or every 3,000–4,000 miles)

Complete all the daily, weekly, monthly and three-monthly checks and then attend to the following.

1. SPARK PLUG CONDITION AND GAP: FOUR-STROKES ONLY

The procedures for servicing spark plugs in four-stroke engines are exactly the same as for the plugs in a two-stroke, but simply need to be done far less frequently. For details of spark plug servicing see pp. 44–8, where the spark plugs in two-stroke engines are discussed.

One further point needs to be made, however, concerning the implications (for the internal condition of a four-stroke engine) of discovering oil-fouled plugs. In addition to the items listed on p. 45, oil-fouled plugs may also indicate: (1) that you are using the wrong grade of petrol; (2) that the valve guides or piston rings have worn; or (3) that there is an excess of upper-cylinder lubricant; while burned electrodes may be the result of a tight inlet valve tappet or a faulty head gasket, both causing air to leak into the combustion chamber.

If this does occur you should check the engine's specifications and internal condition, correct the problem(s) causing this condition and clean or replace the spark plug(s).

2. REPLACE THE SPARK PLUG(S): TWO-STROKES ONLY

As we saw earlier (p. 44), when servicing the plugs in a two-stroke engine the first thing you should do once the plug has been removed, and while inspecting it, is to decide whether or not it is worth cleaning up and resetting the gap. In brief, if a plug has covered 3,000–4,000 miles in a two-stroke engine, it is almost certainly time for a change. Renewing a plug after this distance will undoubtedly reduce fuel consumption and improve both acceleration and engine efficiency. For details of refitting new plugs and the precautions to take, see p. 48.

3. AIR-FILTER CONDITION: FOUR-STROKES ONLY

Ensure that the air filter is clean and undamaged. As with the filter in two-stroke engines, a clogged or damaged filter will result in the mixture burning in the cylinder being too rich.

In most motorcycles with four-stroke engines the air filter is made of paper and so does have a relatively limited life span, especially when compared to the foam filters commonly found in two-strokes (see p. 67).

To clean a paper filter:

1. Gently tap the filter to remove any loose dust.

2. Use high-pressure air, from the inside outwards, to remove any remaining dust. Also, you can try using the air jet from a foot pump if a high-pressure air hose is unavailable.

3. If the paper is torn or ripped, as a temporary measure you can try stapling it together as best you can. This is clearly only a temporary measure, and the element should be replaced as soon as possible.

4. If the paper is oily or greasy and beginning to disintegrate, you should have no hesitation in replacing it immediately.

5. Under no circumstances should you run the engine with the air filter removed – the weakened mixture would cause the engine to overheat and ultimately damage the engine.

4. CHANGE THE ENGINE OIL FILTER ELEMENT

As already indicated (see p. 52), you should change the engine oil and clean the oil filter every three months or 2,000 miles, whichever is the sooner. There is, however, a limit to how much dirt and other harmful particles you can remove by cleaning. If you were to continue using the same filter for a considerably greater number of miles, it would soon reach the stage where the filter was putting more impurities into the oil than it was capable of taking out. As a result, therefore, every second time the oil is changed you should also renew the oil filter.

5. VALVE (TAPPET) ADJUSTMENT: FOUR-STROKES ONLY

Adjusting the valve-operating clearance (or tappet) is a relatively straightforward operation, despite the fear people sometimes have.

The correct clearance – which is the amount of free play required in the mechanism when the valve is fully closed – is there because of the expansion of the metal components when the engine is at its normal operating temperature. The clearance ensures that the valve can still fully close even when hot.

If the clearance is too small, as the metal expands the valve will be held partially open and the hot gases which will be allowed to leak past will eventually burn out the valve seat.

On the other hand, if the clearance is too large, the extra looseness or sloppiness in the mechanism will lead to the parts wearing faster and the engine sounding much noisier.

The procedure for adjusting the clearance varies so much from one motorcycle to another that it is essential you follow the procedure as set out in your owner's handbook or workshop manual. Before you begin, however, there are several things you do need to know (and once again your owner's handbook or workshop manual should be able to supply the necessary information):

1. Which type of adjuster is employed in your motorcycle's engine. Basically there are two types of adjuster: (a) *screw tappets* (see Figure 8a, p. 17), where the adjustment involves varying the operational length of the rocker arm tip or the push-rod; (b) *shim-type tappets* (used with an overhead camshaft (O.H.C.) and often referred to as bucket tappets), where adjustment involves using a little bit of maths and some special shims.

2. Whether the clearances required are to be set with the engine *hot* or *cold*. As a general rule, in alloy engines the clearances are usually set with the engine cold, that is, the engine has not been run for at least twelve hours before you begin.

3. The precise amount of clearance required, and where it is actually to be measured.

Set out below is the very basic procedure for adjusting both types of tappet. Although these notes will give you a broad idea of what is involved and how to go about making any adjustments it would be wise to check first, with a workshop manual or your local workshop, if your motorcycle has any particular characteristics or idiosyncrasies that you should be aware of.

Screw tappet adjustment

1. Remove the spark plugs and valve covers and in some cases remove, or at least move, the petrol tank.

2. Turn the engine until the piston is at T.D.C. on the compression stroke. If either the inlet or the exhaust valve is under pressure, the piston is at T.D.C. on the exhaust stroke and *not* the compression stroke. You will need to turn the crankshaft one full revolution until the piston is at T.D.C. and the valves are fully closed, that is, the rocker arms move like small morse keys; the piston will then be back at T.D.C., but this time on the correct stroke.

3. Select a feeler gauge somewhere in the middle of the acceptable clearance range and check the size of the gap: if there is just the slightest touch of friction as the feeler enters, then the gap is correct; if there is slack, then the gap is too big; and if it is extremely tight, then the gap is too small.

4. To adjust the clearance:
(a) Loosen the locking nut and turn the adjuster as necessary: clockwise will reduce the gap, anti-clockwise will increase it.
(b) Turn the adjuster until the feeler blade slips in and out with only very slight friction.
(c) Hold the adjuster in place and tighten the locking nut.
(d) Recheck the gap with the correct gauge and, as an extra check, try inserting the next largest feeler blade – it should either not enter or be extremely tight.

5. Repeat the operation on the other valve.

6. Move to the other cylinders in turn and use the same procedure as in (4) to bring all the clearances within the specified limits.

7. Refit the valve covers, plugs and the petrol tank.

Shim tappet adjustment

It is far more difficult to give a general procedure for this type of adjuster as the details do differ quite substantially. However, in brief, you will need to:

1. Remove the valve cover, spark plugs, the contact breaker cover and possibly the petrol tank.

2. Rotate the crankshaft until the heel of the cam is bearing on the exhaust valve tappet. In this position the peak of the cam should be pointed upwards.

3. Slide the feeler gauge between the cam and the shim and check that the gap is within the specified limits. If it is incorrect, however, you will need to measure the gap and replace the existing shim – with a thinner one to increase the gap or a thicker one to reduce the gap.

4. To calculate the size of the shim required remove and measure the size of the existing shim and use it to calculate the size of the one now required.

5. Insert the new shim(s) and recheck with the feeler.

6. Repeat the procedure with the other valves.

7. Refit the cover(s), plug(s), contact breaker cover and the petrol tank.

This is certainly more complicated than for screw adjusters, but, once they are set, bucket tappets rarely lose their adjustment between services.

6. FUEL SYSTEM

When servicing the fuel system you should always ensure that there is an uninterrupted supply of fuel to the carburettors, and that there are no leaks within the system.

To do this you need to:

1. Check that the petrol flows freely through the fuel lines: disconnect the fuel line from the carburettor, place a small container beneath the bottom of the tube and open the fuel tap. The petrol should flow freely out of the pipe in a full stream. If it does not flow out freely, try removing the petrol cap; if the petrol flows correctly with the cap off, it is likely that the petrol cap breather vent is blocked. Use a small pin to clean it out.

If the petrol flow still appears obstructed, even with the cap off, you must inspect the fuel lines themselves for any obstructions. There may be dirt or simply a kink in the pipe. If the lines are clean and straight, however, the obstruction is almost certainly occurring inside the petrol tap, and you should turn your attention there.

2. Check that the fuel filter, inside the fuel tap, is clean. To ensure the filter is clean, remove the filter bowl from the petrol tap and clean both the bowl and the filter with either petrol or a cleaning solvent. If the filter has become blocked by varnish-like deposits petrol is unlikely to make much impression on them. If it is a reusable filter, and almost all are, you will need a special carburettor cleanser. This basically consists of a chlorinated hydrocarbon solution. If the filter is old it may not be able to withstand cleaning once again; in which case, the best thing to do is throw it away and buy a new one. Dirty

fuel filters are one of the major causes of carburettor starvation.

3. Inspect the fuel lines and fuel tap ('petcock', as it is sometimes called) for any white stains which will indicate that petrol has been leaking.

4. Examine the fuel lines for any signs of perishing or splits.

5. Make sure, while operating the fuel tap, that it is secure. If the tap is sloppy tighten it up using the screw in the outer plate or replace the tap if necessary.

6. Ensure that the bolts fixing the fuel tap to the petrol tank are secure.

7. Inspect underneath the fuel tank for rust and pay particular attention to the seams for leakages. If you do discover any rust on the tank treat it immediately: remove the rust (and there are many products on the market), prime and repaint it. This is the only sure way to prevent leaks developing.

8. Check that the method of mounting the petrol tank is secure and that the anti-vibration rubbers are not perished.

9. Ensure that any pipes linking the two undersides of a fuel tank are in good condition and securely fitted.

7. CONDITION, ADJUSTMENT AND, IF YOU RIDE A MULTI-CYLINDER MOTORCYCLE, SYNCHRONIZATION OF THE CARBURETTOR(S)

You must ensure that the carburettors are clean, correctly adjusted (sometimes referred to as 'tuned') and, if your engine has more than one carburettor, that they are synchronized (sometimes referred to as being 'in balance').

The carburettor is one of the most complicated items on a motorcycle. Sometimes simply being able to remember the names and distinguish the various adjusters, needles and jets can be quite a feat. Use Figures 40a and 40b, and perhaps your workshop manual or owner's handbook, to help you locate the various key components.

It is important that you tune and balance the carburettors only after you have serviced the rest of the engine: firstly, because it cannot be done accurately until all the other engine adjustments are correct; and secondly, because even if you were to try there is little point in precisely adjusting the carburettor's operation if the other components in the engine are set incorrectly.

Cleaning

Dismantle the carburettor to be cleaned and wash all the parts in petrol or a dirt-removing solvent. You should ensure that the float needle, the float seat, the pilot jet, the needle jet and the main jet are all clean and that the float bowl is free of any dirt or rust particles.

While the carburettor is dismantled it is a good idea to check for wear: scuffing on the airslide or excessive play between the airslide and the carburettor body will both lead to air leaks. If there are any scuff marks on the needle, or it is bent, it should be replaced. If the needle jet hole is oval instead of circular, this too should be replaced.

Also, before tuning and balancing you should ensure that:

1. The filters and sludge traps in the bottom of the float chamber are clean.

2. The float height is correct (you

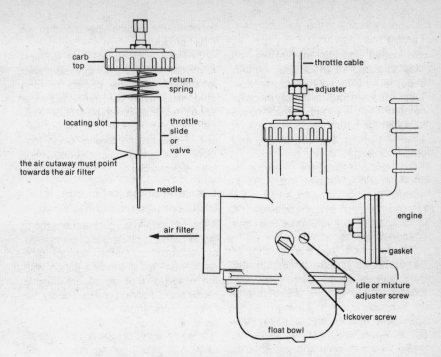

The mixture screw is usually the smaller adjuster and is set flush to or below the surface. The tickover screw is usually larger than the mixture screw and generally above the surface, and it may be knurled for your fingers to grip on

Figure 40a Carburettor layout

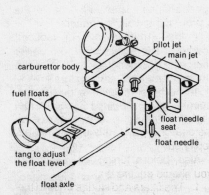

Figure 40b Carburettor with float bowl removed showing layout

should reset it, if necessary) and that the float itself is undamaged. To check whether the float is punctured or not, shake it and listen for the sound of petrol splashing around inside.

3. The needle valves are seating correctly. If they are you should not be able to blow through the fuel line when just the weight of the float is holding the valve closed.

4. The float chamber gasket is in good condition and that, when the securing screws are fitted, there is a petrol-tight seal.

Tuning

Idle speed and idle mixture are the only adjustments which are normally necessary at the six-monthly service. Tuning the carburettor largely involves compromising various characteristics to obtain the optimum blend of power, ease of starting, smooth running and petrol consumption.

To avoid offsetting one alteration by another and disturbing the various mixture settings unnecessarily while refining the carburettor's operation, it is inadvisable to make more than one change at a time.

There is, however, a wide range of carburettors and, although in principle they operate in the same way, the location of the various adjusters and the procedures for adjusting the idle speed and mixture are not always the same. As a very general guide to making these adjustments you should:

1. Ensure that the engine is at its normal operating temperature before you make any adjustments: a cold engine requires a different mixture to a warm one (that is, a cold one may require the choke to be open, and you can't set the carburettor while it is).

2. Slacken off the throttle cable adjusters to remove all the tension from the cable.

3. Turn in the idle-mixture screw, sometimes called the air screw or pilot screw, to its fully home position, then turn it back 1¼ to 1½ turns (depending on the specifications set down for your motorcycle).

4. Turn the idle-speed adjuster until the engine speed slows down and the engine begins to falter.

5. Turn the idle-mixture screw whichever way is necessary to increase the engine speed and make it run smoothly.

6. Repeat steps (4) and (5) and carry on doing so until the idle speed is correct and the engine running smoothly. The recommended idle speed for your machine will be indicated in your workshop manual.

7. Readjust the throttle cable tension to the specifications set down for your motorcycle.

Synchronization (balancing): (multi-carburettor engines only)

Although individual carburettors feeding separate cylinders can be treated as separate units when tuning, each carburettor must be in balance with the other(s), that is, all the throttle slides should open simultaneously (be in synchronization) and by the same amount.

If the carburettors are not in balance, at any throttle opening not only will one cyclinder be doing less work than the others, but the others will be forced to carry it: power output is therefore unbalanced, performance is reduced accordingly and slow running becomes very poor. For maximum performance it is essential that all the carburettors work in harmony.

Indeed, many cases of reduced overall performance and low power output can be attributed to unbalanced (unsynchronized) carburettors.

If the carburettors are out of synchronization, a trained ear can often detect it from the uneven sound of the air intake and engine vibrations. Some mechanics may also diagnose this problem simply by placing a hand over the end of the silencer and feeling for the uneven exhaust pulses. The most efficient and most accurate method, however, is to use a vacuum gauge consisting of two, three, four or six separate gauges, one connected to each cylinder. To balance the carburettors an equal volume reading is required on each gauge. Specific details of how to operate the gauge, the procedure to adopt and the location of the necessary adjuster for the carburettors on your motorcycle will be provided with the vacuum gauge itself, or possibly in your owner's handbook or workshop manual.

If you are fortunate enough to have access to a vacuum gauge, and feel confident enough to use it, it can also be used to monitor any adjustments you make in tuning the carburettors. Using the vacuum gauges in this way is particularly helpful in achieving minimum fuel consumption at relatively high cruise speeds.

For most people, however, buying a vacuum gauge is simply beyond their means – understandably, as they are quite expensive. If you do not have access to a gauge your local dealer or workshop will undoubtedly have the necessary equipment and should be willing to balance the carburettor for a nominal sum. Remember, the adjustment of the carburettors on a multi-carburettor engine is critical and does require a good deal of skill. If you are at all unsure, don't hesitate to visit your local workshop on this occasion. The importance of balanced carburettors cannot be overstressed.

Although there is virtually no other way to balance constant velocity carburettors than with a vacuum gauge, a variety of other methods can be used to balance other types of carburettor.

1. Another device, which is rarely used, consists basically of a U-tube containing paraffin (kerosene). The device connects to the bell mouths of the carburettors and any inequality in the airflow between the two carburettors is revealed by the unequal levels of liquid in the tube.

2. Some carburettors can be balanced by removing a screw from the side of the mixing chamber and opening the throttle until a pip on the airslide can be seen through the hole. The other carburettor in the set can be aligned in a similar way using the cable adjusters or throttle linkages.

3. Finally, for those with experience there are the more intuitive methods. If you have good hearing you can balance the carburettors by holding a tube to the air intake and listening; adjustments should be made so that the air passing over the top of each tube makes the same sound. These methods are clearly only for experienced and confident mechanics, with *good* hearing – they are extremely unsophisticated and difficult to use.

8. REAR-SUSPENSION UNITS

On conventional dual suspension you should ensure that:

1. Both units are on the same damper and spring settings.

2. Both the upper and lower mounting bolts are securely fastened.

3. There are no signs of perishing in the rubber bushes, top and bottom.

4. There are no leaks in the damper units.

On motorcycles with monoshock suspension you must make sure that:

1. Both the upper and lower end-mounting bolts are secure.

2. There are no leaks of gas or oil from the unit.

3. The damping effect is correct. If it is correct, the resistance you feel as you depress the rod should be slight on the compression stroke and considerable on the return stroke.

4. There is no rust on the outer casing. If there is, this should be removed as soon as possible.

IMPORTANT: Monoshock suspension units frequently contain nitrogen under high pressure. You should only ever use nitrogen to refill them and never attempt to disassemble any unit. Also, attempting to burn old units is highly dangerous.

9. SWINGING-ARM MOVEMENT

Check for play in the rear swinging-arm pivot. To do this prop the rear wheel off the ground and pull/push it from side to side: there should be no movement in this direction at all. If there is slight play check the tightness of the pivot spindle securing bolt: the movement may be because this is fractionally loose, in which case tightening it should eliminate any play.

If, on the other hand, there is more than the slightest play, the pivot bearings are worn. You must examine the whole pivot and replace all worn parts.

When you feel confident that the pivot is satisfactory grease the bearings – a grease nipple is usually provided.

10. NUTS, BOLTS AND SCREWS ALL TIGHT

Ensure that all nuts, bolts and screws on the motorcycle – including the cylinder head bolts, for which you will need a torque wrench – are securely fastened.

11. FRAME CONDITION

Make a visual check of the frame for any cracks and rust: you should pay particular attention to the areas around the joints.

Any rust patches which do appear should be taken care of as soon as possible: sand them down, prime and repaint them.

If there is any indication that the frame is cracked or split DO NOT ride it. Under no circumstances should you ever consider riding to the local workshop, which will probably do any welding necessary – either take it on another vehicle or push it there!

12. COOLING SYSTEM: RADIATOR CONDITION

When servicing the cooling system you should:

1. Visually inspect the outside of the core elements of the radiator for possible clogging by dirt, leaves or insects. If necessary you can usually remove any obstructions with a high-pressure air hose.

2. Ensure that none of the fins are bent; sometimes these can be straightened with a screwdriver, for example, but be gentle.

3. Check the hoses for splits or cracks, particularly where the circlips tighten onto the rubber. Leaks here may be cured by tightening the clips, but if not, you will probably have to replace the pipe.

4. Check for leaks at the thermostat feed pipes and the coolant drain plug.

YEARLY CHECKS
(or every 8,000–10,000 miles)

Complete all the daily, weekly, monthly, three-monthly and six-monthly checks and then attend to the following.

1. CLEAN AND ADJUST BOTH FRONT AND REAR BRAKES

Ensure that both brakes, whether they are disc or drum types, are clean and operating correctly.

Disc brakes

1. Remove and inspect the pads. Ensure that they are not exessively or unevenly worn, and that there is no oil or grease on the friction surface – the pads will need to be replaced if any significant traces are found as braking will be impaired.

Your owner's handbook or work-shop manual should indicate how to remove and replace the pads on your motorcycle.

2. Dismantle the caliper and clean any dust or rust particles from the recesses into which the pads fit. Take care that none of the particles, which are likely to contain asbestos dust, get into your lungs or eyes and wipe the caliper with a clean, dry rag.

3. Ensure that there are no signs of rust on the exposed area of the pistons and use a *soft* wire brush, but *not* a solvent and *not* a stiff wire brush, to clean up any which are there. You should also make sure that the piston is not seized and moves freely in and out as required. If one pad is worn more than the other, this may be an indication that the piston behind the least worn pad is sticking – this pos-sibility should be investigated. Infor-mation on how to remove, clean and replace a seized or sticking piston should be supplied in your owner's handbook or workshop manual.

When you are satisfied the piston is clean and free, lightly lubricate it with a smear of hydraulic fluid.

4. Before replacing the pads smear a small amount of high-melting-point grease or copper slip on to the *back* of the pad (NOT the friction side) to prevent brake squeal.

5. Inspect the disc plate for scoring or any other damage. It is unlikely, however, that the disc itself will require attention unless it is badly scored, when braking efficiency will be reduced. If necessary, the disc should be replaced by a new one.

Drum brakes

1. Dismantle the brake drum, inspect the drums and clean out any dust or rust particles. Use a clean dry cloth to wipe away any particles.

2. Examine the inside surfaces of the drums for cracks, grooves, scoring or any other damage. If the drum is marked or warped slightly it is possible to have it cleaned up on a lathe by a specialist. However, if the scoring is too deep or the warpage too severe, a new drum will be necessary.

3. Inspect the brake shoes and ensure that they are not excessively or unevenly worn. Also, make sure that there is no oil or grease on the friction surface: if there is, they will need to be replaced.

4. Examine the brake return springs and ensure that they are not worn, pulled or collapsed: if they are, they must be replaced. The normal free length of the brake return springs on your motorcycle should be indicated in your owner's handbook or workshop manual.

5. Inspect the brake cam and plate for any signs of wear or damage: if necessary, they should be replaced.

It cannot be stressed too greatly that detecting wear on the component parts of the braking system is critical if full braking efficiency is to be maintained.

More information about braking problems and cures can be found on pp. 231–4.

2. REAR-BRAKE PEDAL: POSITION ADJUSTMENT

Ensure that the position of the rear-brake pedal is correct and comfortable. If you need to lift your foot off the foot rest to reach the pedal, the pedal is in the wrong position. It's worth while spending the few minutes required to reset the position and make operation both easy and safe.

Normally the pedal is secured by the combination of a spline and spindle secured by a small screw at the fulcrum. To reset the pedal, simply pull it from the spline and refit it one or two notches up or down, depending on whether you want it higher or lower. Any adjustment should move the pedal so that it now sits neatly under your foot while you are in your normal riding position.

Adjusting the position of the brake pedal may have disturbed the brake and brake light adjustment: these should be checked and suitably adjusted if necessary. Precise and final positioning of the pedal is a matter of choice, but you should always make sure that the brake does not bind when the pedal is fully returned. In readjusting the brake light you must ensure that it comes on the instant the brakes begin to operate: any delay in indicating you are slowing down may cause an accident. Drivers unfortunately do not always travel far enough behind to allow for even a split-second's delay in braking.

3. CHANGE THE BRAKE FLUID IN A HYDRAULIC SYSTEM

Brake fluid is hygroscopic, that is, it absorbs water, which in this case can actually find its way through the wall of the brake hose: the result is contaminated fluid. When the brake is operated, the water within the system heats up and vapour locks form, destroying the brake's efficiency.

Changing the fluid on a regular basis can prevent this; you will require: (1) a tin of fresh fluid; (2) a jam jar or bottle to catch the old fluid; (3) a length of plastic pipe – the bore must be small enough to fit tightly over the bleed nipple and long enough to reach the jar on the ground; (4) the correct spanner to fit the nut on the bleed nipple.

To change the fluid

1. Remove the rubber dust cap from the bleed nipple and push the pipe tightly into place.

2. Place the lower end of the pipe into the jar.

3. Open the bleed nipple.

4. Remove the master cylinder reservoir cap and the diaphragm.

5. Squeeze and relax the brake lever or pedal. As you do so, fluid will be pushed out of the pipe. Continue to squeeze and release until you have expelled all the fluid in the system.

6. Once you are satisfied the system is empty, close the bleed nipple and top up the system. Do take care, however, to protect the paintwork in

the vicinity of the reservoir – remember, brake fluid is a good paint remover and any spillage could be costly.

7. Open the nipple again and operate the lever (or pedal) until the fluid leaving the nipple is the same colour as the fluid entering the reservoir. While you are doing this you must ensure that the reservoir level remains constant by continually adding more fluid.

8. Bleed out any air which may have found its way into the system while you are emptying it.

To bleed a hydraulic system you must:

1. Make sure that the reservoir is full.

2. Ensure that the hose is still attached to the bleed nipple and that the lower end is immersed in the jar of old fluid.

3. Open the bleed nipple with one hand and slowly operate the brake lever (or pedal) with the other.

4. As the movement of the lever (or pedal) is coming to an end, close off the nipple and let the lever (or pedal) slowly return. Closing the nipple fractionally before you allow the lever (or pedal) to return ensures that the old fluid (or air) cannot be sucked back up into the system.

5. Check the level of fluid in the reservoir and ensure that it is still within the minimum and maximum levels marked on the reservoir wall.

6. Open the bleed nipple again, operate the lever (or pedal) and again close the bleed nipple before the lever (or pedal) comes to a stop.

7. Between all successive strokes of the lever (or pedal) make a quick visual check of the reservoir fluid level. If you allow it to drop below the required level and operate the brake

you risk air being drawn into the system – the very substance you are trying to remove.

8. Continue bleeding until no more bubbles appear in the jar. This should be an indication that the system is completely air-free.

9. Close the bleed nipple securely and replace the dust cap. If you don't have one, buy one.

10. Replenish the reservoir to the required level, refit the diaphragm and screw on the cap.

4. STEERING-HEAD BEARINGS

Check and adjust the steering-head bearings (Figure 41). If they are too loose the vibrations at the front wheel will make riding uncomfortable and unsafe. On the other hand, if they are too tight this will not only interfere with your driving, making it more difficult and more tiring than it need be, but will also lead to premature bearing failure because of excessive wear.

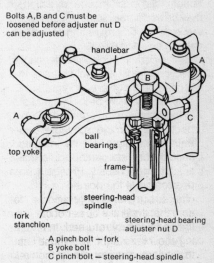

Bolts A,B and C must be loosened before adjuster nut D can be adjusted

handlebar

A

B

A

C

ball bearings

top yoke

frame

steering-head spindle

fork stanchion

steering-head bearing adjuster nut D

A pinch bolt – fork
B yoke bolt
C pinch bolt – steering-head spindle

Figure 41 Steering-head bearing layout

For some reason, however, this task is often overlooked, despite its being so simple.

To check if they are too loose:

1. Raise the front wheel off the ground.

2. Either place your fingers on the head cap (the upper bearing) and rock the forks backwards and forwards, or hold the forks near the wheel spindle and gently pull and push them backwards and forwards. In neither case should there be any significant movement or free play.

To check if the forks are too tight:

1. With the front wheel still off the ground set the forks centrally and tap one end of the handlebars with your fingers. The forks should turn to full lock under their own weight.

2. Recentralize them and this time tap the other end of the handlebars to test the other lock.

Having observed the forks turn you will have to interpret what you find yourself. For example, if the forks appear stiff only in one direction, it may be that some clumps of stiff wiring are slowing or preventing full movement in any one direction.

Stiff operation in both directions, however, almost certainly means that the head bearings are too tight.

The solution in both instances – whether they are too tight or too loose – is the same: the movable upper bearing will have to be adjusted. Unfortunately, the procedure to make this adjustment does vary slightly from one motorcycle to another.

The recommended procedure for your motorcycle will be set out in your owner's handbook or workshop manual. Follow the instructions to the letter and continue checking the tension and adjusting until you are satisfied it is correct.

5. CONDITION AND ADJUSTMENT OF FRONT AND REAR WHEEL BEARINGS

Make sure that both the front and rear wheel bearings are not excessively worn.

To check if they are worn you need to take hold of the wheel rim – placing your hands to the left and to the right of the wheel spindle – and try rocking the wheel about the spindle. There should be no movement at all – although, if there is slight movement, this does not necessarily mean that the bearings are worn out. First check the wheel spindle nut, if necessary tighten it and then recheck the bearings. If there is still movement in the wheel and the spindle is now fixed, the bearings are worn and will need replacing shortly. Clearly, however, the extent of the wear can be estimated by the amount of movement you observe. If you do decide that, although they are worn, it is not yet excessive, you should now keep a closer eye on them and check for wear every couple of weeks. It is hard for us to specify just how much movement is permissible on your motorcycle before you must change them, but let us say this: worn bearings are dangerous and it is far better to change them immediately you discover wear – even if they may possibly have run another couple of hundred miles – than to leave it too late.

6. FRONT AND REAR WHEEL SPINDLES CLEAN AND WELL GREASED

Having once established that the wheel bearings are satisfactory you now need to ensure that both the front and rear wheel spindles are clean and well greased.

Taking one wheel at a time:

1. Remove the split or spring pin and screw off the spindle nut.

2. Withdraw the wheel spindle from one side and simultaneously replace it with a metal bar or a long screwdriver from the other: this will allow you to leave the wheel in place while you clean and lubricate the spindle.

Removing stubborn spindles (Figure 42). If a spindle has not been removed for some time, quite often it becomes rusted into place and can be very difficult to knock out (especially without damaging the thread). The problem can easily be solved with a solid wall, a block of wood, measuring will drive the spindle *from*. When you now hammer out the spindle (taking care to protect the threads), the bike will be solid and there is far less chance of any damage being done to either the swinging arm or the fork leg.

3. Clean off the old grease with a rag and, if necessary, a solvent cleaner.

4. Remove any signs of rust with fine emery cloth.

5. When you are satisfied it is clean, cover the spindle with a fresh coating of grease.

6. Remove the metal bar or screwdriver and replace the spindle.

7. Replace and tighten the spindle nut and use the wheel-bearing check to ensure it's tight enough – but don't

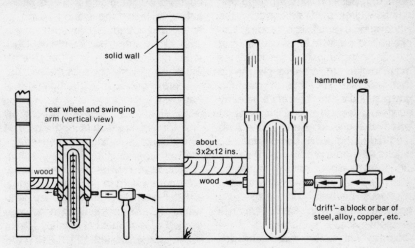

Figure 42 Stubborn wheel spindles

about 2×3×12ins., and a friend. Place one end of the wooden block against the wall and position the bike so that the other end of the block is against either the swing arm or the fork leg (depending, of course, on whether you need to remove the rear or front spindle) on the side opposite the one you make it over-tight.

8. Refit a *new* split pin or the original spring pin.

7. WHEELS BALANCED

Ensure that both wheels are perfectly balanced.

Some parts of a wheel, such as the tyre valve, are heavier than others and this extra weight in one section of the wheel makes for an asymmetric load. As soon as the wheel begins to rotate, that section of the wheel tries to fly outwards and its path tends to become elliptical instead of circular: the result is that the suspension for that wheel begins to bounce up and down. And, the faster you travel, the more exaggerated that movement becomes. Balancing the wheels will prevent this happening.

On modern motorcycles this is normally done in the factory as the wheel is being built; lead weights are attached around the wheel rim until it is in balance. While these weights remain in position, and provided that any new tyres are fitted correctly, the wheel should remain in balance indefinitely. The problem is, of course, that the balance weights do sometimes move or fall off. We strongly advise that you take your motorcycle to a professional for this part of your yearly service. Although it can be done at home, the checking and rechecking required to rebalance can be done so much faster on a proper jig or with the aid of dynamic balancing machines that it is hardly worth all the trouble you would have to go to – especially as there should only be a small charge for the service.

However, if you are a dedicated do-it-yourself motorcyclist, here's one way of checking and rebalancing your wheels:

1. You either (a) make a special jig to hold the wheel or (b) do the job with the wheel still on the motorcycle.
2. If you elect to use system (b), you must first remove the brake caliper, or brake drums, and disconnect any other items that may cause drag, such as the rear chain or the speedometer cable.
3. Raise the wheel you intend to balance clear of the ground and ensure that it can spin freely.
4. Spin the wheel and let it rotate until it comes naturally to rest.
5. Mark the lowest point with chalk.
6. Spin the wheel again and when it stops once again mark the lowest point.
7. You will probably soon discover that one particular section of the wheel is always at the lowest point once the wheel has stopped: this will be the heaviest section of the wheel.
8. Strictly you should use lead weights to counter this uneven distribution of weight, but an excellent alternative is lead tape wound round a spoke and adequately secured.
9. Using either lead weights or lead tape, add extra weight to the side of the wheel directly opposite the section you previously identified as being the heaviest.
10. First fit the smallest weight, or one turn of lead tape, and test the wheel again, spinning and marking.
11. If the original heavy section continues to stop at the lowest point add more weight to the opposite side.
12. Given time and patience you will arrive at a moment when no one section of the wheel constantly stops in the lowest position. When that happens your wheel is in balance and you can replace the caliper or drums and any other items you disconnected.

8. CHANGE THE FRONT-FORK OIL

Before you commence draining the forks take two seconds to inspect the fork seals for any signs of leakage which might indicate that the seals were worn out and required replacement. However, if you are confident that the seals are satisfactory:

1. Remove the large bolt at the top of the fork leg. This bolt is under pressure from the fork spring, so be careful when you come to the final few threads. If you change the oil in one leg at a time you can avoid the front of the bike collapsing. Otherwise you will need to raise the front of the motorcycle clear of the ground.

2. Remove the drain screw, usually located at the bottom of the fork leg on the outside edge, and drain out the old oil.

3. Once you are sure all the oil has drained out replace the drain plug.

4. Refill the fork leg with the required amount of the correct oil. It is important here that you put the same amount of oil into each leg and that it is of the correct viscosity for your motorcycle and the type of riding you intend to do. Refer to your owner's handbook or workshop manual if you are unsure.

5. Replace the top bolt – until the first few threads catch hold you will have to press down quite hard to compress the spring while still turning the bolt.

6. Repeat operations (1) to (5) on the other leg.

7. Ensure that the top bolts and drain screws are tight and that no oil is leaking out.

8. If your motorcycle has air-and-oil forks, pump the fork to the recommended pressure for how you intend to use the motorcycle. Again you may need to refer to your owner's handbook or workshop manual for this information.

9. REPLACE PAPER-TYPE AIR FILTERS

With continued use dirt steadily gathers in the vanes of a paper air filter and, despite your more frequent checks, these deposits eventually become virtually impossible to remove. It is advisable, therefore, to fit a new filter once a year.

Remember, a partially blocked air filter will increase your petrol consumption and reduce the motorcycle's performance, as the engine will be running too rich.

10. FUSES AND THE FUSE BOX

Ensure that all the fuses are sound and that all the electrical leads from the fuse box are not rusty, trapped or kinked.

11. LUBRICATE THE FINAL-DRIVE ASSEMBLY OF SHAFT-DRIVE MOTORCYCLES

Check and, if necessary, lubricate the gear mechanism of the drive shaft.

Although this system of final drive is virtually trouble-free and maintenance-free, especially when compared to chain drive, there are a couple of items you do need to attend to on a regular basis: (1) replenish the level of oil in the gear housing; and (2) regrease the drive shaft joint.

The oil level

As with a gearbox, the drive shaft mechanism also requires the oil level to be maintained within given limits. You should make a yearly check and replenish the oil supply as required. It is extremely important, however, that you use only the correct grade of oil – usually an extreme-pressure gear oil often known as hypoid oil. For the correct procedure, and grade and amount of oil necessary for your motorcycle, refer to your owner's handbook or workshop manual.

Regreasing

Greasing the drive shaft joint is usually done separately by means of a grease nipple on the gear housing. Simply attach a grease gun to the nipple and pump in three or four measures of multi-purpose lithium-based grease.

TWO-YEARLY CHECKS
(or every 15,000–16,000 miles)

Complete all the daily, weekly, monthly, three-monthly, six-monthly and yearly checks, and then attend to the following:

1. REMOVE AND CLEAN OIL PUMP STRAINER

Remove and clean the oil pump strainer.

However, because the location of the pump and the procedure for removing it and its strainer do vary from one motorcycle to another, it is impossible for us to give any detailed information on this item of servicing. What we can say is that having removed the strainer you should wash it and the inside of the pump thoroughly in petrol (or another suitable solvent), and make sure that any collections of dust, dirt or rust particles are removed before you replace it.

2. CHANGE THE OIL IN A SHAFT-DRIVEN FINAL-DRIVE ASSEMBLY

Like all oils, the hypoid oil in a drive shaft mechanism eventually wears thin, becomes contaminated and so needs to be replaced. Although there are minor differences from one motorcycle to another (and you should certainly check your owner's handbook or workshop manual before you begin), below is a brief outline of what you should do:

1. Place a suitable container underneath the drain plug in the drive shaft gear casing.
2. Remove the filler plug and then the drain plug.
3. Allow all the oil to drain out.
4. When you are satisfied that all the old oil is out, replace the drain plug.
5. Fill the gear housing with the required quantity and grade of hypoid oil (the specific requirement for your motorcycle will be indicated in your owner's handbook or workshop manual).

You must take great care as you pour in the oil that no foreign material enters the gear casing and that none of the oil spills on to the braking system.

3. CHANGE THE COOLANT IN A LIQUID-COOLED ENGINE

Drain and flush out the old solution and refill the radiator with fresh coolant. To do this you must:

Draining

1. Ensure that the motorcycle is level – put it either on the centre stand if it has one, or on some form of prop.
2. Remove the radiator cap. Unfortunately, on some motorcycles you do need to remove both the petrol tank and seat to gain access to the cap. Check in your workshop manual for the procedure on your bike. If you have been running the motorcycle and the engine is hot, it is important that you place a thick rag over the cap and turn it just slightly at first – this will allow any pressure that has built up to escape. It would certainly be unwise to try removing the cap from a hot radiator without a rag. Moreover, if you remove the cap immediately, the rapid pressure drop causes the liquid to boil and shoot out of the filler hole in a scalding fountain which will not only damage any paintwork it touches, but, more importantly, will also burn you! Ideally, of course, you should allow the engine to cool thoroughly before you begin.
3. Place a suitable container under the radiator, remove the drain plug and ensure all the liquid is drained.

Flushing

4. With continued use the build-up of scale and other deposits on the inside walls (particularly if you haven't used distilled water) steadily renders the radiator more and more inefficient. Because of this you should flush out the entire system each time you change the coolant. To do this:
   (a) Refit the drain plug.
   (b) Refill the system with clean water and flushing agent. Take great care in doing this not to use an agent for iron engines in an aluminium engine.
   (c) Run the engine for about ten minutes and drain out the flushing solution.
   (d) Repeat the procedure twice more with clean water.
5. Ensure that the drain plug is fitted securely and that the hose clips are tight.
6. Slowly add the recommended solution (as we saw on p. 40, this is likely to be a 50/50 mixture of distilled water and anti-freeze, but you should check first with your owner's handbook or workshop manual).
7. When the radiator appears full, run the engine at a low r.p.m. for a few moments – thirty seconds should be enough to release any trapped air pockets – and replenish the coolant level once more.
8. When the coolant level reaches the full mark, replace the radiator cap and refit items you have had to remove to allow you access.

MAINTENANCE OF MOTORCYCLES USED OFF THE ROAD

After *every* ride on the dirt (off the road) you should clean your bike and check several key items. These checks certainly need to be done before you go out again and, although you will probably be tired (if it was a good ride), it is advisable to clean and service your motorcycle soon after you return. This way:

1. Your bike is ready if a friend suggests you go for a ride at short notice.
2. Any mud or dirt does not have time to go hard.

3. Moisture in the dirt or mud has less time to corrode nuts and bolts, etc.

4. If you find anything broken or worn you have time to repair or replace it.

After every ride, then, you should:

1. Wash and dry the whole motorcycle.

2. Check, adjust and lubricate the controls and cables.

3. Check the wheels, tyres and spokes.

4. Clean and, if required, oil the air filter.

5. Check the condition and gap(s) of the spark plug(s).

6. Clean, lubricate and check the tension of the final-drive chain.

7. Apply fresh coatings of grease or oil to all the lubrication points.

These simple tasks don't take long and they will ensure your motorcycle looks good and performs well for much longer.

CHAPTER THREE
SOLVING ENGINE PROBLEMS

DON'T PANIC!

Problems always seem to occur in awkward situations, or when you are late, and try as you will the bike just won't start. If your natural reaction is to keep on kicking (or pushing the start button) until you collapse (or until the battery is completely flat), try to resist the temptation. If the motorcycle won't start with relative ease, that is, with the first couple of tries, it is unlikely to start at all. Continually working the kickstart or electric start will probably be just a waste of time.

The key is to keep calm and not to panic – even if you are miles away from home: review the situation and set about tracing the cause in a methodical manner. Problem solving does not have to be a major crisis for even the inexperienced motorcyclist.

Always keep in mind: (1) what your engine can and cannot do; (2) that a motorcycle is (despite your love affair with it) a machine and can do no more than its component parts will allow it to; (3) it is incapable of thought and is certainly incapable of conspiring against you, despite what you may think sometimes; and (4) that nothing mechanical can occur without a reason.

There is certainly no need to feel intimidated by your motorcycle, even if it is rather strange to you technically. Simply follow the suggested procedures and continue to keep calm: you will be surprised at your own ability to identify, isolate *and* remedy almost any problem in a reasonable time.

Whereas a professional mechanic frequently has the advantages of modern diagnostic equipment (which can virtually explore the inside of the engine for him) and a wealth of mechanical experience to draw on – both of which help him to go to the heart of the problem quite quickly – for the amateur mechanic, tracking down the cause of a problem often requires going through a painstaking process to eliminate all the *possible* causes until he has traced the *actual* cause of the problem. Moreover, he is frequently forced to rely on more old-fashioned methods: common sense, a logical approach to the situation and, above all, patience.

Also involved in the *art* of problem solving is keeping your mind simple – resist the temptation to let your imagination run away with you, and don't get complicated in your thinking too soon. If you do, you will undoubtedly overlook the 'simple' (maybe even facile) little thing which is at the bottom of it all. A good example of this is the engine cut-out switch. If we had a pound for every time a motorcyclist, and not only an inexperienced one has pushed a bike into a workshop with the complaint 'It won't start' or 'It just stopped', only to have the switch put to 'on' and the motorcycle started immediately, we'd be rich, to say the least. A basic motorcycle repair motto, if you like, is 'Think simple first'.

Start thinking immediately you suspect a problem. When you are investigating problems it is important to always keep in mind that the internal-combustion engine needs four basic elements to operate: (1) a fuel/air mixture reaching the combustion chamber in the correct proportions; (2) an adequate level of compression; (3) a good strong spark at the right time, to ignite the compressed mixture; and (4) sufficient lubrication to prevent overheating, rapid wear and seizure.

In essence your engine consists of four basic systems: (1) a fuel/carburation system; (2) a mechanical system; (3) an ignition system; and (4) a lubrication system. If all these systems are in order, your motorcycle should operate satisfactorily: the chances of your problem being caused by a failure/defect elsewhere are slight. In fact, probably 90 per cent of all the faults that will cause you problems will be in the engine unit, this being the major part of your motorcycle.

When it comes actually to investigating problems and their causes you should begin doing so even before the motorcycle has come to a stop (assuming, that is, that you managed to get it going in the first place). You should begin by making some preliminary checks; for example:

1. Look at the engine 'kill-switch' – a gloved hand can easily knock it into the 'off' position without you realizing it.

2. Look at the ignition switch to make sure it is still on.

3. Check the ignition light, the indicators and the lights – if you had been modestly travelling down the road and the engine suddenly cut out, it is quite likely to be an ignition problem.

4. Check the oil warning light.

5. Look at your odometer or tripometer and calculate how much fuel you have left – if any (see p. 29). If the engine slows down gradually, for example, before it stops altogether, this is likely to be a symptom of a fuel supply problem.

6. Listen carefully for any unusual noises (see pp. 260–63).

Certainly, paying attention to these kinds of things before you actually come to a halt can give you a fair indication of the cause of the problem.

Although there are almost as many approaches to problem solving as there are motorcycles, our approach is to take a particular problem, isolate the potential accompanying symptoms and to rank the possible causes in terms of probabilities and priorities. Instead of laboriously checking through each system in turn, it is far easier to use the symptoms which describe a problem to help you identify the most likely possible causes – regardless of the system involved. If you work through the 'possible causes' lists in a logical manner you should have relatively little trouble resolving the problem.

Quite a difficult situation can arise, however, when a problem is due to two causes, neither of which would have caused trouble on its own – you should always be on the look-out for these situations and keep the idea that more than one cause may be responsible. Although regular servicing is one way to try and prevent this happening, problems like this do still occur. The best advice we can give when you are making your checks is to assume that nothing is correct or properly adjusted; then, having reset them, you can be sure that all is well.

Finally, it is perhaps worth pointing out before you begin your investigation that, if you have been trying to start the engine for some time before you traced the actual cause, you may actually have created another problem if you were not careful. One of the most common 'created' problems, for example, is a flooded combustion chamber and/or fouled spark plug. If the engine still refuses to start, or continues to perform poorly, after you have rectified what you suspect to be the original problem, you must try to rethink what you did to the engine while trying to get it started – operating the choke or repeatedly twisting the throttle, etc., will affect the situation. You now also have to diagnose and remedy these situations too.

The next two chapters both deal with engine problems. Chapter 4, 'Engine failure problems', deals with situations where the engine won't start, where it fails after initially starting satisfactorily and where it is continually difficult to start; and Chapter 5 deals broadly with problems of engine performance.

CHAPTER FOUR
ENGINE FAILURE PROBLEMS

Although a complete engine failure is probably the most annoying problem, frequently it is certainly not the most difficult to resolve, especially when compared to an intermittent misfire, for example, which often has the hardest causes to locate. Because the engine refuses to run, you can be sure that something or other is definitely faulty or defective and, provided you follow a logical pattern when checking, this defect should not be too difficult to track down.

HOW TO USE THIS CHAPTER

In this chapter three basic problems are examined:

Problem 1. The engine won't start.

Problem 2. Having started, the engine subsequently stops.

Problem 3. The engine is repeatedly difficult to start.

Each problem is accompanied by a series of related symptoms which help to describe the problem in more detail and so to direct you to the most likely possible cause(s) far more quickly than if you were forced to work your way through each of the four systems until you discovered the actual cause.

The detailed causal explanations and the appropriate remedies are set out after problem tables 1, 2 and 3 under the motorcycle's four basic systems.

All you need to do is turn to the table concerned with the particular problem you are having and look through the list of symptoms set out in the left-hand column until you find the one which best fits the details of your situation; the list of possible causes to check, and the pages on which they are discussed (along with their remedies), are set out in the right-hand column. All you need to do is turn to the appropriate page and get to work.

For example: if your engine refuses to start, although it has been driven recently and the engine is still hot (for example, you may have ridden to the shops, stopped the bike and, when you return, it won't start), you should turn to the first table, where you will find 'Problem 1: "The engine won't start" '; looking down the list of symptoms you find that No. 2 is almost identical to your situation. So, beginning with 'The ignition and/or cut-out switch position', on p. 100, you now need systematically to work your way through the list of possible causes set out on the right of the table. If the switches turn out to be satisfactory, and are in the 'on' position, move on to 'Insufficient fuel in the tank', discussed on p. 101, etc.

PROBLEM 1   THE ENGINE WON'T START

SYMPTOMS	POSSIBLE CAUSES TO CHECK	Page
1 ... after the motorcycle has been left standing (for at least eight to twelve hours) and the engine is cold. It may be, for example, that you drove home last night and now it won't start to take you to work.	1.1 Ignition and/or engine cut-out switch position	100
	2.1 Insufficient fuel in the tank	101
	2.2 Fuel switch position	101
	3.1 Choke position and operation	103
	4.1 Spark plug gap and condition	107
	4.2 Spark plug defective	110
	4.3 Spark plug cap defective	112
	4.4 Contact breakers (points) faulty	113
	4.5 H.T. (ignition) coil defective	116
	4.6 Condenser defective	117
	4.7 Spark too weak	117
	4.8 Spark plug shorting out	118
	4.10 Deficiency in the H.T. coil	119
	6.6 Starter motor (if fitted) defective	131
2 ... after the motorcycle has been driven recently and the engine is hot. It may be, for example, that you have ridden to the shop, stopped the bike	1.1 Ignition and/or engine cut-out switch position	100
	2.1 Insufficient fuel in the tank	101

SYMPTOMS	POSSIBLE CAUSES TO CHECK	Page
and, when you return, it won't start.	3.1 Choke position and operation	103
	4.2 Spark plug defective	110
	4.3 Spark plug cap defective	112
3 . . . after the motorcycle has not been used for some time. It may have been stored for the winter, for example, and now spring is here you want to take it out for a spin.	1.1 Ignition and/or engine cut-out switch position	100
	2.1 Insufficient fuel in the tank	101
	2.2 Fuel switch position	101
	3.1 Choke position and operation	103
	3.6 Stale fuel	107
	4.1 Spark plug gap and condition	107
	4.2 Spark plug defective	110
	4.3 Spark plug cap defective	112
	4.4 Contact breakers (points) faulty	113
	4.5 H.T. (ignition) coil defective	116
	4.6 Condenser defective	117
	6.5 Ignition switch defective	130
4 . . . and there are no lights or horn, etc.	5.1 Battery insufficiently charged	122
	5.2 Loose terminal connections or battery earth wire	124
	5.3 Corroded terminals	124

SYMPTOMS	POSSIBLE CAUSES TO CHECK	Page
	5.4 Internal short circuit	124
	6.1 Blown fuse	125
5 . . . after the motorcycle has been washed.	**1.1** Ignition and/or engine cutout switch position	100
	6.2 Ignition system damp	125
	3.3 Dirt or water in the carburettor	104
	6.5 Ignition switch defective	130
	6.6 Starter motor (if fitted) defective	131
6 . . . and backfires when you try to turn over the engine, using either the kickstart or the electric starter.	**4.2** Spark plug defective	110
	4.3 Spark plug cap defective	112
	3.3 Dirt or water in the carburettor	104
7 . . . and there is little kickstart resistance.	**7.1** Leaking or blown cylinder head gasket	133
	7.2 Damaged pistons/piston rings	133
	7.3 Sticking valves (four-strokes only)	134
	7.4 Decompressor (if fitted) fouled or incorrectly adjusted	135
8 . . . and the kickstart feels jammed.	**10.1** Petrol has seeped into, and filled, the cylinder and engine casing	143

PROBLEM 2 HAVING ONCE STARTED, THE ENGINE SUBSEQUENTLY STOPS

	SYMPTOMS	POSSIBLE CAUSES TO CHECK	Page
1	. . . the motorcycle engine simple slows down, dies and now won't start.	**1.1** Ignition and/or engine cut-out switch position	100
		2.1 Insufficient fuel in the tank	101
		2.2 Fuel switch position	101
		3.1 Choke position and operation	103
		2.3 Fuel filter and/or lines blocked	102
		5.1 Battery insufficiently charged	122
		6.1 Blown fuse	125
		4.1 Spark plug gap and condition	107
		4.2 Spark plug defective	110
		4.4 Contact breakers (points) faulty	113
		6.3 Breaks in the power cables	127
2	. . . the engine simply cuts out while you are riding along normally.	**1.1** Ignition and/or engine cut-out switch position	100
		2.2 Fuel switch position	101
		6.1 Blown fuse	125
		4.1 Spark plug gap and condition	107
		4.2 Spark plug defective	110

SYMPTOMS	POSSIBLE CAUSES TO CHECK	Page
	4.4 Contact breakers (points) faulty	113
	4.5 H.T. (ignition) coil defective	116
	4.6 Condenser defective	117
3 ... as the motorcycle slows down, approaching traffic lights for example, the engine dies and then stops, but is soon restarted.	**2.4** Fuel cap vent blocked	103
	5.1 Battery insufficiently charged	122
	3.4 Carburettor manifold loose or cracked	106
	6.4 Electrical short circuit	127
4 ... the engine continues to misfire and cut out in wet weather.	**4.3** Spark plug cap defective	112
	6.2 Ignition system damp	125
	3.5 Air intake restricted	107
5 ... the engine cuts out as you accelerate – as you set off from traffic lights, for example – is soon restarted, but continues to cut out each time the motorcycle accelerates.	**3.1** Choke position and operation	103
	2.3 Fuel filter and/or lines blocked	102
	4.3 Spark plug cap defective	112
	3.3 Dirt or water in the carburettor	104
	3.5 Air intake restricted	107
6 ... the engine runs well at tickover, but misfires and dies once the throttle is opened.	**3.1** Choke position and operation	103
	5.1 Battery insufficiently charged	122

SYMPTOMS	POSSIBLE CAUSES TO CHECK	Page
	4.1 Spark plug gap and condition	107
	4.2 Spark plug defective	110
	4.4 Contact breakers (points) faulty	113
	4.6 Condenser defective	117
	3.3 Dirt or water in the carburettor	104
	4.9 Ignition timing incorrect	119
7	. . . the engine cuts out when you are turning to the left or the right, is soon restarted, but fails again as you are turning (left or right).	**6.3** Breaks in the power cables	127
		6.4 Electrical short circuit	127
8	. . . the engine fails to start with the electric starter but always starts with the kickstart.	**4.3** Spark plug cap defective	112
		4.5 H.T. (ignition) coil defective	116
		4.9 Ignition timing incorrect	119
		5.1 Battery insufficiently charged	122
		6.6 Starter motor (if fitted) defective	131
9	. . . the engine backfires and stops shortly after the cylinder has been decoked.	**10.2** Spark plug tip fouled by carbon	144
10	. . . the engine stops dead and locks the rear wheel.	Engine seizure: unlike all the other symptoms discussed, if your engine seizes, not only do you have to establish the cause – and correct it – you must also	

SYMPTOMS	POSSIBLE CAUSES TO CHECK	Page
	correct any damage the seizure itself has caused – especially to the barrel(s) and piston(s). For more information on repairing the damage, see 'Engine seizure', pp. 252–5. The possible causes of a seizure you should check for are:	
	Two-strokes **8.1** Auto-lube oil tank empty	136
	8.2 Incorrect proportion of two-stroke oil in pre-mix petrol	137
	8.3 Oil delivery pump control cable broken	137
	8.4 Delivery pump setting incorrect	138
	8.5 Loose, cracked, broken or blocked oil delivery pipes	138
	8.6 Incorrect type of oil in the auto-lube system	139
	8.7 Delivery pump failure	140
	8.8 Leaking crankcase joints	140
	Four-strokes **9.1** Engine oil level too low	141
	9.2 Cracked, loose or blocked oil delivery pipes	142
	9.3 Oil pump strainer and/or filter blocked	142
	9.4 Oil pump failure	142

SYMPTOMS	POSSIBLE CAUSES TO CHECK	Page
	If you are satisfied none of these are responsible for the seizure, any of the following are also capable of causing the trouble, regardless of whether the engine is a two- or four-stroke:	
	4.9 Ignition timing incorrect	119
	3.3 Dirt or water in the carburettor	104
	3.4 Carburettor manifold loose or cracked	106
	7.1 Leaking or blown cylinder head gasket	133

PROBLEM 3 THE ENGINE IS HARD TO START		
SYMPTOMS	POSSIBLE CAUSES TO CHECK	Page
1 . . . when the engine is cold, starting is *extremely* difficult, but even when it is hot, starting is still a problem.	Although the engine does ultimately start, and so strictly speaking it is not a question of engine failure, the range of causes which are capable of making starting difficult is almost as wide as of those which prevent the engine starting at all. However, although the explanations of these causes are in principle the same, the consequences are different, which is less of a	

SYMPTOMS	POSSIBLE CAUSES TO CHECK	Page
	problem, because each is far less severe. Of the possible causes the *most likely* to be the source of your problem are:	
	4.1 Spark plug gap and condition	107
	4.4 Contact breakers (points) faulty	113
	4.3 Spark plug cap defective	112
	4.9 Ignition timing incorrect	119
	5.1 Battery insufficiently charged	122
	5.2 Loose terminal connections or battery earth wire	124
	5.3 Corroded terminals	124
	3.1 Choke position and operation	103
	7.2 Damaged pistons/piston rings	133
	7.3 Sticking valves (four-strokes only)	134
	3.2 Carburettor adjustment	104
	3.4 Carburettor manifold loose or cracked	106
	3.5 Air intake restricted	107
	8.8 Leaking crankcase joints	140

POSSIBLE CAUSES TO CHECK

1. Ignition and/or engine cut-out switch position

Cause 1.1

The ignition and/or engine cut-out switch may be in the 'off' position: in both cases the engine will not start (Figure 43).

Remedy 1.1

Ensure that the ignition is on and check the position of the cut-out switch. If the cut-out is off, simply return it to the 'on' position: the engine can then be started in the normal manner. Checking the position of these switches is the first thing you should do whenever the engine refuses to start or stops while you are driving along. Once you have satisfied yourself that both switches are in the

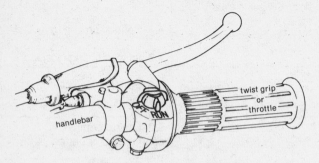

If your machine will not start, make sure the cut-out switch is in the 'run' position. This switch is easily knocked to 'off' as you take your hand from the twist grip.

Figure 43 The dreaded cut-out switch

If the engine stopped while you were riding along, check the ignition key – sometimes the weight of the key fob may suddenly turn the engine off or pull out the key.

Moreover, this simple cut-out switch has caused many motorcyclists to scratch their heads for some considerable time puzzling through the possible reasons why an engine will not start.

It is much easier than you imagine to catch this switch with a gloved hand or your coat sleeve, etc., without realizing it.

correct position, you can then proceed to give consideration to diagnosing another possible cause.

THE FUEL SYSTEM

In checking the fuel system you must ensure that there is enough fuel in the tank, that it is reaching the carburettors and that the mixture being drawn into the combustion chamber contains the correct proportions of fuel and air. An engine will not start or, if it does, will run poorly if there is either too little or too much fuel in the mixture.

These two sets of problems are elaborated in the 'Fuel supply' and 'Incorrect fuel/air ratio' sections respectively.

2. Fuel supply

Cause 2.1

Insufficient fuel in the tank. One of the first things you should check if your engine refuses to start, or dies, is that there is sufficient fuel in the tank. Don't necessarily assume that you can't have run out simply because you drove it home O.K. last night, for example – it may be that you arrived home as the last drop was being used. Moreover, don't discount the possibility of having insufficient fuel even if your calculations (see p. 29) tell you there should be some left. Calculations do go wrong and petrol tanks do leak!

Remedy 2.1

Remove the petrol cap and shake the tank: if you can't see or hear any petrol, the problem is almost certainly one of starvation. Even though the symptoms of insufficient fuel can sometimes appear to be those of spark plug fouling, it is important that you make this check of the fuel tank.

Before you add petrol to the tank put the petrol tap to the 'off' position; this will ensure that raw fuel is not forced from the carburettor into the cylinder by the rush of petrol into the system as you fill up. (This is particularly important on engines with a single cylinder or, more accurately, a single carburettor.) After the petrol is in the tank switch the petrol tap to the 'on' position and either wait ten to fifteen seconds to allow the fuel to flow into the system or, if the carburettor has an accelerator pump, twist the throttle a couple of times to pump fuel to the carburettor; then start as normal. If you are out of petrol and the next garage is some miles away you can sometimes travel a few more miles by laying the motorcycle right over on the petrol tap side to try to get the last few drops which may be trapped in the other side of the tank. It is also useful to carry a length of tubing in your tool kit, or attached to some part of the motorcycle: it will come in handy for siphoning petrol from a friend's tank into yours. It is also useful to keep in mind that many petrol tanks are detachable: if you do have to leave your motorcycle to get fuel and you don't have a container (and not all garages have spare containers to give away), take your tank with you. See your owner's handbook or workshop manual for details on how to remove it.

If you run out of petrol because your petrol tank is leaking, clearly you will need to take it to your local workshop or dealer for repair. A temporary repair, however, is possible: a really well-chewed piece of gum will block any leaking petrol tank and enable you to drive home or to the workshop.

Cause 2.2

Fuel switch position. If you have satisfied yourself that there is fuel in the tank, it may be that the fuel tap (sometimes known as the 'petcock') is not in the 'on' (or open) position, or that the fuel level is extremely low.

Remedy 2.2

Firstly, you need to check the position of the fuel tap and, if necessary, to move it to the 'on' position. Wait a few moments for the petrol to flow into the system, or again pump it in with the throttle twist grip, and try starting the engine. If it still refuses to start it is possible that the fuel level is too low to reach the outlet hole with the tap in this position: move it to the reserve position and try starting the engine again.

If it does fire up you should make a beeline to the nearest petrol station and fill up. Although most reserve tanks will take you a reasonable distance, especially if you take your time, it is certainly not worth risking running out altogether just to put off spending a few pence. The size of your reserve tank should be indicated in your owner's handbook or workshop manual. Using this information, and your estimate of how far your motorcycle will travel on a gallon, you can quickly estimate how far your reserve fuel will take you.

Cause 2.3

Fuel filter and/or lines blocked. If you are sure that you have plenty of fuel, and that the tap is in the correct position to allow it to flow, it may be that:

1. There is a kink in the pipe.
2. Particles of rust or dirt have been sucked from the bottom of the fuel tank (especially if you run low on fuel) into the fuel filter – in the fuel tap – or fuel line (the pipe from the petrol tank to the carburettor). A blockage in either of these places will cause the petrol/air mixture to be too weak.

Remedy 2.3.1

Inspect the path of the pipe from the fuel tap to the carburettor and ensure that it follows as near a straight path as possible, and certainly that it has no sharp bends or kinks in it – if it has, disconnect the pipe, straighten it out and replace it in a new path.

Remedy 2.3.2

Disconnect the fuel pipe from the petrol tap, place something underneath it to catch any fuel and switch the tap on for a few seconds. If only a few drops of fuel come out instead of a good, even flow, the petrol filter is blocked. The answer is to remove the filter (see your owner's handbook or workshop manual for details, or see pp. 71–2) and wash and clean it. However, don't wash the filter in water unless you have time to let it dry thoroughly before you replace it. Otherwise wash the filter in petrol: it can then be replaced immediately. Failure to do this correctly could result in you having the same problem, but with a different cause (see 3.3 below).

If the filter in the fuel tap appears clear, however, you must now suspect the fuel line. Reconnect the fuel pipe to the tap and disconnect it at the top of the carburettor. If you now put your container under the bottom end of the pipe and turn on the fuel for a few seconds, and petrol only trickles out of the pipe, clearly it is blocked somewhere along its length. To clear it, disconnect the upper end from the fuel tap and try blowing down it. If that fails to dislodge the blockage, try poking a length of wire down the pipe to push it out of the other end. Reconnect the pipe to the tap and recheck that there is a sufficient flow. If for any reason you can't unblock the fuel pipe (although this is rare), or if your inspection reveals it to be cracked rather than blocked, the length of pipe you carry for siphoning can often be used to replace the damaged fuel pipe.

The older the tank, the more likely it is to have rust or dirt particles floating around in it; periodic checks for this are essential (see p. 72). New tanks, however, are not immune from dirt particles. Indeed, any new tank should be thoroughly washed out with petrol before it is used.

Cause 2.4

Fuel cap vent blocked. If both the fuel filter and fuel lines are clear and yet the only flow is in intermittent bursts, it is possible that the air vent in the petrol filler cap is blocked. Usually the vent is located on the underside of the cap itself, but sometimes it is on the perimeter of the crown. Check with your owner's handbook or workshop manual to establish where it is on your motorcycle.

Remedy 2.4

Although you can easily check if a blocked cap vent is the problem by riding a few miles with the filler cap removed, or loosely attached – in which case the problem would be eliminated – it is quite a straightforward task to clean out the vent hole with a needle, pin or paperclip, etc. Indeed, because of the potential danger involved when riding with the filler cap removed, it is something you should attempt only if you have nothing to clean out the hole with; even then you should take great care and only make your way home very slowly. A safety pin would, of course, be another very useful addition to your tool kit.

3. Incorrect fuel/air ratio

Cause 3.1

Choke position and operation. If the engine refuses to start when it is cold, it may be that the choke is in the wrong position – that is, it needs to be opened – to enrich the mixture, or that the choke is stuck in a closed position and won't open (sufficiently) even when the choke is switched on.

On the other hand, if the engine refuses to start, or subsequently stops after having initially started with little or no difficulty, it may be that you have left the choke open (in the 'on' position) and that the mixture is too rich for normal running conditions, or that it is stuck in the 'open' position and fails to close regardless of the switch position.

Remedy 3.1

Check the position of the choke switch and ensure that it is in the appropriate position for the conditions in which you wish to operate the engine. If the engine was running too rich, you may have to wait a few moments for some of the excess fuel to evaporate. You should then be able to start your engine in the normal way – bearing in mind the prevailing conditions, of course. Your owner's handbook or workshop manual will give you details of how and when to use the choke on your motorcycle – read them carefully!

Signs that your engine is running too rich will be given by:

1. Thick sooty deposits on the spark plug firing tip (in both two-stroke and four-stroke engines). These are distinctly different from the more oily, black carbon deposits associated with an oil problem.

2. Black smoke from the exhaust (of a four-stroke only) leaving soot deposits inside the silencer. If you put your finger inside, it will come out black.

The sooty deposits in both these places will build up very quickly if your engine is running too rich.

It may be, however, that you have persisted in trying to start the engine with the choke open and this has flooded the engine and left the spark plug firing tip soaked in petrol (or petrol/oil, in the case of two-strokes). If there is a very strong smell of petrol, it is quite likely that this is what you have done. Before the engine will start in this situation you will need to dry and clean the spark plug (See 'Spark plug gap and condition', pp. 107–9).

However, before you replace the clean plug you must expel the excess petrol fumes pumped into the combustion chamber by the choke. To do this, ensure the ignition, choke and petrol are all off, open the throttle fully, and kick the engine over three or four times with the kickstart. This will draw large volumes of air through the carburettor(s) and combustion chamber(s), flushing out the excess fumes.

You can now replace the clean plug and plug cap, turn on the ignition (*not* the petrol or choke) and try starting the engine in the normal manner. If it fires, you can now turn on the petrol.

If you unfortunately do not have a kickstart fitted to your motorcycle, you must be patient and wait for five to ten minutes for the fumes to evaporate.

If you suspect that the choke is sticking – and it should be said that this is *not* a common occurrence, and indeed will only occur where the choke lever is cable-operated – you will need to trace the system from the switch all the way through; look out for kinks in the cable, or signs of cracking or wear in the outer casing, as these may mean that the cable has become frayed or rusted. Check that the cable is attached at both ends, and that as you operate the choke lever the choke is actually opened or closed at the carburettor.

If your choke lever is mounted on the body of the carburettor, it is far more likely that there is a malfunction inside the carburettor.

Cause 3.2

Carburettor adjustment. It may be that the carburettor is incorrectly adjusted (and here we are basically referring to idle speed and idle mixture). Moreover, if your engine has more than one carburettor, they may also be out of synchronization.

Remedy 3.2

You must reset (or have your local workshop or dealer reset) the idle speed and idle mixture. If you do ride a multi-carburettor motorcycle, they will need to be synchronized. Unfortunately, as there are no tests you can do to verify if carburettor adjustment is the cause, you must actually go through the necessary tuning and synchronizing procedures. See 'Condition, adjustment and . . . synchronization of the carburettor(s)', pp. 72–5, for a more detailed discussion of the procedures.

Cause 3.3

Dirt or water in the carburettor. If the petrol is reaching the carburettor and the choke is operating correctly, and yet there is still a strong smell of (excess) petrol, it is likely that the float needle (needle valve) which controls the supply of fuel to the float bowl is stuck open or is being held open by a particle of dirt or rust. It may also be, however, that the float is punctured and is being weighted down by petrol which has leaked inside.

On the other hand, if there is no clear smell of (excess) petrol, it is more likely that particles of rust or dirt, or even a droplet of water (which may have found its way from the petrol tank or may even be the result of condensation), are blocking the float chamber vent or one of the jets (commonly the main jet), preventing the fuel from circulating through the carburettor.

A further complication to the problem is that these particles or droplets don't always stay in one place. As the motorcycle is moved, for example, they may be temporarily dislodged, allowing the engine to run with no apparent problem, only to be sucked back into the jet later. The result is that dirt or water in a carburettor will not simply prevent a motorcycle starting, but may allow it to start only to cause it to stop soon after. Then, as the engine dies, the particles drop away from the jet, unblocking it and allowing it to start once again.

The carburettors on two-stroke engines are prone to a further problem: small amounts of oil sometimes find their way into the carburettor and collect under the main jet.

It should be noted, however, that whichever of these is the cause of your motorcycle's problems it is only likely to result in a single-carburettor engine failing to start, or stopping after having once started. Dirt or water in one of the carburettors on a multi-cylinder, multi-carburettor engine will only lead to a misfire and reduced performance. For a more detailed discussion of engine misfires see pp. 181–9.

Remedy **3.3**

If your motorcycle has only one carburettor, obviously there can be little question about which you should suspect. The situation is not so clear-cut on a multi-carburettor engine. If you do suspect that there is dirt or

water in the carburettor, the problem is which one, or ones, as the case may be. There are two simple checks you can use to help you with this problem:

1. Cautiously touch the exhaust pipes soon after they leave the cylinders: if any are cooler than those at the normal operating temperature, the carburettor supplying that cylinder should be examined. Do be careful in doing this – the cylinders will be hot: spit on your finger first.

2. If you find it difficult to detect any temperature differences, a brief inspection of the spark plugs will indicate exactly what is happening inside your engine. In brief, if the plug is white, there is a lack of fuel in the mixture reaching the combustion chamber, and if the plug is black and/or wet (and perhaps oil-coated in the case of two-strokes), there is an excess of fuel in the chamber. Under normal operating conditions, where the combustion chamber is being supplied with the appropriate petrol/air mixture, the spark plug firing tip will have light brown, greyish deposits and a small build-up of carbon.

If you do suspect that water or dirt is causing the problem, a sharp blow to the top of the carburettor body, with an appropriate soft tool (not a hammer!), is often sufficient to dislodge the offending particle. You should then remove the drain plug at the base of the carburettor and empty out all the contaminated fuel. On multi-carburettor engines each suspect carburettor will need to be tapped and drained individually.

Should tapping the carburettor fail to clear the problem, and yet you still suspect that water or dirt is blocking one of the jets, then, depending on how many carburettors the engine has and the precise nature of the problem, there are two other possible remedies.

1. *To be used primarily on single-carburettor engines*:

(a) Switch off the fuel and disconnect the fuel pipe at the tap.

(b) Remove the drain plug and empty the fuel from the carburettor.

(c) Blow down the pipe to dislodge the blockage.

(d) Refit the drain plug and open the fuel tap to refill the float chamber.

(e) Switch the fuel off and again drain the carburettor.

This final filling and draining will increase the likelihood of any particles being flushed out of the carburettor passages or jet.

2. *To be used on multi-carburettor engines (or single-carburettor engines where the jet is only partially blocked)*:

(a) With the engine running, turn the throttle twist grip to rev the engine.

(b) Switch the choke on and off a few times; this may help clear a small blockage.

If all these – tapping, blowing, revving or draining – fail to resolve the problem, there is no alternative: you will have to remove, dismantle and clean the carburettor and its components (Figure 44). When you are doing this take particular care not to bend the needle valve, and never use a pin or wire to clean out the jet holes – always blow down them. Their diameter is critical and even a slight alteration can dramatically affect an engine's performance. If, when you're checking, the components are damaged, that is, the float is leaking or the needle valve is bent, you should have no hesitation in replacing them.

Before you remove the carburettor and begin to work on it, read the

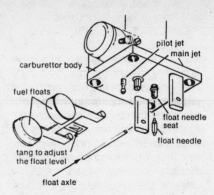

Figure 44 Carburettor with float bowl removed, showing layout

section on cleaning the carburettor, on pp. 72–3, where you will find the procedures discussed in much more detail.

Cause 3.4

Carburettor manifold loose or cracked. The carburettor is connected to the cylinder on one side and to the air-filter box on the other by two rubber hoses – the manifold – and a couple of ring clips. Problems will arise if either of these joints or the manifold is not airtight. If air enters the system on the carburettor/cylinder side it will be drawn directly into the cylinder instead of via the carburettor. Any petrol/air mixture eventually reaching the combustion chamber will obviously be too lean to ignite correctly, if at all.

Remedy 3.4

You must check and, if necessary, tighten the ring clips securing the manifold to the carburettor and inspect the manifold itself for any cracks or splits which will allow air to pass: any defective manifold should be replaced – repairs are difficult and often ineffective.

Cause 3.5

Air intake restricted. If the intake tract becomes clogged or the filter damaged, the mixture being burned will be over-rich – that is, there will be a higher proportion of petrol to air than is required for maximum efficiency.

The result will be a significant loss of power, increased petrol consumption, fouled spark plugs and a smoky exhaust. Indeed, if the blockage or damage is severe, it can prevent an engine starting.

Which of the three main types of filter is fitted to your motorcycle, and how you gain access to it, will be indicated in your owner's handbook or workshop manual.

Remedy 3.5

You must ensure that the intake tract is clear and that the air filter is clean and undamaged. For information on how to clean the various types of filter see pp. 66–7. However, if your filter has been cleaned several times already, or if it is damaged, it should be replaced immediately. Under no circumstances should you consider running the engine with the air filter removed. See pp. 148–9 for further discussion of this issue.

Cause 3.6

Stale fuel. If you store your motorcycle during the winter, for example, by the time you want to use it again in spring it is quite likely that condensation forming on the inside of the tank will have contaminated the petrol with water. Even if you were lucky, however, and it remained uncontaminated, you should remember that petrol loses its potency after being left to stand for long periods.

Remedy 3.6

In both these situations you should drain off the old petrol from the whole system – the tank, the fuel lines and the carburettor – preferably before the motorcycle goes into storage, but certainly before you try to run it again. Then, when you return to your motorcycle, you can start with a system full of fresh fuel and all should be well.

THE IGNITION SYSTEM

The ignition system in a motorcycle exists to do only one thing: to produce a spark between the electrodes of the spark plug at precisely the right moment and therefore ignite the compressed mixture. Any failures or imperfections within this system have immediate effects on the engine's performance – either it won't start or, if it does, it performs poorly. Indeed, deficiencies within the ignition system are by far the most common cause of engine problems.

4. Component defects

Cause 4.1

Spark plug gap and condition. At the heart of any ignition system is the spark plug: it is essential that it is kept clean and the electrodes kept at the correct distance. If (1) the gap between the electrodes is incorrect, or (2) the firing tip is in poor condition, no engine will perform correctly, if at all.

Remedy 4.1

In brief, the plug(s) should be removed from the engine, the electrodes cleaned and the gap checked with the correct feeler gauge. The correct operating gap for the spark plugs will be indicated in your owner's handbook or workshop manual.

Remedy 4.1.1

When it comes to checking the electrode gap, although it is unlikely that it will be too narrow on a used plug there is no reason to assume that the same can be said of a new plug – certainly don't assume the gap will be correct simply because the plug is new. The wear and tear of continued use, however, will result in the gap steadily widening (approximately 0·002 ins. per 1,000 miles). To reset the gap carefully bend the earth electrode towards the centre until the correct feeler gauge will fit in with only slight friction (see 'Setting the gap', pp. 47–8).

Remedy 4.1.2

If the spark plug is in poor condition you will need first to solve the immediate problem to get you home, and then to assess what needs to be done to correct the underlying problem which caused the plug to be fouled.

The quickest solution to the immediate problem is to replace the defective plug and clean it at a more convenient time – if it is worth it. Motorcyclists are often inclined to throw away old plugs, and in many cases this is the only thing to do with them – especially when the plug is simply worn out. However, if the plug is merely fouled by oil or carbon, it can be sufficiently cleaned to be reused. Although carbon-fouled plugs can be cleaned relatively easily with emery paper and a wire brush, those that are oil-fouled are a little more difficult. The most effective way to dry and clean wet and oily plugs is either to put them in the oven or to hold them over the ring of a cooker until no more smoke is being given off. When you're doing this, do remember that the heat from the firing tip will be conducted along the plug body, so take care to protect your hand in some way. When the smoke does stop, remove the plug from the heat and let it cool *very slowly*. A plug dried out in this way can frequently be used again. The heat not only removes the wetness but also makes it far more likely to fire if you refit and use it right away. If any heavy deposits are left on the electrodes after heating, however, it is worthwhile taking a minute or two to clean them off before you refit the plug.

If you don't have any of the 'kitchen' facilities available, or a new plug, you will have to improvise and hope that you can supply sufficient heat to do the job. Two of the more obvious things to use are matches or a cigarette lighter. Although these will clearly not supply the heat of a cooker (or the equivalent), they are capable of providing sufficient heat and are worth trying.

If the situation is even more desperate – either you don't have a plug spanner or you have no cleaning materials – all is still not lost. It is still possible to relieve the problem temporarily. Having detected the plug(s) you suspect (by touching the exhaust pipes to find which are cooler), switch the engine off, lift off the plug cap and replace it loosely over the plug. Replacing the cap loosely in this way means that the spark has to jump to the top of the plug from the inside of the cap and so increases the strength of the spark at the plug tip. Indeed, if you are at the roadside and only have matches or a lighter to dry the plug, refitting the cap loosely will further enhance your chances of getting home.

It is essential that you only apply the throttle very gently to ride home steadily. Frequently, after running like this for a while, the faulty plug will steadily improve and eventually dry out.

This method of loosening the plug cap will also work on single-cylinder engines occasionally, but the secret here is to keep the engine revs very low until the engine is dry. Even though things may appear satisfactory when you get home, it is still advisable either to dry out the plug using the greater heat of the rings on your cooker, and then clean it, or perhaps even to replace the plug if you feel that it is beyond salvation.

If the plug is simply worn out, you have nothing to worry about, and it can simply be replaced. On the other hand, if a particular condition continues to reoccur you must trace the problem and rectify it (see 'Spark plug condition and gap . . .', pp. 44–8).

If you are in any doubt about the condition of your plug(s) throw them away. They are quite inexpensive items but they are very important to a smooth-running engine.

Ignition system defects

If the spark plug is clean and the gap is correct, and still the engine fails to work, it may be that there is a defect in the ignition system, that is, a spark is not occurring at the plug or, if it is, it is too weak to ignite the mixture in the combustion chamber.

When considering the ignition system as a possible problem source, however, it is important to remember that whereas a faulty plug, H.T. lead, contact breaker or coil, etc., on a single-cylinder motorcycle will almost certainly prevent your motorcycle from starting, on a multi-cylinder engine the consequence will depend on how many plugs are triggered by the defective contact breaker, coil or magneto, etc. If they all are, the engine is unlikely to start. However, if not all the plugs are affected – two out of four, for example – this is far more likely to lead to a misfire and reduced performance.

To test the spark

The first thing you need to do if you suspect there is a problem in the ignition system is to check that there is a good spark at the plug. To do this you should:

1. Remove the spark plug from the cylinder head and reattach it to the spark plug cap.

If you have been trying to start the motorcycle for some time, not only is there a problem of your flattening the battery (if you do use an electric starter), but the plug will probably have become wet with petrol and you will need to dry it before you can expect to see a spark. It is also a good idea to clean the plug before you do this test.

2. Earth the spark plug by laying it on the cylinder so that its base makes a good contact (Figure 45).

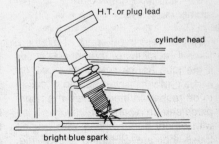

Figure 45 *Laying a spark plug on the cylinder head to check for a spark at the plug tip*

3. With the engine switched on, look at the spark plug gap and spin the engine, using the kickstart (if fitted) or the pedals, if you ride a moped. If your motorcycle is only fitted with an electric-starter system, remember the heavy drain this makes on the battery and take care not to over-use that little button.

4. Your next move depends entirely on what you observe in the gap between the two electrodes.

(a) If there is a fat blue spark in the gap as the engine turns over, the spark plug and indeed the ignition as a whole are *almost* certainly not at fault. Unfortunately we can only say *almost* because there are two instances when, despite the presence of a fat blue spark, the ignition system remains the source of your problem. It may be that the spark is occurring at the wrong time or that, once the plug comes under pressure in the cylinder, the spark runs to earth prematurely (that is, before it reaches the firing tip). Both these possibilities are discussed in more detail on pp. 118–19.

(b) If the spark is orange or, still worse, red, the condenser is almost certainly faulty, or at least on the verge of complete failure, and you can turn your attention immediately to that component (see item 4.6 on p. 117).

(c) If there is no spark at all, there are a number of potential causes between the plug and the coil (or magneto) which you should check in turn: test each time to see if a spark occurs at the spark plug.

No spark at the plug

Assuming that there is no spark at the plug, Chart 1 sets out how you should proceed to locate the cause. Although there is a slight difference in the detailed procedure you must follow, depending on whether your motorcycle has a coil-based or magneto-based system, in principle you will need to check every component in the system and ensure that it is not defective.

Cause 4.2

Spark plug defective. It is virtually impossible to detect whether a spark plug is defective simply by looking at it, unless there are obvious problems with the firing tip. The porcelain may be cracked, for example, or there may be an internal short circuit, and although electrical equipment does exist to test a spark plug, the price of plugs these days means that such testing is simply not worth the time, effort or cost.

Certainly, you shouldn't expect your plug(s) to last 10,000 miles and still perform efficiently – whatever the manufacturers say. The older the plug (in terms of elapsed time or miles), the more likely it is to break down under pressure – the electrical pressure it is put under when starting an engine. For more information see 'Spark plug condition and gap . . .', pp. 44–8.

Remedy 4.2

The simplest way to remedy a defective plug, or even a plug you suspect is defective, is to replace it. Indeed, replacing the spark plug is always a good move to make if you suspect your problem lies in the ignition, just to be on the safe side. The electricity required by a new plug to create the fat blue spark is considerably less than that required by older ones. For example, whereas 5,000 volts may be sufficient to fire a new plug, the demands

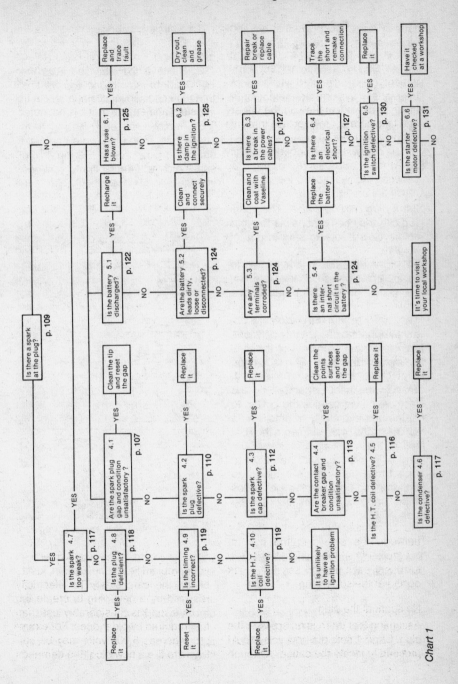

Chart 1

made by an old plug (whether starting the machine or travelling at high speeds) are likely to be twice that amount, that is, close to 10,000 volts. Because of this, a new plug is far more likely to fire, even if there are other 'slight' deficiencies somewhere within the system. You can always take a close look at the system later once you are home and have better facilities.

Cause 4.3

Spark plug cap defective. The spark plug cap may be responsible for your motorcycle's failure to start in one of two ways:

1. It may be that its connection to the spark plug or the H.T. lead is loose, and hence there is a break in the circuit.

2. It may be that the electrical pathway through the cap itself is deficient. Like most other elements of the ignition system, the plug cap has to cope with high voltages passing through it. Steadily, the heat generated by the electrical power causes the plastic to harden and eventually to crack. As a result, instead of passing from the H.T. lead to the spark plug, some of the current is sidetracked: the reduced current may then not be sufficient to jump the gap between the electrodes at the firing tip – consequently, no spark.

Remedy 4.3

The first thing you should do is ensure that the cap is firmly fixed to the spark plug and to the H.T. lead, and test again for a spark at the plug tip.

If the cap is firmly attached at both points, and the plug still fails to spark, you will need to test the cap itself by eliminating it from the system.

To do this you should:

1. Ensure the ignition system is switched off.

2. Remove the plug cap from the H.T. lead. In most cases you will find that the cap has simply been screwed into the end of the wire.

3. Remove the outer casing from about ½ in. of the H.T. wire and twist the bared wire around the top of the spark plug while it is firmly screwed into the cylinder (Figure 46).

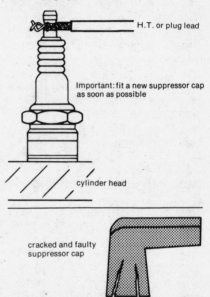

Twist the bared end of the H.T. lead directly onto the plug top

H.T. or plug lead

Important: fit a new suppressor cap as soon as possible

cylinder head

cracked and faulty suppressor cap

Figure 46 Eliminating plug cap failure

4. Switch on the ignition and try starting the engine as normal.

If the engine does start with this arrangement, the plug cap is clearly defective and should be replaced. If you are far from home, with no replacement (cap) available, you can drive home with the H.T. wire connected directly to the plug so long as you take your time and drive carefully. You should certainly ride no further than absolutely necessary in this condition, and fit a new cap as soon as possible.

If you don't have a knife or any other tool to bare the end of the wire with, and so are unable to attach it to the plug, hold – or better still place – the H.T. lead so that the bare end (after you have removed the cap) is about ⅛ in. from the cylinder head, use the kickstart (or pedals on a moped) to spin the engine over (if necessary use the electric starter, but sparingly) and check for a spark between the wire end and the head. If there is a spark, electrical power is clearly reaching the end of the H.T. lead and the circuit is breaking down at a defective plug cap. Once again, if the cap does appear defective, it should be replaced. There is no way to repair these caps (and besides, they are not expensive).

IMPORTANT: To avoid a nasty shock, hold the wire only by the insulation and, if the lead is dirty or wet, wrap a rag around it to protect yourself. If you do feel a shock or see a spark run along the cable, however, clean the lead and renew the cap – the system is obviously providing power which is being stopped at the plug cap.

Cause 4.4

Contact breakers (points) faulty (Figures 47 and 48). It should be made clear at the outset that, these days, not all motorcycles use contact breakers to trigger the spark. An increasing number of new motorcycles are fitted with 'pointless' transistorized ignition systems. Check with your owner's handbook or workshop manual if you are unsure.

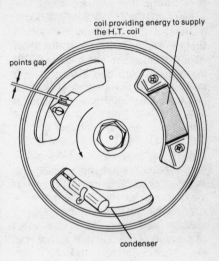

Figure 47 Contact breaker location in a flywheel/magneto ignition system

Figure 48 Contact-breaker layout in a coil/generator ignition system

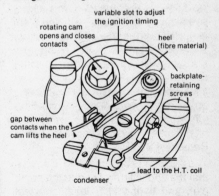

Before you make any assumptions about the possibility of defects in your contact breaker assembly you must test the points: the results will tell you how to proceed, that is, what may be wrong with the points, or where else the cause may be outside the contact breakers.

To check the points themselves:

1. On a D.C. coil/generator system: (a) remove the points cover; (b) rotate the engine, to move the contact breaker arm, until the points are fully *closed*; (c) switch on the ignition; (d) flick open the points with your finger or a suitable tool and check to see if a spark jumps across the opening.

2. On an A.C. flywheel/magneto system: (a) remove the points cover; (b) turn the engine over using the kickstart or electric starter; (c) while the engine is turning, check to see if a spark is leaping the open gap.

Note: See pp. 120–21 for a full discussion of the differences between D.C. coil/generator and A.C. fly-wheel/magneto systems. Your owner's handbook or workshop manual will indicate which system your motorcycle uses.

Cause 4.4.1

No spark at the points. If you do not see a spark, the source of the problem is either at the contact breaker or somewhere between the points and the battery (for information on the latter see pp. 127–8). At the contact breaker itself you must ensure: (1) that the points are in good, or at least satisfactory, condition; (2) that no breakdown of electrical current is occurring within the assembly.

Cause 4.4.1.1

Points in poor condition. As we saw on pp. 60–62, if the points are burned and/or pitted, or coated in dirty greases or oil, it can be almost guaranteed that they will fail to work.

Remedy 4.4.1.1

To inspect the points, open the gap by moving the arm as far as possible against the resistance of its retaining spring. Points' surfaces should be clean – free from dirt or oil – and smooth – without high spots or pits. For a full discussion of how to deal with oily, dirty or damaged surfaces, and how to clean and dress them, see pp. 60–61.

As a temporary solution, points in poor condition, especially if they are covered in oil, can be sprayed with a penetrating oil. This may allow your motorcycle to run for a little while – by helping the spark to leap the gap – and enable you to get home. Indeed, the engine may run for two or three days after you've sprayed, but be assured that it is only a temporary measure and certainly not a permanent solution.

Cause 4.4.1.2

A part in the contact breaker assembly may be defective (D.C. coil/generator systems only). With the ignition on, try earthing across the two points arms (not the points themselves) with a screwdriver blade (Figure 49). If you get a spark with this test, but didn't get one when you opened the points manually, the very tips of the points themselves are defective.

If you also fail to get a spark with this second test, it may be that a section of the wiring within the contact breaker is earthing on to some part of the assembly.

Note: This test is only appropriate for D.C. coil/generator systems. A flywheel/magneto system has no power in it unless the engine is spin-

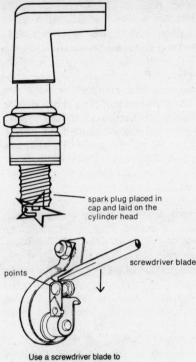

spark plug placed in
cap and laid on the
cylinder head

points

screwdriver blade

Use a screwdriver blade to
short across the points arms –
if a spark appears at the plug, the points
faces may be dirty and preventing
contact, and hence there is no spark
when you kick the engine over or
use the electric starter

Figure 49 Checking for a spark at the
spark plug, using a screwdriver across
the points arms (having had no spark
while turning the engine over)

ning. It is impossible, therefore, to do
this test on an A.C. system: the easiest
thing to do is replace the contact
breaker assembly.

Remedy **4.4.1.2**

If you satisfy yourself that it is the tips
of the points that are defective, there
is no real solution other than to replace
them with a new set.

On the other hand, if you decide that
the source of your problem is a wire
shorting-out into the assembly mechanism, it may be possible to locate the
short and cover it with insulating tape,
thereby preventing the electrical current running to earth. At the same
time, however, you must also try to
find out why the short developed in the
first place. If the wire was trapped and
the outer covering chafed, then redi-
recting it may be possible and sufficient to resolve the problem.

Cause **4.4.2**

There is a spark at the points. If you
do see a spark across the points as
you flick them open, the source of the
problem is either the contact breaker
assembly itself or somewhere
between the points and the spark
plug(s). At the contact breaker
assembly you should check that the
points are actually opening and closing
fully while the engine is turning, and
that the gap between the points when
they are at their widest is within the
tolerance limits set down by the manufacturers.

Cause **4.4.2.1**

Points gap incorrect. Either the points
may have worn so much that the
erosion of material has left the gap too
wide, or they may have closed up
(frequently, the gap closes slightly
soon after you have fitted them as the
nylon heel wears down to bed itself in
– so beware!).

Remedy **4.4.2.1**

With the points fully open, use the
correct feeler gauge (indicated in your
owner's handbook or workshop manual) to check the gap between the two

point surfaces. Reset the gap to the recommended size, or replace excessively worn points, as necessary. For a more detailed discussion of the points gap and resetting it see pp. 60–62.

Two small tips to bear in mind, however, while you are checking the size of the gap: always make sure that the feeler gauge is clean – grease or oil will easily be transmitted to the point surfaces as you move the gauge around to judge the friction you feel; also, always ensure that you insert the feeler gauge squarely and not at an angle.

Cause 4.4.2.2

The points do not move from a fully closed position as the engine rotates. There are several reasons why the points may not open and close as they should while the engine is rotating: it may be that although the crankshaft is turning, the contact breaker cam (which is driven by the crankshaft) is not; the return spring may be weak or broken; or the cam may have worn so much that it cannot open the points sufficiently.

Remedy 4.4.2.2

You must inspect the whole contact breaker assembly very closely and observe the entire mechanism as you rotate the crankshaft.

If the cam is loose on its drive shaft, you must take the necessary steps to secure it; if the points return spring is weak or broken, you must replace the whole breaker assembly; if the cam is worn, it too must be replaced. Indeed, any other adjustments or replacements which appear necessary should be made immediately.

For a discussion of the problems which may occur between the points and the plug(s) or the points and the battery, that is, the ignition system wiring and/or switches, see pp. 127–8.

Cause 4.5

H.T. (ignition) coil defective. If you get this far in the checks and the engine still won't start, the coil should now be suspected: that is, power is not reaching or leaving the coil either because the terminal connections are loose or dirty, or because the coil itself is defective.

A coil actually has two coils of wire inside it: the 'primary winding' carries battery power and the 'secondary winding' carries the high voltage, which is induced by breaking the primary circuit at the points, to the spark plug.

In brief, the coil converts current from the battery or generator to high-tension current which then flows through H.T. circuits to the spark plug.

Having no moving parts, the coil requires very little maintenance; really, all you need to do is occasionally check that the connections are secure.

Remedy 4.5

If you do suspect that the coil is the source of your motorcycle's problems, and you have checked that all the terminal connections are secure, the coil itself can easily be checked.

1. With a battery/coil (or D.C., as it is more often called) ignition system (and you should check in your owner's handbook or workshop manual to determine how your system is constructed), you should disconnect the secondary lead (between the coil and the points), using the connector you'll find located near the coil.

2. With the spark plug attached to

the plug cap, lay it on the cylinder head, as described in the spark plug test on pp. 109–10.

3. Turn on the ignition.

4. Ground the lead coming from the coil to the engine or frame, and at the same time check to see what happens at the firing tip of the spark plug.

If the spark leaps the electrode gap, the coil is in a satisfactory working condition.

If there is no spark at the plug, the coil has probably failed and must be replaced.

Should you feel at all unsure about this test, or simply don't have the necessary tools to earth the terminal, a more certain way to check your existing coil is to replace it. New H.T. coils, however, are very expensive. Although you could try borrowing one from a friend, or even having your own tested at a reputable workshop, often the easiest solution is to purchase a secondhand coil from the breaker's yard. This should be guaranteed to be in working order, cost substantially less than a new one and eliminate your problem – if the coil was the culprit.

Cause **4.6**

Condenser defective. Most commonly, when a condenser is defective, the fault means that it is unable to build up sufficient energy to create a spark at the plug. Although in almost 90 per cent of cases this will result in a severe misfire, there are occasions when a faulty condenser will prevent an engine firing.

Remedy **4.6**

To examine the condition of the condenser, you must check the colour and strength of the spark at the points:

1. Turn on the ignition.

2. Spin over the engine, using the kickstart, electric starter or pedals, as appropriate, and at the same time look closely at the points gap.

If you see a bright blue spark, the source of the problem is almost certainly the condenser. Firstly, check that the wiring to the condenser is in good condition and that the terminal connections are secure. If those connections are satisfactory, it is likely to be the condenser itself which is defective, and it should be replaced.

On the other hand, if you see a slight white or red spark, the condenser is satisfactory and the problem must lie somewhere else.

If there is a spark at the plug

If we now assume that there is a spark at the plug when you test it, your (initial) conclusion may be that the source of the problem must therefore lie outside the ignition system, and in 95 per cent of all cases you would be correct. Unfortunately, however, there are occasions when the ignition system may still be the source of your problem, even though there is a spark when you test the plug.

Cause **4.7**

Spark too weak. Although a spark may be visible between the electrodes, it may be only very weak and insufficient to ignite the compressed mixture in the combustion chamber. When you test the plug by laying it on the cylinder head, as described above, you must be able to see a strong, bright blue spark. If you can see the spark leap the electrode gap in full daylight, you can almost certainly assume that it is strong. If, on the other hand, the only way you can see a spark is by shading the plug or working in a darkened garage, more than likely it is too weak. Although this general rule of thumb will help you make up your mind, clearly it must ultimately be left to your judgement: for example if it is an extremely bright, sunny day, some degree of shade may be necessary to see even a good-strength spark. You must judge for yourself.

Remedy 4.7

If you have any doubt about the condition of the plug you are using, change it and try the test again before you decide there is a deficiency somewhere in the ignition system.

Having satisfied yourself that the spark plug itself is in good condition and the gap is correct, you will be almost compelled to conclude that, although the ignition is functioning to a degree, there is still a problem somewhere in the system. It is certainly possible for a deficiency within the ignition system to result in a weak spark when the plug is laid on the cylinder head, and for nothing to occur when the plug is under pressure in the combustion chamber.

To test the strength of the spark travelling down the H.T. lead, unclip the plug cap, disconnect it from the H.T. lead and try to get the spark to jump across a reasonably sized gap (say, ⅛ in.) between the bare H.T. lead and the engine. A weak spark will only be able to leap a small gap (that is, $1/16$ in.), and then only just. A good-strength spark should be able to clear ⅛ in. quite easily.

If you decide that the spark is not up to strength, one thing you can try, as a temporary cure, is to remove any suppressors that are in the system.

You will cause interference all the way home, but at least it may enable you to get home, where you can rectify the source of the problem. Also, as we mentioned on p. 110, simply inserting a new plug may do the trick, because of its smaller electrical demands. Once again, however, you will have to establish the source of the deficiency and rectify it.

In brief, the source of a weak spark can lie anywhere in the entire ignition system: dirty or incorrectly adjusted points; damp wiring or switches; a deficient coil or condenser; a discharged battery; corroded terminals; or poor connections throughout the system are all potential sources. Unfortunately, you must make the same thorough check of the entire system for a weak spark as you would for no spark at all, that is, causes 4.1–4.6, 5.1–5.4 and 6.1–6.5.

Cause 4.8

Spark plug shorting out. If there is a spark at the plug, and you think it is strong enough, it must be that once the plug is screwed into the cylinder head, and comes under pressure in the combustion chamber, the spark breaks down, or 'shorts out', inside the plug before it reaches the firing tip. Electricity will always take the shortest path to earth: if it can find earth before it reaches the earth electrodes at the firing tip – and it is likely to try to do so with that electrode under pressure – then, be assured, it will do. A deficiency in the spark plug, such as an oily film or dampness on the porcelain, cracked porcelain, or breaks or fractures in the centre electrode, etc., will all allow the voltage to take that shorter path.

Remedy 4.8

The only solution, if you suspect that the spark plug is breaking down under pressure, is to replace it: either with a new one, or with a used one you are sure of.

You can check to see if it is the spark plug or ignition system which is at fault by replacing the suspect plug with either a new one or, if you ride a multi-cylinder motorcycle, by a plug you know to be good from another cylinder.

If the replacement plug operates correctly, the original plug was obviously breaking down and must be thrown away and replaced.

Cause 4.9

Ignition timing incorrect. If all your investigations to this point have revealed nothing faulty, or even suspicious, in the ignition system, there is the possibility that although a strong spark is occurring at the tip, even under pressure, it is *severely* out of time – that is, the spark is being triggered far too early or too late to ignite the mixture. Signs that this is happening are sometimes given by the engine backfiring as you try to start it, but unfortunately the absence of this signal does not mean that the timing is correct. It should be stressed, however, that the timing will rarely become so far out of line that the engine won't start without you first noticing the deterioration in performance. If this ever does happen, you should not only reset the timing but immediately investigate how on earth it became so far out so quickly.

Remedy 4.9

Roadside failures rarely occur in a situation where you will have access to the proper equipment you will need to reset the timing. The best you can do in these circumstances is to check that the points (if fitted) are opening when the piston is roughly at T.D.C. on its compression stroke. Although accuracy to within a thousandth of an inch is not vital, in that an engine should run – albeit poorly – even with considerable inaccuracies, you should do your best to get it as close as possible. Use a dial gauge to achieve T.D.C. if you have one with you (see 'Ignition timing', pp. 62–3). If you don't have one to hand, use a pencil, screwdriver or length of old spoke, down the spark plug hole, to make a rough estimate.

If you do have access to more substantial facilities, or a workshop is close by, by far the best solution is to use a strobe wired into the ignition to reset the timing precisely (see 'Ignition timing', pp. 62–3).

Cause 4.10

Deficiency in the H.T. coil. This final possible cause will only be the source of your motorcycle's refusal to start if it is a single-cylinder, and if the ignition system relies on a flywheel/magneto to supply the power.

Situations sometimes do arise on motorcycles of this description where the engine appears to be in good working order – that is, there is plenty of clean fuel, and it is reaching the plug in the correct proportions (see items 3.1–3.6 on pp. 103–7); there is plenty of compression (see item 7 on pp. 132–6); the spark appears a lovely blue colour – but none the less the engine still won't start: deficiencies in the H.T. coil are usually to blame.

Remedy 4.10

Check that the terminal connections are all secure: if they are, the problem is within the coil itself. By far the simplest and cheapest way to resolve this is to replace the coil with one from a reputable bike-breaker. It should carry some guarantee that it is in working order, and will be substantially cheaper than a new one.

Note: This possible cause is inapplicable to motorcycles fitted with C.D.I or transistorized ignition systems.

5. Battery condition

A point we should make clear at the outset of this section is that not all motorcycles use the battery in the same way, and there are some motorcycles which don't have a battery at all (although these are almost always machines designed for competition riding – and there are also some mopeds that have no battery). The difference basically depends on whether the ignition system uses a D.C. coil and generator or an A.C. flywheel/magneto.

The D.C. coil/generator system

In this system the battery feeds power to the coil where it is energized into high-tension power, to supply the spark plug, as the contact breaker operates. Power needs to be drawn from the battery when you start the engine because the charge generated is insufficient. In effect, the generator power needs to be supplemented by power from the battery if the engine is to start. Once the engine is running, however, the generator replaces the battery's drained power.

The battery in this system may be of either 6 or 12 volts. However, because

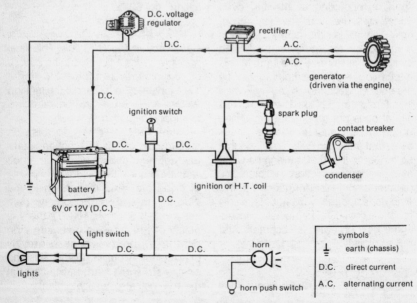

Figure 50 A basic wiring diagram for a D.C. coil/generator type ignition system

of the demands which are made upon it to aid starting, most manufacturers design their systems around a 12 volts battery. A general D.C. system is set out in Figure 50.

The A.C. flywheel/magneto system

Although this system is fitted with a battery, it is quite capable of providing enough power to start an engine without drawing any from the battery – indeed, the engine would still start if the battery were removed. The power is generated by the flywheel/magneto and fed from there to the A.C. coil, where it is boosted to high-tension current. This operation is sometimes referred to as being a self-contained generator ignition system. A general A.C. ignition system is set out in Figure 51.

A battery is included in this system simply to power the lights, indicators, horn, etc. As with the D.C. ignition, some of the power generated – by the magneto in this case – is used to replenish any power that the battery has lost in powering the electrical system.

If you are unsure which system is employed in your motorcycle, it should be quite easy for you to distinguish the two simply by looking at them. In the A.C. coil system, unlike the D.C. system, the contact breaker assembly is surrounded by the flywheel/magneto (Figures 47 and 48). However, if you still feel unsure, don't hesitate to check in your owner's handbook or workshop manual *before* you begin to inspect the battery and to make assumptions about why the engine won't start.

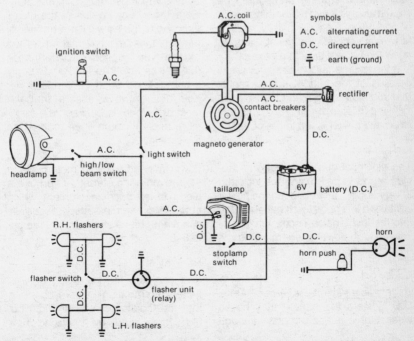

Figure 51 A basic wiring diagram for an A.C. flywheel/magneto type ignition system

In brief, if your motorcycle is fitted with a flywheel/magneto you can discount the battery as being a source of the engine's refusal to start. On the other hand, the condition of the battery may prevent your engine from starting if the ignition system uses the D.C. coil/generator method.

The level of power required to start a motorcycle, however, depends entirely on the method of starting you use.

Electric starting

When you use a starter motor the drain on the battery is enormous. It is virtually the same as shorting the battery directly to earth and, as such, the demands it makes are enough to flatten the average motorcycle battery in less than two minutes. Even during your normal starting procedure you should always leave a breathing space of about ten seconds initially, and up to twenty seconds if it fails to start, to allow the battery time to recover.

If the engine fails to fire after a few presses of the button, it is essential that you stop using it and revert to the kickstart (if fitted) if you are to conserve what little power is left in the battery.

Kickstarting

The electrical current needed to provide a good spark using the kickstart is very small – indeed, even the power contained in a good torch battery wired into the low-tension circuit would provide enough power to energize the coil for kickstarting.

Cause 5.1

Battery insufficiently charged. On a D.C. system the battery may be so weak that it doesn't contain enough power to start or turn over the engine:

1. *Using the electric starter.* If this is the case, the pitch and level of the noise made by the starter motor will be different from usual: the motor will be sluggish and sound laboured. Indeed, if the battery is too low you may only hear a clunk (when you press the button) as the starter motor switch engages and nothing from the motor itself.

Immediately you suspect the battery is low on power, switch to the kickstart.

2. *Using the kickstart.* If the engine fails to fire using the kickstart, it must be that the battery is totally drained of power.

As we discussed on pp. 38–9, sustained care of your battery is essential. If, when you inspect it, the electrolyte level has fallen below the level of the plates, you must refill it immediately. Remember, any portion of the plates exposed to the air will be permanently damaged, and each damaged cell will reduce your battery's performance (that is, its ability to hold and supply a charge) and shorten its useful life. You must always ensure that the electrolyte level is between the maximum and minimum lines marked on the casing.

Indeed, insufficient ability to hold power may cause your motorcycle to stop, even once started, if you use a piece of electrical equipment which puts a drain on the battery, especially if that item has a short circuit (see pp. 225–6).

Remedy 5.1

You can test the condition of your battery by sounding the horn, checking that the indicators not only light but also flash, and by checking how bright the lights are. If the horn is not up to standard, the indicators light but do not flash or there is little or no glimmer from the headlight, then the battery is almost certainly not holding a charge sufficient to start the engine.

1. If the engine refuses to start with the electric starter motor, you should not hesitate to switch to the kickstart – persistence will only flatten the battery even more and perhaps make it too weak even to fire with a kick. If kickstarting does do the trick, a relatively short drive, say, eight to ten miles, should fully charge the battery. It is a good idea to check the charge when you return just to ensure the generator has been working correctly. If the battery is still in the same condition, that is, will start with the kickstart but not the electric starter, you have an electrical-recharging problem somewhere in the system (see item 15.1.1, p. 225).

2. On the other hand, if the engine also refuses to start using the kickstart, or if your motorcycle is not fitted with a kickstart, you will need either to bump-start (push) or to jump-start the motorcycle. See pp. 234 and 240 respectively for a more detailed discussion of these two last-resort methods.

Once again, however, if the engine does start, ride the motorcycle for a few miles (perhaps for a little longer this time, say, ten to fifteen miles) and recheck the battery's condition. After a trip of that distance it should be fully charged. If it is not, once again you have a recharging problem and should see item 15.1.1, p. 225.

If the battery is fully charged immediately you return and yet is flat again the next morning, it is clearly discharging itself somehow while not being used (see item 15.3, pp. 225–6).

To measure the electrical charge you can use either a battery charger, on which you will be able to read off the amount of charge on the gauge provided, or a hydrometer, to measure the specific gravity of the electrolyte surrounding the plates in each cell. A normal, fully charged motorcycle battery should have a specific gravity of $1 \cdot 260$–$1 \cdot 280$. If the reading you obtain is lower than that, the battery is undercharged. On the other hand, if the reading is higher, there is a problem inside the battery itself (see item 5.4 below).

If you do decide that the battery needs to be recharged, you should:

1. Remove it from the motorcycle and set it down in a secure place. If it is inconvenient to remove the battery it must, at least, be disconnected from the electrical system. Failure to do so risks damaging the generator.

2. Ensure that the electrolyte level is between the recommended maximum and minimum levels.

3. Do not replace each cell hole cover until the battery is fully charged.

4. If the charger is designed for both 12 and 6 volt systems, select the correct voltage for your motorcycle.

5. Connect the charger to the battery and leave it 'on slow charge' for the required period.

6. Disconnect the charger and replace the cell hole cover(s).

7. Secure the battery in the frame and reconnect the terminals.

Finally, a point worth making at this stage is that if you have been trying for some time to start the engine before tracing the possible cause to the battery, you may have flooded the cylinder and wet the spark plug. So, if the motorcycle also refuses to be bump- or jump-started, a flat battery is now not the only cause of your engine's failure. You should try to rethink what you've done to the engine while trying to get it started: operating the choke or twisting the throttle, etc., will all affect the situation. Clearly, further investigation of these possibilities may now be required.

Important: If there is the slightest sign of weakness in the battery, remember to switch off the lights or any other equipment before you try to start the engine again.

Cause 5.2

Loose terminal connections or battery earth wire. If either of the two terminal connections – to the top of the battery – or the earth wire attached to the frame are loose, the flow of current to the coil may be interrupted, and will almost certainly be insufficient to gen- erate the necessary H.T. power at the plug to leap the electrode gap.

Remedy 5.2

Ensure that both terminal connections are secure and that the earth wire is firmly fixed to the frame. If you are unsure, the location of the battery's earth will be indicated in your owner's handbook or workshop manual.

Cause 5.3

Corroded terminals. If there are any signs of white or greenish-white deposits around the terminal connec- tions, they are being corroded – that is, gradually eaten away, possibly by a small seepage of electrolyte (an acid) from the battery, or possibly by the climatic conditions. Whatever the cause, terminals that are corroded have a high electrical resistance and so give the impression that the battery is flat when you come to use it.

Remedy 5.3

Any sign of corrosion on the battery terminals or lead connections should be removed immediately. Surprisingly, pouring a small amount of boiling water over the terminals will often help remove built-up corrosion. You can then either rub the terminals (or con- nectors) with a wire brush, or scrape them with a knife, and then rub them over with a piece of emery paper to remove any final signs.

Finally, before and after you remake the connections, coat the terminals and the connectors with Vaseline to protect them from any future attacks.

Cause 5.4

Internal short circuit. As we pointed out in section 5.1, the cells of a nor- mally charged battery should have a specific gravity of $1·260–1·280$. Although a lower reading indicates that the battery is undercharged, a higher reading does not mean that the battery is overcharged, but rather indicates that there is an internal short circuit, reducing the battery's capacity and therefore reducing the possible power output.

Remedy 5.4

Unfortunately, there is nothing to do except replace the battery.

6. Switches and wiring

If you are satisfied that the individual components in the ignition system are operating satisfactorily, there is a final set of problems in the ignition system which may be preventing your engine from starting. You must ensure that the wiring, which is used to transmit the electrical power from one component to another and finally to the spark plug itself, is intact and securely connected to the flow of electrical power.

Any interruptions or hindrances to the flow of electrical power will certainly result in performance problems and will probably prevent your engine from firing at all.

Cause 6.1

Blown fuse. A blown main fuse will bring a complete shutdown of the motorcycle operation.

Although a blown fuse may be evidence of a short circuit in the system, it is more likely that the fuse was old. The life expectancy of a fuse does vary according to the level of current flowing through it, but sooner or later fuses can fail even if the electrical system is in perfect condition. The location of the fusebox and the main fuse will be indicated in your owner's handbook or workshop manual.

While at the fusebox inspect the fuse-holder for signs of dirt or corrosion. Even if the fuse hasn't blown, a holder in poor condition will inhibit the current flow and may be the cause of your problems (see p. 83 for more information on fusebox servicing).

If the motorcycle is stationary, with the engine off, a blown fuse will prevent it starting. On the other hand, if the motorcycle is in motion, with the engine running, when the fuse fails, the ignition system will die instantly and the engine will fade rapidly.

Remedy 6.1

Certainly a blown fuse should be replaced, but you should also give consideration to the possible cause of its failure. There are many reasons for a one-off fuse failure – old age (perhaps the primary one), excess vibration, etc. – but if a new fuse blows, and replacements continue to do the same, you will need to look further into the electrical system to discover an electrical fault severe enough to burn out the fuse.

If you do suspect anything other than old age, *do not* replace the fuse until you have traced the problem's source. (See 'Continually blowing fuses', pp. 223–4).

Cause 6.2

Ignition system damp. Most ignition systems are highly susceptible, and sensitive, to water or dampness: riding in heavy rain, leaving your motorcycle ungaraged (or uncovered), on a damp night or using a pressurized hosepipe carelessly while washing your motorcycle (see also pp. 235–7) are just three of the more common situations. As a result of any of these the engine is unlikely to fire and, even if it does, it will run with a severe misfire (see pp. 181–9).

If you do suspect that there is damp in the ignition, you should particularly check for:

Cause 6.2.1

Water or damp collecting around the spark plug, the spark plug cap, the plug leads (H.T. leads), the points or the coil(s). Dampness here often contains traces of metallic particles which can leak the current to earth or sufficiently divert its course to weaken or prevent the spark. Indeed, with the engine running on a wet night sometimes the current can actually be seen sparking along the length of the H.T. cable(s).

Remedy 6.2.1

The problem of wetness or damp in the ignition can be solved temporarily by wiping all the equipment with a rag which has been soaked in methylated spirits, or by spraying the components with a penetrating oil or one of the many damp-start products on the market.

For a longer-term solution you will need to replace the spark plug cap(s) with a waterproof type and give the whole system an added layer of protection, either by smearing a thin coat of grease (which will need to be replaced every two to three months) over the components, or by using one of the sprays currently on the market which puts a thin coat of rubber sealant over the entire system.

When deciding which protectant to use it is worth noting that, although grease is cheaper, the rubber spray-on sealants do last longer.

Important: Whichever you decide to use, it is essential that all the items are perfectly clean and dry *before* you apply the protective coating – otherwise you will simply be trapping the moisture in.

Cause 6.2.2

Loose fittings between the components in the H.T. circuit, particularly the H.T. cable–coil, and H.T. cable–spark plug cap connections. Any slackness here will allow water or damp to seep into the cable and once again divert the current flow from the inner core of the cable.

Remedy 6.2.2

Ensure that there is a tight fit at the point where each of the various components is joined. Although the spark plug cap (which is screwed into the end of the H.T. lead) is designed to link the spark plug and H.T. cable, while also keeping water off the plug's terminal, it sometimes works loose: you should check that it is securely attached.

If you do discover a loose connection, however, do not simply retighten the component's securing devices. Remember, you are having problems with your motorcycle because moisture has entered the ignition system: always disconnect the cables and clean and dry both areas – perhaps apply a light coating of grease – and then remake the joint.

Don't forget to protect this new joint with a smear of grease or rubber sealant spray.

Cause 6.2.3

Water or dampness which may have gathered under the suppressor built into the spark plug cap (these are designed to stop your motorcycle interfering with radios and televisions as you ride past).

Remedy 6.2.3

If the suppressor is the metal shield type (and it is only with this type that you will have this particular problem), the best advice we can give is to remove the metal shield with a pair of pliers, leaving only the plastic cap, or to replace the cap with one of the non-shielded, waterproof type. Indeed, it is perhaps best to do this before the problem occurs (see 'Metal-shielded caps' p. 267).

Cause 6.2.4

Water in the cut-out switch. The cut-out switch is designed to instantly shut off the engine when necessary. If water or sufficient dampness finds its way into this switch, the circuit will be broken, even while the switch is in the 'on' position.

Remedy 6.2.4

As a temporary measure you can always try spraying a water-repellent spray into the switch, but if this is ineffective you will need to: (1) dismantle the switch; (2) clean and dry the contact surfaces; (3) pack the inside of the switch casing with grease; and (4) rebuild and refit the switch.

Cause 6.3

Breaks in the power cables. Although there are various wiring arrangements in the different ignition systems, they all require that both the primary circuit – that is, the battery to the coil(s) and the coil(s) to the contact breaker assembly(-ies) – and the secondary circuit – that is, the coil(s) to the plug(s) – should always have continuity from one end to the other. If the wiring in either circuit is corroded or broken, the flow of electrical power will itself be broken.

Although the H.T. cable is heavily insulated to prevent current escaping, age does steadily cause the casing to perish or wear, and eventually cracks or holes may begin to appear in that outer insulation.

The power will also be prevented from reaching the plug terminal if any of the connectors are broken or loose.

Remedy 6.3

Check and, if necessary, secure all the connections: at the coil(s), condenser(s), spark plug cap(s), breaker assembly, etc., and examine the condition of the H.T. cable casings in the secondary circuit.

In the primary circuit you can use the rough circuit tester described on pp. 201 or 235 to check for dirty connectors and for cracks or breaks in the wiring.

Find a point in the system which is live and move from there through the system either until you reach a point where no current is detected or until the current you detect is substantially weaker.

The obvious conclusion is that between that point and the previous one tested there is a break in the wiring.

Any cables in the secondary circuit that appear in the least bit cracked or worn should be replaced immediately.

If the problem occurs while you are away from home, as a temporary solution several layers of insulating tape wound around this area may help. It is a good idea, however, periodically to replace these cables (beware – some cannot be replaced!), regardless of their apparent condition, to prevent these types of problem occurring.

Cause 6.4

Electrical short circuit. If a short circuit exists anywhere within the ignition/electrical system, the electrical power designed to leap the gap between the spark plug's electrodes will either be drained off to earth via some point on the cycle frame or be stopped by a break in the circuit.

Some of the more likely sources of an electrical short circuit you should check for are:

Cause 6.4.1

Loose or fractured connectors. These may arise because:

1. Steady vibrations over time may have caused a connector to work loose.

2. If you have been fitting new electrical equipment or making changes to existing equipment you may not have securely replaced a connector.

3. The connectors may have been continually exposed to moisture so that they become corroded and finally fractured.

4. A connector may also be at fault because of a break at the joint where it is crimped on to the wire, especially if it is subjected to excessive vibrations.

Remedy 6.4.1

Ensure that all connectors within the system are securely fitted and inspect them all for any signs of corrosion, cracks or fractures. If you do suspect any connector, by and large it is a waste of time to try to repair it, unless you are away from home and have no choice. In this situation a hefty binding of insulating tape may hold it together long enough to get you home, but that is all it should be used for; the most simple solution is to replace it. Even though it is likely that only one side of the connector will be fractured, it is still best to replace the whole connector. The other side will undoubtedly also be worn, and perhaps even on the point of breaking. Replacing both sides now will prevent you having problems in the future.

Cause 6.4.2

Breaks in the electrical wires themselves. Electrical wires are frequently gathered into long plastic sleeves (known as looms), and it is rare that a fracture will occur inside the loom. Single lengths are therefore more suspect.

One of the most common locations for a fractured wire, and one which is often associated with very particular symptoms, is where a wire passes around the headstock. If your engine stops or severely misfires while you are turning either left or right, or while you are manoeuvring it at the kerbside, you can be almost certain that one of the wires passing around the headstock has either worn excessively (that is, down to the wire itself) and is therefore shorting to earth, or fractured, because of the continued stretching, and is therefore breaking the electrical flow each time you turn.

Remedy 6.4.2

Check all electrical wires – paying particular attention to those running singly and/or in exposed areas – for cracks, splits or worn sections. In brief, you need to examine each length of wire for any section which may allow the inner wire to contact to earth.

If nothing becomes apparent after a short inspection, try using the test lamp (see p. 235) to check each section in turn. Checking the entire system can be a very time-consuming process and you will need to be both methodical and logical in how you go about it; unfortunately, there are no short-cuts. If the bulb lights at the start of a section and not at the end, the source of your problem clearly lies within that section.

If the problem does appear to be associated with a particular action, however – when you turn left or right, for example – you should direct your attention to the most likely problem area first. If you do suspect the head-stock: (1) centre the handlebars; (2) start the engine but leave the motor-cycle stationary; and (3) move the handlebars from full-left to full-right lock. If the engine stops (or misfires), you need look no further.

If you do find evidence of splits, cracks or wear they should be covered with several layers of a good insulating tape. Moreover, if the problem occurred because of wear it would be a good idea to redirect the wire. On the other hand, if the outer cable appears unbroken (and the connec-tors are secure), but you are satisfied the problem lies in that section, it may be that the wire has fractured inside the casing. Unless you can ascertain the exact location of the break (which can be very difficult), where you can then cut the wire and insert a connec-tor to make a secure joint, you may find it easier simply to replace the section with a new length of sound wire.

Cause 6.4.3

If the engine fails only when you use a particular piece of equipment it is likely that there is a short in the elec-trical system serving that item. If the engine fails or misfires each time you use the brakes, for example – that is (to be precise), each time the brake light comes on – then either the light unit, the wiring to the unit or the switch is shorting out.

To detect a situation such as this, however, you need to be aware of your motorcycle at the time you are riding. As we pointed out in the intro-duction to this chapter, immediately you sense a problem or something unusual try to remember and analyse

everything you have just done – no matter how small – and ask yourself if it can possibly be related to the current problem. If the engine has misfired on several occasions during your ride (before it failed totally), and you sus-pect it is related to applying the brakes, for example, you can test this possi-bility by applying each brake *individu-ally* until the brake light is on. If the engine fails again, and you are confi-dent the battery is sufficiently charged (see pp. 122–3), you have not only been able to establish the brake light as the source of your problem, but which specific brake light circuit.

Remedy 6.4.3

A temporary solution which will get you home, but one which should cer-tainly not be used any more than necessary, is to disconnect the switch which operates the problem circuit. (Some items of equipment are not always essential to your safety, and if this is the case it may be sufficient simply to stop using it for the remainder of the journey. Brakes clearly don't fall into this category, however.)

IMPORTANT: If you do disconnect the brake light switch, don't forget to use the necessary hand signals when you're slowing; otherwise, you may put yourself and others in unnecessary danger.

To resolve the problem permanently you will need to use the test lamp again and check the flow of current through the defective circuit until you can trace the area at fault. If it is a section of wire it can be taped, recon-nected or replaced; defective switches are best replaced; and lamp units (or any other item of equipment) will need to be either repaired or replaced.

Cause 6.5

Ignition switch defective. If, when you switch on the ignition, none of the indicators on the instrument panel light up, and you have checked (and are satisfied) that the ignition circuit – especially the main fuse – is intact, then unfortunately your ignition switch is likely to be defective. In brief, the ignition circuit is not being completed when you turn the key. This occurs most frequently because: (1) damp, dirt or corrosion (sometimes referred to as 'verdigris') has gathered on and around the contact surfaces and is preventing a good connection; or (2) the contact surfaces and/or other internal switch components are excessively worn and no longer make contact as the switch is turned on.

Remedy 6.5

The complication in solving this problem is, of course, that while you are looking from the outside, it is almost impossible to determine whether the contacts are dirty or worn – the only potential guide you may have is if you know the age of the switch and/or whether or not it has been cleaned recently. Although this kind of information should enable you to make a more educated guess than no information at all, it may not be any more than that: a guess.

As a first step, and one which may only be a temporary solution, spray penetrating oil down the keyhole and down a small hole you should find on the switch body (spraying down the key hole will lubricate the key action but will do little to the contacts). This should remove any dampness which may have gathered and may also dislodge any particles of dirt. Moreover, sometimes simply jogging the key around in the slot will do the trick (to get you home at least), although even if it does work this time the problem will get steadily worse and cause eventual failure, and that will undoubtedly be at the most inconvenient moment.

A permanent solution – and the one you will be forced into if the temporary ones don't work – involves dismantling the switch and cleaning the contact surfaces with solvent and a dry cloth (or emery paper if the dirt or corrosion is heavy). Before you rebuild the switch, however, it is always a good idea to spray all the components with a lubricating or anti-corrosion spray, just to give an added layer of protection.

If, when you have dismantled the switch, the contact surfaces are clearly worn, unfortunately the only practical solution is to replace the switch. You might consider trying to build up the contact surfaces with solder, etc., and filing them square, but unless you feel competent you may be just wasting your time. Also, solder is very soft and will only be useful for six to eight starts, after which it will have worn out. Really, then, solder is only good to tide you over until you can get a replacement switch. Before you consider replacing the switch with a new one (or after you have considered it and discovered the rather high price), give your local breaker's yard a call – he may have just the item you are looking for and it should be substantially cheaper.

One final situation you may come across is that when you open the switch there are no signs of dirt or corrosion and no real evidence of excessive wear. Try rebuilding the switch: it may be that some of the internal components were loose and rebuilding will secure them.

Cause 6.6

Starter motor (if fitted) defective. If, when you press the starter motor button, all you hear is a click as the solenoid switches on, and yet the lights stay bright, it is likely that the starter motor is defective.

Listen carefully to the noise and make sure you don't confuse it with the clunk of a starter motor failing to turn over because of a flat battery. If you feel at all unsure, just put your ear close to the solenoid as you press the starter button (your owner's handbook or workshop manual should indicate its location) and then try the lights or horn, etc. A basic difference between the two situations is that if the problem is with the starter motor, the lights, etc., will still be strong.

Remedy 6.6

The majority of motorcycles with a starter motor are still also fitted with a kickstart: if yours is, you will have no problems getting home – use it!

Unfortunately an increasing number of motorcycles (some of which are very popular) don't have this back-up to the starter motor, in which case you will have either to bump- or jump-start the motorcycle (for a detailed description of bump-starting see p. 234–5; for jump-starting, see p. 240).

A further complication with some motorcycles, however, is that as well as being dependent on a starter motor, they are shaft driven, and for those of you who haven't tried it, bump-starting a shaft-driven motorcycle is quite a task. If you are in this situation we suggest you try jump-starting first. Remember, any other vehicle's battery (provided its ignition system is of the same voltage as your motorcycle) can be used. In fact, the battery you use need not be in another vehicle at all: provided it has sufficient charge you can use it free-standing.

When it comes to resolving the starter motor problem itself, you will need, in brief, to repair or replace it. For a detailed assessment of the situation, that is, when and how it may be repaired and when it will need to be replaced, see p. 228.

THE MECHANICAL SYSTEM

As we saw in Chapter 1, the internal-combustion engine requires the petrol/air mixture to be compressed at the top of the cylinder, that is, in the combustion chamber, before it is ignited. Once it is ignited the compressed mixture burns and expands rapidly, forcing the piston down the cylinder and so transmitting power to the crankshaft and, via the final drive, to the rear wheel. For this process to occur effectively, it is essential that the combustion chamber is completely airtight. If there are leaks, problems will occur:

1. On the compression stroke, instead of the mixture being compressed correctly (that is, the original volume being reduced to the combustion volume specified in the compression ratio – see Glossary for more information) some of the petrol/air vapour will be pumped out into the atmosphere, reducing the combustion

chamber pressure, and therefore reducing the force of the explosion and the power behind the downward thrust of the piston.

2. On the power stroke, gases will rush out of the leak, reduce the force on the piston crown and therefore once again reduce the power behind its downward thrust.

Reduced compression will therefore lead to reduced power and, if the compression loss is substantial, the engine will fail to start. Indeed, in the most extreme case, a total lack of compression will mean a total lack of power.

The principal mechanical reason for an engine's failure to start, therefore, is a total, or certainly a substantial, lack of compression. This problem is only likely with older machines, although, as usual with engines, this general rule of thumb does have its exceptions. If the compression loss is less than substantial, however – and what that means in reality varies so dramatically from one motorcycle to another that it is virtually impossible to be more specific at this stage – your problem will be one of *reduced power* and hence *reduced performance*: the subject of Chapter 5.

7. Lack of adequate compression

If your engine fails to start, and you suspect that inadequate compression is the cause, there are a couple of simple tests you can use to check its compression.

Although the more experienced amongst you can actually assess an engine's condition manually by simply pushing the kickstart or by sticking a thumb over the spark plug hole, the majority of us may feel a little more confident if that rough-and-ready check was verified by a compression gauge.

Compression checks

1. *Manually.* (a) Push down the kick-start lever by hand and assess the resistance you feel: if it is slight (and a good example of this would be if one gentle push spins the crankshaft of a large single-cylinder engine several times) your suspicions were correct and you do have a compression problem. However, although you can use this method roughly to gauge the condition of all engines, it is really only practical on single-cylinder engines. On multi-cylinder engines further testing would be required to determine which cylinder(s) is (are) causing the trouble.

(b) Alternatively, remove the spark plug and place your thumb over the plug hole, depress the kickstart (or press the electric starter button if a kickstart is not fitted) and feel for pressure. Once again, if it is minimal or non-existent (as described above), inadequate compression is the source of your problem. Unlike test (a), this second test can be used on multi-cylinder engines: simply test each one in turn to determine which is (are) causing the trouble.

2. *Using a compression gauge.* (a) Normally, this would be done with the engine warm. Obviously, you can't operate the engine to warm it up. Therefore you'll need to do the test with the engine as it is. (b) Remove the spark plug from the cylinder to be tested and clean away any dirt or grease which may prevent the gauge seating correctly. (c) Insert the tip of the gauge into the hole and ensure that it is sealed correctly and firmly. (d)

Open the throttle fully. (e) Turn the engine over several times – use the kickstart if possible (to save battery power) – but if not the electric starter will do just as well – and record the highest pressure reading on the gauge. In brief, readings under 100 p.s.i. mean trouble. (f) Repeat the test on any other cylinders.

If any of these tests do indicate that compression is inadequate, clearly you will need to investigate further and establish the precise reason for the compression loss. In carrying out any further investigations, however, it is useful to bear in mind that a gradual loss of power, or increasingly difficult starting, generally indicate wear, whereas a sudden loss of power and/or a refusal to start generally indicate that something has broken.

Cause 7.1

Leaking or blown cylinder head gasket. If the cylinder head gasket is leaking, or has blown completely, the escaping gases will leave tell-tale signs – dry, black, carbon deposits with four-stroke engines and wet, oily patches with two-strokes – on the outside of the cylinder and on the cooling fins.

As a quick way of checking that these marks are the result of a damaged head gasket, place your hand over the area of the joint you suspect and turn the engine over: you should be able to feel the escaping gas on your hand as it rushes out, if the seal is leaking. Unfortunately, however, on multi-cylinder engines the leak may be between the cylinders and into the cam-chain tunnel: this problem can only be diagnosed if the cylinder head has been removed.

Remedy 7.1

Firstly, try screwing down the cylinder head bolts as they may have become loose. Beware, however, that you don't overtighten them: you may distort the cylinder head (and this is far easier to do than you think) by applying too much pressure. Always use a torque wrench to ensure that you exert no more than the required amount of pressure to seal the joint satisfactorily. The extent of the pressure you should use, and the order in which the bolts should be tightened, will be indicated in your owner's handbook or workshop manual. If no specific order is indicated, they should always be tightened in diagonal pairs – never consecutively.

If tightening the bolts fails to cure the problem, however, unfortunately you will need to remove the cylinder head and inspect the gasket and the jointing surfaces. If the gasket is not made of copper, do not hesitate to replace it; if the faces of either the barrel or the head are in any way uneven they will need to be skimmed flat (at your local workshop) before a secure head joint can be achieved.

Cause 7.2

Damaged pistons/piston rings. If the petrol/air mixture is to be contained above the piston crown, it is essential that the piston rings form a gas-tight seal with the cylinder wall. If either the piston, the bore or, more particularly, the piston rings become damaged or excessively worn, the resultant loss of compression will almost certainly cause your starting problems. Even if the engine started, its performance would be drastically reduced.

Because of the operational procedures of two-stroke engines, their piston rings tend to seize, break or simply become gummed up with oil or carbon far more frequently than four-strokes, and all these seriously reduce compression.

Remedy 7.2

Unfortunately, the only foolproof way to verify if the compression loss is due to a piston or piston ring defect is to dismantle the engine and inspect the components individually. However, using a compression tester and a squirt of oil will at least signpost whether the compression is being lost at the piston rings or the valves, and you can begin your investigations with this in mind. Taking each cylinder in turn:

1. Use the compression tester to take a reading.

2. Inject one or two squirts of oil into the cylinder through the spark plug hole.

3. Use the compression tester again to take a second reading.

4. If: (a) the second reading is *higher* than the first, the *piston rings* are the more likely problem; (b) the second reading is the *same* as the first, the *valves* are the more likely cause.

Certainly, any items which are damaged or worn need to be replaced immediately. On the majority of motorcycles in this situation you will find that the rings are broken, and replacing them should clear the problem.

If the rings are intact, however, and nothing appears to be worn excessively, the best advice is to have both the piston and the bore checked by your local workshop – measuring these components accurately requires specialized precision tools and more than a little experience. If they are worn to excess, the piston can be replaced, but the cylinder will need to be rebored or relined – a job for the expert. On the other hand, if you are satisfied the piston, the rings and bore are all satisfactory and you ride a four-stroke, it may be that the valves are sticking.

Cause 7.3

Sticking valves (four-strokes only). Whether as a result of poor adjustment, or of excessive carbon deposits on the stem, either the inlet or the exhaust valve of a four-stroke engine may fail to close fully, or to seat itself correctly. As a result, instead of the vapour being compressed by the rising piston, it is simply pumped into the atmosphere through the open valve.

Remedy 7.3

The first thing you should do is ensure that all the valve tappets are correctly adjusted (see pp. 69–71 for a full description of the various types of tappet and how to adjust them). The required clearance will be specified in your owner's handbook or workshop manual.

If you are satisfied that the gaps are correct, but the problem persists, you can be fairly confident that carbon deposits are the source of your problem. Although the location of the valves and the procedure to gain access to them do differ (and sometimes quite dramatically) from one motorcycle to another, in general you will need to:

1. Remove the cylinder head. On some engines this may necessitate removing the engine from the frame

first (the Honda CB750, for example); if it does, and you feel at all uneasy about the task, you should at least consult your local workshop before you go any further. If you still intend to tackle the job yourself, ensure that you are certain of the procedure for your motorcycle as set out in the owner's handbook or workshop manual.

2. Decarbonize the valve seats, the ports and the valves – particularly the stems. To remove any excess carbon you will need either a stout brush, or an electrically driven wire brush or even a good concentrate of soda. However, if you do decide to use soda, don't forget what it can do to alloy cylinder heads or pistons (see pp. 63–6).

3. Replace any valves which are defective, for example those which are cracked, chipped, pitted or burned.

4. Regrind the valve seats with valve-grinding paste until they are smooth, but no more. It is important that the seats are smoothed out but not effectively reduced in size. Because of this, valve grinding is often best left to the expertise of your local workshop.

5. Reassemble and adjust the clearances (again, these will be indicated in your owner's handbook or workshop manual).

Cause 7.4

Decompressor (if fitted) fouled or incorrectly adjusted. The decompressor, or compression release as it is sometimes known, is designed to reduce the compression in the combustion chamber *slightly* to make (kick)starting easier. On some motorcycles it is operated automatically, and on others you are required to operate it manually. To be functioning correctly – that is, releasing the correct amount of pressure at the correct time – it must be correctly adjusted and not fouled by excesses of carbon, for example.

Not all motorcycles are fitted with this device, so consult your owner's handbook or workshop manual before you go any further.

1. *Four-stroke engines.* The surplus compression is released through one of the exhaust valves. In some instances a mechanical device coupled to the valve (and mounted on the handlebars) allows you manually to open the valve whenever necessary, whereas in others the release is automatically operated via the kickstart.

2. *Two-stroke engines.* Because of the absence of valves in two-strokes, decompression is achieved by mounting a separate valve, generally on top of the cylinder head, although sometimes you may find it mounted on to the side of the cylinder above the exhaust port. As with the four-stroke, however, either the valve will need to be operated manually (by a handlebar-mounted lever) or it will be opened automatically (via the kickstart), depending on the type of motorcycle.

Compression problems will arise on both types of engine if this device is incorrectly adjusted, that is, if it has insufficient free play in the cable; moreover, on two-strokes there is the additional possibility – indeed it is almost a probability – that the valve will fail to operate correctly because it is fouled by carbon.

Remedy 7.4

On two-strokes the first thing you should do is examine the cylinder-mounted mechanism; if there are signs of carbon fouling, remove the valve and decarbonize it. Various methods of removing carbon deposits from engine components are discussed in full on pp. 63–6. Briefly, it involves scraping off the carbon with a wooden scraper or the rounded end of a hacksaw blade (depending on how stubborn the deposits are – indeed, if they are very stubborn, you may need to use a wire wheel attached to an electric drill), polishing the valve with wire wool or saucepan cleaning pads to remove any final traces and then lightly polishing.

However, if you are satisfied that carbon fouling is not the problem (and four-stroke riders can be pretty sure of that before they even look), you will need to readjust the slack in the cable between the actuating mechanism (either the manual lever on the handlebars or the automatic one at the kickstart) and the valve.

Your owner's handbook or workshop manual will indicate the correct adjustment procedure and required clearances for your motorcycle.

THE LUBRICATION SYSTEM

By acting as a barrier between an engine's moving parts, where there would otherwise be metal to metal contact, oil reduces the friction which causes an engine to overheat and its components to wear rapidly. Consequently, it is important that you ensure that an adequate supply of oil is always available, and (equally importantly) that it is able to reach the required areas as and when necessary (see 'Oil levels', p. 39, as well as 'Change the engine oil and clean the oil filter', pp. 52–3). Failure to make these checks will almost certainly mean that the lubrication system will be the source (or at least a contributory cause) of your motorcycle's current problem.

As we discussed in Chapter 1, the lubrication systems in four-stroke and two-stroke engines are quite different. In the four-stroke engine, oil is pumped from the oil tank to all parts of the engine where it is required and then circulated back to the oil tank to be used again. In the two-stroke engine, on the other hand, the question of lubrication is solved by adding oil to the petrol/air mixture and burning it in the combustion chamber once it has done its lubricating job. Unlike the four-stroke, therefore, the lubrication of a two-stroke engine operates on a total-loss basis. (That's why you need to keep such a close eye on the two-stroke oil tank whenever you fill up with petrol.) Two-stroke oil is either poured directly into the petrol tank or stored in a special reservoir tank from which correct quantities are then automatically fed into the mixture by an oil pump. Your owner's handbook or workshop manual will indicate the method used on your motorcycle.

Exactly how the lubrication system may be responsible for your motorcycle's problem therefore depends on its operational cycle.

8. Fuel/oil ratio incorrect (two-strokes only)

Cause 8.1

Auto-lube oil tank empty. Obviously, if the oil tank is empty, no oil can be pumped into the petrol/air mixture; as a result, the engine lacks lubrication, and the internal components – especially the piston – will begin to overheat and eventually to seize.

Remedy **8.1**

Check the oil tank (a small window is often provided on the side of the tank for this) and, if necessary, refill it with the correct grade of oil. If you find the tank is completely empty, be sure to bleed the oil pump of any air, which may have been drawn in behind the last drips of oil, before you go any further (see 'Auto-lube systems . . .: Air locks', p. 231).

Cause **8.2**

Incorrect proportion of two-stroke oil in pre-mix petrol. If your engine requires that you mix the petrol and oil manually, it is essential that you add *no more* and *no less* than the amount required – either can be extremely harmful.

1. *Too much oil.* A higher proportion of oil than that specified will result in heavy carbon fouling of the spark plug, piston crown, exhaust ports and exhaust system – eventually stifling the engine to the point of failure.

2. *Too little oil.* If the petrol lacks sufficient oil to do its job effectively, excess wear, rapid overheating and ultimately engine seizure are not only likely, but probable.

Remedy **8.2**

Ensure that you use only the grade and proportions of oil specified in your owner's handbook or workshop manual.

Also, make sure the oil and petrol are well mixed: by simply pouring the oil into the petrol tank you do run the risk of it sinking and lying on the bottom (as a result, the oil supply would be intermittently excessive and deficient) – so shake it up well before you ride off.

You may also need to remedy any damage caused by the disproportionate oil supply. That is either:

1. Too much oil. Decarbonize the spark plug (you may need to replace it if it is too bad), the silencer and, if necessary, the exhaust pipe and exhaust ports (see pp. 63–6).

2. Too little oil. Check the spark plug's condition for signs of overheating and possibly melted electrodes, and replace it if necessary.

Cause **8.3**

Oil delivery pump control cable broken. On almost all auto-lube systems the rate at which oil is pumped into the petrol/air mixture is determined by how far the throttle twist grip is opened. The more you open it (to increase your speed or to climb hills, for example), the more revolutions the engine will spin at and, therefore, the more oil your engine will require. The most common way of ensuring that the rate of oil delivery is related to the engine's speed is to link the throttle and the oil pump with a control cable. Should this cable break, however, the oil pump's rate of delivery will *not* increase as the throttle is opened, but will remain at the rate required for tickover. Immediately you move off, therefore, the delivery rate will be insufficient to cope with the speed at which the engine is now turning.

Unfortunately there are rarely any outward signs that the cable has broken, but the consequences can certainly be serious: once again, without sufficient oil the temperature of the internal components, particularly the piston and bore, will increase dramatically, rapidly reaching the point of total seizure.

Remedy 8.3

Check the condition of the cable and, if necessary, replace it with a *new* one.

To check the cable simply: (1) remove the oil pump cover (its position will be indicated in your owner's handbook or workshop manual); and (2) observe the oil pump while you twist the throttle slightly.

If the cable attached to the pump doesn't move while you turn the throttle, you don't really need us to tell you that there is a break somewhere along its length. Sometimes it becomes evident that the cable is broken immediately you remove the cover; the nipple securing the end of the wire to the pump may have come loose, or the cable itself may appear too loose to be attached at the twist grip end.

Refer to your owner's handbook or workshop manual for the new cable's specifications and for the particular replacement procedure for your motorcycle.

Secondhand replacements will probably be available at your local breaker's and, as usual, they will be cheaper. Unless you are planning to sell the motorcycle soon, fitting a used cable would be a false economy: you have no way of knowing what it looks like inside the sleeve.

Cause 8.4

Delivery pump setting incorrect. If the engine is to operate correctly, oil must be supplied to the petrol/air mixture in just the right proportions: too much will cause plug fouling and excessive carbon build-up on the piston crown, whereas too little oil (and this is more likely to happen) will lead ultimately to engine seizure. If neither of these are to happen, accurate adjustment of the auto-lube is very important.

As with all other cables, however, the oil pump control cable will stretch over time and, as it does, the pump setting will begin to slip, steadily reducing the amount of oil being pumped into the mixture at any throttle setting. Once again, the consequences can be very serious.

Remedy 8.4

Check and, if necessary, reset the oil pump. Generally, to do this you will need to take up any slack which may have developed in the cable and ensure that the two guide marks are in line at the appropriate time. More details on auto-lube adjustment can be found on pp. 58–9.

Your owner's handbook or workshop manual will indicate the correct procedure and setting for your motorcycle.

Cause 8.5

Loose, cracked, broken or blocked oil delivery pipes. If the two-stroke oil is leaking from cracks in the pipes or loose joints, or is being prevented from reaching the inlet tracts or crankshaft bearings because the pipes are blocked, the proportion of oil being mixed with petrol will be insufficient for it to do its job correctly. And, as we have already seen above (item 8.1), the consequences of that can be serious.

Remedy 8.5

Visually inspect the pipes and joints: where possible, run your finger around the joint and along the length of the pipe to feel for any traces of oil.

If there does appear to be oil seeping from around a joint or connections, check that they are securely located and tighten any that are loose.

If you find traces of oil seepage along the length of a pipe, it is likely that it is cracked or severely split. Cracks may be a little difficult to locate precisely, unless the pipe is clean. So, if you do suspect any length, wipe it with a rag that has been soaked in methylated spirits, or a degreasing solution, and check again.

Any cracked, split or broken pipes should obviously be replaced with *new* ones immediately.

On the other hand, if all the joints appear secure, there are no signs of damage to the pipes and you feel confident that the pump is adjusted correctly, it may be that one of the pipe lengths is partially or even totally blocked. To check if there are any blockages in the system:

1. Drain the reservoir.

2. Remove the first length of pipe in the system.

3. Blow down it and, if possible, peer down it to check for any signs of sludge or dirt.

4. Clean out any blockage that may be there and replace the section.

5. If the first section appears clear, move on to the next and repeat the operation.

6. Clearing a blocked section depends on what the blockage consists of: dirt or rust particles caught on a bend, for example, are relatively easy to remove by flexing the pipe and blowing down it. Those blocked by sludge, on the other hand – especially if that sludge is the result of mixing mineral-based and vegetable-based oils (see p. 241 below) – can be extremely difficult, and really the best advice in that situation is to replace that section of pipe with a new length.

7. If you do find a section which is blocked, *do not* assume that it is the only blockage, but continue on through the entire system, removing and checking each section in turn.

8. When you are satisfied that the system is clear, don't forget to bleed the auto-lube pump (see p. 231 for precise details) and adjust the delivery rate setting (as discussed in item 8.4).

9. Replenish the system with the correct quantity of the oil recommended for your motorcycle.

Cause 8.6

Incorrect type of oil in the auto-lube system. Using the incorrect oil is likely to be a problem because:

1. Two-stroke oil normally contains a small proportion of paraffin or white spirit to help it mix with the petrol; other oils don't have these additives, and so mixing them thoroughly is a problem. However, the mixing *must* be very thorough, otherwise the engine will be under-oiled one moment and over-oiled the next.

2. In a pre-mix system, even if you do shake the mixture vigorously, the oil may separate out and steadily sink to the bottom of the tank. Consequently, either neat petrol will flow into the carburettor and crankcase, in which case the lack of lubrication will quickly cause the engine to seize, or the layer of oil will prevent the petrol flowing through the tap, quickly causing the engine to stop because of fuel starvation.

3. Although the auto-lube system may not need the self-mixing ability of two-stroke oil, the pump is only

designed to deliver this two-stroke filtration oil; any others – 20/50 engine or gearbox oil, for example – are too thick to pass through the pump and the system.

4. All oils are designed not only to lubricate, but also to do other things as they move around the system. Some of these tasks are common to all types of oil, but the emphasis is different in each, and each has its own particular jobs to do. For example, two-stroke oil is not required to fight oxidation or foaming, but it does need to reduce plug whiskering and carbon fouling of the exhaust port. Moreover, most other oils are not designed to have the sticking power that the oil in a two-stroke engine requires to do its principal job of lubrication correctly.

Using the incorrect oil, therefore, can have a variety of effects throughout the engine which manifest themselves in many different ways.

Remedy 8.6

Immediately you realize you have put the wrong oil into the system:

1. *On auto-lube systems*. Completely flush out the oil tank, the oil lines and the pump, and refill the system with the recommended grade of oil (see your owner's handbook or workshop manual for the specifications). Once again, don't forget to bleed the air from the pump after you refill the reservoir – or it won't work (see p. 231).

2. *On pre-mix systems*. Flush out all traces of petrol (or even collections of pure oil) from the petrol tank, fuel tap, fuel lines and carburettors, and refill the petrol tank with petrol mixed in the correct proportions with the recommended oil (again, your owner's handbook or workshop manual will give you the specifications you require for your motorcycle).

Cause 8.7

Delivery pump failure. If you have checked items 8.1–8.6 above, you should now suspect the pump itself. Although generally the oil pump is quite a robust little component, it is not uncommon for the drive shaft to shear off, particularly on older machines.

Remedy 8.7

Have the pump checked by a competent mechanic. If the damage is slight, it may be reparable, but, in our experience, if there is any sign that it is defective, replace it. The most cost-effective thing to do is to check with your local breaker to see if he can help you; if he doesn't have one, it will have to be a new one, unfortunately – really, repair is often not worth the time and money.

Cause 8.8

Leaking crankcase joints. As an engine heats and cools, the jointing compound, or gasket, between the mating surfaces expands and contracts. Eventually, because of this, holes or cracks may develop which will break the airtight seal around the crankcase which is so important on two-stroke engines. If this airtight seal is broken, then:

1. As the piston rises (which acts as an induction stroke in the crankcase, remember), extra air will be drawn into the mixture through the leak instead of via the carburettor (where it would be mixed with petrol). The result is a mixture which is too lean.

2. As the piston descends (on its power stroke), some of the mixture in the crankcase, which should be pushed up the transfer ports to the combustion chamber, blows out of the leak, leaving a smaller quantity of petrol/air in the chamber.

Signs that the seal is leaking will be given by:

1. Dark oily patches on the outside of the crankcase. These will be left by the mixture as it blows out.

2. Hesitancy in the speed with which the r.p.m.s descend to a tick-over: that is, as you throttle back, they will tend to hover at around 3,000 r.p.m. momentarily (regardless of the size of your motorcycle), before dropping to tickover and then, normally, fading out altogether.

3. Difficulty in starting the engine.

Remedy 8.8

The only way to solve the problem of a blown crankcase joint is to: (1) split the engine casing; (2) remove all traces of the old sealant or gasket; (3) clean the jointing surfaces and ensure they are flat and true; and (4) fit a new gasket or sealing compound and rebuild the casing.

For more information on leaking crankcase joints see p. 40, and if you are at all unsure about the detailed procedures you should follow to change the seal on your motorcycle, your owner's handbook or workshop manual should be able to help you out.

9. Engine/transmission lubrication failure

Although on many four-strokes the transmission is included in the engine oil circulation system, sometimes the gearbox, or the bevel box on a shaft drive, is lubricated separately (as it *always* is on a two-stroke). Your owner's handbook or workshop manual will indicate which system is used on your motorcycle. With a separate system the gearbox housing is simply filled with gear oil so that the cogs dip into it and splash it around as they turn. You should have no problems with the transmission so long as you remember to keep it topped up to the required level (not more, otherwise you will put undue pressure on the seals) and change the oil every 2,000 to 3,000 miles.

However, when it comes to four-stroke engine lubrication, or a situation where the engine and transmission are lubricated by the same oil, you will need to check the following if you suspect that a defect in the lubrication system is the cause of your problem.

Cause 9.1

Engine oil level too low. If the level of oil circulating in the system falls too low, its ability to cool the engine will decline and, as a result, the oil, along with the engine, will become hot and begin to 'thin'. As it does so, its ability to lubricate the moving parts satisfactorily will be reduced, and further heat rise and excess wear will result.

If the oil pressure – determined in part at least by the amount of oil in the system – is allowed to drop still further, a total seizure becomes all the more likely.

Remedy 9.1

Check the engine oil level daily and, if necessary, replenish it with the recommended oil to the specified level.

Cause 9.2

Cracked, loose or blocked oil delivery pipes: Clearly, cracked, loose or blocked oilways will interfere with the circulation of oil throughout the system, either by depleting the supply sooner than you expect, thereby causing you to run with too little oil (see item 9.1 above), or by preventing the circulation, and thus cooling. Some oilways inside the engine are particularly small and highly susceptible to blockage by metal particles or filings.

In either situation the oil would rapidly become too hot and too thin to function effectively, with the obvious consequences of excess heat and wear in the engine.

Remedy 9.2

Inspect all the joints and hoses in the system, as discussed in item 8.5 above. However, if you suspect that one of the oilways inside the engine is blocked (and these are unique to four-stroke engines), you should have the situation thoroughly checked by a competent mechanic.

Note: If you plan to switch from a mineral-based oil to a vegetable-based oil (of the 'R' type), or vice versa, you must first strip the engine completely and remove all traces of the original oil. Mineral and vegetable oils *do not* mix and will form a rubber-like solution that will block all the internal oilways immediately they become hot.

Cause 9.3

Oil pump strainer and/or filter blocked: Attached to the oil pump is a gauze filter to prevent dust particles or metal filings entering the pump. Eventually (like all other straining systems), the gauze will become blocked with matted dirt and other particles, preventing sufficient oil from entering the pump and hence resulting in insufficient oil being delivered to the lubrication system. Although some pumps do have a bypass valve which will allow unfiltered oil to pass in such circumstances, they are not fitted to all machines and, moreover, it is clearly unsatisfactory to have unfiltered oil flowing through your pump for any length of time. This will simply cause further problems elsewhere.

Remedy 9.3

Inspect the oil pump filter screen and, if necessary, remove and wash it thoroughly in petrol. It is essential that you make sure any collections of dust, dirt or metal particles are removed before you replace it. See Chapter 2 for details on the timing of this. Really, you should never allow a filter to get into such a condition that it blocks the oil flow. Regular maintenance is the best way to prevent such problems before they begin (see p. 84).

Cause 9.4

Oil pump failure. The failure of an oil pump in a four-stroke engine means that the oil is no longer being circulated around the system and, as with any other blockage in the system, the consequences are that the oil trapped in the engine will rapidly rise in temperature, become thin and eventually be unable to protect and cool the engine's components.

Remedy 9.4

Often, the cause of an oil pump's problems is mechanical failure in the drive mechanism, and checking it could involve stripping the engine (which you may or may not have already done if the engine has seized), checking the pump's drive components and replacing the damaged parts or the whole pump. Essentially this is a job for an experienced and competent mechanic. The strident do-it-yourselfer may still want to tackle the job, but take your time and remember that logic and patience are the keys to success.

10. Miscellaneous causes of particular problems

Cause 10.1

Petrol has seeped into, and filled, the cylinder and engine casing. On motorcycles with vacuum-type fuel taps – that is, where the tap positions are marked 'on', 'res' and 'pri' – the fuel is automatically switched off when the engine is not running (see p. 257).

However, if you leave the tap in the 'pri' position – that is, the one used to prime the engine with fuel before starting – unfortunately, after only three or four hours either: (1) the cylinder(s) may become flooded (and indeed this is the most likely); or (2) in the more extreme, but not uncommon, situation the entire engine may fill up with petrol.

A quick check of the fuel tap's position will tell you if either of these is a possibility for, if the switch is not in the 'pri' position, it is highly unlikely that either will have occurred. If the tap is in the 'pri' position, on motorcycles fitted with:

1. *A kickstart.* Simply try again to start with the kickstart. If the lever comes to a dead stop before the full stroke is completed, it is likely that the engine case is full of petrol. The lever comes to such a sudden stop because of the pressure created by the movement inside the casing.

2. *An electric starter.* The starter will suddenly stop shortly after beginning to turn and appear to be defective. Once again, it is the pressure of the petrol preventing the pistons moving. Certainly, if the starter shows these symptoms, you should consider the possibility of the engine casing having filled with fuel before you turn to the electrical starter itself.

While this problem is more common with vacuum-type taps, it can also occur with traditional taps if you leave them in the 'on' position.

Remedy 10.1

If you are forced to conclude that the casing is full, quite simply the whole engine will need to be drained of both petrol and oil and then flushed out. Briefly:

1. Return the fuel tap to its correct position.

2. Remove the spark plug and the cap to the supply of transmission oil. This will allow air to enter the top of the engine and so assist in the draining.

3. If possible unscrew the sump drain plug and let the petrol and oil mixture drain out into a tin. (Unfortunately few two-strokes have a crankcase drain plug, in which case the engine will need stripping down to gain access to the flooded compartment.)

4. Pour a small quantity of oil (say, half a pint) into the crankcase, and let it drain through the system.

5. Refit the drain plug, replenish the oil with the required amount and refit the oil caps.

6. Make sure there is fuel in the tank; if there is none, replenish that too.

7. Start the motorcycle in the normal manner.

Note: Two-strokes can be drained by removing the head and barrel and then using a small rubber hose to siphon the fuel from the crankcase. You will need to lubricate the moving parts with oil before reassembly.

On the other hand, if both the kick-start and the electric starter operate but fail to start the engine, you may have got away with only a flooding.

However, although you will probably detect a stronger smell of petrol than normal, there will be little else, other than the position of the fuel tap, to indicate this as the source of your problem.

If your diagnosis is that the engine is flooded:

1. Ensure the ignition, choke and petrol are all at 'off'.

2. Open the throttle fully.

3. Kick the engine over two or three times. This will draw large quantities of air through the carburettor(s) and combustion chamber(s), flushing out the excess fuel.

4. Turn the ignition on but *not* the petrol.

5. Return the throttle to the 'off' position.

6. Start the engine as normal; on two-stroke motorcycles, using 'full throttle' may assist starting in this situation. If this fails, try using a half and then a quarter throttle until it does. When the engine fires, you can turn on the petrol.

Note: If the engine seems to be severely flooded, removing the spark plug(s) before you kick over the engine will give you the additional aeration it needs to do the trick.

Cause **10.2**

Spark plug tip fouled by carbon. Occasionally, after a two-stroke has been decarbonized, the engine fails soon after starting because very small particles of carbon, sucked back through the exhaust system, become lodged between the spark plug electrodes (Figure 52). No damage is done to the spark plug, or to the engine, but it is a nuisance.

Remedy **10.2**

To remove the carbon, simply use

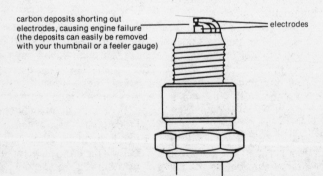

carbon deposits shorting out electrodes, causing engine failure (the deposits can easily be removed with your thumbnail or a feeler gauge)

electrodes

Figure 52 Plug fouling after decarbonizing of a two-stroke

your fingernail or a feeler blade to knock it out. The engine will restart immediately, but don't be surprised if it happens again in the next few minutes. Despite your efforts to clear out every speck of dust after a decoke some pieces may still be trapped in the system as you rebuild it. So, after a decoke, especially on two-strokes, don't forget to carry your plug spanner everywhere you go.

If you have exhausted all the possible causes we have discussed, and your motorcycle still fails to start, you should visit your local workshop, describe all the symptoms to the mechanics in detail, tell them all the items you have considered and checked, and ask their advice. If you have reached this stage it is likely to be an electrical/ignition problem and it would be worth while to have a mechanic check it out thoroughly.

CHAPTER FIVE
ENGINE PERFORMANCE PROBLEMS

There is seemingly an endless number of symptoms which describe engine performance problems: we have chosen twenty-five of the most common. They represent a cross-section of problems which are likely to occur in all the areas of an engine unit, and were selected to provide a broad idea of how to approach problems in general, enabling you, we hope, to tackle problems we are unable to cover.

Problem table 4, on pp. 147–8, contains a list of the twenty-five symptoms and indicates the pages on which the possible causes and their remedies are explained. So, if your motorcycle continues to run, but unsatisfactorily, all you need do is turn to this table, find the symptom which best fits your situation and turn to the page indicated in the right-hand column. On turning to the appropriate page you will see that the possible causes and their remedies are ranked in order of probability and priority. Basically, all you need to do is to work your way through the list until you identify the actual cause.

However, although we strongly recommend you to stick to the ordering we suggest, when referring to the lists you must use your own judgement and decide whether, under the circumstances, it should be changed slightly.

For example, if it begins to rain, or you've ridden through some deep puddles, and your engine then fails to respond to the throttle, clearly it is far more likely to be damp in the ignition circuit or water in the carburettor than a broken throttle cable – even though a broken cable is listed above either ignition or carburettor system problems.

Essentially, you should use this material as a guide to your thoughts. Always consider what has happened, what you have done (or not done as the case may be), what the weather conditions are like, whether you have been fiddling around (tampering) with or dismantling an item, etc. A few moments' thought may allow you to detect the actual cause without it being necessary to run through too many possibilities.

PROBLEM 4: POOR ENGINE PERFORMANCE

	SYMPTOMS	Page
1	The engine will not pull to climb hills, or will only run successfully in the lower gears	148
2	The engine runs well at tickover, but will not respond to the throttle as it is opened	151
3	The engine runs well at above quarter-throttle, but will not tick over	155
4	The motorcycle is erratic or jerky when accelerating	159
5	The engine won't reach maximum r.p.m.	162
6	The engine performs normally, but occasionally slows down rapidly; after the throttle is closed, the engine performs normally for a while and then slows down rapidly again	162
7	The engine seems to die momentarily when the throttle is opened, and then recovers	163
8	The engine runs unevenly	164
9	The engine feels rough while operating below 4,000 r.p.m. when you are slowing down	165
10	The idling speed is too high	165
11	The engine runs badly, and: (1) blue smoke comes from the exhaust (a) on a four-stroke; (b) on a two-stroke; or (2) black smoke comes from the exhaust (four-strokes only)	167
12	Fuel consumption is excessive	172
13	Oil consumption is heavy, with no external leakage	174
14	The oil pressure warning light comes on	175
15	The engine never reaches its correct operating temperature, that is, it underheats (water-cooled engines only)	176
16	The engine overheats	176

	SYMPTOMS	Page
17	Misfires	181
	17.1 Intermittent misfire	182
	17.2 Misfires at certain throttle openings	183
	17.3 Misfires under load or while accelerating	184
	17.4 Misfires and running is jerky and/or erratic	185
	17.5 Misfires and is spitting back	186
	17.6 Engine backfiring	187
	17.7 The engine pulls well at tickover, but misfires at full or high throttle openings	187
	17.8 Misfires in wet weather	188
18	The gears are difficult to engage/change	189
19	The gear lever does not return to its original position	190
20	The engine repeatedly jumps out of gear	191
21	Gear changing is jerky and the motorcycle creeps forward even when the clutch is withdrawn (that is, pulled in)	192
22	The engine speed (shown on the tachometer) increases, but the motorcycle does not respond with an increase in speed	193
23	Clutch operation is stiff	196
24	The kickstart slips	197
25	The kickstart lever does not return to its 'rest' position after the engine is turned over	197

1. The engine will not pull to climb hills, or will only run successfully in the lower gears

Cause 1.1
The intake of air is restricted: (1) by an obstruction in the flow of air to the filter; or (2) by a partially blocked air filter.

Remedy 1.1.1
The first thing to do if you suspect that the flow of air to the engine is restricted is to inspect the hole where air is drawn into the system. The hole's

precise location does differ from one motorcycle to another, but it will be indicated in your owner's handbook or workshop manual.

1. If the air is drawn in from under the seat, you should ensure that you have not inadvertently placed gloves, waterproofs, rags or a plastic bag, etc., where they would impede the flow of air, or that they have not fallen into such a position. Frequently, motorcyclists do store items under the seat, which is all well and good, but you must take great care that they cannot cover the air intake.

2. If the air is drawn in elsewhere, you must make sure that it is not being blocked by, for example: a long scarf you may be wearing; a rag you accidentally left stuffed there when you were cleaning; a collection of dead leaves, etc. (particularly if you are trial or trail riding).

Any objects you suspect may be preventing the free flow of air should be removed (and, if necessary, relocated) immediately.

Remedy 1.1.2

Check to see if the air filter is dirty or damaged: full details of how to clean the various filters (paper, foam, metal or cloth) are described on pp. 66–7 and your owner's handbook or workshop manual will indicate the type fitted to your motorcycle and how to gain access to it.

If your filter has been cleaned several times already (paper ones in particular will eventually become too blocked to clean), or if it is damaged, it should be replaced.

Never consider running the engine with the air filter removed for longer than a few moments – doing so risks severe damage to the cylinder(s) and piston(s).

Cause 1.2

Blocked or partially blocked exhaust systems.

1. *Four-stroke engines.* Sometimes the interior packing of the silencer becomes loose and blocks the silencer opening, hindering the exhaust gases as they leave the system.

2. *Two-stroke engines.* Periodically, the exhaust system on a two-stroke becomes so clogged up with deposits of carbon that the exhaust gases are unable to escape unhindered. The silencer's exhaust baffle (which fortunately is often removable) and the cylinder exhaust port are by far the most prone to this problem and, as such, should be given regular attention.

Whatever its cause, however, a blocked or partially blocked exhaust results in the system gradually being choked up with spent gases which should have been expelled.

Remedy 1.2.1

Four-stroke engines. Bend a piece of sturdy wire into a hook shape and use it to pull any loose material out through the rear exit hole. This will enable the exhaust gases to exit freely; if the noise level increases substantially, you must repack (if possible) or replace the silencer.

Remedy 1.2.2

Two-stroke engines. In brief, both the silencer and the cylinder must be decoked or, to use the correct term, decarbonized. However, your problem is far more likely to be at the silencer baffle than at the exhaust port (unless, of course, you recently decoked the silencer), so begin your investigations there and progress to the exhaust port only if this fails to solve the problem.

Full details of how to decarbonize both the silencer and the port are on pp. 63–6. It is essential that you satisfy yourself that both areas are totally clean. If you don't, and you leave the slightest sign of carbon, especially around the port, the hole will close up with remarkable speed. Before you know it, the engine will refuse to run above tickover. See item 2.7 below.

Note: After the silencer or the exhaust port have been decoked, a two-stroke engine may cut out or misfire. This is due to a small piece of carbon being drawn back down the exhaust system and fouling the spark plug electrodes. See item 10.2 on pp. 144–5 for more details.

Cause 1.3

Points gap incorrect. If the gap between the points is either too large or too small, the electrical power generated in the coil, and therefore the current reaching the spark plug tip, will be reduced. As a result, full combustion will be inhibited and thus the power developed to thrust the crankshaft around is diminished.

Remedy 1.3

Reset the gap to the manufacturer's specifications. These will be set out in your owner's handbook or workshop manual. See 'Contact breaker (points) condition and gap', pp. 60–62, for full details of how to check and adjust the points gap.

Cause 1.4

Ignition timing incorrect. When the engine is running correctly, the spark occurs at the plug a fraction of a second before the piston reaches T.D.C. on the compression stroke. Although this is only one thousandth of a second, it does give the petrol/air mixture time to ignite. If the spark were to occur at any other time, the piston would either still be rising as the explosion exerts force on the piston, or it would already be on its way down; in both cases the power output would be reduced.

Advanced ignition timing means that the spark is occurring too early and the mixture is being ignited before the piston reaches T.D.C. The resulting explosion means that the upward motion of the piston is resisted by the expanding gases. Clearly, the implications of this depend on just how early the spark occurred; certainly, the whole motion of the engine is slowed up, which generally doesn't do it any good, and a pinking sound can be heard from the area of the combustion chamber.

Retarded ignition timing means that the spark occurs after the piston has passed the correct ignition position and has started down the cylinder. The exploding mixture in this situation has lost valuable fractions of a second in which to accelerate the piston's descent. As a result, the engine will tend to run hot, with a substantially reduced performance if it performs at all.

For the most part, a retarded ignition is likely to result in reduced performance, although if it is too retarded the engine will not start. Indeed, some ignitions, particularly those in high-performance two-strokes with more than one cylinder, are especially sensitive when it comes to ignition timing.

The engine is more likely to pull

successfully in the lower gears because it is not under load and the revs are higher. Finally, although either advanced or retarded ignition will cause problems, difficulty in climbing hills is perhaps more likely to be the result of over-advanced ignition.

Remedy 1.4

Reset the ignition timing. See 'Ignition timing', pp. 62–3, for full details of how to check and reset your timing either with the engine static or with the aid of a strobe light wired into the ignition.

Cause 1.5

Binding brakes. If for any reason the brake shoes or pads begin to bind on the drum or disc, you will certainly experience problems in climbing hills or making normal progress in a gear when the revs are low. Running in a lower gear will increase the engine's speed, and this may be sufficient to overcome the drag of the brakes.

Remedy 1.5

Taking each wheel in turn, you will firstly need to check which, if any, of the brakes are binding (or sticking, as it is sometimes called). To do this, raise the wheel to be checked clear of the ground and spin it, to check that it rotates freely.

Ideally, the wheel should turn with little or no resistance, although you may be able to hear a very light rubbing sound as the pad catches the rotating disc slightly. Far from this being something to worry about, your brakes will perform best if they are adjusted to that point.

However, if, on the other hand, the wheel only moves with difficulty, or only spins a few inches, you must inspect the brakes. (Beware, however, when you are checking the rear wheel. If the chain is too tight, it may be this that is preventing the wheel rotating. For an accurate check you should remove or at least slacken the chain.)

Details of the reasons why your brakes may be binding are given on p. 232, and information on how to regulate and clean poorly adjusted or dirty brakes can be found on pp. 48–52 and 77–8.

2. The engine runs well at tickover, but will not respond to the throttle as it is opened

Cause 2.1

A broken throttle cable. If the throttle cable is broken, operating (turning) the throttle twist grip will have no effect on the amounts of petrol or air being drawn into the carburettor: as the slide needle will not be lifted, the engine speed will remain unchanged – at tickover.

Usually, this cause should be easy for you to detect because of the excessively slack feeling at the twist grip – far more than the free play normally required for accurate throttle cable adjustment (see pp. 41–2 for details of throttle cable adjustment).

Remedy 2.1

Replace the broken cable. Your owner's handbook or workshop manual will set out the precise procedure for your motorcycle; and on p. 245 there are a couple of useful tips you should keep in mind if your cable should break.

Cause 2.2

A loose handlebar grip on the throttle.

The grip may have become so loose that it can simply turn around the throttle and not turn the throttle with it.

Grips may become loose because they: (1) are wet or damp inside; or (2) have stretched over time and are now too large for the throttle twist tube.

Remedy 2.2.1

The cure for wet or dampness is to: (1) remove the grip; (2) dry the throttle twist tube and the inside of the rubber with a tissue or a clean, dry cloth; (3) refit the grip – this will be made much easier, and the grip will remain more secure, if you first coat the inside of the rubber grip with petrol (see 'Refitting grips', p. 239).

Remedy 2.2.2

If the rubber appears to have stretched, that is, if it slips even though it is quite dry inside, then really the pair of grips ought to be replaced. See the items on removing and refitting grips on pp. 238–9. Increasing the diameter of the throttle twist tube with sticky tape, however (as described in item (2) of 'Loose grips', p. 239), will suffice as a temporary measure until you have the time and/or the money to replace them. A final measure – and permanent, in that they will be extremely difficult to remove – is to fix the grips with one of the impact adhesives freely available.

Cause 2.3

A wet, or otherwise fouled, spark plug. An engine will only work correctly if the spark plugs are clean and dry.

If all is running satisfactorily (that is, the engine, ignition and carburettor), the electrodes will have light brown or greyish deposits, a very small build-up of carbon and there will be no signs of abnormal gap wear.

If your spark plug is in any other condition, it is quite likely that this may be a cause of your problem.

Remedy 2.3

In brief, any spark plugs which are defective will need to be either cleaned (and the gap checked) or replaced by a plug which is known to be good.

The details of how to clean and adjust the gap of a spark plug are given on pp. 47–8, and some points to bear in mind if you decide to replace a plug are set out on p. 48.

Unfortunately, however, the poor condition of your plug(s) may also indicate that your engine has another problem. As we discussed in 'Spark plug condition and gap' (on pp. 44–8 for two-strokes and p. 68 for four-strokes), the condition of an engine's spark plug(s) will tell you a great deal about its operating condition. The situations which will lead to a plug becoming fouled by oil, carbon or lead – or defective in other ways – are also examined on those pages.

The result is that you not only have to solve the immediate problem of a defective spark plug, but you also must take steps to identify and resolve the underlying problem which caused the plug to become fouled.

Cause 2.4

Points gaps too small. Although an engine is unlikely to tick over if the gap between the points is too wide, it will still tick over satisfactorily if it is slightly too small. The problem with a small gap occurs when you want to accelerate: there is insufficient electrical power to provide a satisfactory spark. Moreover, because there is a close relationship between the points gap and the ignition timing, the spark will not only be too weak but too late, that is, it will be retarded. (If the gap is too wide, the timing will be advanced.) The result is that you will have problems accelerating.

Remedy 2.4

Reset the points gap to the manufacturers' specifications. Your owner's handbook or workshop manual will indicate the precise setting for your motorcycle and its recommended tolerance limits. Finally, turn to 'Contact breaker (points) condition and gap', pp. 60–62, for a full description of how to check and readjust the gap.

Cause 2.5

Water droplets or dirt particles at, or around, the carburettor main jet. Any particles of dirt or droplets of water floating around the carburettor main jet will be drawn towards that jet immediately the throttle is turned and more fuel demanded, thus hindering the circulation of fuel through the carburettor.

Remedy 2.5

See 'Dirt or water in the carburettor', pp. 104–6, where detailed explanations of how to identify which carburettor may be contaminated (on a multi-carburettor engine) and how to solve the problem – temporarily or permanently – are set out.

Presumably you are now wondering how dirt or water in the carburettor can be responsible for two quite distinctive problems with different symptoms (an engine failure and an engine's refusal to respond to the throttle), and hence why the remedy for one can also be recommended as a remedy for another. The answer is quite simple: in the case of engine failure, the petrol in the carburettor is far more contaminated than the petrol in the other situation, and hence it causes different problems.

In either situation, however, the particles or droplets must be either dislodged from the main jet or (preferably) cleaned out of the carburettor altogether.

Cause 2.6

Defective carburettor slide needle. At the carburettor end of traditional carburettors, that is, those that are not vacuum operated, the throttle cable is attached to the carburettor slide needle. Thus, if the system is operating correctly, when you turn the throttle twist grip, the cable will pull the slide and needle upwards inside the carburettor body and cause more air and fuel to be drawn through.

Occasionally, however, the security clip which actually attaches the needle to the slide fractures and ultimately breaks. When this happens, the needle drops into the carburettor, completely blocking the flow of fuel through the main jet. The cable itself will still only contain the required amount of free play and so give you no indication of the problem within the carburettor, but although the engine will continue to idle satisfactorily, turning the throttle will have no effect on the needle's position, no extra fuel will be drawn in, and hence your engine's speed will remain unchanged – or may in fact go down.

Remedy 2.6

The only cure for a broken slide needle security clip is to replace it with a new one. Your owner's handbook or workshop manual should indicate the location of this clip on your motorcycle, how to gain access to it and how to replace it. As a temporary measure, a twist of very fine wire in the appropriate groove will suffice until a new clip is available (Figure 53). Indeed, if you are really stuck, even chewing gum will hold until you get home.

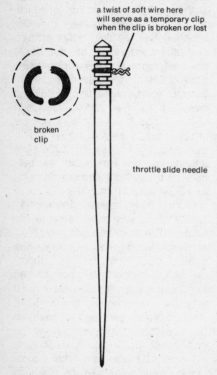

a twist of soft wire here will serve as a temporary clip when the clip is broken or lost

broken clip

throttle slide needle

Figure 53 A temporary method of retaining a throttle slide needle

Cause 2.7

Totally blocked exhaust baffle or exhaust port (two-strokes only). In all two-strokes the exhaust baffle in the silencer and the exhaust port in the cylinder head are highly susceptible to carbon fouling. As they start to become blocked (that is, they are partially blocked), problems will begin to occur (see item 1.2 above). If you allow the situation to continue, or fail to clean these areas adequately, ultimately the holes will become so small that only the quantities of waste gas produced at tickover can escape fast enough to prevent the engine being choked. When it comes to acceleration, the volume of gas becomes too much for the small hole and the system becomes choked up with its own fumes.

Remedy 2.7

As with item 1.2, begin your investigation with an examination of the silencer baffle – it is quite likely that this will need decarbonizing. However, if the engine has become so restricted that it cannot operate at above tickover, you must also decoke the exhaust port. For the situation to have reached this point (and assuming carbon to be the source of your problem) you have clearly been neglecting the items we recommend to you in the three-monthly service. The only real solution may be to decoke the entire system (see pp. 63–6).

Cause 2.8

Cracked or split rubber diaphragm on C.V. carburettors (four-strokes mainly). If you are unsure, clearly the first thing you should do is find out if your motorcycle is fitted with the vacuum-type carburettor, sometimes known as constant-vacuum or constant-velocity carburettors. This type of carburettor is now increasingly being used as an alternative to the traditional cable-operated slide needle, particularly on motorcycles over 250 cc. Your owner's handbook or workshop manual will tell you the type used on your engine.

Unlike traditional carburettors, where the slide needle is pulled up by the throttle cable, in the C.V. carburettor the slide needle is automatically operated. With this system your throttle is linked to a pivoted flap, known as a butterfly, and it is this which controls the throttle.

In normal circumstances, as the engine is started, the pressure in the venturi falls to below that of the outside air. Because the vacuum chamber above the diaphragm is linked to the venturi, the pressure there also falls, while the pressure below the diaphragm remains the same. This pressure difference therefore causes the diaphragm to be pushed upwards, lifting the slide and needle with it and hence increasing the supply of fuel to increase the engine speed. Any cracks or, still worse, splits which develop in the diaphragm will mean that the pressure in the vacuum chamber (above the diaphragm) will not fall sufficiently (if it falls at all) below that of the outside air to cause the diaphragm to be pushed upwards: the slide needle will therefore not be lifted and hence the supply of fuel will not increase.

The precise response of the engine to the throttle will be determined by how badly the diaphragm is damaged. For example, if there is a clear split which allows the two pressures to equalize almost instantly, the diaphragm – and hence the needle – will not move at all: the engine speed will remain at tickover. On the other hand, if the diaphragm is only cracked and the two pressures never *completely* equalize, the diaphragm – and hence the needle – will be lifted, but only slightly. This limited increase in fuel supply will cause the engine's response to be sluggish.

Despite damage to the diaphragm, however, the engine will continue to idle because, in the same way as the traditional carburettor, the C.V. carburettor has a slow-running jet which passes the idling mixture into the induction tract on the engine side of the butterfly. The air to be mixed with this is fed in through a small intake jet in front of the butterfly valve. Both these jets are unaffected by a damaged diaphragm.

Remedy 2.8

If you do suspect that the diaphragm is defective, you will need to dismantle the carburettor and actually inspect the diaphragm. If it appears to be in anything other than very good condition, remove it and fit a new one. Your owner's handbook or workshop manual should indicate the precise location of the diaphragm, how to gain access and how to replace it on your motorcycle.

3. The engine runs well at above quarter-throttle, but will not tick over

Cause 3.1

Choke not fully closed. If the choke is not *fully* closed, once the engine has reached its correct operating temperature the amount of petrol entering the carburettor will be far greater than is required to mix satisfactorily with the air being drawn in at tickover or below quarter-throttle. The mixture entering the cylinder, therefore, will be too rich to burn, and the engine will not fire.

At above quarter-throttle, however, this extra petrol is minimal when compared to the amount now required and, because it can be incorporated into the larger petrol flow with negligible effects on the mixture's proportions, the engine will continue to fire – and probably do so quite satisfactorily.

A further point to note is that if the choke is the cause of your problem there will be a noticeable increase in the level of fuel consumption – you are doing far fewer miles on each gallon. Take a look in the tank or, if you are lucky enough to have one, the petrol gauge, and check just how much you have been using. Even a rough approximation should be enough to give you an indication of whether the choke is fully closed or not.

Remedy 3.1

If you suspect that the choke is the source of your problem, you will need to ensure that: the switch or lever is fully closed; and the choke mechanism is *actually* off when the switch is in this position. This may involve you in (1) lubricating dry cables or linkages (see pp. 42–3), or (2) freeing a cable and/or a linkage which may be fouled in some way. Because there are a multitude of problems, you must use your own initiative to resolve whatever you find – but it is unlikely to be serious.

Certainly (1) and (2) are capable of preventing the choke from closing regardless of the switch position, so do not assume that the choke is off just because you have switched it off.

Cause 3.2

Blocked carburettor pilot jet. The pilot jet in a carburettor is the one which allows fuel to flow through when the throttle, and therefore the main jet, are closed. Quite simply, if the pilot jet becomes blocked, the engine will not be supplied with petrol unless or until the throttle is opened to beyond quarter-open, when fuel will begin to flow through the main jet.

Remedy 3.2

Dismantle the carburettor and clean out the pilot jet – blowing through it is often all that is required. Peering down the pin-size hole in the jet, you should be able to see daylight at the other end if it is clear. Finally, refit the jet, rebuild the carburettor and secure the carburettor in position.

If you are unsure of the pilot jet's location within the carburettor fitted to your motorcycle, it will be indicated in your owner's handbook or workshop manual.

Cause 3.3

Carburettor mixture screw too far in. We have known more than a few motorcyclists who have had this adjuster tampered with in their absence, or who, in fact, have 'tampered' with it themselves in the belief that it was 'loose' and needed to be tightened.

The correct position for the mixture screw is 1¼ to 1½ turns out from a fully home position, depending on the specifications for your motorcycle. Anything less than that and you will certainly have problems in getting your engine to idle satisfactorily – if at all.

Remedy 3.3

Briefly: (1) screw the adjuster lightly into its fully 'home' position; (2) unscrew it 1¼ to 1½ turns (see your owner's handbook or workshop manual); and (3) adjust the idle screw until you achieve the required tickover speed. For a far more comprehensive description see the section on tuning the carburettor, pp. 74–5.

Cause 3.4

Points gap too wide. There are two aspects to this particular cause. Firstly, if the points are opening too wide, the build-up of energy to the coil will be inhibited. This will produce an unsatisfactory spark at the plug, which in turn will result in incomplete combustion and so reduced thrust.

Coupled with this, however, is the second factor. Because the gap between the contact breaker's points is related to the ignition timing (in that if the points gap is too narrow, the timing will be retarded, and if it is too wide, the timing will be advanced), not only will the spark's strength be reduced, but it will also occur too soon. This, in brief, means that the explosion (which will itself be reduced in strength) will be expanding against the still-rising piston – thus, in effect, trying to prevent it going over T.D.C.

At below quarter-throttle the expanding gas succeeds and the engine fails. Above this point, however, the extra momentum instilled in the piston, and the increased levels of petrol and air being drawn into the engine, will force it to operate successfully but inefficiently – despite these competing forces. For more details on advanced and retarded ignition timing see item 4.9 of 'Ignition timing incorrect', p. 119.

Remedy 3.4

Reset the points gap. See 'Contact-breaker (points) condition and gap', pp. 60–62, for full details of how to check and reset your engine's contact breakers.

Cause 3.5

Valve clearances too small. If the clearance between the valve and the tappet is too small, then as the engine becomes hot and the metal expands, the valve will be held partially open – the gases will be allowed to leak past, thus reducing the engine's compression and, in the long run, burning out the valve seat.

If the throttle is set to 'idle', this loss of compression prevents combustion. With the throttle opened beyond quarter-open, however, the speed at which the operational cycles take place means that momentum is able to overcome compression loss and keep the engine running. The longer this situation is allowed to continue, however, the worse it will become, until eventually your engine will refuse to start at all.

Remedy 3.5

Check the valve (tappet) clearances and reset them to the specifications indicated in your owner's handbook or workshop manual.

Full details of how to measure and reset valve clearances for screw and shim-type tappets are given in 'Valve adjustment' on pp. 69–71. If you are in any doubt about the valve clearances on your motorcycle, don't hesitate to call your local workshop mechanic and ask him to do a compression test and possibly to check the clearances for you.

Cause 3.6

Air leak at the carburettor intake manifold. Normally, the air going into the carburettor draws petrol through the jets. With an air leak (which may be caused by loose manifold joints, or even cracks in the manifold (Figure 54)) in front of the carburettor – that is, between the carburettor and the engine – extra air can be drawn into the mixture leaving the carburettor immediately before it enters the cylinder. When the engine is operating at low r.p.m. – at tickover, for example – the mixture is extremely lean – too lean, in fact, for the engine to operate – because the system draws a large proportion of the air entering the cylinder through the manifold air leak and not through the carburettor (where it would otherwise have been mixed with atomized petrol).

At above quarter-throttle, however, the throttle slide (which controls the

Figure 54 Carburettor manifold leaks

flow of *air* through the carburettor) is open much more, the main jet is in operation and, by and large, the engine cannot help drawing in sufficient fuel to ˉenable the engine to operate.

Remedy **3.6**

You must check and, if necessary, tighten the screw(s) securing the manifold to the carburettor and to the engine. Also, inspect the manifold itself for any cracks or splits which may allow air to pass. A defective manifold should be replaced – repairs are difficult and often ineffective.

Cause **3.7**

Cracked exhaust system. A crack in the exhaust pipe prevents the burnt gas being completely expelled. As a

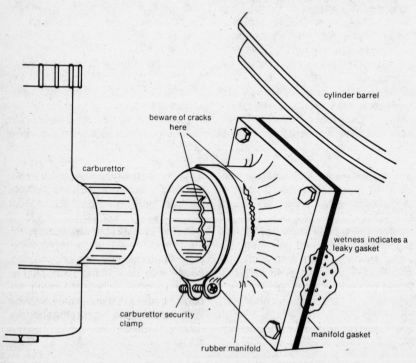

cylinder barrel

beware of cracks here

carburettor

wetness indicates a leaky gasket

carburettor security clamp

manifold gasket

rubber manifold

result the chambers become so contaminated with the old gas that proper combustion cannot take place.

Once the throttle is opened beyond quarter-open, however, the engine is virtually forced to overcome the problem; as it opens: (1) the inward rush of the fresh charge and outward draw on the burnt gas become greater; and (2), partly as a result of (1), the burnt gases now form a smaller proportion of the charge ignited in the cylinder.

Remedy 3.7

If you detect any signs of blowing within the system:

1. Inspect all the joints in the system, tighten any that are loose, and replace any seals which have blown.

2. Examine the length of the system for cracks or holes in the pipes. If they cannot be closed by welding, you will have to replace that section.

4. The motorcycle is erratic or jerky when accelerating

Cause 4.1

Spark plug loose. A spark plug which is only loosely fitted into the cylinder head will allow the mixture or burning gases to leak out, so reducing the compression (and for that you can read power) available to drive the piston.

Remedy 4.1

Tighten the spark plug. To do this, first make it hand-tight and only then use a plug spanner to turn it an additional ¼ to ⅓ of a turn. See p. 48 for more details on securing spark plugs.

Cause 4.2

Spark plug problems. If a *good strong* spark is prevented from leaping the electrode gap because the spark plug is in poor condition (that is, the gap is incorrect or the firing tip is fouled in some way), or because it is beginning to 'break down' occasionally (that is, to short circuit), the increased pressure of acceleration will exaggerate the situation. The engine will consequently become jerky or erratic as the spark plug increasingly begins to miss a beat.

Remedy 4.2

Having removed the suspect spark plug from the cylinder head (see p. 44):

1. Make sure that the firing tip is in good condition, that is, that it has light brown or greyish deposits and only a small build-up of carbon. If it is in any other condition, not only will you have to clean it up to solve the immediate problem, you must also take steps to discover and rectify the situation which caused it to be in that condition. See 'Spark plug condition and gap', pp. 44–8 for two-strokes and p. 68 for four-strokes.

2. Ensure that the gap between the electrodes is correct. Your owner's handbook or workshop manual will indicate what that should be for your motorcycle.

For a more detailed description of how: (a) to adjust the gap, see 'Setting the gap', pp. 47–8; and (b) to clean the firing tip, see 'Plug cleaning', p. 47.

3. If (1) and (2) are satisfactory, yet the symptoms still occur, replace the plug with a new one or a known good one. It may be that the spark plug is breaking down when the firing tip comes under pressure in the combustion chamber (see 'Spark plug shorting out', pp. 118–19).

Cause 4.3

Ignition wiring defects. If there is any point in the ignition system where cable/wire insulation is worn or fractured, or the connectors are even slightly loose, the increased demand for power and the vibrations during acceleration may cause the electrical power destined for the spark plug tip to be persistently interrupted, and hence for the spark plug repeatedly to miss a beat: erratic or jerky performance is the result.

Some of the more likely explanations for these interruptions are:

1. Loose connections: particularly the H.T. lead to the coil and the low-tension leads to the points; the coil to the battery; the battery to earth; and the spark plug cap to the H.T. lead.

2. Worn or fractured H.T. lead insulation.

3. Chafed wiring in the contact breaker assembly.

Remedy 4.3.1

Ensure that all connections in the system are secure and inspect them for any signs of corrosion or dirt. Any that do appear loose and/or dirty should be cleaned and refitted securely. If any connectors appear fractured or cracked, they should be replaced. Although it is possible to hold them together with hefty bindings of insulating tape to get you home, you should certainly not travel any further than is necessary with connectors in this condition.

At the battery make sure that both terminal connectors are secure and that the earth lead is firmly attached to the frame. Your owner's handbook or workshop manual will indicate the location of the battery's earth if you are unsure.

To check the spark plug cap–H.T. lead connection, remove the spark plug cap from the spark plug and detach it (which usually means unscrew it) from the end of the H.T. lead. Having done that, you now need to make a couple of checks: that the screw inside the cap is satisfactory; and that the hole in the end of the H.T. lead is not too big to take the plug cap's threaded end. The results will tell you how to proceed.

1. If both the screw in the cap and the cable end are satisfactory, refit the cap *securely.*

2. If there appears to be *any* problem with the cap, replace it.

3. If the end of the H.T. lead seems to be at fault, cut ½ in. off the end and screw the cap securely into the new end. Unfortunately, however, many H.T. leads these days are cut just long enough when the motorcycle leaves the factory, and removing even half an inch may make them too short. Should this be the situation with your motorcycle, you must replace the whole lead back to the coil.

Unfortunately, this too may be a problem, as in many cases the H.T. lead is permanently fixed to the coil, that is, it is *not* detachable. However, although twisting and taping an extra length of H.T. lead to the existing one is far from satisfactory, it will probably suffice to get you by.

Remedy 4.3.2

Examine the lead for any signs of wear or fracturing in the outer covering, especially near the frame. With the engine running you can do a visual check if you rev up the engine to about 2,000 or 3,000 r.p.m. – to put a load on the circuit – and observe the H.T. lead while the revs are high. If there is a short you will see sparks leaping from the lead to earth. Obviously these sparks will be far easier to see in a darkened place.

Three possible solutions if you see sparks jumping are:

1. Re-route the cable so that the worn parts are not near an earth, that is, it is too far for a spark to jump.

2. Cover the H.T. lead with a length of thick-walled, unused petrol piping with an inner diameter similar to that of the cable. To do this, remove the spark plug cap, push the H.T. lead into the pipe and replace the plug cap, ensuring it is secure.

3. Replace the H.T. lead.

Solution (2) is particularly useful if you cannot do (1) and if the lead is not detachable from the coil, in which case solution (3) would be particularly expensive.

Remedy 4.3.3

Inspect all the wires inside the contact breaker assembly for signs of wear or chafing by moving mechanical parts, for example, the points cam or the flywheel on a flywheel/magneto.

As a temporary measure, a few windings of insulating tape should hold it for a while, although for long-term security you should replace that section of wire *with the same type of wire*.

Cause 4.4

Faulty condenser. Within the electrical system the condenser acts as a little storeroom for electrical power with only one door. Usually, when it becomes defective the problem is that it does not store sufficient power to energize the plug. As a result, the contact breaker points become burned, the spark at the plug is too weak, combustion is poor and, consequently, the power output is reduced.

Jerky or erratic running while accelerating is probably an indication that the condenser is beginning to break down, and the extra demands for power during acceleration are accentuating the fact.

Remedy 4.4

Fortunately there is a quick and easy test to check if it is the condenser. Remove the cover protecting the contact breaker assembly and start the engine. Now observe the points as they open and close: if you see a bright blue spark, the condenser needs to be replaced. This test can be important, so watch carefully. The spark may be yellow for a while, with blue sparks occurring for only a few moments: this shows that the condenser is beginning to break down, and the problem will become more severe as the engine gets hotter.

If the connections from the condenser to the points are good, you must replace the condenser.

Cause 4.5

Particles of dirt or droplets of water in the carburettor. Should you get minute particles of dirt or droplets of water in the carburettor that are small enough to pass through the main jet, then each time one of these is drawn through the jet, petrol is not. As a result, the engine will miss a beat and therefore appear jerky or erratic during acceleration. The problem will become more noticeable during acceleration because the suction power – towards the jet – is stronger.

Remedy 4.5

The carburettor must be removed from the motorcycle, dismantled, thoroughly washed in fresh clean petrol, reassembled and refitted.

For more details see item 2.5 on p. 153, and item 3.3 on pp. 104–6.

5. The engine won't reach maximum r.p.m.

That is, the engine holds back short of what you know to be the maximum.

Cause 5.1

Clogged exhaust baffles. In brief, the problem here is that any blockage in the silencer prevents the waste gases escaping, and this causes a back-pressure in the system. In this situation the system rapidly becomes so choked that fresh mixture entering the combustion chamber is being mixed with useless exhaust gas and the engine's efficiency is dramatically reduced. As a result, the engine is unable to produce enough power to reach its maximum r.p.m.

On two-strokes the problem is most likely to be carbon fouling the holes in the baffle, whereas on four-strokes it is far more likely that some of the packing has come loose.

Remedy 5.1

Unfortunately, on four-strokes you will almost certainly have to replace the silencer. You may be lucky enough to have one in which the interior is replaceable, but these are quite rare. If you suspect yours may be, check with your owner's handbook or workshop manual to be sure.

On a two-stroke engine the silencer will need to be decoked; details of how to do this can be found on pp. 63–6. It is unlikely that a two-stroke silencer will need replacing: the perpetual coating of oil on the inside prevents rusting, unlike four-strokes.

Cause 5.2

The air intake is restricted. If the intake of air into the system is restricted for any reason – an obstruction in the intake tract or a dirty filter, for example (see item 1.1 on pp. 148–9) – the mixture entering the combustion chamber will be too rich (that is, it will have a lower than necessary proportion of air), combustion will be impaired and the resultant reduction in performance prevents the engine turning at its maximum r.p.m. in any gear.

Remedy 5.2

Check and clean the air filter, and remove any obstructions from the air intake tract.

See remedy 1.1 on pp. 148–9 for more details.

6. The engine performs normally, but occasionally slows down rapidly; after the throttle is closed, the engine performs normally for a while and then slows down rapidly again.

Cause 6.1

Blockages are being temporarily drawn into positions which restrict the supply or exit of fuel, air or waste gas. Three main suspects are:

1. *Fuel*: particles of dirt or droplets of water in the carburettor. In this situation the dirt or water is only occasionally being sucked against the main jet, and therefore only occasionally causing the problem. When the throttle is closed the particle drops away.

2. *Air*: obstructions in the air intake tract. As you accelerate, an object such as a scarf, a rag or a plastic bag may be drawn against the intake hole, only to fall back as you close off the

throttle. The air intake operates something like a vacuum cleaner hose gripping and releasing any object as the cleaner is switched on and off.

3. *A blocked exhaust*: (a) on a *two-stroke* this may be loose carbon in the silencer baffle, which is only occasionally blocking the exit; (b) on a *four-stroke* there may be loose silencer baffles or packing, which are only obstructing the waste gases occasionally.

Remedy 6.1.1

Dismantle the contaminated carburettor (if your motorcycle has more than one, you will first need to check which it is – see item 3.3, pp. 104–6, for details) and wash all the components with fresh clean petrol. When you are satisfied it is clean, rebuild and replace it. For more details of this operation see item 3.3 on pp. 104–6.

Remedy 6.1.2

Inspect the air intake tract and remove any potential obstructions (see item 1.1, pp. 148–9).

Remedy 6.1.3a

Although removing the silencer and tapping it on the ground may shake the offending carbon out (and you should try doing this first), if this fails you will need to decarbonize the silencer and its baffle. For details of how to do this see pp. 63–6.

Remedy 6.1.3b

Pull the loose packing material out through the end of the silencer with a length of sturdy wire, such as a coat hanger, bent into a hook shape. If you are unable to remove the material this way, or if, when you do remove it, the engine noise level increases substan-tially, unfortunately you will need to replace the silencer.

Cause 6.2

'Whiskering' plug. In this situation 'whiskers' (flakes) of carbon become detached from the piston and attach themselves to the spark plug's electrodes, causing the gap to close and hence running problems to begin. Shutting the throttle, however, causes these particles to fall away, re-establishing the correct gap and therefore allowing the engine to operate normally, for a while.

The problem usually occurs when the engine is running hot (if you have a cracked silencer, for example), or if you use a plug of the wrong heat range. Check your owner's handbook or workshop manual to verify which grade of plug you should be using in your motorcycle.

Remedy 6.2

If you are using the correct grade of plug, you will need to investigate and rectify the overheating problem: this will almost certainly stop the 'whiskering' (see 'The engine overheats', pp. 176–81).

7. The engine seems to die momentarily when the throttle is opened, and then recovers

Cause 7.1

Contaminated fuel. As you accelerate, the demand for more mixture causes an extra rush of fuel through the carburettor main jet. If the petrol in the system is contaminated in any way, each time you open the throttle this extra rush will not only draw and trap particles against the jet opening but may also force them up the jet – and the moment it does so the mixture will become lean and the engine will die. Once you have reached a cruising speed, however, and the draw of fuel through the main jet has stabilized, the contaminating particles will sink to the bottom of the float bowl, allowing the engine to perform normally.

Remedy 7.1

Dismantle and thoroughly wash all the carburettor's components in fresh, clean petrol, and try blowing through the jets just to make absolutely sure they are clear. If your engine has more than one carburettor, you will first need to check which of them is (or are) causing the problem. For details of how to do this, and for information on how to clean a carburettor, see 'Dirt or water in the carburettor', item 3.3, pp. 104–6.

Cause 7.2

Worn carburettor slide. If the carburettor slide is worn there will be irregular variations in the metering of fuel and air at the lower end of the throttle opening – that is, the carburettor may momentarily stop sucking fuel, but keep drawing air, into the mixture. As a result, the mixture will momentarily be lean and so cause the engine to die until the correct proportions are re-established at the slightly higher throttle openings.

Remedy 7.2

Dismantle the carburettor and inspect the slide for any signs of wear. If you are at all unsure how to dismantle the carburettor and where to find the carburettor slide, don't hesitate to consult your owner's handbook or workshop manual. Any slide which appears to be worn must be replaced, although if you feel in need of a second opinion, you can take it along to your local workshop and ask the mechanic for his opinion. Indeed, if it is too bad, the whole carburettor may need to be replaced.

Cause 7.3

Carburettor manifold is loose. Under normal circumstances the air to be used in combustion is drawn through the intake tract and mixed with the petrol in the carburettor. However, if either of the manifold joints is loose (or, indeed, if the manifold itself is cracked or split), extra air can be drawn into the mixture leaving the carburettor, thus causing the mixture that enters the combustion chamber to be lean and the engine to die. As you continue to open the throttle, however, the quantities of fuel and air passing through the carburettor increase; the amount of air coming in through the loose manifold will therefore form a smaller and smaller proportion of the mixture reaching the combustion chamber, until it is inconsequential – at which point the engine will pick up.

Remedy 7.3

Check the manifold gaskets and replace any that are damaged; inspect the securing screws and tighten them if necessary; finally, inspect the manifold itself for cracks or splits – if it is damaged in any way, it must be replaced.

8. The engine runs unevenly

Cause 8.1

Intermittent misfire. A motorcycle runs unevenly basically because the engine is misfiring intermittently.

Remedy 8.1

See symptom 17, 'Misfires', especially items 17.1 to 17.4, pp. 182–6.

9. The engine feels rough while operating below 4,000 r.p.m. when you are slowing down

Cause 9.1

Final-drive chain too tight. You may be thrown off the scent of this cause initially because the engine may also become overheated, but the tight chain is the primary cause of the problem: the overheating is simply a by-product.

Remedy 9.1

Slacken off the chain to its recommended tension (see 'Chain tension', pp. 31–3).

Cause 9.2

Loose engine-mounting bolts. Although the bolts may appear tight, in that they are not 'finger loose', the engine may be allowed to move slightly as you pass what seems to be the rather critical r.p.m. level (4,000 r.p.m.) when slowing down.

Remedy 9.2

Tighten the bolts.

10. The idling speed is too high

Cause 10.1

Throttle stop screw in too far. It is certainly not difficult to find motorcyclists who have returned to their motorcycle only to discover (sooner or later) that the throttle stop screw has been tampered with in their absence. However, it is even less difficult to find motorcyclists who tampered with the screw themselves, believing that it was loose and needed to be tightened.

If the screw is turned in too far, the carburettor slide will be held too high in the carburettor body; more fuel than is required by the carburettor for a satisfactory tickover will be allowed in; and, as a result, the engine's idling speed will be too high.

Remedy 10.1

Readjust (that is, wind out) the throttle stop screw until the idle speed is correct. If you are unsure, consult your owner's handbook or workshop manual for the precise location of this screw and the recommended idling speed for your motorcycle. If you are unable to find out the recommended idling speed, set it to 1,000 r.p.m. – generally speaking, this will be satisfactory.

Cause 10.2

Carburettor top loose. If the top of the carburettor is loose, the suction of air through the carburettor may hold the slide against the carburettor body and so prevent the slide return spring returning the slide fully home. As a result the slide will not be fully closed when the throttle is set at tickover; the idle speed, consequently, will be too high.

Remedy 10.2

Ensure that the top of the carburettor is securely fastened.

Cause 10.3

A lean mixture. The idling speed of an engine which is burning a lean mixture is always slightly higher than that of an engine running on a mixture with the correct proportions of petrol and air. Consequently, anything which results in the mixture being too lean will affect your engine's idling speed. Three of the more likely causes are: (1) a loose or cracked carburettor manifold; (2) a leaking cylinder base gasket (two-strokes only); (3) leaking crankshaft seals and/or crankcase joints (two-strokes only).

Cause 10.3.1

A loose or cracked manifold will result in a lean mixture because, as the correctly proportioned mixture passes through the manifold on its way from the carburettor to the cylinder, extra air will be drawn in through the opening and so increase the proportion of air in the mixture finally entering the combustion chamber.

Causes 10.3.2 and 10.3.3

Leaks into the crankcase. As we saw in Chapter 1, for a two-stroke engine to operate correctly the crankcase must be totally airtight, so that the mixture can be pumped from there, via the transfer port, to the combustion chamber. If a leak develops, either at the cylinder base, around the crankshaft seals or along the crankcase joint, the pump action of the descending piston will force mixture not only up the transfer port, but also out of the defective gasket or seal. As a result, when the reduced charge reaches the combustion chamber and mixes with the air already there, the mixture ultimately ignited will be lean.

Remedy 10.3.1

Ensure that the carburettor manifold connections are all securely fastened and that any gaskets are intact.

Finally, if your inspection of the manifold itself reveals signs of cracks or splits, you must replace it immedi-ately: a repair is really out of the question.

Remedy 10.3.2

Make a visual inspection of the cylinder base and check for any signs of oily wetness or damp patches: either of these usually indicates that the gasket is leaking (Figure 55). If it is leaking, there can be no question but that it must be replaced as soon as possible.

In brief, replacement will involve: (1) removing the barrel(s); (2) cleaning off the old gasket; (3) fitting a new gasket; and (4) replacing the barrel(s), being very careful to tighten the bolts down in the correct sequence and only to the recommended pressure.

However, although the procedure may be this straightforward on some motorcycles, on others it may involve several other operations before you can actually reach the barrel(s) (removing the engine from the frame, for example). Before you begin, therefore, consult your owner's handbook or workshop manual and be sure you are conversant with the details of the procedure for your motorcycle, and that all the necessary replacement components are available.

Remedy 10.3.3

If you suspect the crankshaft seals or the crankcase joint may be the problem, once again you will need to check for any signs of oily wetness or damp patches around the seals: if there are any, you can be sure the seals are defective and need replacing. As with the cylinder base gasket, discussed in 10.3.2. above, the procedure for changing the crankshaft seals or remaking the crankcase joints will differ from one motorcycle to another.

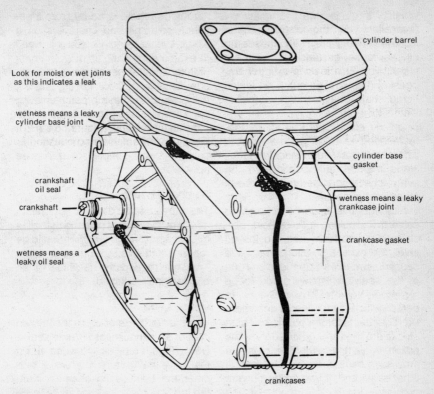

Figure 55 Two-stroke joints, gaskets and seals

So, before you begin it is essential that you consult your owner's handbook or workshop manual and make yourself conversant with the details of the procedure, and that any components which will need replacing are available.

11. The engine runs badly, and: (1) blue smoke comes from the exhaust (a) on a four-stroke; (b) on a two-stroke; or (2) black smoke comes from the exhaust (four-strokes only)

Cause **11.1a**

Blue smoke from a four-stroke. The basic problem here is that oil is entering the combustion chamber and being burned along with the mixture.

Cause **11.1a.1**

Too much oil in the sump. Although it is important you check the oil level regularly to ensure it is not too low (at least once a week, see p. 39), it is essential that you never add oil beyond the recommended level. Overfilling in this way will increase the oil pressure within the engine dramatically (especially as the engine speed increases), and may ultimately force oil past seals, gaskets and even the piston rings into the combustion chamber.

Remedy 11.1a.1

Drain the sump until it is at the recommended level. If you are unsure where this is, although there is usually some method of indication on the sump, check your owner's handbook or workshop manual.

Although this *may* be enough to solve the problem, if the smoke persists after you have reduced the oil level, the excess pressure may have caused permanent damage to any one of the seals, which will need to be replaced. Your task now will be to detect which one. Two of the more likely suspects for the problem of blue smoke are the valve guide seals or the piston rings. However, the pressure may have caused damage to several other seals and, if you are to prevent problems in the future, these too should be checked. To do this may require a partial or total engine strip. If you have the time to do this methodically, there is no reason why you should be unable to detect and replace the damaged component(s). If you feel it is beyond you, don't hesitate to visit your local workshop for help.

Cause 11.1a.2

Worn cylinder bore. Ultimately the continual motion of the piston may cause the cylinder wall to become excessively worn: the seal between the piston rings and the wall will then become increasingly ineffective and oil will begin to seep from the crankcase into the combustion chamber.

Although there is no problem identifying contaminated chambers on a single-cylinder engine, you will need to examine the firing tip of each spark plug to establish which is defective on a multi-cylinder. If oil is being burned, the plug will have a black insulating tip, a layer of carbon over its nose and a damp oily film over the firing tip. For more details of problem diagnosis using the spark plugs see pp. 44–7.

Remedy 11.1a.2

The cure unfortunately is not cheap: *all* the cylinders (not only the defective one on a multi-cylinder) will need to be rebored and oversized pistons fitted. This will require the facilities of an engineering workshop.

Cause 11.1a.3

Worn valve guide oil seal. If either an inlet or an exhaust valve guide seal is worn (Figure 56), oil will seep down the valve guide, past the valve, and enter the combustion chamber from the top.

Examining the spark plugs of a multi-cylinder engine will indicate which cylinder is causing the trouble: its firing tip will be oil-fouled.

Remedy 11.1a.3

In brief, you will have to replace the defective seal. However, there are a number of points to bear in mind. Although only one of the seals may be defective, you would be best advised to replace all the seals on one cylinder. Moreover, on a multi-cylinder it is well worth your time inspecting the seals in the other cylinders just to make sure they are not too worn. Obviously, if they are, they too should be replaced.

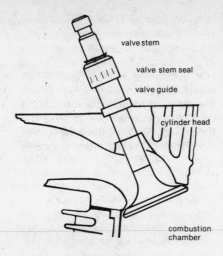

A worn valve seal allows oil to enter the combustion chamber down the inlet valve, or to enter the exhaust port down the exhaust valve

Figure 56 Valve seal layout

Cause 11.1a.4

Piston ring(s) seized or broken. Occasionally the piston rings in an engine break or become so fouled with carbon that they stick in the ring grooves around the piston and therefore don't push out against the wall sufficiently. Consequently, oil is able to seep past the weakened (or broken) ring into the combustion chamber. The more severe the problem – and, clearly, broken rings are the most severe – the greater the amount of oil entering the chamber and the more smoke there will be.

Remedy 11.1a.4

The top of the engine – the cylinder head and barrel(s) – will need to be dismantled and any defective rings cleaned or replaced. The precise procedure for gaining access and removing the piston rings will vary from one motorcycle to another, and you should consult your owner's handbook or workshop manual before you begin. For more details of cleaning (decarbonizing) the rings see pp. 65–6.

Cause 11.1b

Blue smoke from a two-stroke. Limited blue exhaust smoke is normal on a two-stroke. However, if the engine performs poorly and you get large volumes of blue smoke, *excess* oil is being burned in the combustion chamber.

Cause 11.1b.1

Air intake restricted. If the air intake tract is obstructed or the air filter is blocked, the engine will be forced to run on a rich mixture, which will itself reduce performance. However, because greater throttle openings are required to maintain normal speeds (and because the oil pump is controlled via the throttle), an excess of oil will be pumped into the mixture. As this burns in the rich mixture the resultant gases will appear far more blue than normal. Moreover, if you allow this situation to continue, the spark plug will become oil-fouled and there will be an excessive build-up of carbon in the combustion chamber, which would possibly cause hot spots and pre-ignition.

Remedy 11.1b.1

Ensure that nothing is blocking the air intake tract, and clean or replace the air filter if it is dirty or damaged. See item 1.1, pp. 148–9, for a more detailed discussion of the problem, and see 'Air-filter condition . . .', pp. 66–7, if you are unsure how to go about it.

Cause 11.1b.2

The oil pump setting is incorrect. The problem here is quite simple: the oil pump is over-adjusted and too much oil is being pumped into the mixture.

The common problem with the oil pump is that the actuating cable has stretched so much that insufficient oil is being supplied. The current situation – over-adjustment – is almost always the result of someone incorrectly re-adjusting the pump – perhaps they were trying to take up cable slack or to clean the pump.

Remedy 11.1b.2

Recheck and, if necessary, readjust the pump's setting. This time, how-ever, consult your owner's handbook or workshop manual for the *correct* procedure on your motorcycle and follow it to the letter.

Cause 11.1b.3

Oil from the gearbox is entering the crankcase (crankshaft oil seal is faulty). If the air intake is clear, and the oil pump setting correct, extra oil may be being drawn into the crankcase through a defective crankcase oil seal. If you suspect this seal, monitor the oil level in the gearbox; should there be a noticeable reduction after only a day or so, without external leakage, you can be pretty sure the oil is seeping past the seal.

Remedy 11.1b.3

The crankcase seal will need to be replaced as soon as possible. Con-tinuing to burn oil in this way will only lead to further problems.

Consult your owner's handbook or workshop manual for detailed instruc-tions on how to change the seal on your motorcycle.

Cause 11.1b.4

The petrol tank contains two-stroke petroil and not straight petrol (in an auto-lube system). This may be a mistake by the previous owner, or by the garage, if you have just purchased the motorcycle from someone who didn't know what they were doing. Whatever the reason, adding oil to the mixture twice – once via the auto-lube pump and once via the petrol – cer-tainly means there will be far more than is necessary, and that the exhaust gases will be far more blue than normal.

Remedy 11.1b.4

Drain the petrol tank and refill it with straight petrol. Any drops of oil left within the system will have a minimal effect and will soon work themselves out. If you are a perfectionist, and have the time, you could drain and wash out (with petrol) the carburettor, although it is not absolutely necessary.

Cause 11.1b.5

The petroil in a pre-mix engine con-tains too much oil. It is important that you only add the specified proportion of oil to the petrol in order to make up petroil: there is certainly no advantage to be gained by adding more – on the contrary, it is not only a waste of money but it will also impair your engine's performance. If you change from the recommended oil to a higher-performance oil (and unless you are going to take part in competition riding there is no reason why you should, especially as this oil can cost consider-ably more), the ratio may change – but again you must add only the specified proportions.

Remedy 11.1b.5

Drain the petrol tank (and, if you wish, the rest of the fuel system) and refill it with a fresh supply of petroil – mixed in the correct proportions. The recommended grade of oil and the oil/petrol ratio will be indicated in your owner's handbook or workshop manual if you are unsure.

Cause 11.2

Black smoke from the exhaust (four-strokes only). Primarily this occurs because the mixture is too rich, that is, it contains too much petrol.

Cause 11.2.1

Choke mechanism on. If the choke is not fully closed, then as the engine reaches its normal operating temperature the amount of petrol entering the mixture will be disproportionately high for the quantity or air, that is, the mixture will be too rich. Consequently, the exhausted gases will contain a higher proportion of unburnt petrol gas, and it is this which colours the exhaust fumes black.

Remedy 11.2.1

You must ensure that: (1) the choke switch or lever is fully closed; and (2) the choke mechanism is actually closed when the switch is in the 'off' position. Making sure that the choke mechanism really is closed may involve you in: (1) lubricating dry cables; or (2) freeing a cable and/or linkage which is fouled in some way. See item 3.1, pp. 155–6, for a fuller discussion of this problem.

Cause 11.2.2

Carburettor flooding. Normally as the float rises (on the mounting level of fuel within the float bowl), it pushes the float needle into the float seat, switching off the fuel supply until the petrol within the bowl is used, which in turn allows the float to fall, the needle to drop and more fuel to enter – rather like the float mechanism in a toilet cistern.

The most likely causes of carburettor flooding are: (1) that a dirt particle is preventing the float needle valve from seating correctly; or (2) that the float has developed a leak, in which case the weight of petrol (now inside the float) prevents it from rising to its fully home position. Both situations will allow unwanted petrol continually to flow into the carburettor. As a result, the mixture entering the combustion chamber will be too rich.

Remedy 11.2.2

Briefly, having first established which carburettor(s) is (are) faulty, on a multi-carburettor engine (see item 3.3, pp. 104–6), dismantle the carburettor and wash it out thoroughly with petrol, and check the float for any signs of damage. The quickest way is to shake it: if you hear petrol inside, it is obviously punctured and must be replaced.

See the section on cleaning the carburettor, pp. 72–3, for more details.

Cause 11.2.3

Carburettor float level too high. As parts of the carburettor become worn, the level at which the float pushes the float needle fully home – thereby stopping the flow of petrol into the carburettor – will become steadily higher. Ultimately this will allow the carburettor to become flooded before the fuel supply is stopped.

Remedy 11.2.3

Dismantle the carburettor and reset the float level – which is usually done by bending the 'tang' on the float *upwards* – to the manufacturer's specifications. Details of these specifications and the precise readjustment procedure for your motorcycle should be in your owner's handbook or workshop manual; and, for details of how to establish which carburettor(s) is (are) defective, see remedy 3.3, pp. 105–6.

Cause 11.2.4

Air intake restricted. If the flow of air into the carburettor is restricted – because either: (1) the intake tract is obstructed; or (2) the air filter is dirty or damaged – the mixture will consequently contain less than the required amount of air; the resultant mixture will therefore be too rich.

Remedy 11.2.4

Remove and, if necessary, clean the filter (see 'Air-filter condition . . .', pp. 66–7, for a full description). Should you discover the dirt to be unremovable, or the filter to be damaged in any way, you will need to replace it.

You must also inspect the air intake tract and remove anything which may be causing an obstruction.

See item 1.1, pp. 148–9, for a more detailed discussion of this problem.

Cause 11.2.5

The pilot or main jet is loose. The problem here occurs because fuel passes through the jet's retaining threads instead of being drawn in through the end of the jet. If either the pilot jet or the main jet works itself loose, the mixture will immediately become extremely rich, perhaps wetting the plug tip, but certainly causing a reduction in performance and large volumes of black smoke to stream from the exhaust.

Remedy 11.2.5

The only way to rectify this problem is to dismantle the carburettor, having first determined which is (or are) faulty on a multi-carburettor engine, and tighten the jets.

If you are unsure how to dismantle the carburettor and/or unsure what these jets look like or where to find them, etc., see pp. 73–4, or your owner's handbook or workshop manual.

12. Fuel consumption is excessive

Cause 12.1

Air intake restricted. Any restrictions on the air intake – a dirty or damaged filter, or an obstruction in the air intake tract, for example – will reduce the supply of air to the carburettor and so result in an over-rich mixture. Consequently, the engine will be burning far more fuel than is necessary for efficient engine operation.

Remedy 12.1

Ensure the intake tract is free from any obstructions and that the air filter is clean and undamaged. For a more detailed discussion of this problem see item 1.1, pp. 148–9, if you are unsure how to remove greasy dirt from the filter.

Cause 12.2

Carburettor setting incorrect. Yet again, the problem is the result of a rich mixture; however, on this occasion it occurs because of an excess of petrol (not a deficiency of air, as in 12.1). This excess will occur if either the idle-mixture screw is too far in (see item 3.3, pp. 156–7) or the float level is too high (see item 11.2.3, pp. 171–2).

Remedy 12.2

Of the two principal causes, the mixture screw is the easier to check, and you should ensure it is correctly adjusted before you dismantle the carburettor to examine the float level.

To adjust the mixture screw you must: (1) screw the adjuster lightly into its fully home position; (2) unscrew it 1¼ to 1½ turns – consult the owner's handbook or workshop manual for the precise specifications for your motorcycle; and (3) adjust the idle-speed screw until the required number of r.p.m.s (at tickover) is achieved. For more details of this operation see the section on tuning the carburettor, p. 74.

If the problem persists, however, that is, black smoke is still coming from the silencer of a four-stroke, you will need to dismantle the carburettor and reset the float to the recommended level. How to gain access to the float, and the precise readjustment procedure for your motorcycle, should be indicated in your owner's handbook or workshop manual.

Cause 12.3

Petrol is leaking from the fuel system.
1. From the petrol tank or supply lines, where – either as a result of someone tampering or, more commonly, as the motorcycle gets older – various components in the fuel supply system – particularly the seams of the petrol tank, the petcock valve and the fuel lines – may fail and you will begin to lose fuel.
2. From the carburettor: yellowish-white stains on the outside of the carburettor body are a clear indication that you are losing fuel through a defective joint or seal.

Remedy 12.3.1

Inspect the fuel lines, the fuel tap (petcock) and the petrol tank – especially the seams – for any signs of wetness or yellowish-white stains which will indicate that petrol has been leaking.

If any part of the fuel lines shows signs of splitting or perishing, it should be changed immediately. Rust on the petrol tank may be covering a hole or crack and should be treated immediately, that is, remove the rust, solder the hole or crack, and prime and repaint the metal. You will only need to flush the tank if you are planning to do any welding and will therefore be using a naked flame on the tank.

Remedy 12.3.2

Visually inspect all the joints, screw adjusters and the drain plug, and replace any gasket or seal which appears to be leaking, that is, where you see signs of wetness or the yellowish-white stains. Your owner's handbook or workshop manual will indicate the procedure for replacement on your motorcycle.

Cause 12.4

Final-drive chain too tight. Not only do you increase the risk of breaking the chain if it is too tight, but the binding effect of the increased tension means you will also need to have the throttle open far wider than necessary at a given speed. Consequently, to make normal progress you will use more petrol.

Remedy 12.4

Check the chain's tension and, if necessary, readjust it. See 'Final-drive chain . . . : Adjustment', pp. 30–33, for details.

Cause 12.5

Binding brakes. If any of the brakes begin to bind against the drum or disc, you will be forced to open the throttle wider than normal to attain a given speed: that is, you will have to use the engine's power to advance the motorcycle not only against the wind and gravity, but also against its own braking power.

Remedy 12.5

Raise and spin each wheel separately to establish which brake is defective: the wheel should rotate freely, with only the slightest contact between the friction material and the disc (or drum). If you do suspect the brakes are defective, they will need to be dismantled, cleaned and readjusted. Details of these operations can be found on pp. 48–52.

13. Oil consumption is heavy, with no external leakage

Cause 13.1

Engine oil. Essentially the problem here is that oil is being burned in the combustion chamber: the more oil that is burned, the more blue smoke will be blown out of the exhaust.

Cause 13.1.1

Cylinder walls excessively worn. Basically, because the cylinder wall has worn, the piston rings can no longer satisfactorily seal the combustion chamber, and oil is entering from below.

Remedy 13.1.1

Unfortunately, this is one of those problems that it is extremely difficult to rectify at home. Briefly, you need to check the cylinder bore for signs of excess wear and, if necessary, rebore and fit an oversize piston. If you do decide to attempt the dismantling and reassembly yourself – and many amateur mechanics do – it is essential that you familiarize yourself with the procedure and ensure you have all the necessary parts and equipment before you begin.

See item 11.1a.2, p. 168; where the problem is discussed in more detail in relation to exhaust smoke.

Cause 13.1.2

Wear in the valve mechanism (four-strokes only). Excess wear in the valve mechanism – whether it is the valve guide seal, the valve guide or the valve itself – will allow oil to seep down into the combustion chamber, where it is burned.

Remedy 13.1.2

Having first checked the spark plug to establish which cylinder(s) is (are) burning the oil (see pp. 44–7 for more details), you must remove the valve covers and examine the whole valve mechanism for any signs of wear or damage. Any components that are worn will need to be replaced as soon as possible. If you are unsure how to gain access to the valves, and how to determine if any wear you discover is excessive, you must check the actual measurements against the specifications set out in the owner's handbook or workshop manual for your motorcycle.

Cause 13.2

Two-stroke oil. The problem here will almost certainly be that an *excess* of oil is being burned in the combustion chamber.

Cause 13.2.1

Auto-lube pump incorrectly adjusted. Quite simply, the oil pump is over-advanced, and more oil than is required is being pumped into the mixture and, consequently, burned in the combustion chamber.

Remedy 13.2.1

If too much oil is being supplied, the most likely reason is that the pump has been incorrectly set. You will need to recheck the alignment of the adjustment marks and, if necessary, readjust to the correct setting. For details of the general procedure see pp. 58–9.

14. The oil pressure warning light comes on

This is not so much a performance problem in itself, but indicates that one may be about to occur: if you are to ensure it doesn't you should investigate the possible causes immediately.

Cause 14.1

Insufficient oil in the lubrication system. The oil pressure warning light is activated by a pressure switch. If the light comes on, it may mean that a lack of oil is causing the pressure in the engine to drop and so the warning light to come on.

Remedy 14.1

Stop the engine *immediately*, check the oil level and top up (with the recommended oil, which will be indicated in your owner's handbook or workshop manual) if necessary. It is important, however, not to overfill the system, as this too would cause problems (see p. 39).

Cause 14.2

A defect in the lubrication system itself. If you feel confident that the lubrication system is satisfactorily topped up, and yet still the light comes on, it is essential that you ride no further until you have investigated the reason, as the damage you can cause may be extensive (that is, expensive).

Although it may be only the switch which is defective (in which case no damage would be done), it may be that there is a blockage in the system obstructing the oil's circulation. The potential for damage in this case is extremely high.

Remedy 14.2

If you suspect the wiring or switch to be defective, you should first check the wiring to the switch. To do so, you must: (1) disconnect the wiring from the switch; (2) switch on the ignition:

(a) if the oil light still comes on, you have a wiring problem and this will need to be checked; or (b) if the light now stays off, the switch is at fault. If this is the case, you must: (1) remove it from the engine; (2) wash it thoroughly in clean petrol; and (3) blow it dry with a pressurized air hose.

Unfortunately, however, starting the engine to check if this was the source of your problem may be just enough to cause the extensive and expensive damage, if your suspicions about the switch were *incorrect*.

Ideally, the oil pressure and the entire lubrication system should be checked by a competent mechanic if you are to be sure.

15. The engine never reaches its correct operating temperature, that is, it underheats (water-cooled engines only)

Cause 15.1
Thermostat defective. The thermostat in a liquid-cooled engine controls the temperature of the liquid, and so the temperature of the engine, by controlling the liquid's rate of flow through the system. The wider the thermostat gap, the faster the liquid is allowed to circulate, the more times it will pass through the radiator and the cooler it will become. Consequently, the narrower the gap, the higher the temperature of the coolant.

Therefore, the engine will be unable to reach its correct running temperature if: (1) the thermostat is jammed open; (2) the incorrect grade of thermostat is fitted; or (3) the thermostat is omitted entirely from the system.

Remedy 15.1
The first thing you need to do is to remove the thermostat cover (your owner's handbook or workshop manual will indicate the precise procedure for your motorcycle) – what you do after that depends on what your investigation reveals.

If the thermostat is jammed open – and you can check this by immersing it in a bowl of cold water (whereupon it should close) – it will need to be replaced.

On the other hand, if it does close and open when immersed first in cold and then in hot water, it may be the incorrect grade of thermostat for your motorcycle – if it is, you will have to replace it. The correct grade for your motorcycle will be indicated in your owner's handbook or workshop manual.

Finally, if you remove the thermostat cover and find the thermostat has been removed, fit one of the correct grade as soon as possible.

You now need to renew the thermostat cover gasket (it is often a good idea to secure it with liquid gasket or gasket cement), replace the thermostat cover and replenish the liquid to the 'full' mark. For a while after this job it is advisable to check around the joint occasionally for signs of wetness: if any appear, your seal is defective and you will have to remake it. Losing too much coolant may result in your engine overheating.

16. The engine overheats
The easiest way to confirm your suspicions that the engine is too hot is to inspect the spark plug: light grey or mid-white chalk deposits on the nose

tip, and burned electrodes, are a clear indication that the plug is overheating and burning itself out prematurely (see 'Plug condition: burned electrodes', p. 46, for more details).

The first thing you need to do is to verify that the spark plug you are using is of the correct grade: if it is, you will have to investigate further.

Cause 16.1

Incorrect spark plug fitted. Fitting a spark plug of the wrong grade, that is, one that is too hot, will cause the engine rapidly to overheat.

In brief, whereas 'cold' plugs conduct heat away from the plug tip quickly, 'hot' plugs retain their heat for far longer (see p. 264). For a fuller discussion of the spark plug heat range, and the problems associated with fitting an incorrect plug, see p. 48.

Remedy 16.1

Replace the existing spark plug(s) with one(s) of the correct grade. There is a specific heat range plug for your engine and, unless your engine has been modified, you should abide by the manufacturer's specifications set out in your owner's handbook or workshop manual.

Cause 16.2

Ignition timing advanced. Because the spark occurs too soon, the piston is compelled to climb up to, and over, T.D.C. against the force of the exploding mixture – indeed, in doing so it is forced to compress expanding gases. It is this action which results in the engine overheating because of the excess load which is placed upon it.

Remedy 16.2

Check and, if necessary, reset the timing: for an explanation of how to go about this see 'Ignition timing', pp. 62–3.

Cause 16.3

Fuel/air mixture is too lean. If the mixture being ignited is too lean – that is, the proportion of air is too high – the power of the resultant explosion will be significantly reduced, and the load placed upon the engine will increase substantially; as a result, the engine is likely to overheat. A good indication that the mixture is too lean is that the engine speed will be higher than usual at tickover.

Some of the more likely causes of a lean mixture (and hence where your investigation should begin) are:

Cause 16.3.1

Incorrect main jet. If you or the previous owner (should you have recently purchased the motorcycle) have tampered with the carburettor main jet – in an attempt to 'tune' the carburettor – it may now be too small to allow the required amount of petrol through the venturi to mix with the air being drawn in. Consequently, the proportion of air will be high and the mixture will therefore be lean.

Remedy 16.3.1

Dismantle the carburettor(s) concerned and examine the main jet: its size will be marked on it. If it is smaller than the main jet size specified in your owner's handbook or workshop manual, screw it out and replace it with one of the correct size. Examining the spark plug(s) on a multi-cylinder engine will tell you which of them is overheating – although, if someone has tampered with one jet, they will have probably tampered with them all. Therefore, all the cylinders will be too hot.

Cause 16.3.2

Air leaks in the inlet manifold. Any air leaks in the inlet manifold – that is, between the carburettor and the engine – as a result of loose manifold joints or cracks in the manifold, will allow extra air to be drawn into the correctly proportioned mixture as it travels from the carburettor to the cylinder. Consequently, the mixture entering the combustion chamber will contain too much air – that is, it will be lean.

Remedy 16.3.2

Visually inspect the manifold and replace it if there are any signs of splits or cracks which may allow air to pass: effective repairs to this component are virtually impossible. Winding insulating tape over the damaged area will reduce the air intake, and so reduce the engine's temperature, allowing you to ride home, but it is certainly not a long-term solution. Also check and, if necessary, tighten the fasteners securing the manifold to the carburettor and the engine.

Cause 16.3.3

Air filter is disconnected or damaged. All adjustments of the carburettor are made with a good air filter, securely in position, to control the supply of air into the system. If the filter becomes loose, or if cracks develop in the intake tract – after the air filter – more air will be allowed into the system than the carburettor is adjusted to cope with. The result is a lean mixture.

Remedy 16.3.3

Ensure that the air filter is in good condition and securely fixed in its correct position (see 'Air-filter condition . . .', pp. 66–7), and inspect the air intake tract – particularly between the filter and the carburettor – for any signs of cracks or splits which would allow air to enter the system. Winding insulation tape over any problem areas will relieve the situation a little, enabling the engine to cool sufficiently for you to ride home (carefully!), but in the long term the section will need to be replaced.

Cause 16.3.4

Crankcase seal defective (two-strokes only). A defective crankcase seal will not only allow the charge to be pushed out – as the piston descends to transfer the mixture from the crankcase to the cylinder – but will also allow extra air to be drawn into the crankcase during the subsequent stroke (that is, when the piston ascends, compressing the mixture in the combustion chamber and drawing fresh mixture into the crankcase). Consequently this increases the proportion of air in the mixture, making it lean. A good indication that the crankcase seal is the source of your problem is if the revs stay high as you close the throttle, and then rapidly die away. Moreover, you will almost certainly be experiencing severe starting difficulties.

Remedy 16.3.4

Check the crankcase and cylinder base joints for signs of wetness, and replace any gaskets or seals which are defective.

Cause 16.4

Lack of coolant (liquid-cooled engines only). Unlike air-cooled engines, which are fitted with fins to disperse the heat, a liquid-cooled engine transfers its heat to the liquid coolant continuously circulating around it. The liquid then passes through the radiator and is itself cooled by the rushing air.

Any significant reduction in the amount of coolant in the system means that: (1) the remaining liquid is insufficient to accept all the heat being produced by the engine; and (2) the liquid spends less time in the radiator than it normally would. As a result, the temperature in the engine and the liquid steadily increases.

Remedy 16.4

A word of caution before we go any further: NEVER remove the radiator cap while the engine is hot – the liquid is likely to spurt out in a boiling fountain and severely scald you.

When the engine and radiator are *cool*, remove the radiator cap and check the coolant level: if it is below the recommended level, it must be replenished with the recommended liquid immediately.

Your owner's handbook or workshop manual will indicate how you gain access to the radiator (on some motorcycles, unfortunately, you have to remove the petrol tank) and what proportions of water and anti-freeze (the normal constituents of motorcycle coolant) are required by your motorcycle. It will almost certainly be a 50/50 mix. See 'Liquid cooling system: top up', pp. 39–40, for more details.

If the coolant level was so low that the engine began to overheat, you should suspect, at least, that there is a leak somewhere in the system; set the engine running and, when it reaches its normal operating temperature, make a visual check of the radiator, the hoses and all the connections for any signs of wetness.

Although leaking joints may be cured by tightening the fastener, and the radiator may be reparable, split hoses will need to be replaced.

Cause 16.5

Coolant not circulating correctly. If you are satisfied that there is sufficient coolant in the system, it may be that the liquid is unable to circulate through the radiator and so to cool down, in which case the temperature of the engine and the liquid will soar rapidly. Some of the more common obstructions are: (1) a thermostat not opening correctly; (2) a blocked radiator; (3) collapsed hoses; (4) a blowing cylinder head gasket.

Remedy 16.5.1

Defective thermostat.

1. Remove the thermostat and place it in a saucepan of water.

2. Whilst bringing the water to the boil, continually check the thermostat to see if it opens. If it *does not* open, this is almost certainly the cause of your problem, and it will need to be replaced. On the other hand, if it *does* open, replace the thermostat cover but leave the thermostat out, and try running the engine. If the overheating persists, there is clearly a more serious problem elsewhere. Replace the thermostat and continue your investigations.

Remedy **16.5.2**

Blocked radiator. Briefly, this will need to be flushed and cleaned. This may or may not involve removing the radiator, depending on the motorcycle concerned.

1. *Blocked on the inside.* Drain and flush out the scale, and other deposits, which with continual use will have built up on the inside walls. See 'Change the radiator coolant . . .: flushing', p. 85, for more details.

2. *Blocked on the outside.* Visually examine the radiator fins to see if they are damaged or clogged with dirt: blocked fins can usually be scraped clean with a screwdriver, or blown clear by a high-pressure hose; bent fins can usually be straightened with a screwdriver, so long as you are gentle.

Remedy **16.5.3**

Collapsed hoses. Quite simply, if any hose is collapsed or, indeed, damaged in any other way, the only effective solution is to replace it.

Remedy **16.5.4**

Blowing cylinder head gasket. Unfortunately, there is no other solution than to remove the cylinder head and fit a new gasket. Certainly any attempts to patch it up with gasket cement would be a waste of time. Your owner's handbook or workshop manual will indicate the procedure you must follow to remove and replace the cylinder head. Finally, be extremely careful not to let any scraps of the old gasket fall into the cooling system as you clean the jointing surfaces.

Cause **16.6**

The engine oil level is too low. Because oil has the ability to disperse any heat it picks up as it passes through the engine, it helps cool as well as lubricate the engine. If the oil level drops too low, there is: (1) an increase in the likelihood of metal to metal contact and therefore an increase in the heat generated; and (2) a decline in the means of disposing of this increased heat.

Ultimately, if the build-up of heat continues, the two surfaces may become so hot that they weld themselves together, that is, the engine will seize (see pp. 252–5 for a more detailed explanation of engine seizure).

Remedy **16.6**

Check the level of oil in the lubrication system and replenish with fresh oil of the correct grade (which will be indicated in the owner's handbook or workshop manual) if necessary.

Remember that in a two-stroke engine you will need to check both the two-stroke oil and the gearbox oil.

Cause **16.7**

Inadequate supply of two-stroke oil into the mixture. Although it is possible that the two-stroke oil is being obstructed in the oil lines – between the reservoir and the pump, and the pump and the crankcase – the problem is more likely to be that the pump-actuating cable has stretched, leaving the pump incorrectly adjusted, that is, it is supplying less oil than is required by the fuel/air mixture at any throttle setting.

Remedy 16.7

Check and, if necessary, readjust the auto-lube pump to take up the slack which has developed in the cable. Briefly, you will need to ensure the two alignment marks line up; more details on auto-lube adjustment can be found on pp. 58–9. Your owner's handbook or workshop manual will indicate the precise procedure for your motorcycle.

Cause 16.8

Idling for too long in traffic. An air-cooled engine relies on air rushing through its cooling fins and picking up the heat the fins are designed to dispose of. Although the fins will be able to disperse some of the heat when the motorcycle is standing still, this will certainly be insufficient in heavy traffic, and especially in hot weather. If you are idling, especially in traffic, not only is there an absence of cool, rushing air, but it is also likely that the air around will be steadily heating up itself – as it becomes full of exhaust fumes and picks up the heat from the surrounding vehicles.

Remedy 16.8

If you can't manage to move through the traffic – and it must be extremely dense if it prevents a motorcycle making progress – the only other solution is to switch off whenever possible to give the engine a few moments to cool.

Cause 16.9

Blocked cooling fins. This is perhaps a problem which only dirt bikes will come across, and only in muddy terrain at that. Simply, the problem is that the fins become so blocked with mud,

dirt or wet leaves that the passing air is unable to travel between the fins and so disperse the engine's heat. If the going gets muddy, have a look down occasionally, as the problem is easy to prevent before it happens simply by being attentive.

Remedy 16.9

Stop the engine and use anything which is available – a screwdriver, a thin spanner, even a stick – to clear out the fins.

17. Misfires

A misfire, regardless of its accompanying symptoms, is one of the hardest problems to track down – especially if it is intermittent: the fault is never there when you are looking for it. Knowing your motorcycle, its particular idiosyncrasies, its performance potential and its history will clearly be of enormous help to you, but is not vital.

Basically, tracking down a misfire involves you in being a detective. If you are to identify the problem's source, you need to: (1) collect all the information you can about the circumstances in which the fault occurs; and (2) examine these clues using a process of logical deduction.

For example: if you have a single-carburettor, twin-cylinder engine and the fault is an intermittent cutting-out in one cylinder, you can immediately assume that the carburettor is not at fault, since that one component feeds both cylinders. Similarly, if one set of points is used to trigger the coil for both cylinders, because the ignition coil feeds power to *both* cylinders, it too is unlikely to be defective. However, as the cylinders each have separate H.T. leads, plug caps and spark plugs, etc., any one of these could be at fault, and it is here that you should begin your investigation of this particular problem.

Finally, you can determine which, if any, of the cylinders on a multi-cylinder is at fault simply by cautiously touching each exhaust pipe near the engine. Beware when doing this – the exhaust will be hot! Perhaps spit on your finger first. If any one appears significantly cooler than the other(s), it is likely to be at fault. Also, on a multi-cylinder system, silencers may give you important clues. If all is well, and the exhaust gases are normally constituted, then after a good run – that is, not in town conditions – the end of the silencer will be matt grey.

On the other hand: scaly black deposits indicate that oil is being burned; sooty deposits indicate an over-rich mixture and cold running; white ash deposits suggest a weak mixture and overheating.

These and the other clues you can obtain by a brief inspection of the spark plug's firing tip (see pp. 44–7) will be of great help in the deduction process.

Symptom 17.1 Intermittent misfire		
Possible causes	Remedies	See page(s)
17.1.1 Weak spark at spark plug (a) Fouled spark plug (b) Generator defective and/or battery discharged (c) Loose or faulty spark plug cap	17.1.1 (a) Clean the electrodes or replace the spark plug (b) Check the generator output and recharge the battery (c) Secure or replace the spark plug cap	 107 225 112
17.1.2 Defect in contact breaker assembly	17.1.2 Check and reset the points; check that all wires are intact and connections are secure	113
17.1.3 Short circuit along the H.T. leads	17.1.3 Clean and dry the leads or cover them with a length of fuel pipe. If this is unsuccessful, replace the lead	127
17.1.4 Faulty condenser	17.1.4 Replace	117

Possible causes	Remedies	See page(s)
17.1.5 Battery deficiencies (a) Loose connections at terminals or the earth (b) Recharging system defective	17.1.5 (a) Inspect and, if necessary, clean and tighten (b) Ask your local workshop to check the electrical system; replace any defective components	124

225 |
17.1.6 Contaminated fuel	17.1.6 Drain the tank, carburettor and the fuel pipes. Refill the system with fresh fuel	107 and 163
17.1.7 Incorrect oil or fuel/oil ratio (two-strokes only)	17.1.7 Reset the oil pump (on an auto-lube system), or empty the petrol tank and mix a fresh batch of petroil in pre-mix systems	137
17.1.8 Cracked/loose exhaust	17.1.8 Check the length of the system; secure any sections which are loose, weld any cracks or replace the system	158

Symptom 17.2 Misfires at certain throttle openings

Possible causes	Remedies	See page(s)
17.2.1 Worn slide needle and/or needle jet	17.2.1 Lower the needle one notch and try the motorcycle, or replace the needle and the jet	164
17.2.2 Cracked diaphragm on C.V. carburettor	17.2.2 Replace the diaphragm	154

Symptom 17.3 Misfires under load or while accelerating		
Possible causes	Remedies	See page(s)
17.3.1 Defective spark plug (a) Gap incorrect	17.3.1 (a) Reset the gap. See your owner's handbook or workshop manual	47
(b) Electrodes in a poor condition	(b) Clean the electrodes and rectify any underlying problems	44
(c) Plug is of incorrect heat range	(c) Replace the existing plug with one of the correct heat range. See your owner's handbook or workshop manual	48
17.3.2 Over-rich fuel/air mixture (a) Air filter blocked or damaged	17.3.2 (a) Clean or replace the filter	66
(b) Slide needle maladjusted	(b) Lower the slide needle one notch at a time. Road test in between each change. Pay particular attention to the condition of the plug electrodes!	72
17.3.3 Ignition timing incorrect	17.3.3 Check and reset the points gap and the ignition timing. See your owner's handbook or workshop manual for specifications. Also check the plug – it may have been damaged. Replace it if necessary	119 and 150

Symptom 17.4 Misfires and running is jerky and/or erratic

Possible causes	Remedies	See page(s)
17.4.1 Ignition system defects	17.4.1	
(a) Spark plug gap and conditions incorrect	(a) Clean and reset the gap or replace the plug	107
(b) Contact breaker gap and conditions incorrect	(b) Ensure that the points are in good condition and, if necessary, adjust the gap between them	113
(c) Battery terminal or earth connections loose	(c) Ensure that all three connections are securely fixed in position	124
(d) Short circuit on an H.T. cable	(d) Inspect the lead(s) for cracks, wear or signs of possible water penetration	127
(e) Battery insufficiently charged	(e) Recharge the battery. If it refuses to hold a charge, replace it. If you are in any doubt, have the battey checked by a workshop	122
(f) H.T. coil defective	(f) Check the spark plug for signs of a spark; if none are evident, the coil may have failed and must be replaced	116
(g) Condenser defective	(g) Check the colour of the spark at the points; if it is bright blue the condenser will need replacing	117
(h) Ignition timing incorrect	(h) Reset the timing	119 and 150
(i) Breaks in the ignition wiring	(i) Check the ignition and circuit for signs of damage and repair or replace any suspect sections	127

Possible causes	Remedies	See page(s)
17.4.2 Carburettor defects (a) Dirt or droplets of water in the carburettor	17.4.2 (a) Dismantle and clean the carburettor, particularly the jets	104 and 153
(b) Carburettor poorly adjusted	(b) Readjust the idle speed and idle mixture and ensure the carburettors on a multi-carburettor engine are synchronized	72 and 104
(c) Partly blocked fuel cap vent	(c) Remove the fuel cap; if the engine then runs satisfactorily the vent is blocked – clean it out	103

Symptom 17.5 Misfires and is spitting back		
Possible causes	Remedies	See page(s)
17.5.1 Leaky or worn inlet valve	17.5.1 You can check the inlet valve by testing for compression. If the valve is defective, it will need regrinding or reseating – really, this is a workshop-level job and we would advise you to have it done there	134 and 157
17.5.2 Worn carburettor slide or body	17.5.2 A replacement slide usually cures this but on older motorcycles the carburettor may need to be replaced. However, a check by your local workshop may be worth while before you spend a lot of money	164
17.5.3 Ignition timing advanced	17.5.3 Readjust the points gap and the timing	150 and 177

Symptom 17.6 Engine backfiring (this is an explosion in the exhaust pipe either when the throttle is opened wide or, more often, when the throttle is shut off)

Possible causes	Remedies	See page(s)
17.6.1 Loose or cracked exhaust, or a poor exhaust gasket	17.6.1 Ensure that the gasket is in good condition and that all the joints are secure. Minor cracks can be welded, but if they are too bad the exhaust will need replacing	158
17.6.2 Weak mixture entering the combustion chamber – probably a result of an incorrectly adjusted carburettor or a worn slide	17.6.2 Ensure that the carburettor is correctly adjusted and replace the slide if it is excessively worn	164

Symptom 17.7 The engine pulls well at tickover, but misfires at full or high throttle openings

Possible causes	Remedies	See page(s)
17.7.1 Ignition system defects (a) Spark plug gap and condition incorrect	17.7.1 (a) Clean and reset the gap or replace the plug	107
(b) Points gap too wide	(b) Reset the gap between the contact breaker points surfaces	157
(c) Short circuit on an H.T. lead	(c) Inspect the lead(s) for cracks, wear and signs of water penetration	127
(d) Ignition timing incorrect	(d) Reset the timing	119 and 150

Possible causes	Remedies	See page(s)
17.7.2 Carburettor defects: (a) Air intake partially blocked, by a dirty or damaged filter, or an obstruction in the air flow	17.7.2 (a) Ensure that the air passage to the filter is clear and that the filter itself is clean and in good condition	148
(b) Contaminated fuel	(b) Empty the fuel tank, fuel pipes and carburettor of all fuel and replace it with a fresh supply	107
(c) Carburettor main jet too large	(c) Inspect the jet; if it is excessively worn or has been tampered with, resulting in it being too wide, the jet must be replaced	177
(d) Carburettor float too low	(d) Bend the tang between the two floats so as to readjust its level in the float chamber	171

Symptom 17.8 Misfires in wet weather		
Possible causes	Remedies	See page(s)
17.8.1 Damp in the ignition system – you should pay particular attention to the spark plugs, the spark plug cap, the H.T. lead, the contact breaker(s) and the coil(s)	17.8.1 Frequently these components can be dried out with water-dispersant spray. Simply spray a liberal coating of the solution on to the principal components in the system. Moreover, spraying the ignition system will safeguard its future	125
17.8.2 Water in the carburettor, which may be entering the system because of a saturated air filter	17.8.2 If the filter is saturated, wringing it out (if it is foam) may solve the problem temporarily, but in the long run it will need to	

Possible causes	Remedies	See page(s)
	be more thoroughly dried. Check the seal around the filter mount. Finally, dismantle and wash out the carburettor to ensure no water is trapped inside	104 and 153

18. The gears are difficult to engage/change

Cause 18.1

Incorrect amount of oil in the gearbox. With too little oil in the gearbox, changing gear is difficult because the gears are unable to slide correctly. On the other hand, if you overfill the gearbox the increased pressure will also make it difficult to change gear.

Remedy 18.1

Readjust the amount of oil in the gearbox to the specified level. If you need to replenish the oil supply, make sure you do it with the correct grade of oil (see your owner's handbook or workshop manual).

Cause 18.2

The gearbox contains the incorrect grade of oil. Using the incorrect grade of oil in your engine may cause clutch drag and, consequently, difficulty in changing gears. Although the problem is most commonly caused by people using oil which is too thick, using an oil which is too thin will also cause problems.

Remedy 18.2

Drain the engine (or the gearbox if it is separate) of all the existing oil and replenish it with an oil of the correct grade. See your owner's handbook or workshop manual for details of where the gearbox drain plug is located (if one is fitted) and the type of oil necessary. (See also pp. 52–3 for information on changing oil.)

Cause 18.3

Clutch lever/cable incorrectly adjusted. If the clutch lever is incorrectly adjusted or, as is more likely, if the cable has stretched, the clutch plates are unlikely to separate sufficiently to allow free movement of the gears. Consequently, changing gear is difficult.

Remedy 18.3

Lubricate the cable thoroughly (see p. 43 for a tip to help you) and readjust the clutch mechanism to remove any unnecessary slack, leaving only the recommended free play. Your owner's handbook or workshop manual will indicate what the free play should be on your motorcycle and should detail the readjustment procedure. (See also

p. 42 for more information on clutch adjustment.)

Cause 18.4

The gear lever is bent and is fouling against the engine casing. If you have fallen off, or the motorcycle has fallen over, etc., the gear lever may have been pushed in towards the engine casing and is now fouling on the engine casing as you attempt to change gear. A quick visual check of the lever or the engine casing – which will probably have tell-tale scuff marks – will indicate what the precise problem is.

Remedy 18.4

Bend the lever back to its original shape or replace it if it is too badly deformed. A large ring spanner slipped over the end, or a large pair of mole-type grips, are both ideal for reshaping a lever while it is still attached to the motorcycle.

Cause 18.5

There is a broken spring in the gear change mechanism. If the gear changes made by moving the gear lever upwards are reasonably smooth, and yet those requiring the lever to be pushed downwards are difficult, it is quite likely that a spring in the gear change mechanism has broken. A sloppy feel to the gear lever is also a good indication of this situation.

Remedy 18.5

You will need to strip the gearbox (or have it stripped for you), find the broken spring and replace it. If you need instructions, you should find them in your owner's handbook or workshop manual (and follow them precisely). There is no reason, provided you have

the correct tools, why this job should be beyond you. Simply use your common sense, act logically and be patient. It is often a good idea to note each part as you take it off, and perhaps make a sketch of where it came from – you don't want to end up with a couple of pieces in your hand after reassembly. If you don't have the correct tools, or if you feel you don't have the time that this job could take an amateur, don't hesitate to visit your local workshop. The mechanic would much prefer to do the job himself than to try to rectify your mistakes, and it will probably be cheaper for you.

Cause 18.6

Selector forks bent. If the selector forks are bent, not only is it difficult to select the gears, but even when you do so they will not be fully engaged. Consequently, they also tend to jump out of gear frequently as the engine's revs increase.

Remedy 18.6

Unfortunately, aside from the additional symptom of frequently jumping out of gear, the only way to check the forks is to inspect them – and that means dismantling the gearbox. If they are bent, they will need to be replaced, unless you can heat them up to straighten them – and even then it is not a good idea: they will be substantially weakened and may fail altogether, creating a far more serious problem.

19. The gear lever does not return to its original position

Cause 19.1

The gear lever return spring is broken. Normally, after you change gear the gear lever returns to the same position because of a return spring (frequently located on the other side of the casing) fitted for just that purpose. If this spring breaks, the lever will no longer feel firm in its action and is unlikely to return to its central position.

Remedy 19.1

Briefly, dismantle the gearbox and replace the return spring(s). Although on some motorcycles this job can be done simply by removing the clutch cover (with the engine in the frame), unfortunately, gaining access to the spring actually quite often requires the engine to be lifted out of the frame. Although such a task is not beyond the correctly equipped amateur, it does require logic, patience and time in large quantities. Unless you can combine all three with the correct tools, we suggest you visit the local workshop.

Cause 19.2

The gear change shaft is bent, dry or corroded. Should the gear lever shaft become bent (because your motorcycle has fallen over, etc.), dry or corroded (because you have neglected to apply grease) at the point where it passes through the final-drive sprocket cover, it is quite likely that the gear lever's movement will be increasingly stiff and that it will be reluctant to return to its central position.

Remedy 19.2

Remove the final-drive sprocket cover and inspect the shaft. If there are any bends, the gearbox will need to be dismantled and the shaft straightened or replaced. It is highly unlikely that you will be able to straighten it while it is in position.

On the other hand, if the shaft appears to be straight, but is dry or corroded, use a wire brush and/or emery paper to clean it up. Finally apply a good coating of grease and replace the cover.

20. The engine repeatedly jumps out of gear

Cause 20.1

The final-drive chain 'snatches' as you open or close the throttle. (1) Excessive free play in the final-drive chain, (2) excessive play in the movement of the swinging arm and (3) very loose engine bolts are all capable of causing the drive chain to 'snatch': that is, because they all cause the tension of the chain to vary irregularly, opening and closing the throttle may cause the chain to jerk. If this jerking action is severe enough, it can cause the gears to jump out of position and leave the engine out of gear.

Remedy 20.1.1

Check and, if necessary, readjust the final-drive chain to remove any excessive free play. See 'Final-drive chain: lubrication and tension', pp. 30–35, for more details.

Remedy 20.1.2

Check the extent of lateral movement in the swinging arm (see p. 76). If this movement is excessive, try tightening the securing bolts to reduce it. Should this fail, unfortunately you will need to replace the bearings. Details of the precise procedure for this operation will be found in your owner's handbook or workshop manual.

Remedy 20.1.3

Check all the engine-mounting bolts, retighten any which are loose and replace (worn) bolts that have been loose for some time – vibrations will have worn a heavy groove around the bolt and subsequently weakened it.

Cause 20.2

The selector forks are bent. If these forks are bent – and this may well have been caused by the motorcycle falling over on to the gear lever when the gears inside were not in a selected position – the gears will *not* be fully engaged when you have completed the gear change action. Consequently, as the revs of the engine increase, the gears separate and the motorcycle is out of gear.

Remedy 20.2

You will need to dismantle the gearbox (or have it dismantled for you) and examine the forks. If any are bent, it (or they) will need to be straightened (so long as they are heated up first – although even then they will be weakened) or replaced.

If you have the correct tools, the time and the patience, there is no reason why you should not tackle this job yourself. On the other hand, if any of these components are in short supply take your motorcycle to the local workshop before you fiddle with it. It is often cheaper for a mechanic to do the whole job than to correct the mistakes of others.

Unfortunately, your inspection of the dismantled gearbox is likely to reveal at least two damaged gears which will have been jumping out before you got around to doing the job. If you do find any damaged gears they will need to be replaced.

21. Gear changing is jerky and the motorcycle creeps forward even when the clutch is withdrawn (that is, pulled in)

This situation is also frequently accompanied by great difficulty in selecting neutral. Essentially, it is a result of clutch drag, which is itself caused by:

Cause 21.1

The clutch cable is dry. If the clutch cable is dry – and this will be indicated by the inner cable appearing white and corroded – the whole clutch operation will be stiff, giving you movement at the lever, but not at the clutch itself.

Moreover, operating with a dry clutch cable for any length of time is likely to cause it to stretch and so exaggerate the problem.

Remedy 21.1

Use the system of cable lubrication described on pp. 42–3 to force oil into the cable sleeve, and grease the cable linkages.

Note: Some cables – nylon ones, for example – cannot be lubricated, and replacement is the only answer. Your owner's handbook or workshop manual will tell you if your cable can be lubricated.

Cause 21.2

Clutch adjustment incorrect. An excess of free play in the clutch mechanism, either because it has been poorly adjusted or because the cable has stretched, means that movement at the lever is unlikely to be transmitted to the plates themselves. The gear-changing problems occur precisely because the plates are not separating sufficiently to allow free gear movement.

Remedy 21.2

Check and, if necessary, readjust the clutch mechanism to reduce the free play to that recommended in your owner's handbook or workshop manual, where you will also find the procedure to be adopted on your motorcycle (see also p. 42).

Cause 21.3

Worn clutch drum/plate drive tangs. Letting the clutch out fast and/or adopting a racing style of riding produces indentations in the clutch drum from the clutch plate tangs (Figure 57). This makes it difficult for the plate to move backwards and forwards in the slots in the clutch drum.

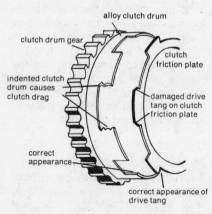

alloy clutch drum

clutch drum gear

clutch friction plate

indented clutch drum causes clutch drag

damaged drive tang on clutch friction plate

correct appearance

correct appearance of drive tang

Figure 57 Clutch layout, showing worn drive parts

Remedy 21.3

Briefly, the drum will need to be examined and, if necessary, repaired or replaced. However, although a good mechanic can carefully dress the drum

with a fine file, replacement is often the only answer. Details of how to gain access to the clutch, extract the plates and remove the drum will be indicated in the owner's handbook or workshop manual.

22. The engine speed (shown on the tachometer) increases, but the motorcycle does not respond with an increase in speed

Cause 22.1

The final-drive chain has snapped. The two principal reasons why a chain may snap are:

1. That it was excessively worn. See pp. 30–33 for details of the various ways of checking if a chain is worn to the point that it needs replacing.

2. That it was too tight. This is particularly detrimental on motorcycles which have long-travel suspension (conventional or monoshock), where the distance between the two sprockets increases as the rider puts his weight on the seat. If the chain is already tight before you mount the motorcycle, you risk breaking it at the first bump.

Remedy 22.1

If you are away from home, the easiest solution is to replace the chain and reconnect it with a split link – something you should always have with you, either fastened to the motorcycle or in your tool kit. To make the reconnection, however, you will almost certainly have to move the rear wheel forward slightly, in which case before you ride off you will also have to readjust the chain tension. Details of how to check and adjust the final-drive chain can be found on pp. 30–33. It is especially important that the tension is correct if the chain is worn: any extra stress on the already weakened chain will undoubtedly cause you problems.

When you arrive home, however, you should remove the chain and check it for wear as soon as possible. If it is excessively worn, replace it immediately. On the other hand, if it still has some miles left in it, clean and replace it (see 'Final-drive chain condition', pp. 54–8, for details).

If you ride a superbike, it will probably be fitted with a continuous chain, in which case the temporary split link will be a weak link: replace it with a rivet, or have your local workshop do it for you.

Cause 22.2

The final-drive chain has jumped off the rear sprocket. If the chain is too loose and/or the rear sprocket is excessively worn, it is not uncommon for the chain to jump off.

Remedy 22.2

Examine both the chain and the sprocket for wear (see 'Chain and sprocket wear', pp. 30–31): if either component is excessively worn it must be replaced. Otherwise, simply replace the chain over the rear sprocket and readjust the tension (see 'Final-drive chain . . .: Chain tension', pp. 31–33).

Cause 22.3

Clutch slip. If a quick visual inspection of the final-drive chain reveals it to be intact and in position, the most likely cause of this symptom is *'clutch slip'*, for which you should suspect:

Cause 22.3.1

Clutch incorrectly adjusted. Although the clutch mechanism should not contain too much free play, the absence of sufficient free play is also a problem. For the full power of the engine's drive to be transmitted through the gearbox the clutch plates must be in full contact: they will not be if there is insufficient play in the mechanism, as each plate will be held off the others (if only slightly).

Remedy 22.3.1

Check the amount of free play in the clutch mechanism, and make any adjustments that are necessary to establish the recommended movement in the mechanism. Although it may differ slightly from one motorcycle to another, there should be approximately ⅜ in. movement at the end of the clutch lever when it is correctly regulated (see p. 42 for more details, and your owner's handbook or workshop manual will indicate how much there should be on your motorcycle). Clutch slip resulting from a poorly regulated mechanism – that is, in the cable – can unfortunately result in the plates themselves being so badly damaged that they need replacing. If adjustment fails to remove the slip, you must examine the plates.

Cause 22.3.2

The clutch friction plates are worn. As the plates in the clutch mechanism become old, they steadily begin to wear and ultimately to slip against each other (although, as we saw in item 22.3.1 above, plates in a poorly regulated clutch will wear much faster). Although this wear can be compensated for to some extent by the two adjustment mechanisms at each end of the cable, eventually plates will become so worn that even this cannot prevent the slipping.

Remedy 22.3.2

Dismantle the clutch, measure the thickness of the friction plates and check these measurements against those required by the specifications (see your owner's handbook or workshop manual): if they are excessively worn (that is, if they are narrower than they should be), you will have to replace them.

Finally, before you reassemble the mechanism, inspect the steel drive plates and ensure they are flat: if they are not, they too must be replaced.

Details of the precise procedure and the tools required to do this job on your motorcycle will be indicated in your owner's handbook or workshop manual.

Cause 22.3.3

Clutch spring tension incorrect. Another problem in an ageing clutch is that, as the clutch springs (which hold the plates together) become old, their tension steadily diminishes until eventually the plates begin to slip against each other.

Remedy 22.3.3

Dismantle the clutch mechanism (or have it done for you) and measure the length of the springs: if any of them are faulty (even if it is only *one*), replace the whole set. Replacing just one or two will cause uneven clutch movement, clutch drag, and difficulty in engaging gears and selecting neutral.

Cause 22.3.4

An extremely dry clutch cable. Often, the movement of an *extremely* dry/rusty cable can become so stiff that the clutch is held partially open even when you think it is closed. If the cable has become as dry as this, however, the strands which are wound together to make the cable may have begun to break and are now getting caught inside the sleeving. For a more detailed discussion of trapped, damaged or frayed cables see item 23.2 below.

Remedy 22.3.4

Lubricate the inner cable thoroughly by using the method described on p. 43 to force oil into the sleeving. Should lubrication fail to resolve the problem, disconnect the cable at both ends, withdraw the inner wire (if possible) and examine it for signs of damage. As a temporary measure, you can trim off these frayed pieces so that it functions correctly; if there is sufficient room on the inside of the sleeve, one twist of insulating tape around the wire may help prevent the problem recurring before you have time to change it. In the long term, however, the problem will return and you will have to replace the cable.

Cause 22.3.5

Use of oil additives in a wet clutch. Most of the oil additives sometimes suggested for addition to your engine oil are far too slippery for wet-plate clutch mechanisms – so slippery that they cause the plates to slip against each other (see p. 241 for more details).

Remedy 22.3.5

Briefly: (1) drain the engine of all its oil; (2) dismantle the clutch – your owner's handbook or workshop manual will tell you how (or have it done for you) – and thoroughly wash the plates with paraffin or petrol; (3) rebuild the clutch and refill the engine with the grade of oil recommended in your owner's handbook or workshop manual.

23. Clutch operation is stiff

Cause 23.1

Handlebar lever too tight. If the clutch lever doesn't automatically move back to its fully home position after you have used the clutch, that is, you have to push it back to its 'off' position, the clutch lever bolt is too tight.

Remedy 23.1

Slacken off the pivot nut and/or locking nut. Also, if necessary, remove the lever and regrease the pivot.

Cause 23.2

The control cable is trapped or damaged (frayed, for example).

1. *Trapped.* The inner wire will become stiff and even trapped within the outer sleeve of the route if the cable contains curves which are too sharp.

2. *Frayed.* Cracks or splits in the outer sleeve frequently result in the inner wire becoming rusty. Ultimately, with continual movement to and fro, some of the strands (which are intertwined to make the wire) break, the wire becomes frayed and these protruding strands catch on the inside of the outer sleeve, hindering movement.

Remedy 23.2.1

Check the cable's route and re-route it if it contains bends which are not sufficiently gradual. The sharper the bend, the more likely it is to cause a problem.

Remedy 23.2.2

Disconnect the cable at both ends, withdraw the inner wire (if possible) and inspect it for any signs of fraying.

If there are some broken strands, as a temporary measure you can: (1) trim off any troublesome strands; (2) cover the damaged section with *one* twist of insulation tape if there is sufficient space in the sleeve; (3) lubricate the wire thoroughly; (4) wind *several* layers of insulating tape over the damaged area of the *outer sleeve* (not the inner wire); (5) replace the central wire in the sleeve. This should relieve the problem until you can replace the cable – which you should do as soon as possible.

Most inner cables, however, have a nipple at both ends which makes it impossible for it to be withdrawn. All you can do in this situation is: (1) inspect the outer sleeve – if it is cracked, split or worn, etc., at any point, you can be pretty sure that if the cable is frayed, this is the place; and (2) move the inner wire back and forth within the sleeve while listening very carefully – if you hear a metallic flicking noise from inside the cable, it is frayed and must be replaced. Unfortunately, although there are numerous things you can try to relieve the problem, none will cure it – for that you will need to replace the cable.

Cause 23.3

Clutch push-rod is bent. If, on your motorcycle, the push-rod is near the final-drive sprocket and the chain breaks or jumps off the sprocket, it may bend the push-rod, preventing full and free movement. Incidentally it may also produce oil leaks from the push-rod seal. A careful inspection is required if you are to spot this.

Remedy 23.3

Examine the push-rod and, if necessary, straighten or replace it. Also, if there are any signs of wetness around the push-rod seal, this too must be replaced (the precise location of this seal will be indicated in your owner's handbook or workshop manual).

24. The kickstart slips

Cause 24.1

Ratchet assembly worn. The ratchet assembly is the mechanism which allows the kickstart to turn the engine as it is pushed down and to return freely to its rest position. If the teeth of this assembly become worn (rounded), as they often do when the motorcycle gets old, they are no longer able to engage correctly. As a result, although the kickstart lever descends and the shaft rotates, the action is not transmitted to the engine.

Remedy 24.1

As with many other jobs in this part of a motorcycle's engine, repairs can be daunting to the amateur. Briefly, you will need to gain access to the gearbox, dismantle the kickstart assembly and renew any parts which are worn. If you have time to be patient and the ability to be logical/methodical in your approach, provided you have the necessary tools (and this can be extremely important for gearbox repairs) there is no reason why you should not tackle the job yourself. You will need to read the procedure set out in your owner's handbook or workshop manual carefully, and be sure of the steps you need to follow before you begin. If you feel at all unsure, take the motorcycle along to your local workshop. Frequently it is cheaper to have the mechanic do the repair than to help sort out any problems you have got yourself into.

Cause 24.2

Kickstart lever and shaft splines are loose or worn. The problem here arises because the pinch bolt securing the kickstart lever to the shaft is loose and so not holding the splines tightly together, or because the teeth on one or both components are so worn that they are no longer able to prevent the kickstart turning around the shaft.

Remedy 24.2

Check the tension of the pinch bolt and, if necessary, tighten it. If it is secure, unfortunately you will need to replace *both* the lever and the shaft. Whereas replacing the lever is simply a matter of loosening a bolt, lifting off one and fitting another, to replace the shaft requires the gearbox to be at least partially dismantled.

Never replace only one of these items. In the long run it would be a false economy as the problem would repeat itself quite soon. As in item 24.1, logic, patience and the correct tools are what you need – if you don't have them, ask your local workshop to help you out.

25. The kickstart lever does not return to its 'rest' position after the engine is turned over

Cause 25.1

Broken or poorly tensioned return spring. Normally, the lever is returned to the 'rest' position by a return spring; obviously, if this spring is broken or poorly adjusted, the lever will not return.

Remedy 25.1

The only way to rectify the problem is to readjust or replace the spring.

Before you begin, however, the first thing you should do is check with your owner's handbook or workshop manual and find out precisely where this spring is located on your motorcycle. Depending on its location, you may be able to get away with just removing the casing, although, on the other hand, you may also have partly to dismantle the gearbox. Your owner's handbook or workshop manual should set out the precise procedure for your motorcycle and indicate if any special tools are required – follow it carefully!

Cause 25.2

Kickstart shaft sticking in its locating hole. If it is not serviced correctly, the kickstart shaft can become so dry or corroded at the point where it passes through the final-drive chain sprocket cover that the strength of the return spring is insufficient to return it, and consequently it sticks.

Remedy 25.2

(1) Remove that part of the engine casing through which the shaft passes (if necessary remove the kickstart lever first); (2) clean (with a wire brush and/or emery paper) and grease the shaft; (3) replace the cover and the lever.

Cause 25.3

The kickstart lever is fouling on the silencer, a footrest, etc. The situation here should be obvious from a quick visual inspection. Assuming that you have not modified the silencer or changed the position of the footrests, etc., the problem must be with the lever – it will probably be bent.

Remedy 25.3

Replace the lever if it cannot be reshaped or at least bent into a usable position.

CHAPTER SIX

ELECTRICAL PROBLEMS

For many people, electricity and electrical systems can be quite baffling, principally because you cannot see the electricity flow. You can only discover if the current has reached a particular point by using a voltmeter or a test lamp. This invisibility, together with an apparently confusing tangle of components and multi-coloured wires, frequently causes even the most ardent D.I.Y. mechanic to telephone his local workshop.

In our opinion, however, if you approach the system in a logical manner, and armed with some basic information, there is absolutely no reason at all why you should be unable to resolve most electrical problems.

MOTORCYCLE ELECTRICS

The electrical system on most motorcycles (and exceptions are by and large confined to some mopeds and competition motorcycles) basically consists of:

1. A battery to provide the electrical power required for ignition or lighting, or both.

2. A generator to replace the power that the battery uses during ignition. Frequently this component is part of, and is driven by, the engine unit.

The generator consists of a rotating magnet passing very close to coils of copper wire, creating electricity in the coils. Unfortunately, however, the type of electricity produced (A.C., or alternating current) by the generator is unacceptable to the battery, which will only take direct current (D.C.). *Alternating current* simply means that the electrical flow rate is not constant but pulsating, so that every time the magnet passes the copper coil, a pulse of electricity is produced. *Direct current*, on the other hand, is a continuous, non-pulsating supply of electricity of the type you get from a battery, though on some models the generator is connected directly to the components and the battery is omitted. This system is called 'direct electrics' because the ignition and lighting only work when the engine is running.

3. A rectifier to convert the A.C. electrical power leaving the generator to the D.C. power acceptable to the battery. Once this component is inserted into the system it becomes self-supporting, in that electrical current provided is continually fed back into the battery to replace the power used by operating the various electrical components, that is, the battery can be continually 'topped up' while the engine is running. Unfortunately, a further problem occurs: the faster the engine turns, that is, the higher its r.p.m., the more power is produced by the generator. Coupled with this (it may seem too obvious to mention), we can only top up the battery as we take power out. Therefore, when the engine

is revving quite high, the system will have more electricity than it needs.

4. A voltage regulator to control the flow of electricity into the battery. This component ensures the battery will only receive the precise amount of power required to top it up, the remainder being switched to earth.

5. A series of wires, units and switches designed to provide the lights, horn, indicators, etc., with the electrical power required when operating.

ELECTRICAL FAULT FINDING

Because they are often hidden – in the form of a broken wire, or a dirty or loose connection – electrical faults can be amongst the most frustrating to deal with.

A basic principle you should always keep in mind as you approach an electrical problem is that, for a current to flow, there must be a complete and unbroken circuit from the power source to the component and back again: otherwise known as *electrical continuity*.

The outward journey to each component is made along a separate wire which begins at the power source, and passes through a variety of connections, switches and fuses, etc. Having passed through the component, current must then make its return journey to earth. This is achieved by contacting any point on the motorcycle frame which is free from dirt or corrosion. Most components, however, are earthed at or near their location. Any breaks or hold-ups in this round trip mean the circuit will be incomplete and, hence, that the component(s)

within it will not work. Discovering precisely where these breaks or blockages occur is the frustrating part.

Some 'simple' failures such as a blown bulb are also simple to cure (replace the bulb), but their diagnosis (why the bulb blew in the first place) can be far more difficult. It is certainly a question worth spending your time on, however, if you are not to be continually replacing bulbs. Other failures can be more awkward to cure in that they are not only difficult to diagnose but also to locate. The best way to pinpoint these faults is to test the circuit for continuity with either a test lamp, a voltmeter, an ohmmeter or a circuit tester.

THE TEST LAMP

By using the test lamp described on p. 236 you can check whether or not power is reaching a particular point in the circuit. If it is, the test lamp bulb will light; if it is not, the bulb will remain off, and you will need to move down the wire (towards the power source) to the next convenient point and check again. Once you find a point that is live you can be pretty sure that the problem is between that live point and the dead one you previously checked.

THE VOLTMETER

A problem with the test lamp is that it only tells you if current is reaching a specific point – it does not tell you how much current there is.

The voltmeter will not only tell you *if* power is reaching a point, but also *how much*. This is useful in that the implications of a reduced reading are different from those of no reading at all. Although in both cases you must move progressively back through the system (towards the power source) until you get a satisfactory reading, having once obtained this reading your next course of action will be different. If there was originally no reading at all, you may infer that there was a breakdown of the circuit in the problem section, whereas if the original reading was reduced, this is far more likely to be the result of a poor (dirty or corroded) connection.

THE OHMMETER

Like the test lamp and the voltmeter, the ohmmeter is also used to check wiring or components for electrical continuity. However, unlike the other two, the ohmmeter uses its own power source and operates independently of the motorcycle's power. Also, whereas the first two instruments operate to determine how far around the circuit power has reached, the ohmmeter will check the continuity of any section of the circuit or a component which is placed between its probes. Where there is continuity it reads zero; if the circuit is broken, it will read infinity.

Moreover, because it is designed to measure the resistance in a circuit and not the power, the ohmmeter can also be used to check earth connections. It is important to note, however, that because it does have its own power source, the ohmmeter should never be used in a live circuit; the two power sources together will cause irreparable damage to the meter.

THE CIRCUIT TESTER

Constructed of a bulb, a length of wire, a metal probe, a crocodile clip and a battery, the circuit tester is a self-contained unit which, like the ohmmeter, operates independently of the circuit's power to test for continuity (Figure 58). If there is electrical conti-

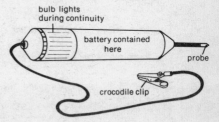

Figure 58 Self-powered circuit tester

nuity in the wiring or component placed between the clip and the probe, the tester's own circuit will be completed and its (that is, the tester's) battery power will light the bulb.

When using either the ohmmeter, the circuit tester or, indeed, any other measuring instrument which contains a battery, always check that it is operating correctly before you use it. The simplest way to do that is to touch the two probes together – you should get a reading of perfect continuity: if you don't, examine the instrument and rectify any problem before you go any further. It will probably just mean replacing the battery.

ELECTRICAL PROBLEMS

	LIGHTING: FAILURE	Page
	Filament broken: Symptoms	
1	The filament is broken in the centre, and the bulb glass is clean or has a yellowish-brown tint on the dome	204
2	The filament has melted in the centre, and the bulb glass is blackened	205
3	The filament is broken, and the glass is clear	205
4	The filament is broken, and the bulb glass is yellowish-green	206
5	The bulb glass appears quite clear, but the inside has melted into a blob	206
6	A bulb repeatedly burns out	207
	Filament unbroken: Symptoms	
7	The filament is intact, and the bulb glass is clear	207
8	All the lights fail at the same time, and their filaments are intact	211

	LIGHTING: PERFORMANCE	Page
	Symptoms	
9	A light flickers	212
10	The lights go out if you turn the handlebars to the left or right	213
11	The lights are dim, with the horn or starter inoperative, but: (1) they *do* become brighter as the engine is revved up; (2) they *don't* become brighter as the engine is revved up	214 215

LIGHTING: TIPS	Page
Headlight failure	215
Taillight failure	216
Bulb failure in direct-lighting systems	216
Defective bulbs	216
How to improve lighting	216
Sticking bulbs	217

ELECTRICS IN GENERAL	Page
Symptoms	
12 — The horn operates very quietly or not at all	217
13 — Indicator problems:	
(1) One lamp not lighting	218
(2) Two lamps on one side not lighting	219
(3) Four lamps not lighting	219
(4) Four lamps lighting but not flashing	221
(5) Four lamps lighting very dimly, but not flashing	222
(6) Flasher unit buzzes continually when the indicators are used	222
(7) Flasher unit buzzes, but only when the indicators on one side are used	223
14 — Continually blowing fuses	223
15 — Battery problems:	
(1) The battery runs down quickly while you are riding, but recovers a little if the engine is left switched off for a while	225
(2) The battery runs down quickly, and remains completely flat until recharged, after which it runs down again	225
(3) The battery runs down quickly after being recharged and reconnected to the motorcycle – even though nothing electrical is being used	225
(4) The battery runs down only when the lights are being used	226
(5) The battery constantly needs topping up	227
16 — The oil warning light stays on	227
17 — The starter motor is sluggish	227

LIGHTING

The bulb

Constructed from a coil of heat-resistant tungsten wire – a filament – encased in a glass envelope filled with a mixture of inert gases – argon, krypton and nitrogen – a bulb provides light because the wire glows white hot as electrical current is passed through it. Its enclosure in these inert gases, however, is crucial. If the filament were exposed to air, it would burn out instantly.

Although the majority of bulbs on a motorcycle are still the tungsten filament type, headlamps are increasingly being fitted with bulbs which have a compound of halogen (usually iodine or bromine) added to the other inert gases. The addition of halogen compounds, accompanied by the higher gas pressure in the envelope made possible by constructing the envelope of quartz, far stronger than glass, allows the filament to attain considerably higher temperatures without burning out: the result is a much more brilliant light.

As we will see below (pp. 206–7), however, you do have to be extremely careful when handling halogen bulbs. Inadvertently touching the envelope or the glass can easily cause the bulb to overheat and burn out.

LIGHTING: FAILURE

Should a bulb fail to light when switched on, the first thing to do is check if the filament has broken. Only then should you begin to check the circuit and its components for continuity.

FILAMENT BROKEN

Firstly, let's assume that a bulb will not light because its filament is broken – that is, the bulb has 'blown'. It would be foolish simply to replace the bulb before giving at least momentary consideration to why it happened. The condition of the filament (where, and in what manner, it is broken) and any discolouration of the bulb's glass can tell you a great deal about what may have caused the filament to break. It will also indicate, therefore, what you will need to do to prevent the same thing happening to the replacement bulb.

1. The filament is broken in the centre, and the bulb glass is clean or has a yellowish-brown tint on the dome

Cause 1.1

Old age. No bulb will last for ever, even in a perfect electrical system. One sign that a conventional (non-halogen) bulb is getting old is that it may begin to darken.

Remedy 1.1

Any bulb which blows as a result of old age should be replaced with one of the same capacity.

One way to prevent this problem, however, is to flick the envelope occasionally with your finger. Although this will have no effect on a sound filament, a weak one will crack and break loose. Clearly, it is inadvisable to try this unless you have a replacement available, but it is better that the filament should break while you are at home rather than on the open road.

2. The filament has melted in the centre, and the bulb glass is blackened

Cause 2.1

A voltage surge. A surge of current through the system will cause the filament to overheat and melt. The extra heat and subsequent melting will cause the glass to become stained black.

Remedy 2.1

Before replacing a bulb that you suspect has blown because of a voltage surge, you must first establish why the sudden surge occurred. If you do not, it will almost certainly happen again, blowing the new bulb.

A sudden surge of current may be the result of:

Remedy 2.1.1

Any loose or dirty connections in the circuit (particularly the earth). Dirt or corrosion on electrical connections have correctly been compared to blockages in water pipes, where the water's flow is restricted or even totally stopped. In an electrical system the current is also slowed down – or stopped entirely – and, consequently, so is the electrical power intended for the component. This excess power (excess because it has not been utilized by the components) then surges through the system, burning out other components in the circuit. Because motorcycles and their electrics are continually exposed to bad weather, we cannot stress enough the importance of making regular checks on the electrical system to ensure that all the electrical connections are clean and tight.

Although you may need to check every connection, you must make especially sure that:

1. The contact surfaces of the bulb and the bulb holder are free from corrosion or dirt.

2. The spring in the holder is strong enough to keep the plunger firmly up against the bulb's base contact. If it appears to be a little stiff, or sticky, lubricate it with a spray cleaner or lubricant.

3. The battery's two terminal connections and the earth connection (at the frame) are all clean and securely fixed.

4. All the fuse connections are satisfactory.

Remedy 2.1.2

A faulty voltage regulator, in direct lighting systems. If the regulator fails to regulate the power from the generator, then, as you rev up, too much power will be produced for the system and will surge through it, melting the bulbs. In other systems the battery will probably be capable of soaking up enough of the extra energy to prevent the surge melting the bulb. Unfortunately, the regulator comes as a sealed unit and repair is really out of the question. The wisest course of action if you do suspect the regulator is to visit your local workshop and ask the mechanic to test it for you. If it is defective, it will need replacing.

3. The filament is broken, and the glass is clear

Cause 3.1

Excessive vibration. Although the lights on most modern motorcycles are mounted with rubber grommets around the bolts, this is not true of all motorcycles still being ridden – and even on those where the lights are rubber-mounted, the rubber doesn't last for ever. As the rubber becomes old and hard, or perished, motorcycle vibrations are increasingly transmitted through the mounting brackets to the lamp unit. This can literally shake the inside of the bulb to pieces.

If any engine bolts are loose, however, the vibrations set up are capable, regardless of the condition of the rubber pads or grommets, of shaking a bulb's insides to pieces.

Remedy 3.1

Before you replace the bulb:

1. Remount any light unit which is not already on rubber pads or grommets, while remembering to ensure that there is a good earth.

2. Check all existing rubber mounts and replace any which are not in good condition, that is, those that are worn, cracked or hard, etc.

3. Ensure that all the nuts and bolts used to secure the lamp unit and its mounting bracket are securely fastened. Don't forget to ensure that the part of the motorcycle holding the bracket is also secure – on rear lamps, for example, your checks should also involve making sure that the mudguard itself is firmly fixed.

4. Ensure that any mounting bracket is intact. If it is cracked or fractured, you will need to have it welded or replace it.

5. Ensure that the engine-mounting bolts are secure.

Generally speaking, in a bulb which contains two filaments – a headlamp bulb, for example – only the filament that is in use (and therefore hot) is likely to fail because of excessive vibrations. So at least you will have one beam to ride home with (see 'Lighting: tips', pp. 215–17).

4. The filament is broken, and the bulb glass is yellowish-green

Cause 4.1

Air leak. The filament of a light bulb is designed to operate in a sealed chamber. If air should somehow find a way in, it will blow immediately, leaving a yellowish-green smoke effect on the inside of the glass.

More often than not, air leaks into the sealed chamber because the bulb has been bounced around or vibrated too much, although you should not rule out the prospect of having been sold a faulty bulb.

Remedy 4.1

If a *brief* inspection of the light unit reveals it to be relatively secure, try replacing the bulb with one of the same capacity. However, if this second one fails in similar circumstances, you clearly have a vibration problem: curing that will cure your lighting problem (see item 3.1, pp. 205–6). When you are satisfied the vibrations are cured, fit a new bulb.

5. The bulb glass appears quite clear, but the inside has melted into a blob

Cause 5.1

Overheating (predominantly in halogen bulbs). Although the halogen bulb does provide excellent lighting, it is very prone to overheating. Whenever you are dealing with this type of bulb, you must take great care not to touch the glass or the quartz envelope: your fingers will leave greasy prints, although you may not be able to see them. As the bulb heats up, the grease forms a hot spot, discolouring the envelope and eventually causing the interior to melt.

If you do inadvertently touch the glass or the quartz envelope of a halogen bulb, you must wash it thoroughly with methylated spirits and either leave it to dry or wipe it with a clean dry cloth before it is fitted into the circuit.

Remedy 5.1

Fortunately, there is no underlying problem to resolve in this situation. Unfortunately, however, you will have to fit a new, and expensive, bulb.

Cause 5.2

A voltage surge. Regardless of the type of bulb being used in a light, a sudden surge in the current passing through the filament may cause it to heat up so much that it simply melts.

Remedy 5.2

Rectify the cause of the surge (see 'A voltage surge', remedy 2.1, p. 205) and then replace the bulb.

6. A bulb repeatedly burns out

Cause 6.1

Using the wrong bulb. Although using the wrong bulb may not *always* result in it blowing, it will if you persistently fit bulbs which are not designed to take the level of power passing through the light unit in question.

Remedy 6.1

Fit the *correct* bulb. Your owner's handbook or workshop manual will indicate the size of bulb you ought to use as a replacement.

Cause 6.2

Failure to rectify an underlying problem adequately. As you can see from the causes for symptoms 1–6 outlined above, there are numerous explanations as to why a bulb may blow – excessive vibrations and loose connections that permit sudden power surges are only a couple of them – but if you do fail to rectify the underlying cause, each successive bulb you put in will simply go the same way as its predecessor: into the dustbin.

Remedy 6.2

If you are confident that you are using the correct bulb, the remedy is easier said than done: you must identify and resolve the underlying problem.

Examine the condition of the bulb closely – its colour and the actual way in which the filament has broken; this, along with the causes set out above for symptoms 1–5, should help you.

FILAMENT UNBROKEN

A broken filament is not the only reason why a bulb will not light. Let us now assume that, although the bulb in question refuses to light, the filament is still intact.

7. The filament is intact, and the bulb glass is clear

Your first thoughts in this situation should be that the bulb is not to blame. To be absolutely sure you could use an ohmmeter or circuit tester to check for continuity, or try the bulb in a circuit you know to be complete. If you are satisfied that the bulb is good, clearly your problem lies elsewhere in the system.

One of the first things it is always useful to do at the first sign of an electrical fault is quickly to check which other circuits are working, or not working, as the case may be. If you can establish whether all the lights have failed, or only those in one circuit, this will help you in your diagnosis. The most likely explanation is that the circuit is incomplete somewhere. The problem is that this can happen anywhere and for a variety of reasons. Some of the more common ones we suggest you look for are:

Cause 7.1

Very dirty, loose or open connections. Any breaks (because of loose or broken connections) or blockages (because the connection is very dirty, corroded or wet) which develop in the electricity supply wire will prevent a bulb from lighting – the electricity simply won't be able to get through to the bulb. You should pay particular attention to: (1) all the connectors in the circuit; (2) the bulb's contacts; (3) the bulb holder and its securing mechanism; (4) the earth connections.

Remedy 7.1

Any connections – and in that we include wire to wire; wire to component; wire to earth; component to component (bulb to bulb holder, for example) – which are:

1. Loose or broken should be remade. If they are insecure because they are excessively worn, they must be replaced. Packing them with Vaseline (and loose bulb holders are a good example of where this will be especially useful) may help temporarily, but in the long term they will need to be replaced.

2. Dirty, corroded or wet should be dismantled, dried (if necessary) and cleaned. If the corrosion is too bad, replace the whole connector. Finally, remake the connection and ensure it is firmly fixed. If a connector is clean, but very damp, spray it with a water dispersant and then a rubber-sealant aerosol.

You can also help protect against future corrosion by smearing all the potential trouble spots with Vaseline.

Cause 7.2

Breaks in the wiring. If the insulation around an electrical wire becomes worn or chafed as a result of being continually rubbed against something, a visual check of the circuit should reveal this with little difficulty.

However, the insulation may still be intact and yet your tests (using any one of the instruments examined on pp. 200–201) continue to indicate that there is a problem in that length of wire. If this is the case, it may be that the wire has been stretched and flexed so many times that the metal wire has broken inside the still intact sheathing.

There are three principal areas you should first suspect for worn or broken wiring:

1. The main wiring harness near the front of the fuel tank, as it bends around the headstock into the headlamp shell. This section of harness is continually bent back and forth with the steering movements: eventually, the insulation becomes worn or the wire breaks.

2. Inside the headlamp shell where the wires vibrate against the metal body of the bulb holder. The point of

entry into the headlamp is also a problem area, and wires have been known to become completely severed at this point.

3. Where the wires pass through the rear mudguard to feed the taillamp, stoplamp or rear indicators.

Remedy 7.2

If you discover a section of wire that is worn, you should either: (1) replace the section; (2) cut the wire at the worn areas and use a connector to remake the join; or (3) temporarily tape the worn area with hefty bindings of insulating tape.

However, whatever you do, you must re-route the wire. If you can re-route it satisfactorily, you will prevent this problem happening again.

On the other hand, if your investigations reveal a section which has a broken wire in it you will need either to: (1) replace the section: this is perhaps the easiest; or (2) discover precisely where the break is, cut the wire and use a connector to remake a secure joint.

Discovering the precise location of such a break, however, can be extremely difficult. Indeed, it is virtually impossible without any measuring instruments. Any of the four instruments discussed on pp. 200–201 will suffice if they have a pointed probe – one that can be pushed through the outer insulation so as to contact the wire. Use the standard techniques of progressing along a length until you narrow it down to the precise point at which the wire is broken. (For a more detailed description of this technique see p. 200.) If you do pierce the outer insulation, it is wise to coat the whole wire with something to prevent

moisture getting into the wire via the holes you have just made: rubber-sealant sprays or Vaseline will do a good job.

Cause 7.3

Blown fuse. Unless it is an in-line fuse – in which case only one light will be affected – not only will the light you are concerned with fail, but so will every other component on that circuit. Check your owner's handbook or workshop manual to establish which other items are linked to the same fuse. If a quick check of these items reveals that they too are inoperative, it is not unreasonable to assume the fuse has blown.

Remedy 7.3

Although the fuse may have failed because of old age, you should never discount the possibility that it did not; so, before you replace the fuse, it is important to consider why it may have blown in the first place. See item 14, pp. 223–4, for more details of why a fuse may blow. Once you are satisfied the circuit is in order, replace the fuse.

Cause 7.4

Switches are: (1) dirty, corroded or damp; (2) defective; or (3) incorrectly adjusted.

Causes 7.4.1,2

A dirty, corroded, damp or defective switch. A complication to (1) and (2) occurs if there is an incomplete circuit within the switch. Test for this with one of the testers discussed on pp. 200–201.

Remedies 7.4.1,2

If you do discover a continuity defect, you will need to dismantle the switch and inspect its internal wiring and contact surfaces.

Remedy 7.4.1

Dirty, corroded or damp switch contacts are a big dissipater of power within an electrical circuit, and they will need to be thoroughly cleaned and dried before you rebuild them. One of the easiest ways to clean the contacts is to scrape the dirt or corrosion away with a screwdriver blade or something similar, and then remove all final traces by rubbing the surfaces with emery paper.

If the surfaces are oily, you may need to spray them with a cleaning solvent before you begin.

Contacts or, indeed, any other parts of the switch which are damp should be sprayed with a water dispersant and then dried with a clean cloth.

Once you are confident the internal circuit and operating mechanisms are satisfactory, pack the inside of the switch with Vaseline or grease, rebuild it and secure it in position.

Remedy 7.4.2

If, having cleaned them, you find the contacts to be so worn that their surfaces no longer touch, or if you discover any other damage, you should replace the switch. Trying to do minor repairs, which are only likely to be temporary, isn't worth the time it takes, unless you have lots of time and no money. Take a trip to your local breaker's yard and ask him if he can help you out by supplying a cheap secondhand unit.

Unfortunately, however, not all switches can be opened for you to examine the inside. If this is the situation on your motorcycle, the best thing to do is to assume that the switch is dirty or damp, spray a lubricant/solvent cleaner into it and hope that this does the trick: if it doesn't, the switch will need to be replaced. Again, your local breaker's yard may be the best place to start.

Cause 7.4.3

Switch incorrectly adjusted. On the other hand, if the circuit through the switch is complete, it may be that the switch is incorrectly adjusted. Brake light switches, for example, are adjustable (Figure 59) and may become incorrectly adjusted as the brake shoes/pads wear down.

Remedy 7.4.3

As an example, let us assume that the brake lamp fails to light when you apply the brakes, and you are satisfied that the switch has a complete circuit through it when it is in the 'on' position.

1. *Rear-brake light failure.* The brake light switch can commonly be readjusted by holding the body of the switch and turning the mounting nut up or down. The lamp will light earlier the more the body is raised, the later the more it is lowered.

Your owner's handbook or workshop manual will indicate the location of this switch on your motorcycle and the precise adjustment procedure. Having made these adjustments, test its operation several times and ensure it is firmly secured in its mount. Finally, check that the bulb lights at the moment the brakes begin to act.

2. *Front-brake light failure.* The first point to make clear here is that not all motorcycles have a light at the rear

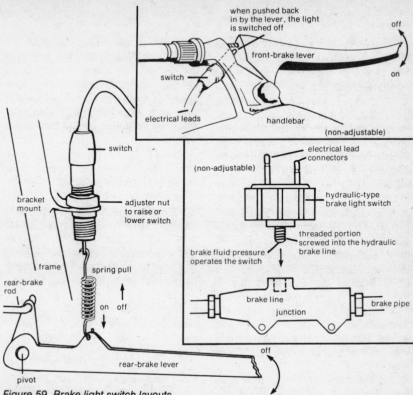

Figure 59 Brake light switch layouts, showing location and adjustment

which is activated by the front brake. Your owner's handbook or workshop manual will tell you if yours has.

On hydraulic brakes the switch will be activated by pressure, and unfortunately these can be tricky to work on – if you are in any doubt, this is one of those occasions when our advice would be to visit your local workshop.

Cable-operated brakes, however, are a different story. Usually, you will find a microswitch in the recess behind the brake lever. The exact location of this switch and the precise procedure for its adjustment do differ slightly from one machine to another, but they will be set out in your owner's handbook or workshop manual. Unfortunately, we can say little more at this point in a book of this nature, but, if you make the adjustments according to the prescribed procedure, the switch should operate correctly.

8. All the lights fail at the same time, and their filaments are intact

Cause 8.1

Blown fuse. Failure of an entire system can frequently be traced to a blown fuse in the power supply wire.

Remedy 8.1

Although your first inclination might be to replace the fuse and try another, in the hope that the existing one failed because it was old, you should resist it and take a few minutes to examine the circuit the fuse was protecting. If you simply replace the fuse, the chances are (unless your initial assumption was correct) that any subsequent fuse you insert into the circuit will also burn out. Moreover, increasing the strength of the fuse, or going as far as replacing it with a nail, etc. (which is not as uncommon as a sensible motorcylist might expect), will only lead you into far more trouble than necessary. The fuse may have blown because there is a problem in the circuit, so if you replace it with a conductor which will not burn out below (or at) the danger power level, something else in the electrical system will – which is likely to cost you a lot of money.

The details of why a fuse may blow are discussed in item 14 on pp. 223–4.

Once the underlying problem is resolved, you can replace the fuse with one recommended for use in that circuit. See your owner's handbook or workshop manual for the fuse specifications in your motorcycle.

As a temporary get-you-home-solution if you don't have a fuse of the correct size (and you are sure you have cured the original problem), a piece of thin wire (obviously, fuse wire is best if you have some) will complete the circuit and, more importantly, will burn out if there is too much current. It is important that you insert the correct fuse as soon as you get home.

Cause 8.2

Isolated battery. The battery will become isolated from the electrical system, and therefore the circuit will be broken, if either of the terminal leads' or the earth strap's connection to the frame becomes broken or extremely dirty or corroded.

Remedy 8.2

Examine the terminal connections and the earth point to see if they are clean, corrosion-free and securely attached to the battery's terminals and the frame (in the case of the earth). Any connections you suspect should be dismantled and thoroughly cleaned (see items 5.2 and 5.3 on p. 124). Finally, before and after you remake the connection, coat the terminals and the connectors with Vaseline to protect them in the future.

LIGHTING: PERFORMANCE

Not all lighting problems occur because a bulb fails to light. It may be that a bulb (or bulbs) flickers, goes dim or only goes off in specific circumstances.

9. A light flickers

Cause 9.1

Old bulb. The bulb may be about to blow: as a bulb becomes old, its circuitry frequently begins to break down before it finally blows and, as a result, it may begin to flicker. This should have no effect on any other bulbs in the circuit, that is, the remainder should light correctly if the problem bulb is flickering because it is defective.

Remedy 9.1

As we saw in item 1.1 on p. 204, old bulbs frequently have a yellowish-brown tint on the dome – if yours is darkened in this way, replace it. Not all bulbs which are about to blow, however, have the darkened dome. If yours doesn't, try flicking the envelope with your finger: the filament on a defective bulb will break off, whereas it should remain solidly in position in a good one.

Any bulbs which are defective should be replaced.

Cause 9.2

The bulb is loose in the holder. If a bulb can move around inside its holder, it may move into a position which breaks the electrical circuit. The motorcycle's movement (or its vibration – especially on older machines) may then cause this to happen so quickly that it causes the light to flicker.

Remedy 9.2

Examine the bulb and the bulb holder and make sure that the spring in the holder is strong enough to keep the plunger firmly up against the bulb's base contact. If it appears to be stiff, lubricate it with a spray cleaner/lubricant. If the spring has corroded and weakened, on the other hand, it will have to be replaced.

While you have the holder apart, check that the contact surfaces – of the bulb and the holder – are dirt-free and corrosion-free. It never does any harm to make a quick visual check.

Finally, before you replace the bulb, pack the holder with Vaseline, which will not only protect the surfaces from corrosion but will help the electrical flow and hold the bulb firmly in position.

Cause 9.3

Loose connections. If you are satisfied that the bulb is secure, you will need to check all the other connectors in that circuit, especially the earth. One of them may be loose and so, because of the motorcycle's movement or vibrations, be disconnecting intermittently. This will cause the bulb to go in and out as the connection, and therefore the circuit, is first complete then incomplete, etc. If this happens fast enough, the result will be a flickering light.

Remedy 9.3

Check all connections in the circuit, especially the earth, and secure any that are loose. For more details of loose connections see item 7.1, p. 208.

10. The lights go out if you turn the handlebars to the left or right

Cause 10.1

A fractured or broken wire at the headstock. If the wires passing around the headstock are not routed correctly, they may be stretched or flexed excessively each time you turn the handlebars to the right or left (which direction causes you most trouble will be determined by how they are routed on your motorcycle). As a result, the metal wire inside the (intact) plastic insulation may have broken. Each time the cable is now stretched, the wire will separate, the circuit will be broken and the lights will go out.

Remedy 10.1

In brief, you need either to replace that length of wire or to trace the precise location of the break (see pp. 208–9 for more detailed information) with a tester, although you may get some clues to where this is by signs of rubbing on the insulation. Now cut the wire at that point and make a secure connection.

Finally, to prevent further problems, re-route the wire to a less strenuous position.

Cause 10.2

Worn insulation. A further problem for wires passing the headstock is that the insulation around the metal wire (which incidentally remains intact) becomes worn or chafed as a result of being perpetually rubbed against the metal. Once the inner metal wire is bared, turning the handlebars causes the wire momentarily to short circuit, and thus the lights to go out. Although any one momentary short circuit may not instantly cause the fuse to blow, eventually it will blow, and then your problem will be accompanied by a blown lighting fuse.

Remedy 10.2

Visually inspect the wires passing the headstock. If there are any signs of wear you will need either to: (1) replace that section; (2) cut the wire at the worn point and remake it with a secure connector; or (3) use insulating tape to bind the worn area (a temporary solution only). Whichever solution you opt for, however, you must also re-route the wire.

Cause 10.3

Multi-pin connector loose. Occasionally, the stretching wire may open a multi-pin connector just enough to break the circuit. However, immediately the pressure is released, the connector may slip back into a position where the connection, and hence the circuit, is complete. As a result, the lights will go out as you turn the handlebars.

Remedy 10.3

Inspect any connectors in the headstock region, and ensure they are corrosion-free and securely clipped together.

Although there is no foolproof way to prevent the connector being opened, you can prevent the pressure on the connection by re-routing the wire. If the existing length of wire is too short, you might consider inserting an additional section somewhere along its length to allow you to feed the wire along a trouble-free path.

11. The lights are dim, with the horn or starter inoperative, but:

(1) they *do* become brighter as the engine is revved up

Cause 11.1

A discharged battery. When a battery is discharged, the electrical power available to operate the components requiring electrical energy is reduced. However, as you rev up, the generator (which is operated by the engine) takes over to provide all the power being demanded. Consequently, the lights brighten and the other components can now operate.

Remedy 11.1

Recharge the battery (for details of how to do this see pp. 122–4). Aside from this, however, you will also need to examine the conditions under which it became discharged and rectify the problem before you refit the newly charged battery.

Some of the reasons why a battery may become discharged are that:

1. The terminal and/or earth connections are loose; these should be cleaned, coated in Vaseline and securely refitted (see p. 124 for more details).

2. It is low on electrolyte: top up the battery to the required level (see p. 38 for more details).

3. The battery itself is faulty: unfortunately, there is little you can do but replace it (see p. 124 for more information).

4. The brake light is sticking on, continually draining the battery of all its power. Here you have a problem with the switch, which, if it cannot be freed by spraying with penetrating/lubricating oil, should be replaced.

(2) they *don't* become brighter as the engine is revved up

Cause 11.2

The charging system is inoperative. In brief, at least one component in the charging system is defective and so the discharged battery is not being recharged. Moreover, the system is not producing the electrical power being demanded by the various components, even when the engine is revved up. It is, in fact, this last point which tells you that your problem is more than a discharged battery, and one involving the whole charging system.

Remedy 11.2

The key components you should suspect are the rectifier, generator and/or regulator. Unfortunately, there are so many types, methods of incorporation into the electrical system and, therefore, possible remedies that we are unable to give a general procedure which would tell you anything worth hearing. Indeed, because of the nature of the components involved, in our opinion it would be quicker and cheaper to go to your local workshop and ask the mechanic to check the entire system.

What is required is that the defective component or components are traced and replaced. The equipment a mechanic has available will enable him to detect precisely which is (or are) defective and to make replacements only where necessary. Unless you have this equipment, replacement may be the only way for you to detect which *was* faulty; by the time you find it using this method you may have been forced to buy the component, and that will be expensive (unless you have a good friend who has a similar item on his motorcycle and will lend it to you).

LIGHTING: TIPS

Headlight failure

If either the dipped or the high beam on the headlight fails, you can always use the other beam to get home or until a replacement bulb can be obtained. The most common situation is when the dipped bulb fails. In this situation you will now have only a high beam, which will dazzle oncoming drivers if you do not angle the headlight down. This can usually be done by hand, holding the top and bottom of the headlamp unit.

Note: Don't forget to readjust the lamp's position once a new bulb is fitted.

Taillight failure

If the taillight fails, as a temporary measure the stoplight switch can be adjusted until it is on all the time. The location of this switch will be indicated in your owner's handbook or workshop manual.

IMPORTANT: Don't forget to give slowing-down signals whenever you slow down, as you have no stoplight, until a replacement bulb is fitted to the taillight.

Bulb failure in direct-lighting systems

Should a bulb fail – for any reason – in a direct-lighting system, it is likely that the excess power available will then surge through the system to the other bulbs and thus cause them to blow as well. Although, unfortunately, you will have to replace all the blown bulbs, do not do so until you have traced and rectified the reason behind the first bulb blowing. Items 1–6, discussed earlier in this chapter, will help you in this, and it is important that you do so. If you don't, you may lose a second and even a third set of bulbs.

Defective bulbs

One possibility you should not overrule in replacing a bulb is that the replacement is defective internally: despite manufacturers' strict quality control regulations, this is not unknown. Although externally it looks to be in good condition, internally there may be some defect which prevents the bulb lighting satisfactorily – if at all. As a result, if you do replace a blown bulb and you still have a problem (or indeed another problem), do not assume that the new bulb is good – check it with an appropriate instrument (see pp. 200–201) or in a circuit you know to be good. Should neither of these alternatives be possible, it may be worth your while trying a second replacement bulb to make sure: it is unlikely that both replacements will be defective.

How to improve lighting

Three of the things you can do to improve the lighting on your motorcycle are: (1) fit a light unit which is more efficient, such as a halogen unit (see p. 204) – this will give you more light for the same amount of electrical power; (2) fit a light unit or bulb with a greater wattage; or (3) fit additional lights.

Unfortunately, there are problems associated with each of these. The easiest solution is to fit a halogen unit – you avoid any complications with insufficient power, etc., by doing this. The problem is that they are not available for all motorcycles and they can be expensive.

The other two solutions, however, also have their problems: in brief, the greater wattage being demanded may stretch the electrical system too far, ultimately causing the battery to run down. Before you replace your existing bulbs with those of greater wattage, or put on extra lights, you must check the manufacturer's specifications or ask your local dealer. You now need to add up the demands currently being made on the system and find out if there is any spare capacity.

Alternators: larger motorcycles frequently have a three-phase alternator which has an output of above 150 W – this will cope with extra lighting with little difficulty. Most motorcycles with this type of alternator, however, usually have satisfactory lighting anyway. Smaller motorcycles are frequently the problem: headlamps often only put out 25–30 W on high beam and the alternator is only capable of producing 100 W. Fitting bulbs of greater wattage than the existing ones, or additional lights, will certainly put a strain on the system.

Batteries: on larger motorcycles, batteries are usually capable of holding and supplying sufficient power. Problems occur again with smaller motorcycles. Often their batteries only have a capacity of 5 amp-hours, and this, combined with low generator output, means there is nothing left for more lights.

The extra strain that your increased lighting capability will put on the battery will not only cause it to go flat, but will also result in dim lights and possibly an engine misfire.

You might consider fitting a larger battery, of, say, 10 amp-hours, which would last longer and perhaps enable you to make some changes, but don't forget that it will be physically bigger – so check that it will fit.

Although fitting a headlamp bulb that is more powerful – say, 40 or 45 W on full beam – into a system which has little to spare may stretch the alternator when you are using the high beam, so long as the low beam is within its capability, *and* you don't use the high beam for too long, you will probably be O.K.

Another way around the problem is to fit an extra light that you only use for short periods, such as spotlamps. Your motorcycle system will probably be able to cope so long as you remember: short periods only!

Sticking bulbs

Using too much pressure on bulbs which are stuck in their holders (because of corrosion, for example) can quite easily cause them to crack or smash. To prevent this, wrap two or three layers of insulating tape (or any other adhesive tape) around the envelope before you begin turning.

A quick spray of lubricant will help too.

ELECTRICS IN GENERAL

12. The horn operates very quietly or not at all

Cause 12.1

Horn push-button defective. The button may be defective because either: (1) the contacts are excessively worn, or are dirty, corroded or damp; or (2) the earth wire is corroded.

Remedy 12.1.1

If possible, strip the switch and examine the contacts; clean any that are dirty or corroded with a solvent cleaner and emery paper. Replace (if possible) any contacts which are excessively worn. If they are not replaceable, the switch itself must be replaced. Once you are sure the inside is satisfactory, pack the switch with Vaseline and reassemble it.

If the switch cannot be dismantled, try spraying a solvent cleaner and/or a water dispersant inside. If this fails to cure the problem, you will need to replace the switch.

Remedy 12.1.2

Inspect the earth wire for any signs of slackness or corrosion. If the corrosion cannot be removed, the wire will need to be replaced. Always ensure that the earth connectors are secure.

Cause 12.2

A weak battery. Quite simply, the problem here is that the battery doesn't have enough power to activate the horn.

Try revving up the engine – if the horn works satisfactorily when the alternator/generator is providing the power, the battery is at fault.

Remedy 12.2

Recharge the battery, but look for an explanation as to why it went flat in the first place and rectify the problem (see item 15, pp. 225–7).

Cause 12.3

Horn incorrectly adjusted. Constant use and vibration can result in the horn becoming incorrectly adjusted. Although this is not a common problem, it is by no means unknown.

Remedy 12.3

Your owner's handbook or workshop manual will tell you if your horn can be adjusted and how to go about this, but in most cases adjustments are made by turning a small locknut on the back of the horn itself. You will need to make adjustments while the horn is sounded, that is, while the button is being pressed. If you cannot do both yourself, you will need to enlist a friend's help. Simply turn the locknut until the horn is loud enough to be heard above the engine noise and in traffic.

Cause 12.4

Horn faulty. Like everything else on a motorcycle, the horn can be subjected to the worst our environment can throw at it: sooner or later these conditions will have an effect. The horn can become so rusted, blocked with dirt or corroded internally that eventually it cannot work.

Remedy 12.4

Try connecting the two horn contacts directly across the battery terminals: if the sound is still unsatisfactory, the horn is defective and you must replace it. Unfortunately there is no realistic way to repair this component. If a new horn is too expensive for you (although they don't cost too much), your local breaker will probably be able to help you out. Don't buy a bigger one than necessary, by the way, in the hope that it will sound louder: it will probably require far too much power for your system and so still be too quiet (if it makes a sound at all).

13. Indicator problems:
(1) One lamp not lighting

Cause 13.1.1

Defective bulb. The first thing you need to do if only one indicator fails is to remove the lens and inspect the bulb. If it has blown, as is likely, the state of the filament and the colour of the glass will tell you what actually caused the bulb to blow (see pp. 204–7).

Remedy 13.1.1

Identify the reason why the bulb blew and, if necessary, cure the problem. When you are satisfied the problem is resolved, fit a new bulb.

Cause 13.1.2

Poor earth. As we pointed out in the introduction to the chapter (see p. 200), it is vital that the current is allowed to return to earth. If it cannot do this because the connection is dirty or corroded, or loose, the component will not operate.

Remedy 13.1.2

Examine the earth connection for the lamp in question; ensure that it is securely fastened and that both the surfaces of the earth connection are clean. See item 7.1, p. 208, for more details on poor connections in general.

Cause 13.1.3

Breaks in the power supply. If you are satisfied that the bulb (see p. 207) and the lamp's earth are both satisfactory, it is likely that power is not reaching the lamp unit.

Remedy 13.1.3

Briefly, you will need to examine the circuit supplying electricity to the defective lamp. Begin at the lamp and work back towards the power supply. Firstly, ensure that all the connectors are secure and clean (see item 7.1, p. 208); secondly, inspect the wiring for signs of wear or other potential continuity problems; and then use a measuring instrument (see pp. 200–201) to check that there are no hidden breaks in the wiring (see item 7.2, pp. 208–9).

(2) Two lamps on one side not lighting

Cause 13.2.1

Defective indicator turn-switch. In the situation where two lamps on one side do not work, it is likely that one contact within the switch is burned or corroded and that, as a result, the electrical continuity to that side is broken.

Remedy 13.2.1

Dismantle the switch and inspect the contact surfaces for any signs of corrosion or burning.

1. A corroded or dirty contact should be cleaned up with a wire brush or screwdriver blade and finally rubbed with emery cloth. Before you reassemble the switch, however, it is always a good idea to pack the inside with Vaseline to prevent similar problems in future.

2. Unfortunately, if the contact is burned, then, because the contacts are usually not individually replaceable, the switch itself must be replaced.

(3) Four lamps not lighting

Cause 13.3.1

Flasher unit defective. The flasher unit (or flasher relay, as it is sometimes called) is the component which supplies power to the lamps in pulses and therefore causes them to flash. Defects in this unit, however, may mean that power is prevented from reaching the lamps at all.

Remedy 13.3.1

The first thing you need to do is to check the unit itself. There is no reason to remove the relay from the motor-cycle to do this – indeed, on the contrary, it is far easier to check while in its operating position. To do this: (1) link connector pin 'B' and pin 'L' (Figure 60) – a short piece of wire or even a pair of snipe-nose pliers (so long as you don't touch anything else) will suffice for this job; (2) switch on the ignition; and (3) operate the indicator turn-switch.

If the lamps now operate with the switch pushed to either the left or the

this lead, L, to the switch and flashers

this lead, B, carries power from the battery

wire loop

this is for earth, if fitted

flasher relay

Using a short length of wire, connect one end to terminal L and the other to terminal B. This trick bypasses the flasher relay and directs power straight to the flasher switch. With the loop connected, if all flashers light but do not flash, the flasher relay is faulty

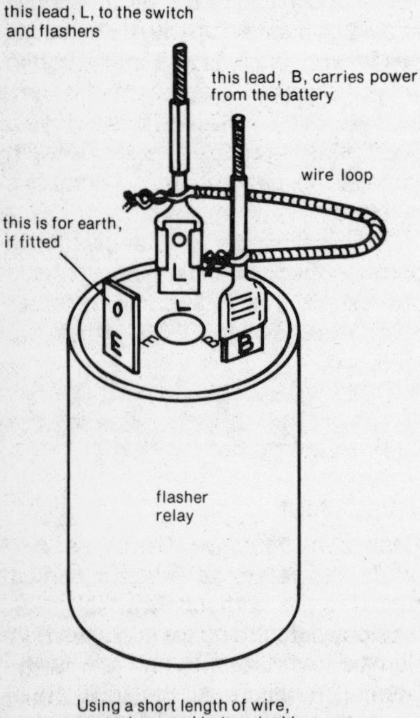

Figure 60 Wire loop test, for when all four flashers are not working

right, the unit is defective and must be replaced. They are supplied as a sealed unit and it is a waste of time even to consider trying to repair the old one.

On the other hand, if the lamps still fail to operate, it is far more likely that the problem is due to a power supply failure. In brief, you must trace and repair the defect.

Cause 13.3.2

Blown indicator fuse (if fitted). Increasingly, indicator circuits are being fitted with their own in-line fuse. If yours has one, and it has blown, none of the lamps will light. Your owner's handbook or workshop man-ual will tell you if your motorcycle has such a fuse and where it is located.

Remedy 13.3.2

Examine the fuse and replace it with one of the same capacity, if it has blown. Before you do so, however, it is worth spending a few minutes to establish why it blew in the first place. If it was on account of anything other than old age, you must identify the specific problem and rectify it (see item 8.1, pp. 211–12, and item 14, pp. 223–4).

Cause 13.3.3

Open circuit. The continuity of a circuit may be broken in several ways: by very dirty, loose or broken connectors; by a worn or chafed section of wire; or by breaks in the metal wiring within the plastic insulation. Any of these are capable of severely restricting, or stop-ping, the electrical flow and hence preventing the indicators from lighting.

Remedy 13.3.3

Visually inspect the indicator circuit for any signs of loose, broken or dirty connectors, which you will need to clean and/or secure, or worn sections of wiring. If you do discover a point or points worn through to the metal wire, you will need either to tape the area (temporarily!) and cut and remake the wire point with a connector, or to replace the worn section with a new length of wire.

Finally, use a measuring instrument (see pp. 200–201) to check for continuity inside what appears to be intact lengths of insulation. In this situation you will need to locate the precise position of the break (see p. 209) and repair it, or simply replace the entire section.

See items 7.1 and 7.2 on pp. 208–9 for a fuller discussion of these possible causes.

Cause 13.3.4

A totally corroded indicator turn-switch. Although this is rarely the cause, it is certainly not unknown. It is rare because usually one side of the switch will become corroded and lead to two lamps on one side not lighting (item 13.2) before it affects both contacts.

On the other hand, if the motorcycle has been stored for some time (the winter months, for example), it is quite likely that both sides will have become corroded.

Remedy 13.3.4

If the switch can be dismantled, do so, and clean up the contacts. Pack it with Vaseline before you rebuild and replace it (see p. 210).

Should you be unable to dismantle the switch, however, try spraying a lubricant cleaner inside and then leaving it for a while to soak in. If this does not solve the problem, unfortunately you will need to replace the switch.

(4) Four lamps lighting but not flashing

Cause 13.4.1

Battery in poor (discharged) condition. The problem here arises because, although it has enough power to light the lamps, the battery simply does not have the energy to activate the relay unit. One way to test for this quickly is to rev up the engine: if the indicators then operate normally, the battery *is* discharged.

Remedy 13.4.1

Recharge the battery (see pp. 122–4 for details of how to do this correctly). However, it may also be necessary to investigate why the power was low in the first place. If the electrolyte level was below what is required, top it up and keep a close eye on the situation throughout the next week. If the problem occurs again, with the electrolyte at a satisfactory level, you will need to identify and rectify the underlying problem. It may be that the battery is old and is simply worn out (which will mean replacement), but you should establish the source of the problem as soon as possible. See pp. 225–6 for more details.

Cause 13.4.2

Poor earth in the circuit. There is an easy way to test if the circuit is earthed correctly; you need to: (1) remove the lenses from the front and rear indicators; (2) switch on the ignition; (3) move the indicator turn-switch to the right-hand side; (4) take a length of electrical wire and hold one end against a clean part of the engine; (5) hold the other end of the wire against the body of the bulb holder in the front lamp.

If this lamp has a faulty earth, the right-hand side should start flashing. If the front right-hand side doesn't start flashing, you will need to test the rear lamp in the same manner. Should the indicator now begin to flash, the earthing problem is at the rear.

Remedy 13.4.2

Having established which of the indicators is causing the problem, you must either check and ensure that its original earth is clean and secure, or fit a secondary earth from the lamp to a clean area of the engine or the frame.

Cause 13.4.3

Faulty flasher unit. If you suspect that the flasher unit is responsible, unfortunately there is no way of confirming that suspicion without checking by replacement.

Remedy 13.4.3

Replace the existing unit with one you know to be good, either new or secondhand (so long as it is guaranteed). If the indicators now operate normally, secure the new relay in position and throw the old one away – it's no good!

(5) Four lamps lighting very dimly, but not flashing

If your motorcycle is suffering from this problem, it is principally because the causes outlined in 13.4 are more severe, so that even less electrical power is reaching the lamps: the result is that they not only fail to flash but are also very dim. See items 13.4.1–13.4.3 for more information on how accurately to diagnose and to resolve this problem.

(6) Flasher unit buzzes continually when the indicators are used

Cause 13.6.1

Poor earth on the flasher unit. If the indicators refuse to flash, and you can hear a buzzing noise from the flasher unit, you can be almost certain that the relay's earth connection is either corroded or loose.

Remedy 13.6.1

How you go about resolving this problem depends on the type of relay fitted to your motorcycle. Some motorcycles have a visible earth connector as a third pin on the front of the relay, and use a wire to make the link to the frame, but others rely on the unit being earthed via its aluminium body.

If the unit on your motorcycle is earthed by the visible wire, inspect the connections and ensure they are clean and secure at the unit and the frame. On the other hand, if your unit relies on being earthed through its body, you can check the quality of the earth by running a temporary secondary earth from the relay body to the engine – it will be sufficient simply to hold it in position with your hands, provided the spots you touch at both ends are clean. If the noise stops and the lamps flash, poor earthing is the problem. You can solve the problem permanently by loosening the grip of the unit's holder, slipping the secondary earth wire under the holder and securing it. However, you must first secure the other end of the wire to a clean point on the frame.

(7) Flasher unit buzzes, but only when the indicators on one side are used

Cause 13.7.1

Shorted power supply to the lamps on the side, causing the buzzing. The fact that the buzzing occurs only when you use the indicators on one side not only shows that the problem is caused by a short circuit, but also tells you which side of the wiring to inspect – the side causing the problem. However, you can narrow it down even more by disconnecting the power supply to the front lamp and switching on the ignition and the indicators. If the rear lamp lights, and the buzzing stops, the short is in the wiring supply to the front lamp. If the buzzing continues, however, you can assume that the short is in the circuit going to the rear lamp.

Remedy 13.7.1

First, visually inspect the wiring supplying the defective section of the circuit. If this reveals nothing, you will need to check the wiring with a test lamp or ohmmeter, etc. (see pp. 200–201). Once you have located the short, you can effect a temporary repair by winding several layers of insulating tape round the wire. For a more permanent solution, however, cut the wire at the short and remake it with a secure connector. You should also try re-routing that wire to prevent it happening again. For more information on tracking down and repairing shorts see item 14 below.

14. Continually blowing fuses

Fuses are an extremely important part of the electrical system. Designed to burn out quickly if too much current passes through, they protect the electrical system from damage. Whenever a fuse blows, it almost certainly means you have a problem within that circuit.

Cause 14.1

Short circuit. Generally speaking, fuses only blow when they are overloaded and not because they deteriorate. What you are looking for if successive fuses blow is a short within the system – either through faulty components or, more commonly, through chafed wires shorting to earth prematurely.

A short circuit occurs when electricity by-passes part of the circuit, resulting in the build-up of heat, and can be likened to a leak from a water pipe which causes damage.

Some points to bear in mind, and areas to check, when you are looking for a short

1. Checking for a possible short circuit can be quite straightforward if you use logical, exhaustive search methods.

2. Did you operate any electrical equipment just before the fuse blew? If so, the fault is probably in the circuit supplying it.

3. Have you just been working on a piece of equipment or a component, or have you fitted any electrical accessories? If so, that circuit should be investigated.

4. Certain sections of the wiring are more susceptible to wear and chafing than others: (a) the headlamp area is

a well-known troublespot – because of the constant pulling back and forth when the handlebars are turned from left to right, the wires are often worn where they pass through the shell of the headlamp; (b) where the rear lighting wires pass through the rear mudguard is also a particular problem area – this problem can be further exaggerated if the mudguard is bent or loose, as this will increase the chafing taking place; (c) where the wires pass through the aluminium wire holders often used to secure them at various points.

5. Most modern motorcycles have separate fuses for the taillight, headlight, indicators and main system, and they are clearly marked as such. In this situation you are directed to the problem circuit at once.

6. Another of the prime problem areas is the battery and its terminals: they, or the earth contact at the frame, may be loose or corroded.

Also, if the battery's terminals are linked by anything metal, such as a screwdriver, this too will short out the system. So if you do store any tools under the seat, that is, near the battery, make sure they are securely held down.

Tracking down a short in the wiring

1. *Visual checks.* If a short is bad enough to cause a fuse to blow, then, once you have located the general area, it will almost certainly be visible. However, if this inspection reveals nothing, you must check the system with a continuity tester.

2. *Instrument checks.* If you do not have a purpose-built continuity tester, you can make one from components on your motorcycle and a couple of other items you will almost certainly have available (see pp. 236–7 for details). It is essential that you work your way through the suspect circuit carefully and logically. Move from one point to another, using the techniques described on p. 200 until the section containing the short is identified. You can then either stop there or continue to work until you find the precise location of the short.

Remedy 14.1

Having located the short you can either: (1) make a temporary repair by covering the area with insulating tape; (2) replace the relevant section between one convenient connector and another; or (3) cut the wire at the point of the short and fit a secure connector to make a good joint.

It is then a good idea to re-route the wire/cable to prevent it happening again.

Once you are satisfied the underlying cause is now cured, you can replace the fuse. Should this situation arise, and you don't have a spare, a piece of thin wire (preferably fuse wire, but any will do) or even a piece of silver paper will suffice to get you home. *Never* replace a broken fuse with an uprated fuse, that is, one which will take more amps, or another piece of metal, such as a nail. Although these blunders are not as uncommon as you may think, and will certainly allow the current to keep flowing, the excess power will ultimately cause another component to break down. It may be something like a voltage regulator, and that would be very expensive.

15. Battery problems

The most accurate way to determine a battery's state of charge is to test the specific gravity of the electrolyte with a hydrometer. If the battery is in good condition, the specific gravity should be between 1·26 and 1·28, depending on the temperature, and it should not vary from one cell to another. A lower specific gravity means that the battery is discharged. When you recharge a battery, always try to do it at the slowest possible rate – 0·5–1 A would be ideal.

For more details of battery servicing see pp. 38–9.

(1) The battery runs down quickly while you are riding, but recovers a little if the engine is left switched off for a while

Cause **15.1.1**

Defective charging system. In brief, the problem here is that the power being taken from the battery is not being replaced, because of a defect in the recharging system. The prime suspects for this defect are: (1) the rectifier; (2) the generator; or (3) a breakdown in the wiring.

However, although it is possible for you to check the circuit wiring, checking the rectifier and the generator is really best left to a mechanic. He will be able to locate the problem precisely and quickly – and hence relatively cheaply.

Remedy **15.1.1**

In brief, replace any faulty components or repair any wiring problems (see items 7.1 and 7.2, pp. 208–9 for more details of wiring difficulties.)

Either do it yourself or, if you have used a mechanic to track down the problem, ask him to effect the repair as well.

(2) The battery runs down quickly, and remains completely flat until recharged, after which it runs down again

Cause **15.2.1**

Faulty battery. There can be little doubt here that the battery is defective. However, one way to make absolutely sure is to recharge the battery (see pp. 122–4 for details on how to go about this) and leave it out of the motorcycle overnight. If, when you return, it is flat again, it is surely defective.

Remedy **15.2.1**

The only thing to do with a battery in this condition is to throw it away and buy a new one.

(3) The battery runs down quickly after being recharged and reconnected to the motorcycle – even though nothing electrical is being used

Cause **15.3.1**

Defective rectifier. It is likely that electrical power is leaking out of the rectifier and so draining the battery, even though no electrical items are being used. You can easily tell if it is the rectifier by isolating it from the system – ensure that the battery is fully charged and disconnect the wire at the rectifier (your owner's handbook or workshop manual will tell you where it is located), but leave the battery connected to the motorcycle's electrical system. When you return to check the battery the next morning, it should still be fully charged. If it is, the rectifier is at fault. If not, the battery itself is likely to be defective.

Remedy 15.3.1

Unfortunately, the only solution to a defective rectifier is to replace it. However, a defective rectifier should not prevent you from using your motorcycle until you can afford to replace it, and that may be some time as they are expensive items. The answer is to leave the rectifier connected while you are riding, but to disconnect it whenever you leave the motorcycle for more than a moment. You could disconnect one of the battery terminals (it would have the same effect), but unplugging the rectifier is probably easier. In this way, you can continue to use your motorcycle and keep the battery charged. Strange as it may seem, it is not unknown for switches to be fitted into the rectifier wiring so that it can actually be switched off – unusual, perhaps, but certainly cheaper than a new rectifier.

(4) The battery runs down only when the lights are being used

Cause 15.4.1

The charging system is operating, but not at 100 per cent. It is possible that although the charging system is operating enough to replace the power used in running the engine, it is not producing enough to replace that being used by the lights. Ultimately, then, the battery will become discharged.

The most likely source of your problem here is a fault in the wiring to the rectifier, or the rectifier itself, although in rare cases it may be the generator which is defective.

Remedy 15.4.1

The first thing to do is to inspect all the wiring and connections running from the rectifier to the wiring harness. Obviously, any broken wires or connectors need to be replaced or resecured, and any dirty connectors should be cleaned thoroughly.

On the other hand, if this inspection reveals nothing, you must suspect the rectifier. However, unless you have a friend with a similar component, who will lend it to you to try in your own motorcycle, you will be forced to go to your local workshop and ask the mechanic to check it for you.

Clearly, if it is defective, it will need to be replaced – although there are temporary ways around this (see remedy 15.3.1). Finally, if both wiring and rectifier are satisfactory, the generator must be checked; again, you will need a mechanic to do it accurately. If it is defective, it must be replaced.

Cause 15.4.2

Excessive lights. If you fit extra lights that are too powerful for the battery, the charging system will be unable to cope and using them will simply flatten your battery.

Remedy 15.4.2

You will need either to reduce the lighting to a level your existing system can cope with, or to increase the capacity of the battery and the generator/alternator to deal with the extra lights. Simply increasing the battery's capacity, however, will not be enough.

(5) The battery constantly needs topping up

Cause 15.5.1

The electrolyte is 'boiling'. If too much electrical power reaches the battery, the electrolyte will overheat and actually boil in the battery. As it does so, the liquid will evaporate. The result is a fall in the electrolyte level.

The two most likely explanations for this amount of power reaching the battery are that: (1) the voltage regulator is defective and not switching sufficient power to earth; or (2) the generator is defective, that is, it is pumping out too many amps for the electrical system to cope with.

Remedy 15.5.1

Really, the best way to resolve this is to approach your local workshop and ask the mechanic to test the two components for you. Once the defective one is identified, either you or the mechanic will need to replace it.

Cause 15.5.2

Battery casing damaged. There is no mystery about this cause. Quite simply, the battery casing is cracked or damaged severely enough for the liquid to leak out. A quick glance under the battery should tell you if this is happening – you should see signs of electrolyte below.

Remedy 15.5.2

Remove the battery from the motorcycle and repair the damage (see p. 38).

16. The oil warning light stays on

Although this may be an electrical problem – the switch may be defective – it is unlikely to be one, and you certainly should not assume such to be the case. You must stop immediately and investigate. The most obvious explanation is likely to be the true one in this situation: you are so low on oil that the pressure has dropped to a critical level. Continuing to ride risks engine seizure, which would do great damage to the engine (see p. 252).

Cause 16.1

Faulty switch. However, if you are convinced that the entire lubrication system is satisfactory, you can suspect the switch.

Remedy 16.1

In brief, the switch will need to be replaced. Your owner's handbook or workshop manual will indicate its precise location and the replacement procedure. This can be a difficult job, and it would be a shame to do it for no reason, so we feel it necessary to stress once again that you make sure the lubrication system is in good order before you suspect the switch.

17. The starter motor is sluggish

Cause 17.1

Discharged battery. Quite simply, if the battery power is diminished even slightly, then, because it demands so much power to operate, the starter motor will appear sluggish and probably fail to turn over.

Remedy 17.1

If your machine fails to start after several presses of the start-button, it is essential that you discontinue using the electric starter and try using the kickstart, if one is fitted. If your machine is not fitted with a kickstart, leave the bike for a few minutes and allow the battery to recover slightly. If it fails to recover sufficiently, however, you will need to either bump- or jump-start the motorcycle to get you home (see pp. 234–5 and p. 240). Once you do get home, you must check the electrolyte level in the battery and recharge it (see pp. 122–4 for details of how this should be done).

Cause 17.2

Worn starter motor brushes. Excessively worn brushes within the motor mean that insufficient power is produced to make it spin. It is unusual for this problem to appear suddenly: it can almost always be detected in advance as starting becomes increasingly difficult and the starter becomes sluggish.

Remedy 17.2

Remove the starter from the engine unit and dismantle it. If, on inspection, the brushes appear excessively worn (and their recommended length will be indicated in your owner's handbook or workshop manual), they should be replaced and the unit refitted.

CHAPTER SEVEN
TIPS AND TRICKS

In this final chapter some of the tips and tricks which help professional mechanics and everyday motorcyclists maintain, repair and enjoy motorcycles have been gathered together.

Although the overall range of these tips and tricks is very wide, they do fall into three broad categories: (1) maintenance and repair; (2) engine efficiency; and (3) motorcycling in general. Below is a list of the specific tips and tricks covered within each category, and for reference convenience they have been arranged alphabetically.

MAINTENANCE AND REPAIR

	Page
Auto-lube systems: two-strokes only	
Air locks	231
Brakes	
Excessive lever/pedal travel	231
Grabbing	232
Sticking	232
Squeal	232
Loss of stopping power	233
Bleeding hydraulic brakes	233
Bulbs and lights	
A better earth, fewer failures	234
Using cheap bulbs	234
Fitting additional lamps	234
Bump-starting	
How it's done	234
Chains	
Old chains	235
	Page
Spare chain links	235
Circuit test lamp	235
Cleaning your motorcycle	
Twelve tips	235
Clutch	
Broken lever	237
Forks	
Bottoming out	237
Gaskets	
Copper head-gaskets	237
Gear levers	
Lost lever	237
Gear-changing difficulties	237
Generator rotor	
Removal	238
Glass fibre repairs	
Surface damage or chips	238
Holes	238
Splits or cracks	238
Handlebar grips	
Removing grips	238
Refitting grips	239
Loose grips	239
Insulation	
Broken wires	240
Jump-starting	
How it's done	240
Lubrication	
The purpose of oil	240
Grades of oil	240
Storing your motorcycle	241
Oil additives	241
Keep the oil clean	241
Changing the type of oil	241
A mobile oil supply	241
Nuts, bolts and screws	
Preventing corrosion	241
Think before you get tough	242

Page

Removing stubborn nuts, bolts
and screws 242
Cleaning the threads 243
Applying heat 243
Stripped threads 243
Broken screws or bolts 243
Putting screws into awkward
places 244
Locating small screws 244
Plastic parts
Removing scuffs 244
Routine maintenance
Do it cool 244
Seat covers
Repairing rips, tears or leaks 244
Silencer baffles
Removal 244
Split pins
Replacing split pins 245
Throttle cables
Broken cables 245
Replacing throttle cables 245
Tyres and wheels
Tyre removal 245
Tyre refitting 246
Tubeless tyres 248
Repairing a puncture 249
Wheel rims 249
How to get more miles per
tyre 250
Washers
Placing washers on difficult
bolts 250

ENGINE EFFICIENCY

Carburettor
Take care when washing your
machine 250
Make sure the carburettor is
securely fastened 250
Petrol leakages 251
Dirt in the float bowl 251
Combustion: normal and
abnormal

Page

Normal combustion 251
Detonation 251
Pre-ignition 252
Contact breakers (points)
The points gap 252
Engine efficiency
One way to improve it 252
Engine seizure: causes and
remedies
What is it? 252
Why does it occur? 252
Running-in 253
Symptoms 253
Are two-strokes more prone to
seizure? 254
A temporary solution: two-
strokes only 254
Repairing the damage 254
Exhaust fumes
Four-stroke engines 255
Two-stroke engines 256
Fuel taps
Traditional or vacuum-
operated 257
Ignition
Transistorized ignitions 258
Instability
The motorcycle is unstable at
high speed 258
The motorcycle wanders at
low speed 259
The front wheel vibrates
and/or jumps when you
brake 259
Noises 260
Pinking 261
Backfiring 261
Spitting back 261
Rattles 261
Rustling or tapping 262
Rumbling 262
Knocking 262
High-frequency noises 262
Ticking 262
High-pitched squeaks 262

	Page
Slapping	263
Screeching	263
Whining	263
A high-pitched scream	263
A heavy thumping in time with the engine	263
Petrol	
Five tips on how to save petrol	263
Spark plugs	
Operating conditions	264
The heat ranges	264
Cold plugs	265
Hot plugs	265
Dimensions	265
Never lubricate spark plug threads	267
Storing your motorcycle	267
Suppressors	
Metal-shielded caps	267

MOTORCYCLING IN GENERAL

	Page
Funnels	
A home-made funnel	267
Riding off-road	
Preparation	267
Spare cables	268
Shabby bikes	268
Everyone falls off	269
Take a friend	269
Sidecars	
Driving an outfit	269
Sidecars and the law	269
Taking care of your sidecar	269
Tools	
Normal day-to-day riding	270
Long-distance trips and touring	270
Tools to be used at home	270
General tool tips	271
Visors, goggles and shields, etc.	271
Misty visors, goggles or glasses, etc.	271

	Page
Scratched visors, goggles, plastic glasses, etc.	271
What to wear	272
In fine weather	272
In the cold and/or rain	272

MAINTENANCE AND REPAIR

AUTO-LUBE SYSTEMS: TWO-STROKES ONLY

Air locks

If for any reason the oil pipes have been disconnected, or the oil tank has been allowed to run dry, when you refill it air will be trapped within the system, particularly the pump. You must bleed this air out immediately, otherwise oil will not be pumped to, and around, the engine. The result – if it has not already happened – will be engine seizure.

Your owner's handbook or workshop manual will give you detailed instructions on how to bleed your particular system but, in brief, you need to locate and remove the oil pump bleed screw – this is usually fitted with a red fibre washer – and allow the oil slowly to run out. After about one minute, all the air locked in the system and pump will have escaped and you can then replace the bleed screw and top up the oil tank.

BRAKES

Excessive lever/pedal travel

Hydraulic brakes

Excessive travel on hydraulic brakes may be caused by one or more of the following: (1) worn disc pads – which you must replace; (2) air in the system

– which you must bleed out; (3) a leak in the master cylinder or caliper seal – which you must replace.

Cable brakes

Excessive travel on cable-operated brakes will occur: (1) when the pads/shoes are worn; (2) if the cables have stretched. If the adjusters fail to take up this travel, you must replace the component at fault.

Grabbing

If, when you apply gentle pressure to the brake lever or pedal, the brake suddenly grabs, this may be because:

1. There is grease or oil on the friction surface of the brake shoe or pad. Many methods have been tried to remove this grease but, generally speaking, none are satisfactory. Really, replacement of the shoe or pad is the only effective solution and certainly the one to be recommended.

2. The brake drum is not round. If this is the case, you will be able to see areas inside the drum which appear high or shiny. The solution is to have the drum machined round again at a good engineering workshop.

3. Dust from the friction material has built up inside the drum. This should be cleaned out as soon as possible. You must take care, however, when doing this – do not blow it out or use an air line, as the material from which the dust comes is largely asbestos, which is highly dangerous if you breathe it in. Gently wipe out the dust using a very clean, dry rag.

Sticking

If your brake shoes are sticking, it may be because:

1. The brake shoes are worn so much that the brake cam, when turning to open the brake shoes, moves too far to be returned by spring tension (as normally happens).

2. A lack of lubrication is causing the brake cam spindle to stick in its locating hole.

3. The brake shoe return springs are broken or weak. These springs are attached to both of the brake shoes and are designed to pull the brake shoes away from the brake drum when the lever or pedal is released.

4. The cables, which operate the brakes, have become stiff because they are dry or rusty inside the sheathing. The continued operation of brake cables in this condition will eventually cause the cable to fray and snap. This can easily be prevented by keeping all cables well lubricated (see 'Routine maintenance', p. 42).

Squeal (Figure 61)

Disc brakes

On disc brakes the squeal is caused by the brake pad vibrating in the caliper: a light smear of high-melting-point grease or a copper brake grease on the *back* of the brake pad (NOT THE FRICTION SIDE) will cure this.

Drum brakes

On drum brakes the squeal is caused by either: (1) dust inside the drum, which you must clean out as soon as possible; (2) the leading edge of the shoe vibrating against the rotating drum – a chamfer filed on the leading and trailing edges of the frictional material (of each shoe) will cure this; (3) a dry pivot and actuating point in the brake drum – a smear of grease on the cam and pivot will cure this.

Figure 61 Brake squeal: brake shoes (top); brake pads (bottom)

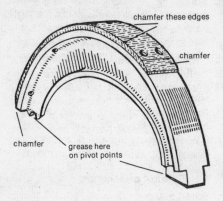

chamfer these edges

chamfer

chamfer

grease here
on pivot points

grease here
to avoid squeal

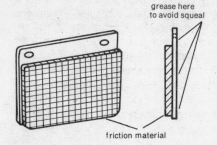

friction material

Loss of stopping power

This may be caused by (1) the lever and/or pedals being poorly adjusted; (2) oil or water on the friction surfaces; (3) the cam spindle, cables or operating linkages being dry or seized; (4) worn-out linings or pads.

Bleeding hydraulic brakes

Because of the positioning of the reservoir and the caliper, pumping air out of the bleed nipple on the hydraulic brake system of a motorcycle is sometimes a problem. Below are some tips on how to make it a little easier.

Front brakes

On the front brake the problem occurs because the caliper is lower than the master cylinder. Attempts to pump the air out of the bleed nipple are often unsuccessful because, each time you release the (brake) lever (after squeezing it to force fluid down towards the nipple), the air simply rises back up the pipe and hence never actually reaches the exit hole on the bleed nipple.

The solution is to close off the bleed nipple and to make the air travel *up* the pipe and out of the master cylinder. To do this you must:

1. Make sure all the pipes, pipe bolts and especially the bleed nipple are securely fastened.

2. Cover all the paintwork in the area of the master cylinder with old rags to prevent any spilt fluid reaching the paint: brake fluid is an excellent paint remover.

3. Fill up the reservoir on the master cylinder.

4. Repeatedly pull in and release the brake lever (you need only pull in about ½ to ¾ in. before you release). Every time the lever is released, the air will rise a little. If you continue to jiggle the lever in this manner, you will eventually see bubbles on the surface as the air escapes.

5. Continue to pull and release the lever until the bubbles stop. The system should now be free from any pockets of air.

6. The fluid remaining in the system, however, will have become aerated. So, for safety reasons, this fluid must either be left to stand for twenty-four hours or removed. To remove the fluid, spoon out as much as you can from the reservoir and refill it with fresh

fluid. The brake will now be safe and should have lost that springy feeling.

Rear brakes

Rear brakes can usually be bled using the bleed nipple, but if there is an upward bend in the pipe, between the master cylinder and the caliper, removing all the air may be a problem. Two basic solutions to this are available. In the first, you must:

1. Remove the caliper-securing bolts and allow the caliper to hang down below the master cylinder, with the pipe as straight as possible.

2. Place a wedge of cardboard between the two brake pads – this will prevent the caliper pistons pushing out too far.

3. Fill the master cylinder and operate the rear-brake pedal in the same way as described for the front-brake lever in items (4) and (5) above.

4. Do not forget to remove the cardboard before remounting the caliper.

In the second method you must:

1. Remove the caliper from the disc.

2. Use a tyre-lever between the pads to force the pistons back into their cylinders, and the fluid up towards the master cylinder.

3. Depress the rear-brake pedal to push the pistons out of the caliper.

4. Again use the tyre-lever to force the pistons back into the caliper.

5. After repeating this operation a few times you should see air bubbles come to the surface of the fluid in the master cylinder. If you continue until the bubbles stop, the system should be free of air and have lost that springy feel.

6. Either leave the fluid to stand undisturbed in the system for twenty-four hours, or spoon fluid out of the master cylinder and replace as much as you can.

BULBS AND LIGHTS

A better earth, fewer failures

Smearing the bulb's metal body with grease or Vaseline will ensure a good earth between the bulb and the socket, lessen the vibrations which cause premature bulb failure and help prevent corrosion.

Using cheap bulbs

Never economize by using a low-capacity pilot bulb. Fit a bulb of at least 6 W, preferably more. A dim pilot bulb is very difficult to see, and dangerous.

Fitting additional lamps

When you are fitting additional lights, a useful pick-up point for the wiring is one of the ammeter terminals. Remember to earth these lights correctly and securely. Also, it may be necessary to use a relay; if you are unsure check with your local dealer.

BUMP-STARTING: HOW IT'S DONE

If, for some reason, your motorcycle refuses to start in the normal way, the engine may turn over and fire if you bump-start it: that is, start your motorcycle without using the kickstart or electric starter.

To bump-start your motorcycle:

1. Pick a quiet spot in the road, preferably with a slight decline.

2. While standing at the side of the motorcycle, engage first gear.

3. Using the handlebars, pull the motorcycle backwards a little until you feel resistance.

4. Pull in and hold the clutch lever.

5. Continue pulling the motorcycle backwards until it moves quite freely. This means that the clutch has fully

disengaged itself. The motorcycle is now ready to be started.

6. Ensure that the ignition and fuel are on, and that the choke is in the appropriate position.

7. Still holding in the clutch, push the motorcycle forward and build up to a speed where you are running.

8. Jump aboard the motorcycle and, at the moment your weight hits the seat, release the clutch. The momentum of the motorcycle should jerk the engine into life, while your weight landing on the seat will help prevent the rear wheel skidding.

9. Once the engine is running, pull in the clutch and use both brakes to stop the motorcycle.

10. Select neutral and run the engine until it is warm. If you use the choke, don't forget to turn it off, and away you go.

CHAINS

Old chains

Don't throw away any old chains: always keep one to help you refit a cleaned or a new one.

Spare chain links

Always carry a spare link or two. Keep one on your key ring and another with your tools or attached to the motorcycle, perhaps to a cable or the helmet lock (if fitted). If you have to use one at any time, replace it as soon as possible.

CIRCUIT TEST LAMP

A quick and easy test lamp can be made from a length of electrical wire, a bulb – from one of the indicators, for example – and a piece of insulating tape (Figure 62): (1) bare both ends of the wire and tape one to the body of the bulb; (2) earth the tip of the bulb on a good, clean metal surface of the motorcycle; (3) hold the other end of the wire against the connector on the lead you wish to check. The bulb will light if power is reaching that point.

Note: By using a bulb from your own

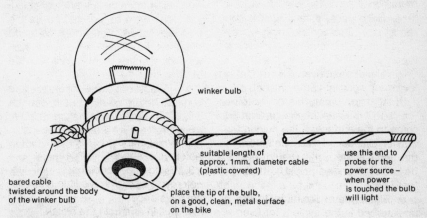

winker bulb

suitable length of approx. 1mm. diameter cable (plastic covered)

use this end to probe for the power source – when power is touched the bulb will light

bared cable twisted around the body of the winker bulb

place the tip of the bulb, on a good, clean, metal surface on the bike

Note! By using a bulb from your machine, you are sure of having a bulb of the correct voltage

Figure 62 Circuit tester

motorcycle you are sure of having one which is of the correct voltage.

CLEANING YOUR MOTORCYCLE: TWELVE TIPS

Twelve tips to help you keep your motorcycle in good condition:

1. You should clean your motorcycle regularly – if possible, once a week.

2. Regular cleaning not only helps you prevent rust and stop corrosion, but also gives you the opportunity to check nuts, bolts and spokes for tightness and to replace any which may be missing.

3. The constant use of chrome cleaner will eventually cut through the chrome on your motorcycle, leaving only the nickel base, which is the colour of brass. The answer is to use chrome cleaner only occasionally, to polish up the surface of neglected chrome. Having done this, you can then keep the chrome looking nice by using an ordinary car body wax. Your chrome will certainly last much longer if you do.

4. Brillo pads, or any similar soap pads, are ideal for cleaning up corroded or rusted chrome and aluminium.

5. Never paint over loose or flaking paint – it will only come off soon after.

6. If any paintwork becomes chipped it must be touched up immediately to prevent rust.

7. If any signs of rust do appear on the paintwork, you should remove them as soon as possible. Rub the area right down to the bare metal, treat it with some form of anti-rust material and respray.

8. Side panels can be covered in clear Fablon to prevent gradual deterioration; or, if you prefer, you could cover the vulnerable areas with colourful stickers.

9. You can protect other exposed and vulnerable parts of your motorcycle by coating them with a thin layer of grease. This is especially useful in winter, when the weather can be particularly hard on chrome and paintwork. Although it may become dirty and black, the grease will prevent any dirt, salt or moisture reaching and possibly damaging the chrome or paintwork. What is more, it can easily be washed off at a convenient time.

Some items you should consider covering are: the mudguards (especially if they are chrome); a carrying rack; the exhaust system; all exposed nuts, bolts or screws; the swinging arm; all springs – for example, on the stands, the rear-brake cable, the rear-brake light switch, etc.; all exposed sections of cable, etc.

10. When you're washing your motorcycle, try to keep water off the carburettor and the electrics, and certainly don't apply the hose pipe directly on to these areas. If the motorcycle won't start immediately after washing, you don't have to look too far for the possible cause. You should also be prepared for a lack of brakes after washing – check them before you ride off.

11. Gunk is an excellent grease and general dirt remover, but it can be difficult to apply in some places. Try using an old paint brush or, better still, pour Gunk into a hand-held garden spray: they don't cost too much and allow you to spray the liquid into the most inaccessible places.

12. Once all the dirt and old grease has been removed, don't forget to apply fresh coats of oil and grease. It is important that the drive chain, swinging-arm bearings, brake and

clutch lever adjusters, and any exposed cables, for example, are all well lubricated after you've finished washing your machine. Your owner's handbook or workshop manual will indicate where the main lubrication points are on your motorcycle.

CLUTCH

Broken lever

On most motorcycles with drum brakes on the front, the brake and clutch levers are interchangeable. The temporary solution to a broken clutch lever is to remove the front-brake lever, turn it upside-down and use this to replace the broken clutch lever. This will allow you to ride home *steadily* using only the rear brake. You must, of course, replace the broken lever before venturing out on the machine again.

FORKS

Bottoming out

If your forks bottom out (that is, they knock when you are going over rough roads or when you brake heavily), they are possibly short of oil and should be replenished with an oil of the correct grade as soon as possible. The capacities of motorcycle forks do differ from one machine to another, so be sure to use the correct amount. Your owner's handbook or workshop manual will indicate which oil and how much of it you will need. Although there are some exceptions (for example, the heavy superbikes or competition dirt bikes), most forks will function quite happily on the general-purpose fork oil sold by most dealers. However, if you can't get hold of a recommended fork oil, automatic transmission fluid will do just as well. Provided you use the correct amount, your forks will perform normally and often this fluid is much cheaper than recommended fork oils.

GASKETS

Copper head-gaskets

Although these gaskets can be reused, they will require softening – 'annealing', to give it its correct name – before you do so. To anneal a gasket the whole thing must be heated up until it is glowing red, and then immediately plunged into cold water. This isn't as difficult as it may sound. It can easily be done by heating the gasket on the kitchen cooker rings and using a pair of pliers to pick it up and plunge it into a sinkful of cold water.

Softening the copper allows it to be compressed when the cylinder head bolts are tightened. As it is being compressed the gasket fills out any slight unevenness in the two joint faces and makes a good gas-tight seal.

GEAR LEVERS

Lost lever

If you lose your gear lever, and a replacement is unavailable, a small pair of mole grips, carried in your tool pack, can be tightly clamped onto the gear-change shaft and used to carry out gear changing.

Gear-changing difficulties

1. Sometimes, gear-changing problems are due to the gear lever fouling on the engine case. Rub or scratch marks on the engine cover are a tell-tale sign this is happening.

2. Gear changing may also seem unusual if you ride your motorcycle wearing different pairs of shoes. If you normally ride in a pair of light boots or

shoes, and then switch to a pair of good stiff boots, the bigger boot may foul under the engine case or engine bars (if fitted) and, if you don't notice, you may have problems changing up the gears.

3. You should never force the gearchange lever. If you can't get into gear or neutral, let the clutch out slightly and try again as you do so.

GENERATOR ROTOR

Removal

The removal of a generator rotor often requires a special tool: an extraction tool. Very often, however, the extraction tool's thread is the same as that on the motorcycle's wheel spindle. To save buying this special tool the wheel spindle can be replaced by a long screwdriver (or any other metal bar) and used as an extractor. After use, simply replace your wheel spindle. Better still, a friend may have a bike with a spindle of the same size, so ask him to lend you his for a short while.

GLASS FIBRE REPAIRS

Surface damage or chips

This kind of damage to glass fibre is easy to repair:

1. With a rasp, scrape an area an inch wide all round the crack.

2. Thin the material enough to accept new glass fibre.

3. Spread on the resin and let it dry.

4. Smooth it out, and apply an undercoat.

5. Rub down the paintwork with wet-and-dry paper and repaint it.

Holes

To repair holes in glass fibre is a little more complicated than repairing surface damage, but not more difficult:

1. Cover the outside of the hole with adhesive tape.

2. Paint a layer of resin on the other side.

3. Apply a first coat of glass fibre and stick it down with resin.

4. As necessary, add one or two more coats of glass fibre and resin.

5. When the resin is hard and thoroughly dry, remove the tape.

6. Fill in any small holes on the outside and rub it down with wet-and-dry paper.

7. Apply an appropriate undercoat and repaint the damaged area.

Splits or cracks

The best way to deal with splits or cracks is as follows (Figure 63):

1. Drill a small hole at the end of the crack; this will prevent the crack from spreading.

2. If the crack is very long, drill a series of small holes (about $1/16$ in. diameter along either side of the crack.

3. Sew the crack together with a piece of soft wire.

If you make the wire tight enough, this repair should be secure for some time, and will certainly survive until you can find a suitable replacement or build a layer of glass fibre over the top.

This method also works very well on splits or cracks in screens.

IMPORTANT: Whatever the damage, you should never attempt to repair crash helmets. *If they do become damaged, replace them*.

HANDLEBAR GRIPS

Removing grips

To remove handlebar grips without cutting or stretching them, spray

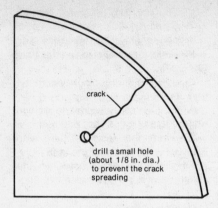

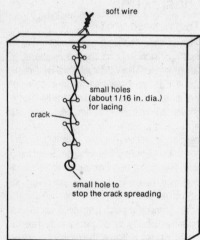

By drilling a series of small holes on either side of a crack you can then lace it with soft wire

Figure 63 Cracks in plastic, perspex or glass fibre items

WD40, or an equivalent lubricating spray, between the handlebar and the grip. The grip should then slide off with relative ease. However, to ensure the grip will be secure when refitted, all traces of WD40 must be removed from both the handlebars and the inside of the grip before it is replaced.

If you don't have a lubricating agent available, heating up the grip with boiling water will cause it to expand slightly, and often this is enough to allow you to slide the grip off.

Refitting grips

Fitting new grips, or replacing old ones, will be made much easier if the inside of the grip is coated with petrol. To do this: (1) pour petrol into the grip; (2) empty out the petrol and fit the grip immediately; (3) after five minutes the grip will be securely attached to the handlebars.

Loose grips

1. Loose grips can be extremely dangerous: for any number of reasons they may cause you to lose control of your motorcycle at a vital moment. It is important that you keep them secure at all times. If your grips do steadily become loose and begin to move in your hand, it may be because they are wet or damp inside. The cure is to remove the grip and dry it with a tissue or small cloth, and then to dry the handlebars or twist-grip tube and finally to replace the grip using petrol.

2. If you are trying to fit a grip which is too big, and using petrol will not secure it, try winding sticky tape around the handlebars to increase their diameter. If the grip is still loose, simply add more layers of tape, as required; it is advisable, however, to add only one layer at a time and to test the grip after each layer. If, on the other hand, you want a permanent fit, you can use any of the impact glues currently available. These glues do provide an excellent solution to the problem of loose grips, but they make grips extremely difficult to remove once fitted.

INSULATION

Broken wires

If a temporary repair is needed for a broken wire and you have no insulating tape, once the ends have been bared and twisted together, a well-chewed piece of chewing gum can be used to cover the connection and prevent the repair from touching any steel parts on the bike. This will prevent blown fuses, but is quite obviously a very temporary measure and the wire should be replaced as soon as possible. Although a twist of insulating tape around the bared wires will suffice, a far better solution is to use electrical connectors, which you can obtain from most electrical shops.

JUMP-STARTING: HOW IT'S DONE

If, for some reason, the battery in your motorcycle is flat and the engine won't start, it is possible to use the battery in another motorcycle. All you need is a pair of booster cables (sometimes known as jump cables): these are two sturdy lengths of cable (usually one red and one black) with a crocodile clip on each end. With both batteries still in place, and wired into their respective ignition systems:

1. Use the booster cables to connect the two batteries. It is essential that you use the first cable to connect one positive terminal to the other positive terminal, and the second cable to connect the two negative terminals. Remember:

Positive to *Positive*

Negative to *Negative*

2. Start the engine of the other vehicle.

3. Start your own engine in the normal manner.

4. After your engine has warmed up sufficiently, disconnect the cables from both batteries, one lead at a time.

Provided the charging system on your motorcycle is in working order, the engine should now provide enough energy to charge up the battery while you are driving around.

If your motorcycle fails to start using another battery, see 'Battery insufficiently charged', p. 122.

LUBRICATION

The purpose of oil

The primary function of motor oil is to reduce friction, and therefore wear, in an engine. The oil does this by acting as a barrier between engine components where there would otherwise be metal to metal contact. As well as acting as a lubricant, however, oil also helps:

1. In keeping the engine free from dirt, because the compounds in modern oils break up the by-products of combustion.

2. In cooling the engine, because it has the ability to disperse any heat it picks up as it flows through hot areas of the engine.

3. In starting the engine when it's cold, because oil, of the correct viscosity, can reduce the additional loading put on an engine as it starts up.

Grades of oil

Firstly, it is important to be aware that the viscosity – the thickness – of oil changes with its temperature. Oils are thicker when they are cold than when they are warm. As a result, an oil thin enough for cold starting may become too thin to be effective when the engine is hot. The development of multigrade oil gets around this problem. A multi-grade oil acts like a mixture of single-grade oils: for example, 20 W/40 will act like a thin 20 W grade when it is cold and like a heavy (thick) 40 W grade when it is hot. The numbers quoted on a multigrade, such as 20 W/40, refer to the oil's viscosity at two standard temperatures $-18°C$ and $99°C$. This ability to change grade with the change in temperature allows you to use just one grade of oil all year round, and in almost all motorcycle engines. Perhaps the two most popular multigrades are 20 W/50 and 15 W/40 and, unless you plan to take part in competition riding, your engine should find both quite acceptable.

Storing your motorcycle

If you leave your motorcycle standing for any length of time, or place it in storage during the winter, for example, it is advisable to run the engine up to operating temperature at least once a week to circulate the oil and help prevent condensation.

Oil additives

These additives frequently contain ingredients which are far too slippery for wet-plate clutches. Even when the brand specifies on the label that it is suitable for motorcycles, this is rarely the case. These products were designed for cars – where the clutch is completely separate from the engine or gearbox oils – or for bikes with dry-clutch systems. It is rare to find motor-cycles with a dry-plate clutch, but if yours has (and we suggest you consult your handbook, or local dealer, to be absolutely sure), there is no reason why oil additives should not be used. They certainly do protect the life of an engine.

Keep the oil clean

It is important not only to change the oil in your motorcycle regularly (see Chapter 2), but also to prevent the oil from becoming contaminated. Always keep your oil in a clean can, and clean the area on the oiltank or gearbox around the filler cap before you add any fresh oil.

Changing the type of oil

Lubrication failures will occur when a change is made from mineral oil to vegetable-based oil of the 'R' type (or vice versa) if the engine has not been completely stripped and all traces of the original oil removed. Mineral oils and vegetable oils do not mix even in normal conditions, but under the action of heat they form a rubber-like sludge that will quickly block the internal oil-ways.

A mobile oil supply

Every motorcycle has a ready supply of oil: in the oiltank, on two-stroke machines, and in the engine and gear-box on four-stroke machines. By dipping a strip of cardboard, a screwdriver, a pencil or the dipstick, etc., into the oil supply, sufficient oil can be removed to lubricate a contact breaker cam, and any dry nuts and bolts or dry cables, etc. (Figure 64).

NUTS, BOLTS AND SCREWS

Preventing corrosion

Whenever you remove a bolt or screw, smear it with grease or Vaseline before replacing it. This will prevent corrosion and make for easier removal and refitting the next time.

Figure 64 A mobile oilcan

Use the dipstick to drip oil onto
dry parts, such as the points, cam, nuts, bolts,
cables, etc.

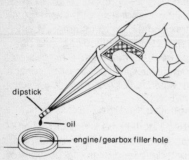

dipstick

oil

engine/gearbox filler hole

Think before you get tough

Brute force is unlikely to get you very far. Always use the correct tools for the job and, if something is unusually stiff, stop and think for a moment – there may be another nut, bolt or screw you have not yet loosened.

Removing stubborn nuts, bolts and screws

Removing either nuts, bolts or screws locked solid by corrosion, or whose ends have become damaged (because you have used the wrong tool), can be a frustrating business, especially if the stubborn one is the last of a series and the others came off with relative ease.

One of the first things you should do is apply penetrating oil liberally and leave it to soak in. If penetrating oil alone fails, there are several things you can do, depending on which type of fastener is proving difficult.

Screws

1. *Impact drivers*. The simplest method of freeing a screw is to use an impact screwdriver. After you have checked that it has the correct bit, and is set for 'anti-clockwise', one sharp blow on the driver will jolt the threads and spin the bit to start unscrewing the screw at the same time. You can then use the impact driver as a normal screwdriver to remove the screw.

2. *Damaged heads*. By using the incorrect screwdriver on a screw you will almost certainly damage the slot, until the screwdriver fails to grip and simply slips round. If this does happen, you will have to re-form the slot. To do this, place a metal bar or punch (with a diameter similar to that of the screw head) on the screw; a few sharp taps with a hammer will flatten the head slightly and allow you to tap the correct screwdriver into the screw. The screw should now be free and turn off with relative ease. If not, add more penetrating oil and repeat the process.

If the screwhead is damaged beyond repair, tap it several times with a hammer (to loosen any rust) and try gripping the screwhead with a pair of strong mole grips. Insert a screwdriver through the grips to act as a tommy bar, and use the grips to turn out the screw. Once these screws have been removed they should never be refitted – new, greased screws should be used to replace them.

Nuts or bolts

1. *Removing stubborn bolts*. Very tight or stubborn bolts will be much easier to remove if you jar them loose with a short, sharp hammer blow while maintaining pressure on the bolt with a spanner. The shock of the blow should free the tightness, while the continuous spanner pressure turns the bolt as it is jarred loose. Alternatively, if you have one, you could use an

impact driver and socket to solve the problem.

2. *Damaged heads*. To prevent either the bolt head or the nut being damaged, a spanner of the correct size should always be used to remove a nut or bolt. If the corners do become rounded, try locking a good pair of mole grips on to the head. Damaged nuts and/or bolts should never be refitted, but replaced by new ones.

3. *Nut-splitters*. Frequently, nuts which are subject to corrosion at high temperatures, such as those which hold exhaust pipes, etc., may become extremely difficult to remove by any normal means. For those of you who are avid tool collectors, a nut-splitter may be considered an investment. It is certainly a sure way to remove very difficult nuts.

To use the tool, merely position it over the offending nut and turn its cutting blade parallel to the stud or bolt from which the nut is to be removed. Then turn the pressure screw on the tool until the nut splits. Forces within the nut will cause it to loosen so that it may be removed easily, leaving the stud or bolt undamaged.

The major, and considerable, drawback to this tool, however, is that it is often rendered useless by the confined spaces in which these difficult nuts most frequently seem to be located.

Obviously, if the nut-splitter cannot be used, the more time-consuming manual methods of penetrating oil and spanner or grips must be used.

Having removed the nut, if you wish to remove the bolt, use a piece of wood or other soft material (for example, aluminium or brass) as a drift to tap out stubborn bolts. Using such materials prevents any damage being done to the bolt's threads.

Cleaning the threads

If you are trying to remove a nut or bolt, make sure that any surface rust is cleaned away from the exposed threads before you begin. This will obviously help the job once the nut or bolt has been started. There is little point in starting a nut or bolt, only to become stuck again on a new section of rusted thread.

Applying heat

Provided it can be done safely (and this must be a primary consideration), applying heat to the spot where the nut, bolt or screw is stuck should enable you to loosen the fastener with the appropriate tool: a screwdriver or a spanner.

Stripped threads

Sometimes, whether by carelessness or from damage in being tapped out, threads become stripped. Often the threads can be cleaned up by running a tap or die through or over them, if you are lucky enough to possess a wide-enough range of tools. The simple solution, however, is to replace the damaged bolt if possible.

Broken screws or bolts

If the head of a screw or a bolt shears off, there are several things you can do to remove the remaining pieces.

1. If the remaining piece is large enough, try gripping it with a pair of mole grips and turning it out.

2. If the remaining piece is too small, you can try filing it into a bolt head shape, or cutting a slot in it to take a spanner or screwdriver.

3. If the head has broken off flush with, or below, the external surface, screw extractors do exist to help you.

They are not difficult to use, but a detailed description of how to use them is provided with each tool. Briefly, you centre-punch the broken part, drill a hole into it (the correct drill size will be marked on the tool), tap the screw extractor into the hole and use a spanner to turn out the broken piece of screw or bolt.

Putting screws into awkward places

If you're trying to replace a screw in an awkward place and find yourself constantly having to pick it up, try putting a blob of grease on the screwhead, to stick it to the screwdriver tip. This is especially useful for short screws when trying to use your free hand tends to hinder rather than help.

Another time when grease can help is if you need to hold a nut inside a socket to use it vertically. The nut will be held in the socket by the grease, allowing you the time to place the socket over the bolt and make those first few important turns.

Those of you who have tried to reassemble a two-stroke engine will already be aware of the problems that arise when it comes to replacing the bolts deep inside the cylinder head fins – 'sticking' the bolt to the socket is a great help.

Locating small screws

It is sometimes difficult to line up very small screws with their holes, especially in awkward places. If you poke the screw through a piece of thin card, it can be held firmly in place while you start it off with the screwdriver.

PLASTIC PARTS

Removing scuffs

Any part of your motorcycle which is made of matt-black plastic, such as headlamps or indicator unit shells, side panels or mirror heads, etc., can easily be cured of scuffs and scratches by vigorously rubbing them with wire wool.

ROUTINE MAINTENANCE: DO IT COOL

When you are carrying out any routine maintenance, the engine should be thoroughly cool before you commence, unless otherwise specified.

SEAT COVERS

Repairing rips, tears or leaks

Sometimes the seams of old seat covers stretch and begin to leak water into the foam padding. The result is a wet rear whenever you sit on the bike. Unless there is an actual hole in the seam, a coat of upholstery cement along the seam should do the trick.

However, either because of old age or spills, splits and tears sometimes appear in the seat covers. A simple, but effective, repair can be made with upholstery cement. This will make a neat job and is relatively inexpensive. If the tear is quite long, the repair will be more secure if you first sew the hole together, using a strong thread, or place a patch underneath, and then apply the cement.

SILENCER BAFFLES

Removal

Never ride your motorcycle with the silencer baffles removed, as the engine will become noisier, and you'll lose power and greatly increase the risk of engine seizure.

SPLIT PINS

Replacing split pins

These act as a safety device by being placed through holes in the end of particular bolts or spindles. They are most commonly found in wheel spindles and brake fittings. When removing these pins, remember that they are only made of soft metal, so always replace them with a new one. They only cost a few pence and, by ensuring that a nut cannot work loose or fall off, they are a cheap and effective safety measure. Finally, after a new pin has been fitted, smear it with grease. This will prevent it from rusting and make removal the next time much easier.

THROTTLE CABLES

Broken cables

If, on machines with twin throttle cables, the pull-cable breaks, as a temporary measure the return cable can be used to replace it and enable you to get home.

Replacing throttle cables

When replacing the throttle cables in a machine with more than one carburettor, be sure to replace the slides in the carburettor from which they came. Frequently these slides are tailored to be right- and left-handed, but are rarely marked as such. A check you can use is to ensure that the cutaway on the base of the slide is facing the rear of the carburettor.

TYRES AND WHEELS

Tyre removal

To many amateurs, changing a tyre seems a most daunting task. In truth, it is far from that. Don't try removing the tyre with the wheel still on the bike – you just cannot do it that way. The first thing you need to do is to remove the wheel carrying the tyre to be changed. Then (Figures 65 and 66):

1. Use the appropriate valve key to remove the valve core (which will deflate the tyre) and a small spanner to remove the valve-retaining nut.

2. With the wheel laid flat on the floor, tread all around the tyre until the wall of the tyre slides into the well of the wheel rim. Having done one side, turn the wheel over and repeat this operation on the other side.

3. While making sure that the tyre bead opposite the valve is as far as possible into the wheel rim well, insert one tyre-lever about two or three inches to the right of the valve and another about two or three inches to the left. Having inserted these levers, prise the tyre out of the well and over the rim of the wheel (in doing this it is important not to pinch the inner-tube between the lever and the wheel rim).

4. Having lifted out this eight to twelve inch section of the tyre bead, withdraw the two levers and reinsert them about six inches to the left and six inches to the right of the freed section. Continue around the wheel, withdrawing, reinserting and prising the tyre over the wheel rim until the final section opposite the valve is freed.

5. Push the valve into the well of the wheel, and carefully remove the inner-tube.

6. The other side of the tyre can be

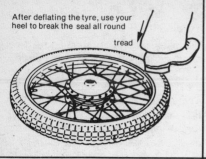

After deflating the tyre, use your heel to break the seal all round

tread

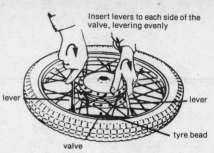

Insert levers to each side of the valve, levering evenly

lever

lever

tyre bead

valve

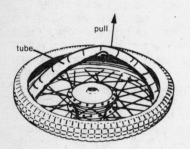

Pull the tube out from the tyre

pull

tube

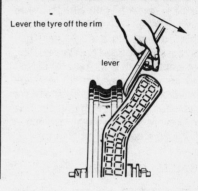

Lever the tyre off the rim

lever

Figure 65 Tyre removal

levered off the wheel using a similar process to that outlined in (3) above. In doing this, however, make sure that the portion of bead opposite that to be levered out is as far into the wheel well as possible. Once more than half of this bead is freed, the tyre can be quite easily removed from the wheel by hand.

7. If the wheel is spoked, you will find a rim tape in the bottom of the wheel well. When you are refitting the tyre, this tape must cover all the spoke nuts to prevent them chafing the inner-tube. Unless you feel the tape would benefit from a wash, you should leave it where it is while dealing with the tyre or inner-tube problem.

Tyre refitting

To refit a tyre, all you need to do is (Figure 67):

1. Cover the inside of the tyre with a generous coating of talcum powder. This will prevent the inner-tube creasing while it is being inflated and reduce any friction between the inner-tube and the tyre during use.

2. Wipe around the bead and wall of the tyre with a 50/50 mix of washing-up liquid and water, which will help you to refit the tyre, and the tyre to seat itself correctly when the tube is inflated.

3. With the wheel laid flat, and using your hands and feet, feed one side of the bead onto the wheel rim. The first

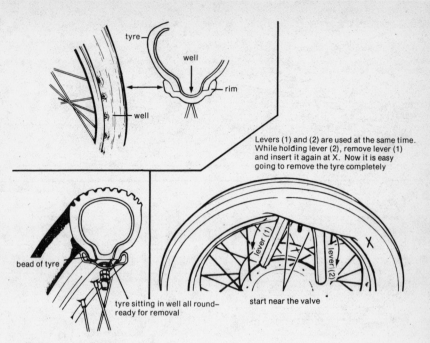

Levers (1) and (2) are used at the same time. While holding lever (2), remove lever (1) and insert it again at X. Now it is easy going to remove the tyre completely

Figure 66 Levering off a tyre

three quarters of that bead should be manageable by hand, but it may become necessary to lever the final section into the rim. Some tyres have a direction-of-rotation arrow, moulded on the wall, indicating which way round the tyre should be fitted for maximum tread life. The recommended direction will be different for the front and the rear wheels, so, when fitting the tyre, you need to be certain that the direction of rotation is correct for where you are using it.

4. Having already refitted the valve core, pump a little air into the inner-tube, sufficient to let the inner-tube take its basic shape.

5. Push the inner-tube neatly into the tyre, making sure the valve is in line with the valve hole in the wheel rim, and smooth out any wrinkles or tucks which might appear in the process.

6. Thread the inner-tube valve through the hole in the wheel rim and wind on the valve-retaining nut a few threads. Once again, ensure the tube is free of creases and pushed well into the tyre all the way round.

7. Now feed the other side of the tyre over the rim. At first it should be relatively easy to do this by hand, but the final section may require the use of a tyre-lever. If you do need to use a tyre-lever, be careful, as it is all too easy for the inner-tube to be pinched and damaged if it is forced against the wall of the tyre or the wheel rim by the lever. Also, while levering this final section, always ensure that the bead

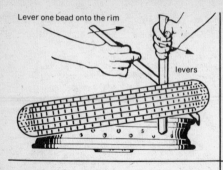

Lever one bead onto the rim

levers

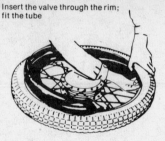

Insert the valve through the rim; fit the tube

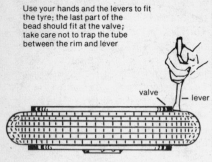

Use your hands and the levers to fit the tyre; the last part of the bead should fit at the valve; take care not to trap the tube between the rim and lever

valve — lever

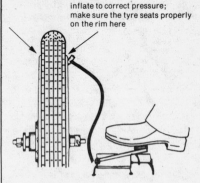

inflate to correct pressure; make sure the tyre seats properly on the rim here

Note! Brushing a soapy solution on the rim and the tyre bead makes for easy tyre fitting

Figure 67 Tyre refitting

already on the wheel rim is as far into the well as possible.

8. After making a visual check, on both sides of the tyre, that the bead is deep into the well and the inner tube is not being pinched, inflate the tyre to about ten pounds over the recommended riding pressure. This will seat the tyre securely onto the rim.

9. Make a final visual check that the tyre has in fact seated itself evenly all round the wheel. To do this, you simply need to check that the wheel rim and a line marked on the tyre are the same distance apart all the way round on both sides. Incorrect tyre fitting will have an effect on the handling of your motorcycle. If the tyre has not seated itself correctly on the rim all the way

round, it will produce an effect similar to a wheel out of balance – in effect, the wheel will become egg-shaped.

10. Once you are satisfied that it is correctly seated, deflate the tyre to the recommended riding pressure (which will be given in your handbook or workshop manual), fully tighten the valve-retaining nut and fit a dust cap.

Tubeless tyres

Although these tyres do have the advantage that they don't require you to be careful with an inner-tube, as you do when changing other tyres, they do have their own disadvantages. By their very nature they are such an exceptionally tight fit on the wheel rims that they are themselves highly susceptible to damage from any tools used to help prise them on. To help ease this problem, you will need to give the tyre beads a very thorough lubrication before fitting.

The area of the rim in which the tyre will be seated must be cleaned meticulously before you replace a tubeless tyre, and the use of tyre-levers must be kept to an absolute minimum. Indeed, it would be far better if you could manage without them at all, although that is almost certainly too much to expect.

Having fitted the tyre, you must initially inflate it hard enough for pressure to build up and correctly seat it. This usually means blasting the beads into place with a pressure airline.

To seat the tyre correctly at home is a much more difficult process, but it can be done. Wrap a rope round the circumference of the tyre and twist it down hard using a peg with the rope to create a tourniquet. This will press the bead into place, while it is possible for sufficient pressure to be built up with a good foot pump.

Repairing a puncture

The first thing to be said about mending a puncture is not to do it unless you have to. Your tyres and inner-tubes are the only point of contact between you and the hard road. Even if it is unavoidable and you have to patch a hole, it is always advisable to replace the inner-tube as soon as possible.

However, if you don't have a tin of Tyre Weld – which injects a solution, under pressure, that simultaneously seals the hole and inflates the tyre – you will need to put a patch over the hole in the inner-tube. To do this you must:

1. Remove one side of the tyre from the wheel with the punctured inner-tube.

2. To locate the hole, inflate the inner-tube and then either immerse it in water and look for bubbles, or try to use your eyes and ears to sense its position.

3. If you have used water, dry the area of inner-tube around the hole.

4. Using a piece of rough emery cloth, clean an area slightly larger than the area of the patch you need to fit. The emery cloth will remove the silicon bloom on the tube's outer surface (this is the silver dust on the outside of the tyre which would prevent the patch from sticking) and put a key on the rubber of the inner-tube. Without this key the patch will not stick properly, or, even worse, it may appear to stick but then come off later.

5. Using a clean finger, spread the glue, sometimes called vulcanizing fluid or rubber solution, all over the area where the patch is to be fitted.

6. Touch the *outer edge* of the glue occasionally to check that it is tacky.

7. When the glue is tacky, peel the backing from the patch, and place it over the hole and squarely in the middle of the glue.

8. Working from the centre outwards, press the patch down until it is completely stuck to the tube.

9. Lightly dust the patch and the surrounding area of the inner-tube with french chalk or talcum powder.

Wheel rims

When repairing a puncture or changing tyres you should always check the condition of the wheel rims and the wheel rim tape. Whether it is actually tape or a rubber ring (which is increasingly becoming the case on modern motorcycles), it may be necessary to remove it and clean the inside of the rim. To do this, brush away any loose rust and, if the wheel is spoked, check for any protruding spoke ends. If there are any protruding, you should either file or grind them down before refitting a tyre as they can easily puncture an inner-tube. While the rim tape or rubber is off the rim, you should wash it and only refit it if it is in good condition. If there is any doubt about it, buy a new one – it may not seem like much but, when the tube is inflated, it takes the shape of the rim well, and the rim tape or rubber prevents the ends of the spokes sticking into the inner-tube.

How to get more miles per tyre

1. Always keep your tyres at the correct pressure – if they are too high, you will get excessive wear in the centre of the tyre and, if they are too low, they will become excessively worn on the edges. Riding with the tyre pressure too low may also damage the sidewalls of the tyre because of the extra flexing.

2. When setting your tyre pressures, always make an allowance for any passengers you may carry. If you are carrying someone behind, increase the rear-tyre pressure by about two to four pounds.

3. Do not try to burn away from every standing start. Rapid acceleration may be fun, but it's dangerous and will reduce the life of your tyres (especially the rear tyre) substantially.

4. Severe braking will also reduce the life of a tyre. Sometimes it is necessary to stop quickly, but remember: each time you skid, or squeal to a stop, rubber is being ripped off.

5. Always keep your tyres clean – remove any objects which may become stuck in the tread. While they are there, you increase the risk of a puncture.

WASHERS

Placing washers on difficult bolts

If you need to drop a washer on to a bolt which is in a difficult position – those located in the bottom of a small narrow hole, for example – the easiest way to do it is to slide the washer on to the blade of a screwdriver which will reach the top of the bolt. All you then need to do is to hold the washer up to the screwdriver handle with your finger, place the tip of the screwdriver blade on the top of the bolt and let the washer drop down the screwdriver's blade and over the bolt.

This should stop you losing too many washers in unwanted places where it is almost impossible to retrieve them.

ENGINE EFFICIENCY
CARBURETTOR

Take care when washing your machine

When washing your machine, be sure you cover the carburettor air intake to prevent water entering the carburettor float bowl and causing starting or, at least, performance problems. If any water does find its way into the carburettor, you must remove and clean the float bowl, main jet and any other part you think may be contaminated.

Make sure the carburettor is securely fastened

Ensure the carburettor top is neither too tight nor too loose, and *be sure* the mounting pinch clips are secure. If not, the carburettor may pivot, possibly causing air leaks, and almost certainly resulting in an improper mixture because the float level has changed.

Petrol leakages

Varnish deposits on the outside of the float bowl are a tell-tale sign that petrol is leaking and that the gasket needs to be cleaned or replaced.

Dirt in the float bowl

Either under normal running conditions or after your bike has fallen or been knocked over, any dirt that is in the fuel may find its way into the carburettor and lodge in the float valve. Whatever its cause, any dirt in the float valve will certainly lead to an over-rich mixture and possibly prevent your machine from starting. As a solution to get you home, try dislodging the dirt by tapping the carburettor lightly with any tool you have at hand. As soon as is convenient, clean the fuel tank, fuel tap filter, fuel lines and the carburettor. Of course, if tapping the carburettor fails to dislodge the obstruction, the carburettor will have to be dismantled and thoroughly cleaned.

COMBUSTION: NORMAL AND ABNORMAL

Normal combustion

The power developed in a combustion engine comes from the expansion of gases which result from the burning of a fuel/air mixture in the cylinder(s) (Figure 1, p. 11). If the 'anti-knock' quality, as indicated by the octane rating of the fuel for that engine, and the ignition timing are correct, the burning process should move evenly across the combustion chamber until all the fuel is burned.

Detonation

Detonation occurs when the octane rating is incorrect for the engine's requirements. As a general rule, engines with higher compression ratios (such as motorcross and road-racing machines) require fuel with higher octane ratings. It is important to remember that, although using a fuel with a higher octane rating than the engine needs does not harm the engine (nor, incidentally, does it provide any extra power), using fuel with an octane which is too low may cause damage to the engine, is certainly uneconomical, and the resultant detonation will certainly reduce the engine's power.

Aside from the octane rating of the petrol, detonation may also be caused by over-advanced ignition timing, or a build-up of deposits in the combustion chamber which prevent the engine cooling quickly enough and cause it to become overheated.

Detonation can occur in several ways, but probably the most common is that, following a spark from the spark plug, combustion spreads only partway across the combustion chamber before the remaining fuel/air mixture 'explodes'. The termination of the combustion process by this premature explosion causes a hammering pressure on the piston crown. The addition of this detonation to the normal heat and pressure created by combustion causes the temperature in the combustion chamber to increase substantially. As a result, the continued pounding is likely to damage the piston and the increased temperature to cause pre-ignition.

Pre-ignition

Pre-ignition is the ignition of the fuel/air mixture in the combustion chamber, before the spark occurs, by any 'hot spot' within the combustion chamber. Carbon deposits, rough metallic edges, incorrectly seated valves or an overheated spark plug are all capable of igniting the fuel/air mixture prematurely in the engine's combustion cycle.

The result is that the piston attempts to compress the gases which are already expanding, and therefore further increases the combustion temperature and pressure, which in the end will damage the engine.

CONTACT BREAKERS (POINTS)

The points gap

On most motorcycles the required gap between the points, at their most open position, is about the thickness of the card used for a standard cigarette packet. If you feel the points may be causing you trouble (see p. 60), and you don't have a feeler gauge, setting the contact-breaker gap to the thickness of a cigarette packet will certainly allow you to ride the machine home.

If you do set the points using this temporary method, they must be reset, correctly, as soon as possible. You must remember that the cigarette packet is only an approximation to the correct gap and that an incorrect gap means incorrect ignition timing, which in turn means reduced performance. Your owner's handbook or workshop manual will tell you the exact size of the required gap.

ENGINE EFFICIENCY: ONE WAY TO IMPROVE IT

The addition of reed valves, between the carburettor and the cylinder, will improve the efficiency of a two-stroke engine at low r.p.m.s (Figure 68).

ENGINE SEIZURE: CAUSES AND REMEDIES

What is it?

Engine seizure occurs when the required clearances between two moving surfaces disappear and the two become stuck fast, or even welded together.

Why does it occur?

Usually an engine seizes because it is too hot or because it lacks lubrication. No matter how smooth the surface of engine components (the piston and cylinder walls, for example) may appear to the naked eye, examination with a magnifying glass would soon reveal just how rough they really are.

A film of oil between these moving surfaces: (1) prevents metal to metal contact and therefore prevents excessive heat being produced; and (2) helps to disperse any heat which does build up, despite the presence of oil, primarily because of the heat generated during combustion.

Consequently, a lack of oil within the system means that: (1) there may be metal to metal contact, and therefore an excessive level of heat being produced; and (2) there is no means of dispersing this increased heat.

If this build-up of heat is allowed to continue, the two surfaces will become so hot that they will weld themselves together, that is, the engine will become seized.

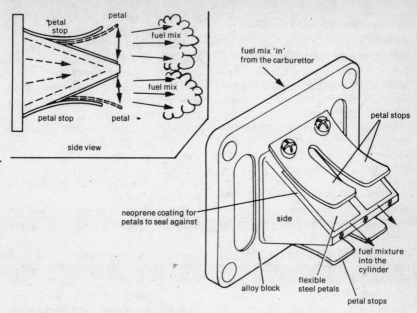

side view

As the piston rises in the cylinder, the petals
are flexible enough to bend away from the block,
allowing the mixture into the cylinder; and as the
piston descends, the petals close, shutting off the mixture supply

Figure 68 Reed valve layout: two-strokes

Running-in

Running-in is vitally important because
the microscopic mountains on the surface of all engine components are
worst when the engine is new. Asking
too much of your engine too soon –
that is, while these peaks are still quite
sharp – increases the likelihood of
there being breaks in the protective oil
film, metal to metal contact, increased
heat being generated and therefore
seizure.

The running-in speed and the limitations for your particular motorcycle
will be set out in either your owner's
handbook or workshop manual: read
them carefully if you're lucky enough
to own a new bike – it would be such
a shame to ruin an engine so early in
its life.

Symptoms

Typically, just before an engine
becomes seized: (1) you will get the
impression that someone has suddenly applied the brakes; and (2) the
engine itself will slow down. If you ever
do suspect that your engine may be
about to seize, shut off the throttle and
pull in the clutch immediately. After a
few moments you can try easing it out
a little and, if the engine fires, you can
carry on. But be careful if it doesn't fire
– manoeuvre the motorcycle over to
the side of the road and investigate.

Are two-strokes more prone to seizure?

Almost without exception two-strokes are more likely to seize than four-strokes: (1) because of the increased likelihood of cylinder distortion, caused by the cylinder ports and piston windows; and (2) because setting up the carburettor(s) correctly on a two-stroke engine is far more crucial to satisfactory performance.

A temporary solution: two-strokes only

Although two-strokes may be more prone to seizure, the damage caused may not always be serious. Indeed, there is a temporary solution which may enable you to ride home, if you are careful. Unfortunately, for reasons you will see, this solution cannot be used on four-stroke engines.

1. Let the engine cool down.
2. Ensure the oil tank is full and that oil is being pumped into the engine. This means checking not only the oil tank, but also the oil pump, oil pump cables and the oil lines.
3. Add about two tablespoons of oil directly to the fuel in the tank and shake it up.
4. Remove the spark plug and put a drop or two of oil down the spark plug hole into the cylinder.
5. While the spark plug is removed, turn the engine over two or three times, with the kickstart, if fitted, to free the piston and lubricate dry surfaces. (If your motorcycle doesn't have a kickstart, you will have to engage first gear and rotate the rear wheel.)
6. Replace the spark plug and start the engine in the normal manner.
7. Provided you are careful, you should be able to ride steadily home, but your engine must be dismantled and thoroughly checked as soon as possible – and certainly before you go out on it again.

The only compensation for the fact that two-stroke engines are more prone to seizure is that they are much easier to dismantle.

Repairing the damage

Having dismantled the engine, examine both the piston(s) and the cylinder(s) for damage (which the seizure will cause).

If the marks or scuffs are not too deep, it is relatively straightforward to remove them: all you need is a light touch and some patience.

1. To clean up the piston: either lightly rub it with grade 400 or 500 emery paper (sometimes known as wet-and-dry paper), just enough to remove any roughness; or carefully dress the damaged area with a very fine file.
2. Once the damaged area is smooth again, rinse the piston in paraffin to wash away any traces of alloy dust or abrasive filings.
3. If the piston was damaged in any way, the cylinder must be examined:

(a) Cylinders which *are not* chrome plated can be cleaned up in exactly the same way as the piston, but don't forget to wash them thoroughly in paraffin afterwards.

(b) Cylinders which *are* chrome plated need to be treated with extra special care and delicacy of touch when you are trying to remove the marks. Rub the walls of the cylinder very gently with grade 600 emery paper; your progress is likely to be frustratingly slow, but with patience and care it is possible to restore the cylinder to a usable condition. Once again, however, don't forget to rinse it thoroughly in paraffin before reassembly.

With a particularly bad seizure, however, the scoring may be too deep to remove, some of the chrome plating may have come away or the material from one of the surfaces may have welded itself onto the other – certainly, it is not uncommon in situations like this for a piece of the piston to become welded to the cylinder wall. Unfortunately, if any of these things have happened, don't even think about repair: the damaged items will need to be replaced.

Finally a word of caution: the complexity of dismantling the top end will vary enormously from one motorcycle to another. Certainly, it will be far more difficult on a large multi-cylinder four-stroke than a mid-range two-stroke.

If you do feel sufficiently confident and competent, and if you make sure you have all necessary tools to complete the job before you begin and follow the detailed description in your owner's handbook or workshop manual, all should go well. Repairing a seizure, however, can be a major piece of surgery and one which you may feel unsure about tackling: if you do, don't hesitate to leave it to a professional on this occasion.

EXHAUST FUMES

A quick and visible guide to the internal condition of an engine is the colour of the gases being emitted by a motorcycle's exhaust. Although the fumes coming from four-strokes and two-strokes may on occasion be the same colour, they do not always mean the same thing.

Four-stroke engines

Blue smoke

A cloud of blue smoke streaming from the exhaust indicates that oil is entering the combustion chamber in some way and being burned within the engine.

On the one hand, it could be that you have overfilled the sump. This is obviously something you should avoid doing, not only because of the heavy soot deposits left throughout the engine and exhaust system, but also because, if the pressure is too great, the excess oil may be forced through the breathing system or – even worse – through the crankcase joints.

On the other hand, if the oil level is as it should be, the burning of oil in the combustion chamber, and the resultant blue smoke, may have come about because of two rather more serious problems. If the problem has developed slowly, the oil is probably entering the chamber via a worn bore or worn valve guide. If the problem occurs suddenly, and the sudden emission of smoke is associated with lost or reduced compression and power, it is highly likely that the piston rings are either seized or broken.

Black smoke

A stream of black smoke from the exhaust pipe means that an excessive amount of fuel is being burned. In this case it may be that: (1) the fuel level in the float chambers of the carburettor is too high, because of either incorrect adjustment or the float needle being stuck; (2) a main jet has worked itself loose and finally dropped into the float chamber; (3) the flap, on the choke-type carburettor, may not be opening properly; (4) the plunger, on bikes with a cold-start device instead of a choke, may be stuck in the open position; or (5) there is an obstruction in the air cleaner, causing a reduction in the amount of air being drawn in, and hence causing the carburettor to supply a mixture containing too high a proportion of fuel.

White smoke or steam

Any white smoke or steam coming from the exhaust is caused by water deposits in the exhaust system itself. The water is caused by carbon monoxide which is produced by the burning gases. This is not a problem – indeed, it's quite natural and nothing for you to worry about.

Two-stroke engines

Blue smoke

Blue smoke will normally appear from the silencer, except after a long run and then the blue smoke is quite faint and hard to see. No smoke at all, however, is a bad sign. It means that the lubricating oil is not circulating through the engine: either the two-stroke oil tank (if fitted) is empty, or the delivery pump is not working. (This may be due to a broken cable or a problem with the internal drive gears.)

Large clouds of blue smoke

An extremely blocked air filter will cause the emission of blue smoke to

Figure 69 Normal-type fuel tap

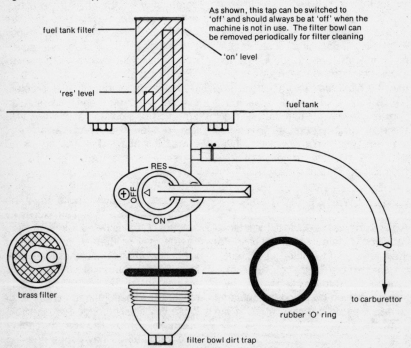

As shown, this tap can be switched to 'off' and should always be at 'off' when the machine is not in use. The filter bowl can be removed periodically for filter cleaning

fuel tank filter

'on' level

'res' level

fuel tank

RES

OFF

ON

brass filter

rubber 'O' ring

to carburettor

filter bowl dirt trap

be greater than normal. The problem is that, because of the lack of air, the mixture becomes too rich and is not being burned completely.

Continual voluminous clouds of smoke

If you continually have great clouds of smoke pouring from the exhaust, and the spark plug is fouling up regularly, this usually means: either (1) the oil pump setting is incorrect and the delivery of oil is too high; or, worse still, (2) that oil from the gearbox is being drawn into the engine – this may be due to a weak or broken oil seal, or possibly a leaking crankcase joint.

FUEL TAPS: TRADITIONAL OR VACUUM-OPERATED

Traditional taps. Always make sure your fuel tap is at 'off' if you leave your machine for more than a few minutes.

Vacuum-operated taps. If your machine has this type of fuel tap, you must never leave it in the 'pri' position.

In both cases, failure to leave the tap in the correct position may result in the engine becoming flooded with neat fuel, making starting extremely difficult. If you are unsure, you should check your owner's manual to find out which form of petrol tap is fitted to your bike (Figures 69 and 70).

Figure 70
Vacuum-operated
fuel tap

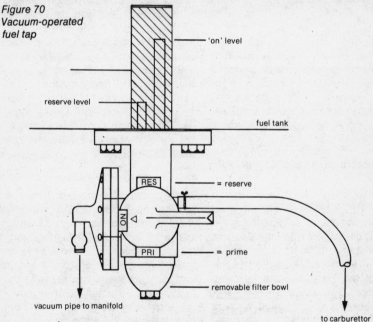

This type of fuel tap has no 'off' position – only 'on' or 'res' need be used. 'Pri' simply bypasses the vacuum switch, allowing the carburettor to be filled after running out of fuel – 10 seconds in the 'pri' position is sufficient to fill the carburettor. Remember: when the engine is off, this type of tap is automatically switched off. Note! If the machine is left with the tap in the 'pri' position, a completely filled engine may result

IGNITION

Transistorized ignitions

If your motorcycle is fitted with a transistorized ignition system and you need to remove the spark plug cap, it is important that you refit the cap securely on to the spark plug. In most cases, if the cap is not fitted correctly and you try to start the engine, the high electrical charge which normally runs through the plug cap to the plug, and to earth, will be stopped by the gap between the spark plug and the cap. Being blocked at the cap, the charge may feed back along the H.T. leads and into the ignition system, causing expensive damage.

INSTABILITY

There are many ways in which a motorcycle may be said to be unstable. Although the three situations highlighted below are only examples, the possible causes listed with them are the primary causes of motorcycle instability.

The motorcycle is unstable at high speed

Tyre pressure is incorrect

Tyres which are either too hard or too soft will cause your motorcycle to 'roll' at high speed. If this has happened to you, you will already know it's no joke. Correct tyre pressures are far more important than many motorcyclists would believe. You will need to check and, if necessary, reset the tyre pressures to those recommended in your owner's handbook or workshop manual. For a more detailed discussion of tyre pressures and the possible problems they can cause see pp. 35–7.

The dampers are defective or incorrectly adjusted

It is important that both front forks contain the same level of oil (and are at the same air pressure if they are air-forks), and that the rear dampers are adjusted to the same height. If they are uneven, you will certainly notice this at high speed.

1. Examine the fork seals for signs of wetness, which is an indication that they are leaking and therefore need to be replaced. Your owner's handbook or workshop manual should detail how to go about this.

2. Ensure that the recommended level of oil is in the forks, and that it is of the correct grade. Again your owner's handbook or workshop manual should provide this information.

3. Ensure that both dampers are at the same level (the adjustment procedure will be in your owner's handbook or workshop manual) and check that there are no signs of leaking from the units themselves: if there are, they must be replaced.

Motorcycle is incorrectly loaded

Many motorcycles these days are fitted with a topbox and/or panniers (behind the rider and/or thrown over the tank) to carry your luggage, and they are indeed very practical. However, if you place excessive weight in one side, or if weighty items in the topbox are free to move around (causing the heavy weight to move from side to side), the motorcycle will be unstable, and not necessarily only at high speed.

Examine the items you have in your panniers and/or topbox and redistribute them. If you have only one heavy item, which cannot be divided and redistributed, you can stabilize the motorcycle by placing anything of a similar weight in the other side to act as a counterbalance – a brick or a bag of sand, for example. Remember, though, if you are delivering the heavy item, it might be a good idea to use a counterweight which is divisible, so that when the item is removed you won't have another stability problem.

Finally, always carry heavy items as far forward as possible and ensure that all weighty items in the topbox are unable to slide/fall around.

Chassis problems, such as a bent frame

A frame can be distorted in many ways, and for many reasons. Two of the more common ones you might suspect are: (1) the frame is bent so that the front-fork angle is wrong, which will cause the wheel to 'castor' at certain speeds; or (2) damage to the frame means that the wheels are out of alignment, which will cause the motorcycle to weave.

When buying a secondhand motorcycle, always inspect the motorcycle's frame from as many angles as possible. Although only a quali-fied/experienced person with the correct equipment can tell for sure if the frame is straight, those problems can be so expensive to rectify that they should certainly be part of the negotiations over price.

The frame will have to be either repaired or replaced. Although replacement is a task the amateur can undertake – 'simply' transfer every-thing from one frame to another – straightening will require the special equipment only a workshop will have.

Perhaps the best advice, however, if you suspect the chassis to be the cause of your stability problem, is to take your motorcycle along to your local workshop and talk to the mechanic about it: the experienced eye may spot a situation amateurs may pass by.

The motorcycle wanders at low speed

The steering-head bearings are too tight

Tight steering-head bearings mean that there is a momentary resistance in the handlebars' movement from left to right (or vice versa) which needs to be overcome. In doing so, the tend-ency may be to over-compensate for this stiffness, which then has to be corrected: the result is weaving or wandering, particularly at low speed. You will need to check and, if neces-sary, readjust (loosen) the steering-head tension: to do so you will need to open the gap between the two sets of bearings. If this fails to resolve the situation, you will need to dismantle the bearings, inspect and repack them with the recommended grease.

The front wheel vibrates and/or jumps when you brake

The steering-head bearings are too loose

Basically, the steering-head bearings are designed to do two things: to hold the front section (the yoke, the forks and the wheel) in position and to allow it to turn smoothly from one side to the other. If the bearings (located at the top and bottom) become too loose, so will the whole front section. This is principally shown up when you are braking, and the slackness of the bearings on the pivot allows the forks, and so the wheel, to 'vibrate'.

Check and, if necessary, readjust (tighten) the steering-head bearings. Remember, this is done by closing the gap between the two sets of ball races. See pp. 79–80 for more details.

NOISES

Often faults may signal their development by a change in the motorcycle's performance, stability, its overall feel or by various noises. Be careful, however – noises are difficult enough to diagnose as it is, so try not to spend time tracing false signals. Although any part of your motorcycle (and noises do not only emanate from the engine – other parts of the motorcycle are also capable of producing an array of noises) may make different noises while running under load, cruising or standing still, not all of them are signposts to problems. You must bear in mind that: (1) a change of helmet, especially from full-face to open-face, may result in previously unheard noises becoming perfectly audible – and beware of different helmets of the same type that can cause noises to differ; and (2) different road surfaces can produce changes in existing noises or cause others to develop.

Clues to the source of the problem can be gained from:

1. The *type* of sound: for example, a heavy thump or a deep rumble is likely to be something large – a big-end bearing perhaps (especially if it is coming from deep inside the engine).

2. The *source* of the sound: that is, whether it emanates from the engine (and, indeed, which part of the engine),

the motorcycle's frame, or the wheels or brakes, etc.

3. *How often* the sound can be heard: for example, if the noise occurs with each revolution of the engine, it may be the big end, small end or pistons, etc.; whereas if it occurs with every other revolution, the valve gear may be suspect.

Basically, noise can be classified into three groups: (1) engine-speed-related noises; (2) wheel-speed-related noises; and (3) 'bump' noises. To check which type yours is, you will need to make instrument checks and/or road tests.

Instrument checks. In well-equipped motorcycle workshops noises are likely to be located and identified by the use of a stethoscope (very similar to the one doctors use to listen to your chest). For most of us, however, there are better ways to spend our money. A cheaper alternative is to use a long screwdriver: put the handle to your ear, block off the other ear and put the point of the screwdriver blade on the engine. The range of noises you will hear will surprise you. You should be able to trace a source for (almost) all of them quite easily, as most are associated with the engine's normal operation – it is those you cannot locate that you need to be concerned with. Really, it is worth while spending a little time listening to an engine you know to be in good condition for, once you are acquainted with its normal noises, identifying the problem noises is so much easier.

Road tests. (1) with the motorcycle stationary run the engine at varying speeds and pull in the clutch occasionally to isolate the gearbox. This will allow you (with the aid of your screwdriver, perhaps) to detect and identify any noises which are coming from the engine unit or gearbox, etc.; (2) some noises may only occur when the machine is under load – to test for these, ride your motorcycle at varying engine speeds, trying all gears and with the clutch engaged and disengaged; (3) running the motorcycle downhill with the engine off will allow you to identify rolling chassis/wheel brake noises and bump noises (provided you go over bumps of course).

Unfortunately, amateur mechanics tend to have problems with noises and this is not surprising: experience must be the watchword in this department, and is perhaps the only way diagnosis can be made accurately.

Noises are hard to differentiate, but they are even harder to describe. Despite this, however, some examples of various noises and the *possible* causes are listed below.

Pinking

The persistent metallic tinkling sound you may hear while accelerating is 'pinking' or, more correctly, pre-ignition, caused by the mixture igniting ahead of time. This may be the result of:

1. Fuel with an octane which is too low.
2. Incorrect fuel/air ratio.
3. Incorrect fuel/oil ratio (on two-strokes).
4. Problems with the ignition system.
5. Inadequate cooling.
6. Incorrect lubrication.
7. Carbon in the combustion chamber(s) becoming a hot spot and igniting the fuel/air mixture prematurely.
8. Over-advanced ignition timing.
9. Engine overloading.

Backfiring

Backfiring occurs when unburned fuel is pushed out of the exhaust. It is, in fact, the opposite situation to pre-ignition. The unburned fuel collects in the silencer and noise occurs when this is ignited by the hot gases passing through.

Although the most likely cause of backfiring is that your mixture is too rich, it may be that you have:

1. A damaged exhaust valve seat.
2. A tappet which is overtight.
3. A leaky exhaust system, with cracked or loose-fitting joints.

Spitting back

Spitting back through the carburettors is caused by gas forcing its way past the inlet valve seat. In this situation the likely causes are:

1. A tight inlet tappet.
2. A damaged inlet valve or seat.
3. Grossly retarded ignition timing.

Rattles

Mostly these noises will not be too serious, but they should be investigated as soon as possible none the less. Some of the most usual rattles come from:

1. A key fob rattling on the machine.
2. Loose tools in the tool box or tray.
3. Loose chain guard.
4. Loose mudguards.
5. Loose headlamp glass.
6. Loose mirror glass.
7. Loose numberplate.
8. A loose kickstart lever.
9. A loose spark plug; but beware – loose spark plugs will cause some very strange noises which sound not unlike broken piston rings.
10. Loose engine bolts.

11. Broken cylinder head bracket to the frame (mainly a four-stroke problem).

12. The safety chain of the petrol cap rattling inside the tank.

13. The battery rattling round in its compartment because its rubber securing strap may have broken.

14. A worn or loose camshaft drive chain.

Rustling or tapping

Rustling or tapping noises usually occur in the valve gear, but you should also check the primary drive and clutch as these too may possibly be the source.

Rumbling

A rumbling sound indicates that the trouble is in the lower end of the motor, and the most likely problem is a faulty main bearing or possibly the clutch.

Knocking

A knocking sound in the bottom end of the engine is usually caused by a big-end failure.

High-frequency noises

Whines or screeches frequently indicate a clutch or gear problem. A continuous whine from the gearbox is frequently the result of worn pinions or an overtight drive chain.

Ticking

Often, when a machine is switched off after it has been running for some time, you can hear ticking noises. There is no need to worry – this is only the exhaust pipes contracting after being hot, and the machine is not about to explode.

High-pitched squeaks

Some of the most likely causes of these types of noise are:

1. A cracked or slack manifold. (This is the pipe connecting the carburettor to the engine.) The squeak occurs when air is sucked in through cracks or loose joints. If you suspect the joints, tighten the clips while the engine is running – if the noise stops, you have obviously found the problem. If the squeaks continue, you must turn your attention to the manifold itself. As a temporary measure, you can use insulating tape to cover any cracks, but obviously you will need to replace the manifold as soon as possible.

2. A dry contact breaker cam. A little oil or grease will easily cure this.

3. A pulsating squeak is a sign of compression leaks at the cylinder head joint. Possibly the head bolts are too loose, or the cylinder head gasket needs replacing. If this is the case, you should check the tightness of the holding-down bolts. Be careful here, however, as these bolts must not be too tight. Having allowed the engine to cool, you must use a torque wrench to ensure the correct tensioning pressure is obtained. The pressures for your machine will be in your owner's handbook or workshop manual. If these bolts are tight, and you do not wish to attempt changing the head gasket yourself, unfortunately a trip to a workshop will be necessary.

4. Dry rear-suspension units. A little spray of penetrating oil on the springs should cure this.

5. Brake squeal. There may be dust in the drum, stones embedded in the disc pads, or they may be worn out.

Slapping

A slapping sound which changes its frequency according to the engine speed is piston slap. This is caused by excessive clearance between the piston and the cylinder wall, when the piston rings or small-end bearings become too worn. If the small-end bearing is the culprit, the noise will rapidly develop into an insistent clank as the gudgeon pin (or piston pin) becomes increasingly loose. Sometimes the noise of these problems might be better described as light tapping – it depends on how bad the problem is.

Screeching

A persistent screeching sound is a clear sign that one moving part (usually one which is rotating or spinning) is coming into contact with another and that the protective coating of oil which is supposed to be between them has become too thin and hence ineffective as a lubricant. If this is the case, then while the noise continues, the parts are being severely worn and you should stop immediately.

Whining

The most likely cause of a whining sound is that the kickstart ratchet is failing to disengage: the return spring will probably have become defective and need replacing.

On the other hand, this type of noise may also be caused by a leaf or a piece of paper trapped between the wheel and the mudguard.

A high-pitched scream

The starter motor clutch rollers may have jammed.

A heavy thumping in time with the engine

This will almost certainly be the big-end or main bearings.

PETROL: FIVE TIPS ON HOW TO SAVE PETROL

1. Always use the correct grade of petrol for your motorcycle's engine. Using four-star premium petrol in a low-compression engine is just wasting money, and using two-star regular-grade petrol in a high-compression engine may save you a few pence per gallon, but in the long run you will lose money because of the increased petrol consumption. It is really only worth using premium petrol in engines with a compression ratio of over 8·5:1. Under that, you will benefit more by using a lower grade of petrol. Your owner's handbook or workshop manual will tell you the compression ratio of your motorcycle's engine.

2. Ensure that your tickover/slow-running mixture is exactly correct (see the section on carburettor adjustment, p. 74). A mixture which is just a little too rich is hard to detect and can increase your consumption considerably.

3. One sure way to waste petrol is to twist the throttle continually, as you stand in a line of traffic or at traffic lights, for example. If your engine won't tick over without you continually having to twist the throttle, you should adjust it until it will.

4. Rapid acceleration, at high revs, causes your engine to drink petrol. Speeding away every time you set off may be fun, but it can be dangerous and certainly costs money.

5. Riding on full throttle will force your engine to consume extra fuel unnecessarily, particularly if you ride a two-stroke. Ease off the throttle – you will probably find that you can go at almost the same speed on half the throttle and, hence, on half the petrol.

SPARK PLUGS

Operating conditions

The conditions under which a spark plug is expected to operate are severe, to say the least. It is essential that the spark plug is able to function correctly, even while being subjected to rapid and extreme changes in temperature and pressure. When the fuel/air mixture in the combustion chamber ignites, the temperature rises, almost instantly, to about 25,000°C – the temperature of a blow torch – and the pressure increases to about 750 p.s.i. Also, while operating, the spark plug must be able to cope with very high voltages: a minimum of 14,000 volts (and a possible maximum of 50,000 volts) is required to produce a spark – such a requirement is approaching the voltage levels carried in the National Grid.

The heat ranges

The spark between the electrodes of each spark plug must be adequate, at all engine speeds and under all conditions of operation, to produce a proper ignition of the (correct) fuel/air mixture.

It is essential that the spark plugs are of the right type for the engine. They must run hot enough at lower speeds to avoid fouling, but they must not overheat and become a potential source of pre-ignition (see p. 252) at high engine speeds. If a spark plug is to operate correctly, the temperature of the firing tip must neither exceed 800°C while you are cruising at high speed, nor fall below 400°C when you are riding around at low speeds (Figure 71).

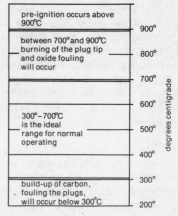

Figure 71 Spark plug temperature range

If the spark plugs are of the wrong type, or are in poor condition, the compressed fuel/air mixture may not ignite efficiently, incomplete combustion results and only part of the fuel is converted into power. Some of the unburned portion goes past the piston rings, diluting the oil in the crankcase, while the remainder goes out through the exhaust system. However, because of the many different engine designs, the amount of heat a plug is subjected to, and therefore the amount of heat it is required to dissipate (if it is to remain within the required temperature range), varies quite substantially. As a result, it is necessary to have a range of spark plugs which are able to operate under these various conditions.

Cold plugs (Figure 72)

These are sometimes referred to as hard plugs. The relatively short nose and short heat path of the cold spark plug means: firstly, that less of the nose is exposed to the combustion

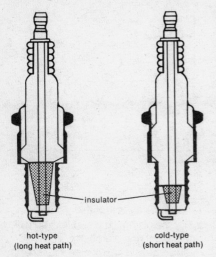

hot-type
(long heat path)

cold-type
(short heat path)

Figure 72 Hot-type and cold-type plugs

gases, and hence it absorbs less heat; and secondly, that it is able to transfer that heat more rapidly into the cooling material. As a result, the plug itself is relatively cool when running and so less able to burn off any combustion deposits.

If this plug were to be used in a cool-running engine, or one that burned oil, the plug would soon become fouled. The cold plug should be used only in high-stress, high-compression and high-performance engines.

Hot plugs (Figure 72)

These are sometimes referred to as soft plugs. On hot plugs the insulator nose and heat path are longer

than on the cold plug. The result is that the plug itself absorbs more of the heat in the combustion chamber and transfers that heat less rapidly from the firing tip to the cooling material. However, because it does operate at a relatively higher temperature, the hot plug does have the ability to burn off any combustion deposits. Consequently, hot plugs are usually used in low-compression or oily engines where the combustion chamber temperature is relatively low.

You should never use a hot plug in a hot-running or highly stressed engine – the plug would absorb so much heat that ultimately the tip would melt. Before this happened, however, the tip would begin to act as a 'glow plug', prematurely igniting the mixture simply because of its heat. (This premature ignition is sometimes called pinking and is discussed more fully on p. 261.) In extreme cases, the heat may become so intense that the piston itself is damaged.

As a general rule, therefore: a *cold* plug should be used in a *hot* engine; and a *hot* plug should be used in a *cold* engine.

Dimensions (Figure 73)

Size

Currently, spark plugs are made in three sizes (that is, thread diameters): 10 mm., 12 mm. and 14 mm. 14 mm. is certainly the most popular, with the other sizes being used only where space for the plug hole is restricted.

Reach

A spark plug's reach is the length of its threaded portion (Figure 74). Clearly, the longer the reach, the greater the projection into the plug hole. With this

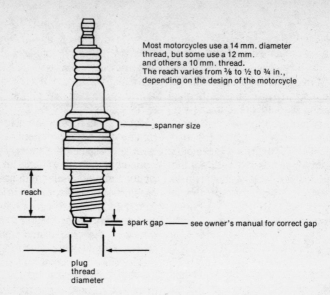

Most motorcycles use a 14 mm. diameter
thread, but some use a 12 mm.
and others a 10 mm. thread.
The reach varies from ⅜ to ½ to ¾ in.,
depending on the design of the motorcycle

spanner size

reach

spark gap ——— see owner's manual for correct gap

plug
thread
diameter

Figure 73 Spark plug dimensions

in mind, always ensure that the plug you are fitting does not have a reach which is too long. Fitting a long-reach plug in a head designed for a short-reach one may end with the plug being hit by the piston – the results would be unpleasant and expensive.

The type and size of plug you require

Figure 74 Spark plug reach

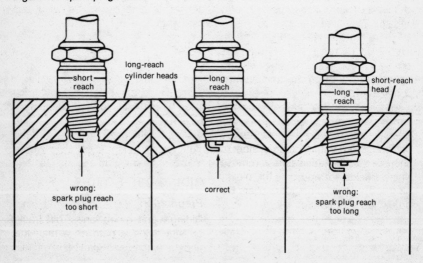

short reach

long-reach
cylinder heads

long reach

long reach

short-reach
head

wrong:
spark plug reach
too short

correct

wrong:
spark plug reach
too long

for your motorcycle will be indicated in your owner's handbook or workshop manual.

Never lubricate spark plug threads

Never put grease or oil on spark plug threads before refitting. Far from helping you to remove the plug next time, the lubricant turns to carbon because of the heat and virtually welds the plug into the cylinder head. If you feel the plug threads do need a little help to ease them in and out, try rubbing soft pencil lead on them: the graphite it contains should help.

STORING YOUR MOTORCYCLE

After being left for long periods (for example, if you store your bike for the winter), petrol tends to lose its potency. Before storing the bike you should always drain off any petrol; if you forget to do this, you must at least change it before you attempt to restart your motorcycle at the beginning of spring.

SUPPRESSORS

Metal-shielded caps

The metal-shielded suppressor caps often found on Japanese motorcycles have frequently been found to be the source of short-circuiting in wet weather. If damp gets between the cap and the spark plug, this metal cap often becomes a convenient path to earth, causing your ignition system to short-circuit. It is advisable to remove these shields, leaving only the plastic plug cap – a pair of standard pliers will do the job adequately.

MOTORCYCLING IN GENERAL

FUNNELS

A home-made funnel

Most oils these days are sold in flexi-bottles with a plastic tube to help you pour the oil into the tank. To make yourself a funnel, simply cut off the bottom of the bottle and screw the plastic tube into place (Figure 75). The long tubular stem on your new funnel will be perfect for putting in fork oil, where the handlebars and cables tend to get in the way of containers.

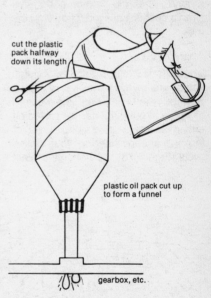

cut the plastic pack halfway down its length

plastic oil pack cut up to form a funnel

gearbox, etc.

Figure 75 Make your own funnel

RIDING OFF-ROAD

Preparation

Riding along green lanes, dirt tracks or over fields is hard on a machine, and the increased likelihood of falls means that prominent items such as direction indicators are far more likely to be damaged than on the road. The main items to remove are the direction indicators and any rear-view mirror; also, if you loosen the brake and clutch lever clamps slightly, there is less chance of their breaking in a fall. To ensure optimum performance and minimum wear and tear, make sure that all the necessary periodic maintenance has been done and that all the pre-departure checks, such as brakes, lights, etc., are all satisfactory. Finally, it is always advisable to waterproof the electrical and ignition systems before you set off. A good spray around with damp-proofer, or perhaps even a coat of Vaseline, should do the trick.

Spare cables

Spare front-brake, throttle and clutch cables are always handy items to have with you when trail riding. The problem of where to put them can be solved by taping the spare cable along the run of the one already fitted to your motorcycle (Figure 76). You should protect

the existing cable snaps, all you have to do is connect the two ends of the spare cable. Enduro-riders often use this trick – not only does it give them somewhere to carry the cables, but also saves time when effecting repairs.

Shabby bikes

Trail riding can be hard on the machine, and pretty soon it can begin to look quite shabby. To protect the painted areas, such as the petrol tank, side panels and any other susceptible areas, try covering them with a clear adhesive film. Your local hardware shop should stock it, or at least be able to tell you where it is available. On the other hand, you could use stickers to protect the tank where your knees will rub, and the side panels where your boots will chafe. To protect the front forks from stone chippings and damage in a fall, fit fork gaiters to cover the chrome work. If you need them, gaiters are also available for the rear shock absorbers.

The point of all this is that the adhesive film or stickers can always be replaced or removed later – if you

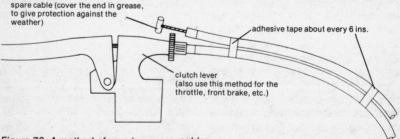

spare cable (cover the end in grease, to give protection against the weather)

adhesive tape about every 6 ins.

clutch lever
(also use this method for the throttle, front brake, etc.)

Figure 76 A method of carrying spare cables

the exposed wire and end nipples from adverse weather conditions by covering them in either grease or tape. If

want to change your motorcycle, for example. If you remove the protection and give it a good wax polish, the paintwork can look like new again and your motorcycle will be worth much more.

Everyone falls off

Off-road riding can be lots of fun if you have the correct bike and have taken some steps to prepare it first. When riding off the road you will almost certainly fall at one time or another. If you don't – well, you are not trying hard enough and therefore not getting the most from this additional pleasure of motorcycling.

Take a friend

Whenever you go trail riding, even if it's not far and you're not going to do much, take a friend with you. Never go trail riding alone. Trails can often be very isolated and, if you have an accident, help may take a long time to arrive – if you're alone!

Also, if a farmer or landowner is kind enough to allow you to ride on his land, respect his property and follow the country code. If you open a gate, close it; slow down near animals and try to make as little noise as possible as you pass them. As always, it is the noisy, disrespectful few who spoil it for the rest of us.

SIDECARS

('The chair', as it is sometimes called)

Driving an outfit

Driving a motorcycle with a sidecar can be a great deal of fun. It is not at all like driving a car – it is still very much a bike – but it is also so very different from driving a solo. Remember:

1. You can't bank it over – you must turn the handlebars.

2. When stopping, if the sidecar is on the left, the outfit may tend to pull to the right, and to the left if the chair is on the right. You must be ready for this.

3. On corners, the sidecar may tend to want to lift when you turn – beware! With the sidecar on the left, you should always accelerate round left-hand corners and throttle back on right-hand corners – simply reverse this if the chair is on the right.

Really, riding with a chair is all a matter of moving your body weight and of *practice*.

Sidecars and the law

1. In the eyes of the law, if you fit a sidecar to a solo motorcycle, the original M.O.T. is invalid. The motorcycle and sidecar, as an outfit, must pass a new M.O.T. However, if you *remove* a sidecar, the M.O.T. on the outfit is valid for the motorcycle as a solo.

2. Although one numberplate is still sufficient, you must have two rear lights and two reflectors on the outfit, as well as a forward-facing pilot bulb.

Taking care of your sidecar

1. Always ensure that the connections between the motorcycle and the sidecar are well coated in grease. Also, pay particular attention to the sidecar body bolts.

2. It may be a good idea to fit a small car battery, especially if you plan to fit a radio, cassette, C.B. radio, or extra lights, to deal with the extra demands. Quite often there is a small space in the rear of the sidecar where this could be located.

3. If your sidecar is fitted with celluloid windows, remember that they don't last for ever. If they do yellow or become brittle, it is always best to

replace them. You can always purchase some clear plastic sheeting and use the old windows as a pattern to cut out the replacements.

4. Pieces of carpet on the sidecar floor and the inside of the nose reduce condensation, retain warmth and make it much quieter for travelling.

5. Another way to reduce the noise level in the sidecar, although it is quite expensive, is to purchase a system that runs all the exhaust pipes into one silencer and to locate it on the offside of the outfit.

TOOLS

Normal day-to-day riding

Every motorcyclist should always have a tool kit with him. Quite obviously, you can't carry everything, but you do need to carry sufficient tools to help you make any necessary roadside adjustments and repairs. The minimum you should consider are:

1. Spare bulbs and fuses.
2. The equipment necessary to remove the wheels and repair any punctures, that is: (a) a tin of 'Tyre Weld' – these spray tins connect to the tyre valve and the tyre is sealed and inflated while it is still on the motorcycle; (b) a spanner fitting the nut in the wheel spindle; (c) tyre levers; (d) a puncture repair outfit – coarse emery paper, glue (sometimes called vulcanizing fluid or rubber solution), patches, french chalk or talcum powder, and a pump of some description.
3. A plug spanner and spare plugs.
4. An array of various spanners – open and/or ring – or an adjustable spanner.
5. A pair of pliers.
6. A screwdriver.
7. A small pair of mole grips.

8. A length of soft wire and insulating tape.
9. A feeler gauge.
10. An electrical circuit tester (see p. 201).

Long-distance trips and touring

For touring, or any other long-distance travelling, you may feel that a more comprehensive set of tools and spare parts is necessary. Certainly you will need to be more prepared; but remember that the amount of carrying space on a motorcycle is limited. If you are touring, in addition to the normal day-to-day equipment you should consider:

1. Spanners and screwdrivers for all nuts and screws.
2. A torch – never rely on breaking down at night underneath a street lamp.
3. And spare: coil; condenser; contact breakers; electrical wire; chain and spring clips; cables; levers; pistons; piston rings; valves.

Tools to be used at home

Although most motorcycles are provided with a tool kit adequate for minor repairs and adjustments, if you wish to do more you will need better and more varied tools. It may therefore be worth while acquiring additional tools to be used at home. Some you may wish to consider are:

1. A hammer.
2. Various screwdrivers.
3. A torque wrench.
4. A socket set.
5. A magnet, to pick up screws and washers from difficult places.
6. An old syringe, to oil cables.
7. Loctite, which prevents nuts from vibrating loose.
8. A silicone jointing compound, to

make oil-tight joints without gaskets.

9. An impact screwdriver.

10. A flywheel puller.

11. An ignition gauge.

12. A timing tester.

13. A timing gauge.

14. A hydrometer.

15. A multimeter or a variable ohmmeter (V.O.M.).

16. A compression gauge.

17. A set of vacuum gauges.

General tool tips

1. Never take any new tools for granted – always try them before setting off with them in your tool kit.

2. With tools, as with most things, the more you pay for them, the better the quality. Take great care with spanners that are pressed out of a metal strip – the edges will be clean cut on one side and rounded on the other. Multi-purpose tools, such as screwdrivers with a detachable handle and numerous blades, are frequently good as gimmicks, but are often expensive and inconvenient to use.

Also, when considering the quality of the tools you are going to acquire, think about when and how often you intend to use them. It may be unnecessary to buy the very best quality every time.

3. Tools are very expensive these days, so perhaps you could consider splitting the cost of highly priced tools with a good friend.

4. Lending your tools to people often turns out to be an expensive business – it's the easiest way of losing them. One way to remain generous, but help prevent losses, is to scratch your initials on them, or mark them with paint.

5. You should always ensure that your tools are neither rusty nor dirty. Each time you've finished with them, wipe them over with a slightly oiled rag before you put them away.

6. When carrying tools around with you, always keep them wrapped in a piece of rag.

7. If it happens that the only available spanner is too large for the nut, try placing a coin or another piece of metal between the faces of the nut and the spanner.

VISORS, GOGGLES AND SHIELDS, ETC.

Eye protection while riding a motorcycle is essential, but all the forms so far put forward tend to develop one problem or another at some time in their lives. Below are a few suggestions on how to alleviate the most annoying ones.

Misty visors, goggles or glasses, etc.

Anti-mist products are quite expensive. A cheap and effective alternative is to use ordinary household washing-up liquid. Using a soft tissue, smear some of the neat liquid on to the inside of the visor, etc., and then wipe clean with a fresh dry tissue. This will usually last all day, and certainly lasts just as long as the special products.

Scratched visors, goggles, plastic glasses, etc.

The scratches that you inevitably get on these pieces of eye protection equipment are not only bothering, but can be dangerous when you are riding at night, and (especially) in the rain. The glare from oncoming car lights, or passing street lights, is increased by the scratches, and the dazzling which results frequently impairs your vision.

One quick and easy way to remove these scratches is to lay the visor, etc., as flat as possible on a cloth and vigorously rub it with Brasso or Duroglit and a clean cloth. Occasionally polish up the visor with another clean cloth and check how much more needs to be done and where the most severe marks remain. Repeat the process until all the scratches are removed.

A final word of advice: don't let your visor, etc., become too scratched or marked – not only does it take some considerable time to remove these defects but, more importantly, it is essential to have good vision at all times.

WHAT TO WEAR

For a short hop over to a friend's house, or on hot sunny days, you may be tempted to ride around in only a tee-shirt, jeans and tennis shoes – don't do it! You must always be adequately protected.

In fine weather

Being adequately protected means *always* wearing: (1) a helmet; (2) gloves; (3) a good pair of shoes or, better still, boots; (4) a sturdy jacket or, if you can afford them, either a one-piece or a two-piece set of leathers.

In the cold and/or rain

Motorcycling in cold or rainy weather will be a very unhappy experience unless you are dressed for it. The motorcycling clothing and accessory industry has made substantial progress over the past few years, and there is now a vast range of protective equipment on the market. Some of the more useful items you should consider are: (1) to protect you from the rain, either a waxed cotton suit or a one-piece or a two-piece nylon suit; (2) a pair of good boots which have been thoroughly coated in dubbin and wax; (3) a pair of silk glove liners; (4) a nylon or silk underhelmet; (5) a set of thermal underwear – if this is too expensive, try wrapping newspaper around your legs and body, underneath your nylon or cotton suit.

For the motorcyclist who plans to ride twelve months a year, or over long distances, good clothing is essential. If you can afford them, all the various combinations possible with thermal underwear, a set of leathers and a wax cotton suit will give you adequate protection in any weather conditions.

Finally, a couple of useful accessories to keep your hands warm are: (1) handlebar muffs – these are strapped over the ends of your handlebars and give excellent protection from the wind and rain; and (2) heated handlebar grips, heated gloves or, indeed, other heated items of clothing – these are a worthwhile investment for winter riding, and your local stockist should be able to supply you with them.

GLOSSARY
OF MOTORCYCLING TERMS

ACCELERATOR PUMP: A component attached to some carburettors to provide a richer mixture during acceleration; a jet of petrol is pumped directly into the inlet tract as the throttle is opened.

ADVANCE: The distance before top dead centre when the spark plug fires.

Although the ignition needs to be slightly in advance, to ensure that the full effect of the explosion is utilized in forcing the piston downwards, an over-advanced ignition means that the piston is still rising and therefore compressing the exploding gases which are trying to expand: in brief, the result is a loss of power.

A.F.: Across flats. A measurement usually of nuts and bolts, between opposite sides. It is also used to indicate spanner sizes, as an alternative to specifying the thread size they are designed to fit.

AIR VENT: A hole which allows air into the fuel tank or float chamber so that fuel can leave.

ALLEN KEY: A metal bar of hexagonal section generally used on socket-headed screws.

ALTERNATOR: A generator of alternating current, used on most modern motorcycles. Basically it consists of a rotating magnet which is surrounded by a number of coils.

AMMETER: An instrument designed to measure electrical current, in amps.

ARMATURE: Usually found in a generator or starter motor, it is the shaft which carries the windings.

AUTOMATIC ADVANCE UNIT: A mechanical device which uses rotating weights and centrifugal force to adjust the timing advance automatically as the engine speeds up.

BAFFLES: Used principally in the silencer to deflect exhaust gases, silencing the engine noise and collecting drips of oil. (Although, in general, a baffle is a plate or obstruction designed to hinder or regulate the passage of elements through an inlet or outlet.)

BALANCE WEIGHTS: Metal weights which act as a counterbalance for moving components.

BALL BEARINGS: Small metal balls used to separate two or more bearing surfaces.

BALL RACE: A device designed to reduce the friction between two surfaces by means of small ball bearings (often packed in grease) held in a track at the top and bottom.

BANJO: The junction between a component and a flexible pipe using a banjo bolt.

BATTERY: A series of connected cells used to store electrical energy. Each cell contains metal (lead) plates and electrolyle (dilute sulphuric acid).

BATTERY ACID: In lead–acid batteries it consists of sulphuric acid and distilled water. The specific gravity should ideally be $1 \cdot 26$–$1 \cdot 28$.

B.D.C.: Bottom dead centre. This is the lowest point in the cylinder reached by the piston – the farthest point from the cylinder head.

BEADS: The wire-reinforced edges of a pneumatic tyre; the beads locate the tyre on the rim.

BEAD WIRE: Wire used to stiffen and strengthen the bead of a tyre. The wire makes it easier for the bead to seat itself correctly in the wheel rim.

BEARING: That part of a surface which supports another surface, although it is usually restricted to parts that are moving in relation to each other.

BEARING BALL: See BALL BEARINGS.

B.H.P.: Brake horsepower. The power out of an engine as measured on a dynamometer in the laboratory.

BIG END: The bearing between the crankshaft and the connecting rod.

BLEED: To remove any unwanted air, usually from a hydraulic-brake system.

BLEEDING: (1) A process to remove air from a hydraulic system. (2) The situation in which a bright colour stains a lighter colour which has been sprayed over it.

BLEED NIPPLE: A small valve in a hydraulic system which, when opened, allows fluid and air to be pumped out – used to remove contaminated hydraulic fluid or air, or both, from a system.

BLOW-BY: The expanding gases developed in combustion escape past the piston, usually because of piston ring failure or a worn bore. The result is reduced engine performance and increased oil consumption.

BOOST PORT: An extra transfer port in a two-stroke engine. Usually this port is open slightly longer than the other main ports.

BORE: (1) The internal surface of the cylinder. Most commonly used to refer to the engine cylinder, but other cylinders, such as the brake master cylinder, can be considered to have a bore. (2) The radius (or diameter) of a cylinder. (3) To machine to the correct size – as in bore out.

BRAKE FADE: The tendency for brakes, commonly drum brakes, to lose their efficiency when they become hot.

BRAKE LININGS: The frictional material attached to a brake pad or brake shoe.

BREAKER POINTS: See CONTACT BREAKER.

BREATHER: A hole or passage into the air, usually from the engine compartment. If that compartment is pressurized, the breather may incorporate some form of valve.

BRIDGE: The material left in the port of a two-stroke engine to support the piston rings.

BRUSH: A carbon block used to transmit electricity to and from rotating parts.

BUCKET TAPPET: A small cylinder, closed at one end, most commonly used in engines with double overhead cams. With the shim inside it, the bucket is over the end of the valve stem. The cam runs on the bucket which in turn transmits the cam's motion to the tappet. The thickness of the shim is varied to adjust the valve clearance.

BURNT VALVE: Usually refers to the exhaust valve, a situation arising because of excessive combustion temperatures.

BUSH: A cylindrical metal lining to a hole, often made of soft metals such as phosphor–bronze.

BUTTERFLY: The throttle valve sometimes used in carburettors; see BUT-TERFLY VALVE.

BUTTERFLY VALVE: A disc, pivoted on the line of its centre and used in a carburettor as a throttle valve.

CAGE: A carrier for the ball bearings in a ball race.

CALIPER: The fixed part of a disc brake which holds the hydraulically con-trolled piston and the brake pad.

CAM: An elliptical lobe formed on a shaft to operate valves.

CAM FOLLOWER: The actual compo-nent moved by a rotating cam; it may be in a slide or pivoted at one end or the middle.

CAPACITOR: Also known as a con-denser, an electrical component to absorb electrical power to minimize the sparking at the contact breaker. In CDI systems it is also used to store electricity.

CARBURETTOR: An instrument for accurately mixing fuel and air in the correct proportions for combustion.

CASTELLATIONS: Slots cut into the head of a nut which allows a spring clip or split pin to be inserted. Once the nut has been tightened, subse-quent movement is prevented.

CDI: Capacitor discharge ignition. An electronic ignition system without contact breakers, and using solid-state devices to trigger a spark at the plug.

CHAIN: A continuous series of metal links used to transmit power.

CHAIN CASE: A protective cover for a chain. They come in two forms, one covering only the top half and the other covering the entire chain.

CHAIN TENSIONER: A device designed to control the amount of slack in a drive chain. They are sometimes fitted to the final-drive chain, most frequently on off-road motorcycles.

CHOKE: An inlet tube in the carburettor which, when opened, increases the proportion of petrol being mixed with the air.

CHROME BORE: Chrome-plated cylin-der walls to reduce friction.

CIRCLIP: A spring clip formed into a horseshoe shape. It fits into a groove, preventing a part from mov-ing. They come as internal or exter-nal types.

CLEARANCE: Any gap between parts.

CLUTCH: Part of the transmission mechanism to engage or disconnect the drive from the engine to the gearbox.

CLUTCH DRAG: A defect in the clutch whereby the plates don't free cor-rectly. Usually caused by incorrect adjustment or problems in the release mechanism.

CLUTCH PLATE: Plain or friction-lined plates used in the clutch which, when pressed together by springs, transmit the drive from the engine to the gearbox.

CLUTCH SLIP OR SPIN: A defect in the clutch whereby the plates don't grip and it will not transmit the drive. It is usually caused by incorrect adjust-ment, worn or bent plates, weak springs or oil on the clutch plates.

COIL: An electrical transformer. It boosts the voltage in the ignition system to provide the spark at the plug.

COLLET: A split collar, sometimes tapered, most frequently used to hold a valve cap to the valve stem.

COMBINATION SPANNER: A spanner with one open and one ring-shaped end.

COMBUSTION CHAMBER: The space, in the cylinder, above the piston when it is at T.D.C., and where the mixture is ignited.

COMPRESSION RATIO: The ratio between the volume (inside the cylinder) above the piston when it is at B.D.C. and T.D.C. The ratio indicates exactly how much the mixture is compressed before it is ignited: for example, in an engine with a compression ratio of 10:1 the mixture will be compressed to one tenth its original volume before being ignited.

COMPRESSION RING: Upper ring serving primarily a gas-sealing function; see also PISTON RING.

CONDENSER: See CAPACITOR.

CONNECTING ROD (CON-ROD): A metal bar connecting the piston to the crankshaft. The bearing at the piston end is known as the 'small end', and that at the crankshaft is known as the 'big end'.

CONTACT BREAKER: A cam-operated electrical switch.

COTTER PIN: A tapered pin, threaded at the narrow end. As you tighten the nut, the pin is pulled into the hole.

CRANKCASE: The main engine casing made in two sections.

CRANK-PIN: Sometimes called a big-end journal on a one-piece crank, it is the circular section of the crankshaft around which the big end rotates.

CRANKSHAFT: The main shaft in the engine which is turned by the piston's downward movement, thus providing the engine's motive power.

CROSSHEAD SCREW: Originally called Phillips, or Posidrive, the head has a crossform slot.

CROWN: The top of the piston.

C-SPANNER: So called because of its shape; it is used on screwed collars with slots or holes instead of flats.

C.V.: Constant velocity.

CYLINDER: A hole in the engine block in which the piston moves up and down.

CYLINDER HEAD: The enclosed end of the cylinder, opposite the crankshaft.

DAMPER: Sometimes used to refer to shock absorbers. Strictly, it is a device which absorbs unwanted movements of a sprung or hinged part.

D.C.: Direct current. An electrical current which flows in one direction.

DEAD CENTRE: The point at which the piston changes direction. Usually abbreviated to T.D.C. and B.D.C.

DECARBONIZE: Sometimes known as decoke; the removal of carbon from the combustion chamber, piston crown, ports and exhaust system.

DECOMPRESSOR: An automatically or manually operated component which releases compression in a cylinder. It is usually used to make starting easier. In a four-stroke it operates via the exhaust valve, by raising it slightly, whereas on a two-stroke a valve is fitted to the cylinder wall.

DESMODROMIC: A method of mechanical operation which relies on cams to open and to close valves. Using a cam both to open and to close a valve means that far higher speeds can be obtained without spring surge or valve bounce.

DIODE: An electrical component which will only allow electrical current to pass in one direction.

DIRECT LIGHTING: An electrical system with no battery; power for lights is supplied directly from the generator.

DISC BRAKE: A circular plate between two friction pads held in a caliper. Hydraulic power presses the pads on to the plate to form the brake.

DISC VALVE: A rotary inlet valve, often used in two-stroke engines to improve performance.

DISTRIBUTOR: A component designed to distribute the electrical power to the spark plugs of a multi-cylinder engine if only one coil is being used. They are rather rare on modern motorcycles.

D.O.H.C.: Double overhead camshafts. One is used to operate the exhaust valves and one to operate the intake valves.

DRESSING POINTS: Cleaning the contact breaker surfaces and making them flat and square.

DRUM BRAKES: Friction material on brake shoes presses on the inside of a hollow drum to slow the wheel.

DRY SUMP: A system of lubrication in which the oil is stored in a tank and, having once been pumped into the top of the engine, falls into the sump. It is then returned to the same tank by another pump.

DWELL: The time that the points are closed while the contact breaker cam is rotating.

DYNAMO: A component which produces electrical power by getting coils of copper wire to rotate in a magnetic field.

EARTH: Otherwise known as ground; connection of a wire conductor with the earth.

ELECTRODE: One of the poles of a galvanized battery. The central rod or the small projection from the bottom of a spark plug.

ELECTROLYTE: A solution of distilled water and sulphuric acid in the lead–acid battery.

ELECTRONIC IGNITION: A solid-state system controlling the current in the coil.

EXPANSION CHAMBER: The section of the exhaust system designed to allow the engine to breathe correctly and enhance engine power.

EXTRACTOR: A tool for removing a part of the engine.

FEELER: A thin piece of sheet metal, used to set the gaps between various components.

FILTER: *Air* – a dry-paper, wire-mesh or oil-coated-foam element to trap dust particles. *Fuel* – a mesh for trapping large particles in the petrol. *Oil* – a cartridge to extract the impurities from the oil.

FIRING ORDER: The sequence of combustion on multi-cylinder engines.

FLAT SPOT: A fault in the carburation – usually an engine misfire during acceleration.

FLOAT: A part of the carburettor which floats in the reservoir of petrol; as it rises, it closes a valve, shutting off the supply of petrol.

FLOAT BOWL: The petrol reservoir in the bottom of a carburettor.

FLOAT NEEDLE: The tapered valve in a carburettor, pushed by the float to close off the fuel supply.

FLOODING: The state of an engine which is over-rich.

FLYWHEEL: A heavy wheel attached to the crankshaft, its inertia keeping the engine running between the power strokes.

FOUR-STROKE: An engine which requires four strokes to complete its cycle.

GALLON: A unit of volume, eight pints or 4·55 litres.

GAP: The space between two surfaces, usually applied to points or spark plugs.

GASKET: A seal. A thin sheet of paper, cork or copper (these are the most common) cut to conform to engine parts. When placed between two joining surfaces it makes a liquid- or gas-tight joint.

GEAR: A steel wheel with teeth around its edge to engage the teeth of another gear.

GEARBOX: The casing containing gearwheels and shafts, although sometimes the whole assembly – casing and gearwheels – is referred to as the gearbox.

GEAR RATIO: The ratio of the differing speeds of two engaged gears, determined by the number of teeth on each wheel.

GEAR-SELECTOR FORKS: A component designed to move gears along a shaft so as to engage and disengage them.

GENERATOR: A device for producing electrical power.

GROMMET: A plug used to block off a hole; it is often soft and hollow to allow you to insert it in the hole. Occasionally it has a hole to allow a cable to be passed through it.

GROUND: See EARTH.

GRUBSCREW: A headless screw, threaded along its entire length and slotted at one end.

GUDGEON PIN: Sometimes called a piston pin or wrist pin. It connects the piston to the connecting rod.

HAIRPIN SPRING: A spiral spring with two parallel arms at right-angles to the spring.

HALOGEN LIGHT: A special bulb with a quartz envelope filled with halogen gas.

HEAT RANGE: The classification of spark plugs by type according to their ability to transfer heat from the firing tip of the insulator to the cooling system of an engine.

HIGH TENSION: The high-voltage secondary current supplied from the coil to the plug.

HOOKED: Damage to sprocket teeth. The top part of the tooth is pulled out of line so that it looks like a hook.

HORIZONTALLY OPPOSED: An engine design with cylinders set on opposite sides of the crankshaft.

HOT SPOT: An exceptionally hot area in the combustion chamber or near the ports. These may possibly cause the fuel/air mixture to ignite prematurely.

H.T. See HIGH TENSION.

H.T. LEAD: The cable(s) carrying the high voltage from the ignition coil(s) to the spark plug cap(s).

HUB: The central part of a wheel.

HYDRAULIC: Operating by means of a liquid.

HYDROMETER: An instrument for measuring the specific gravity of liquids, such as the electrolyte in the battery or the liquid used in a liquid-cooled engine.

IDLER: An intermediate gear or sprocket used for linking two gear wheels when they cannot be brought close enough together; it is used to take up slack on a system while not providing drive.

IGNITION: The process by which the mixture in the cylinder of an internal-combustion engine is ignited. The mixture in a motorcycle engine is set on fire by a spark from a spark plug. The source of power is the coil or magneto. In brief: (1) current passes from the battery through the primary circuit, ending at the points; (2) at the instant the points open (by means of a cam) the primary circuit breaks down; (3) this collapse relieves a high voltage in the secondary circuit, ending in a good strong spark at the plug.

IGNITION ADVANCE: See ADVANCE.

IGNITION COIL: The component which provides the high voltage necessary to provide the spark at the plug tip.

IGNITION SYSTEM: The system of components and wires required to produce the spark for ignition.

IGNITION TIMING: The arrangement to ensure that the points open, triggering the spark, when the piston is in the correct position.

IMPACT SCREWDRIVER: A screwdriver which is rotated by striking it with a hammer. The screwdriver is designed to jar loose the threads and rotate the screw at the same time. A very useful tool for the motorcycle mechanic as the heat of the engine often locks tight many screws.

INJECTION: On motorcycles this usually refers to fuel injection. It is a method of operation in which fuel is squirted under pressure into the system.

INTAKE: That part of the engine between the air cleaner and the inlet valve or port – the passage used by the petrol/air mixture to get to the engine.

JET: A component of the carburettor with a small, accurately sized hole to control the flow of fuel.

JOURNAL: The section of a shaft which rests on the bearings, or around which the bearings are fitted.

KNOCKING: An engine noise caused by a mechanical defect or incorrect ignition timing.

LEADING EDGE: The edge of the brake shoe facing the direction of rotation of the brake drum.

LEADING LINK: A type of front-wheel suspension.

LEADING SHOE: A brake shoe with the operating cam at the leading edge. This arrangement is far more effective than having the operating cam at the trailing edge.

LINER: A cylindrical component often inserted into an aluminium block. It is used to provide a satisfactory bearing surface for the piston and piston rings.

LITTLE END: Sometimes called the small end, it is the end of the connecting rod which is attached, with a gudgeon pin, to the piston.

LONG REACH: A spark plug with a threaded portion of 19 mm. (¾ in.).

LONG-STROKE: An engine in which the length of the stroke is greater than the diameter of the bore.

LOW TENSION: The low voltage in the primary circuit; the 6 or 12 V in the primary circuit can be compared to the 10–30 kV in the secondary circuit.

MAG DYNO: A component, used most frequently on motorcycles made between 1930 and 1960, in which the magneto and dynamo were combined.

MAGNETO: An abbreviation of magneto-electric machine – a machine generating electrical current by magneto-electric induction.

MAIN BEARING: The major bearings on which the crankshaft rotates.

MAIN JET: The principal opening controlling the flow of fuel when the engine is running at full throttle.

MANIFOLD: The pipe(s) connecting the carburettor(s) and the cylinder(s).

MASTER CYLINDER: The main fluid reservoir in a hydraulic system. It is operated by the rider as he squeezes the lever or depresses the pedal. The force generated works the brakes.

METRE: A unit of length, equal to 39·37 ins.

MIXING CHAMBER: The part of the carburettor where the fuel and air are mixed.

MIXTURE: Another way of saying fuel/air mixture. A rich mixture has too much fuel, and a lean mixture has too much air.

MOPED: From 1 August 1977, in the United Kingdom mopeds are defined as motorcycles with capacities of not more than 50 cc., with a maximum speed of 30 m.p.h.

MULTIGRADE: An oil taking on several viscosity grades at different temperatures.

MULTI-PLATE CLUTCH: A clutch with two or more driving plates and two or more driven plates.

NEEDLE ROLLER: A long narrow roller, usually caged while in use. Frequently used at the small end or the gearbox or clutch.

NEEDLE ROLLER BEARING: A roller bearing in which the lengths of the rollers are considerably greater than their diameters.

NEEDLE VALVE: A cone-shaped rod which rises and falls in a hole in order to seal it, and thus to prevent liquid passing through it. It is most commonly used in carburettors.

NEGATIVE EARTH: When the negative pole of a battery is earthed to the motorcycle. This is now almost standard on motor vehicles.

NIPPLE: (1) A part soldered to the end of a cable to allow it to pull; (2) A valve to allow greasing.

OCTANE: The anti-knock properties of a fuel. The higher the octane rating, the greater the petrol's ability to prevent knocking.

ODOMETER: See TRIPOMETER.

O.H.C.: Overhead camshaft. In engines the camshaft is located above the cylinder, thus operating the valves or rockers directly and removing the need for push-rods. Driven by a chain from the crankshaft.

OHM: A unit of electrical resistance.

O.H.V.: Overhead valve. In these engines the valves are located inside the cylinder head and operated by push-rods, the camshaft being near the crankshaft.

OIL CONTROL RING: Otherwise known as a 'scraper ring'; as the lowest of the rings on the piston it is designed – with slots cut into it – to remove any excess oil from the cylinder walls and prevent it reaching the combustion chamber.

OILED UP: When a spark plug becomes fouled with excess oil and/or carbon. This is usually caused by excess oil or petrol, or by using a plug which is too cold.

OPEN-ENDED SPANNER: A spanner (wrench) with an open end, angled to ease entry into awkward places.

'O' RING: A band of rubber or synthetic material, designed to create a seal between two mating surfaces – usually located in a specific groove.

OVERALL GEAR RATIO: The ratio of the rear wheel's r.p.m. to those of the engine, that is, how many times the engine must turn for the rear wheel to turn, in any gear.

OVER-GEARED: A motorcycle on which the gearing, especially top gear, is too high to achieve top speed. Overgeared machines are slower than others – the engine will not have enough power to travel at the maximum speed for the peak r.p.m.

OVERHEAD CAM: See O.H.C.

OVERHEAD VALVE: See O.H.V.

OVERLAP: The setting of the valves so that the inlet and exhaust valves are open at the same time for a brief period.

PENETRATING OIL: A lubricant thin enough to seep through the rust on the threads of a bolt or screw.

PETROIL: The mixture of petrol and oil

used to power and lubricate two-stroke engines.

PILOT JET: A small hole which controls the flow of petrol in the carburettor when the throttle is closed, that is, at tickover.

PINION: A small gear wheel (cog wheel) whose teeth engage those of a larger gear.

PINKING: Sometimes called 'pinging', a small knocking noise in the engine, usually caused by incorrect ignition, overheating, the wrong plug or fuel of an incorrect octane rating.

PISTON: The component moving up and down the cylinder compressing the mixture. The component that is thrust downwards by the force of the explosion.

PISTON PORTED: A description you can apply to a two-stroke engine in which the piston is used to open and close the ports.

PISTON RING: The cast-iron rings around a piston. The compression ring seals the combustion chamber; the oil control ring controls the oil; and the centre ring performs both functions.

PISTON SKIRTING: The lower portion of the piston. If it is cut away, it is usually described as a 'slipper piston'.

PISTON SLAP: A rattling noise caused by excessive wear between the cylinder and the piston.

PLAY: Slack in a mechanical system. Although it may be due to excess wear, it may also be put there deliberately, in which case it is called clearance.

PLUG: See SPARK PLUG.

PLUG CAP: A connector between the H.T. lead and the spark plug. Suppressors are built in and it is shrouded to give waterproofing.

PLUG LEAD: An insulated cable carrying the high-tension current from the coil to the spark plug (see H.T. LEAD).

POINTS: See CONTACT BREAKERS.

POINTS GAP: The gap between the points when they are opened to their maximum.

PORT: Holes and passages through which the petrol/air mixture is inducted, transferred and exhausted.

POWER BAND: The range of r.p.m.s – engine speeds – in which effective power is produced.

PRE-IGNITION: The ignition of the fuel in the cylinder by a hot spot before the spark occurs.

PROP STAND: The side stand on a solo motorcycle.

P.S.I.: Pounds per square inch; a unit of pressure, particularly of tyres.

PULL-OFF SPRING: The springs that pull the brake shoes away from the brake drum.

PUMP: A device for moving liquids.

PUSH-ROD: The rod used to move a part, such as a valve, a rocker or a clutch pressure plate.

RAKE: The angle between the vertical and the steering-head pivot.

RAM EFFECT: The inertia behind gas which causes it to move along a pipe after the pressures have equalized. This effect helps get more mixture into the combustion chamber.

RATCHET: A set of angular or saw-like teeth on the edge of a bar or rim of a wheel, into which a cog, tooth or the like may catch, for the purpose of preventing reversed motion.

REACH: The length of the threaded portion of a spark plug.

RE-BORE: Machining material out of the cylinder when it is worn or when fitting a larger piston.

RECTIFIER: A device for converting an alternating electric current into a direct or continuous one while only passing electric current in one direction.

REED VALVE: A flap-type valve used to control the flow of mixture into an engine.

REGULATOR: A device to control the current; it increases or reduces the generator's output to suit the state of the battery's charge.

RELAY: A high-powered electrical switch triggered off by a lower-powered switch.

REV COUNTER: An instrument for reading engine speeds.

RICH: When the petrol/air mixture has an excessive proportion of petrol.

RIM: The edge of a wheel, carrying the tyre.

RING SPANNER: A spanner with a circular end which is placed over the head of nuts or bolts. The inside of the ring is serrated.

ROCKER: An arm pivoted either at one end or centrally and mainly used to transmit cam motion to the valves.

ROLLER BEARING: A bearing mechanism in which the rollers are cylindrical and not spherical.

ROTARY VALVE: A revolving disc with a portion removed, to act as a valve in two-stroke engines.

ROTOR: The part of an alternator, magneto or pump, etc., which revolves (rotates).

R.P.M.: Revolutions per minute; the number of times the crankshaft of an engine revolves per minute.

RUNNING ON: A defect in the engine causing it to continue running after being switched off. This is usually the result of a hot spot in the cylinder which continues to ignite the mixture.

RUN-OUT: The distortion on a shaft, wheel or other rotating part; the amount by which it is out of line, or out of true, as is sometimes said.

SCAVENGE: The removal of burnt gas during the exhaust cycle, frequently by allowing a new charge of mixture into the cylinder to sweep it away.

SCRAPER RING: See OIL CONTROL RING.

SEALED BEAM: A light in which the reflector, filament and lens are formed into one sealed unit.

SHAFT DRIVE: The transmission of power from the engine to the rear wheels by means of a shaft and bevel gears, rather than by chain.

SHIM: A thin slip of metal used to fill up a space between parts, to reduce play. Frequently they are used to adjust the valve clearances on D.O.H.C. motorcycle engines.

SHOCK ABSORBER: For a general definition see DAMPER, although shock absorbers are sometimes regarded as the more complete suspension system: that is, both the coil spring and damper together.

SHORT CIRCUIT: An electrical fault where the current flows directly to earth.

SHORT-STROKE: An engine in which the length of the stroke is less than the diameter of the bore.

SIDECAR: An attachment to the side of a motorcycle, supported on one side by the motorcycle and by its own wheel on the other. Usually used to carry passengers or luggage.

SILENCER: A component designed to silence or reduce the sound caused by the engine's operation.

SKIRT: That portion of a piston below the gudgeon pin.

SLAVE CYLINDER: A hydraulic cylinder operated by a master cylinder.

SLEEVE: A metal cylinder used to increase an outside diameter (O.D.) or reduce an inside diameter (I.D.).

SLUDGE: A build-up of substances in the lubrication system. Usually this occurs because of contamination from combustion or a breakdown of the oil.

SMALL END: The bearing between the connecting rod and the piston pin.

SNAIL CAM: Used as a chain adjuster, usually it is a cam with a spiral-shaped profile.

S.O.H.C.: Single overhead cam. One camshaft located over the cylinder operating both the inlet and exhaust valves.

SOLENOID: An electro-magnetic switch used to operate an electric motor.

SPARK PLUG: A device with two electrodes, positioned at a precisely determined distance apart. A spark jumps across the gap between the electrodes, igniting the mixture of petrol and air in the combustion chamber.

SPINDLE: A rod, usually of iron or other metal, used as an axis upon which something revolves, such as the wheel.

SPLINES: Regular serrations around a wheel or shaft. The system of joining which allows both longitudinal and rotary adjustment.

SPLIT PIN: A hairgrip-shaped wire pin. It is pushed through holes in the end of spindles, for example; the ends are splayed open and it acts as a security device by preventing the nut from turning itself loose.

SPOKE: A length of stiff wire holding the wheel rim to the hub.

SPROCKET: A toothed wheel which turns, or is turned by, a chain.

STAR RATING: A guide to the properties of a petrol, particularly its octane rating.

STEERING DAMPER: A damper fixed to the motorcycle frame and the forks to prevent steering wobble.

STEERING HEAD: The tube and bearings which connect the forks to the frame; the bearings in which the forks pivot.

STEERING LOCK: (1) The movement of the handlebars and forks to the fully left or fully right position, sometimes measured in terms of the angle between straight ahead and the fully left or fully right position. (2) Anti-theft device built into the steering head, and operated by a key.

STEERING STEM: The spindle rising from the bottom yokes on the forks to, and holding, the steering-head bearings.

STROBOSCOPE: Usually used to check the ignition timing. It is a lamp wired into the ignition system which flashes each time the spark occurs at the plug.

STROKE: The distance the piston moves from B.D.C. to T.D.C. or vice versa.

SUB-FRAME: A combination of brackets and tubes which forms part of an additional part of a structure, in this case the motorcycle frame.

SUMP: The well at the bottom of an engine for the engine oil to drain into. In a dry sump the oil is pumped back into the oil reserve tank, whereas in a wet-sump system the sump itself is used as the reservoir.

SUPPRESSOR: A device designed to prevent a machine's electrical system interfering with T.V. or radio reception.

SUSPENSION: See SHOCK ABSORBER or DAMPER.

SWARF: Metal shavings produced by the operation of an engine.

SWINGING ARM: Sometimes referred to as swinging fork. A kind of fork carrying the rear wheel, hinged to the frame behind the engine and held by suspension units, or a suspension unit in the case of the mono-shock design.

SWITCH: A mechanism for connecting and disconnecting electrical circuits.

TACHOMETER: See REV COUNTER.

TAIL PIPE: The final section of the exhaust system, synonymous with the silencer and often removable.

TAPERED ROLLER BEARING: A bearing in which the rollers are conical and not cylindrical; usually used in steering heads and swinging arms.

TAPPET: The component between the cam and the valve or push-rod, it is usually a sliding block or cylinder which is supported to take side loads.

T.D.C.: Top dead centre. The top point of the piston's travel.

TELESCOPIC FORKS: A form of front suspension combining two sets of two tubes, one able to slide over the other, containing oil to act as a damper and a spring.

TENSIONER: A mechanism designed to take up slack in a chain.

T-HANDLE SCREWDRIVER: A screwdriver with a handle which is 'T' shaped, allowing greater torque to be applied.

THREE-PHASE: Three separate windings are arranged in an electrical generator so that the voltage in each one rises to its maximum in sequence rather than at the same time.

THROTTLE: To check or stop the flow of a fluid in a tube by means of a valve. In motorcycles, used in the carburettor to control the flow of air and hence the power output of the engine.

THROTTLE CUTAWAY: A wedge-shaped section cut out of the throttle valve or airslide in the carburettor.

THROTTLE STOP: A screw adjuster used to alter the idle speed of the engine by changing the position of the airslide. Any adjustment should be done with the throttle closed.

THRUST BEARING: A bearing designed to resist a load along an axis.

TIMING: The point at which ignition or valve opening takes place in relation to the position of the crankshaft. Correct timing, usually measured in terms of degrees from T.D.C., ensures that the valves and piston are in the correct position when the spark occurs.

TIMING CHAIN OR GEARS: The mechanism designed to drive camshafts.

TIMING LIGHT: A lamp connected across the contact breakers indicating when they are open or closed.

TORQUE: A twisting or rotary force in a piece of mechanism.

TORQUE WRENCH: A type of spanner incorporating an indicator to show what torque is being applied.

TOTAL LOSS: A system of lubrication in which there is no way of recirculating the used oil. All two-stroke engines operate in this way.

TRAILING SHOES: A brake shoe where the point of operation is at the trailing edge.

TRANSFER PORT: The passageway in a two-stroke engine connecting the crankcase to the cylinder.

TRANSISTOR IGNITION: Electronic ignition using solid-state parts.

TRANSMISSION: A mechanism for transmitting motive power from one place to another; this may be done primarily using a chain or shaft.

TREAD: Grooves cut into the rubber of a tyre, to increase grip and channel off water.

TRIPOMETER: An instrument used to measure distance travelled, usually in miles or kilometres.

TWIN-LEADING-SHOE: A drum brake mechanism in which both shoes are leading shoes, and in which the servo effect is increased.

TWO-STROKE: An engine type which requires two strokes to complete one cycle.

VACUUM GAUGE: An instrument designed to measure pressure below atmospheric in a carburettor.

VALVE: A component designed to allow gas to pass in and out of the cylinder of a four-stroke engine; also used in tyres to allow air to pass into the inner-tube.

VALVE BOUNCE: The situation in which a valve opens so rapidly that it rebounds, and can occasionally clip the piston.

VALVE CAP: A safety and dust cap used on tyre valves.

VALVE CORE: The central working component of a tyre valve; usually they are interchangeable.

VALVE LIFT: The distance a valve is lifted from its seat.

VALVE SEAT: The area of the cylinder head against which the valve head is seated.

VALVE SPRING: The spring ensuring that the pressure is maintained to control the valve.

V-ENGINE: An engine with its cylinders set at an angle to each other.

VENTURI: A passage of varying section to change the speed of fluid, and cause a pressure drop; usually used in carburettors.

VERTICAL TWIN: An engine with two parallel cylinders.

VISCOSITY: The thickness of oil.

VISCOSITY INDEX: A scale indicating how thin an oil would become when heated.

VOLT: A unit of electrical pressure.

VOLTAGE REGULATOR: A device designed to regulate the supply of electricity to the battery so that the battery remains fully charged.

WATT: A unit of electrical power.

WEAK: A mixture supplied to an engine with an insufficient proportion of petrol.

WET SUMP: A system of lubrication in which oil is either splashed or pumped out of the sump, into which it falls back.

WHEELBASE: The distance between the front and rear wheel centres.

WIRE WHEEL: A wheel built using spokes.

WORKSHOP MANUAL: A book describing your motorcycle and containing service information.

ZENER DIODE: An electrical device operating similarly to a diode, but one that is also voltage sensitive.

USEFUL ADDRESSES

MOTORCYCLE ASSOCIATIONS AND TRAINING SCHEMES

Amateur Motor Cycle Association, Darlaston Road, Walsall, West Midlands (0922 656552)

Auto-Cycle Union (A.C.U.), Millbuck House, Corporation Street, Rugby, Warks. CV21 2DN (0788 70332)

British Drag Racing and Hot Rod Association, 109 Halstead Road, Mountsarral, Loughborough, Leics.

British Motor Cyclists Federation (B.M.F.), 225 Coventry Road, Ilford, Essex (01 554 4244)

British Speedway Promoters Association, Tower Lodge, 2 Trinity Road, London SW19 (01 543 3243)

F.I.M., 19 Chemin William-Barby, 1292 Chambesey, Geneva, Switzerland (Tel.: 022 58 19 60/58 19 61)

Institute of Motorcycling (I.M.C.), 4 Hammersmith Broadway, London W6

Motor Cycle Association of Great Britain, Starley House, Eaton Road, Coventry (0203 27427)

National Drag Racing Club, 104 Essex Road, Romford, Essex (0708 60336)

National Motorcycle Training Scheme, Federation House, 2309 Coventry Road, Sheldon, Birmingham B26 3PB (021 742 4296) (This scheme is often referred to as the STEP or Star Rider system)

Rider Training Scheme, P.O. Box 2, Uckfield, East Sussex TN22 3ND (082571 2896)

Royal Society for the Prevention of Accidents (RoSPA), Cannon House, The Priory, Birmingham B4 6BS (021 233 2461)

Schools Traffic Education Programme (STEP), 2309 Coventry Road, Sheldon, Birmingham B26 3PB (021 742 4296)

Scottish A.C.U., Kippilaw House, Longridge Road, Whitburn, West Lothian (0501 42663)

Trail Riders Fellowship, 39 Warren Road, Thorne, Doncaster (0405 814388)

Vintage M.C.C., 26 Strigley Road North, nr Poynton, Stockport, Cheshire

F.I.M. NATIONAL MOTORCYCLING ORGANIZATIONS*

*Source: Auto-cycle union handbook

F.I.M.
The Secretariat, 19 Chemin William-Barbey, 1292 Chambesey, Geneva, Switzerland (Tel.: 022 58 19 60/58 19 61)

ALGERIA
Fédération Algérienne de Motocyclisme (F.M.A.), 136 bis, Bd Salah Bouakouir, Alger, Algeria (Tel.: 670 13 35)

ARGENTINA
Federación Argentina de Motociclismo (F.A.M.), Campana 5661, Buenos Aires, Argentina (Tel.: 571 5921)

AUSTRALIA
Auto-Cycle Council of Australia (A.C.C.A.), Savoy Buildings, Elgin Street, Maitland, New South Wales 2302, Australia

AUSTRIA
Österreichischer-Automobil-Motorrad-u. Touring Club, (Öe.A.M.T.C.), 3 Schubertring, 1010 Vienna, Austria (Tel.: 72 99 202/52 14)

BELGIUM
Fédération Motocycliste Belgique (F.M.B.), 550 Chausse de Louvain, Boîte No. 7, 1030 Brussels, Belgium (Tel.: 736 99 12)

BRAZIL
Confederação Brasileira de Motociclismo (C.M.B.), Avenida Sao Joao 1, 151 Conjunto 12, Sao-Paulo, Brazil

BULGARIA
Auto-Moto Club Central de la République Populaire de Bulgarie (M.C.B.), 48 Bd Botev, Sofia, Bulgaria (Tel.: 880261/84101)

CANADA
Canadian Motorcycle Association (C.M.A.), 500 James Street N., Suite 201, Hamilton L8L 1J3, Ontario, Canada

CHILE
Federación Chilena de Motociclismo (F.M.C.), Casilla 9844, Vicuna MacKenna 44, Santiago, Chile

CHINA
Moto-Sport Association of the People's Republic of China (M.S.A.P.R.C.), All China Sports Federation, 9 Tiyukuan Road, Peking, China

COLOMBIA
Federación Colombiana de Motociclismo (F.C.M.), Avenida 26, Nos. 17–46 Bogata, Colombia, Oficina 304, Apartados Aerco 14533Y 19519

CUBA
Federación Cubana de Motociclismo (F.C.M.), Hotel Habana Libre, La Habana, Cuba

CYPRUS
Cyprus Motorcycling Federation (C.M.F.), Agathonas 4, Nicosia, Cyprus

CZECHOSLOVAKIA
Ustredhi Automotoklub C.S.S.R. (U.A.M.K.), 29 Opletalova, 11631 Prague 1, Czechoslovakia (Tel.: 22 35 44/22 35 92)

DENMARK
Danmarks Motor Union (D.M.U.), Roskildevaenge 21, 400 Roskilde d., Damotun, Roskilde, Denmark (Tel.: (02) 36 36 26)

ECUADOR
Guayaquil Moto-Club (G.M.C.), Apartado No. 6780, Guayaquil, Ecuador

FEDERAL REPUBLIC OF GERMANY (WEST GERMANY)
Oberste Motorradsport Kommission (O.M.K.), Baseler Platz 6, 6000 Frankfurt/Main 1 (Tel.: 0611 23-10-15)

FINLAND
Suomen Moottoriliito (S.M.L.), Topeliuksenkau 41a A, 00250 Helsinki, Finland (Tel.: 418 – 611)

FRANCE
Fédération Française de Motocyclisme (F.F.M.), 74 Avenue Parmentier, Paris 11ème, France (Tel.: 700-94-40)

GERMAN DEMOCRATIC REPUBLIC (EAST GERMANY)
Allgemeiner Deutscher Motorsport Verband der D.D.R. (A.D.M.V. der D.D.R.), Charlottenstrasse 60, 108 Berlin, G.D.R. (Tel.: 207 1931)

GREAT BRITAIN
Auto-Cycle Union (A.C.U.), Millbuck House, Corporation Street, Rugby, Warks. CV21 2DN (Tel.: 0788 70332)

GREECE
Automobile et Touring-Club de la Grèce (E.L.P.H.A.), 2–4 Rue Messogion, Athènes 610, Greece (Tel.: 7791 615)

GUATEMALA
Federación Guatemalteca de Automovilismo y Motociclismo (F.G.A.M.), Palacio de los Deportes, Guatemala, Guatemala

HUNGARY
Magyar Auto es Motorsport Szovetseg (M.A.M.S.), Romer Floris U4/a, pfH1, 1277 Budapest, Hungary (Tel.: 158 469/355 921)

IRELAND
Motor Cycle Union of Ireland (M.C.U.I.), 11 Glen Crescent, Jordonstown, Newtownabbey, Northern Ireland

ITALY
Federazione Motociclistica Italiana (F.M.I.), 70 Viale Tiziano, 00100 Rome, Italy (Tel.: 396 4309)

JAPAN
The Motorcycling Federation of Japan (M.F.J.), Taisei Bldg, 9–12 1-Chome, Ginza Chuo-Ku-Tokyo, Japan (Tel.: 561-8566)

KUWAIT
Kuwait Automobile & Touring Club, Airport Road, Klaliyah, P.O. Box 2100, SAFAT, Kuwait

LUXEMBURG
Motor Union du Grand-Duché de Luxembourg (M.U.L.), Boîte postale 2442, Luxemburg, Luxemburg

MEXICO
Federación Mexicana de Motociclismo (F.M.M.), Insurgentes Norte No 80-A, Mexico 4 DF (Tel. 547-50-32/547-42-79)

MONACO
Moto-Club de Monaco (M.C.M.), Quai Albert-le-Côté Nord 44, Monaco (Pte)

MONGOLIA
Central Motor Club of the People's Republic of Mongolia (M.P.R.), Central Post P.O. Box 882, Ulan-Bator, Mongolia

THE NETHERLANDS
Koninklijke Nederlandse Motorrijders Verneniging (K.N.M.V.), Zipendaalseweg 1, Arnhem, The Netherlands (Tel.: 450 841)

NORWAY
Norges Motorsykkelforbund (N.M.F.), Hauger Skolevei 1, 1351 Rud, Norway (Tel.: (02) 13 42 90)

PERU
Inca Motor Club del Peru (I.M.C.), Avenida Nicolas Arriola 290 – Of. 312, Lima 13, Peru

POLAND
Polski Zwaizek Motorway (P.Z.M.), U1, Kazimierzowska 66, 02-518 Warsaw, Poland (Tel. 499 3 61)

PORTUGAL
Federação Portuguesa de Motociclismo (F.P.M.), Rua Arco do Cego 90, 6 Esq Salon, 39 Lisbon, Portugal (Tel.: 7662 16)

RUMANIA
Fédération Romana de Motocyclisme (F.R.M.), Strasse Vasile Conta 16, 70139 Bucharest, Rumania (Tel.: 119787)

SAN MARINO
Federazione Samarinese Motociclistica (F.S.M.), Via Scalette Citta 47031, Republic of San Marino (Tel.: 99 21 01)

SOUTH AFRICA
The Automobile Association of South Africa (A.A.S.A.), A.A. House, 66 Dr Korte Street, Braamfontein, Johannesburg 2001, South Africa (Tel.: (011) 28-1400)

SPAIN
Real Federación Motociclista Española (R.F.M.E.), General Pardinas 71-1, Madrid 6, Spain (Tel.: 262 53 42/262 53 43)

SWEDEN
Sveriges Motofederation (S.V.E.M.O.), Stora Nygatan 20, Postbox 2058, 103 12 Stockholm, Sweden (Tel.: (08) 21 25 82)

SWITZERLAND
Fédération Motocycliste Suisse (F.M.S.), 47 Rue de XXXI Decembre, 1207 Geneva, Switzerland (Tel.: 35 34 40/35 36 80)

URUGUAY
Federación Uruguaya de Motociclismo (F.U.M.), Rue Canelones 978, Montevideo, Uruguay (Tel.: 91 59 02)

U.S.A.
American Motorcyclist Association (A.M.A.), P.O. Box 141, Westerville, Ohio 43081, U.S.A. (Tel.: (614) 891-2425)

U.S.S.R.
The Motorcycling Federation of the Soviet Union (M.F.S.U.), P.O. Box 395, Moscow d-362, U.S.S.R. (Tel.: 491-86-61)

VENEZUELA
Federación Motociclista Venezolana (F.M.V.), Centro Comercial El Rosal, Locai No. 4, Urbanizacion El Rosal, Caracas, Venezuela

YUGOSLAVIA
Auto Moto Savez Jugoslavije (A.M.S.J.), 18 Ruzveltova, Post Fah 66, 11001 Belgrade, Yugoslavia (Tel.: 401 699)

AUTO-CYCLE UNION NATIONAL CLUBS*

*Source: Auto-cycle union handbook

BERMUDA
Bermuda A.C.U., The Secretary, P.O. Box 361, Devonshire 4, Bermuda

EAST AFRICA
Automobile Association of East Africa, A.A. House, Westlands, P.O. Box 40087, Nairobi, Kenya

GIBRALTAR
Gibraltar M.C.C., H. E. Smith, 8 Grand Parade, Gibraltar

GUYANA
Guyana Motor Racing Club, Miss Carole Swayne, Palm Court, 35 Main Street, Georgetown, Guyana

MALAYSIA
Automobile Association of Malaysia, Mrs K. S. Lim, P.O. Box 34, Petaling Jaya, Malaysia

MALTA
Malta A.C.U., C. Muscat, Dar Is-Sewwieg, Rabat, Malta

NEW ZEALAND
New Zealand A.C.U., M. M. Cleverley, P.O. Box 968, Hamilton, New Zealand (Tel.: 83 464)

SCOTLAND
Scottish A.C.U., Arnott Moffat, Kippilaw House, Longridge Road, Whitburn, West Lothian (Tel.: 0501 42663)

SINGAPORE
Automobile Association of Singapore, The Secretary General, 336 River Valley Road, Killaney Road, P.O. Box 85, Singapore

SRI LANKA
Sri Lanka Motor Cycle Club, R. Samaraweera, Ranjit Automotives Ltd, 129 Jayantha Weerasekera Mawatha, Colombo 10, Sri Lanka

ZAMBIA
Zambia Motor Sports Association, Mrs S. M. Cooke, P.O. Box 515, Kitwe, Zambia

ZIMBABWE
Zimbabwe Motor Sports Federation, Mr H. A. J. Harris, Competitions Manager, P.O. Box 1350, Gwelo, Zimbabwe

AUTO-CYCLE UNION NON-TERRITORIAL CLUBS*

*Source: Auto-cycle union handbook

Army Motor Cycling Association, Capt. Allen, Depot of Training, Regiment R.C.T., Buller Barracks, Aldershot, Hants.

Bantam Racing Club, Mrs J. Andrews, 6 Kipton Close, Rothwell, Northants. NN14 2DR

British Drag Racing Association, Mrs A. Pallant, 105 Parkfield Crescent, South Ruislip, Middx (Tel.: 01 864 6232)

British Formula Racing Club, J. Milligan, Cronk y Voddy, Rectory Road, Coltishall, Norwich (Tel.: 0603 737370)

British Motor Cycle Racing Club, Miss Barbara Bailey, Bemsee House, 30 Dartnell Road, Croydon (Tel.: 01 654 1684)

Civil Service Motoring Association Ltd, C. V. Devenish, Britannia House, 95 Queens Road, Brighton BN1 3WY (Tel.: 0273 21921)

Classic Racing Motorcycle Club, A. Cathcart, P.O. Box 147, London W5 1AR

Federation of British Police Motor Clubs, B. Rigby, 40 Oakhampton Crescent, Sale, Cheshire (Tel.: 061 969 7640)

G.R.A.S.A., M. Blankart, 12 Tottenham Road, London N1

International Motorcyclists Tour Club (Rally Section), T. Wilkinson, 46 Mowson Crescent, Worral, Sheffield S30 3AG

Morgan Three Wheeler Club, Mr L. Weeks, 43 Greenhill Road, Moseley, Birmingham 13 9SS

Motor Cycling Club Ltd, H. W. Tucker-Peake Cars, 100 High Street, Stevenage, Herts. (Tel.: 0438 54361)

Motorcycling Club of Wales, Fitzroy Allen, 2 Springfield Terrace, Pentyfla, Port Talbot, W. Glam. SA12 8HN (Tel.: 0639 6129)

National Drag Racing Club, Mr S. Copeland, 241 Humberstone Lane, Leics. LE4 7JR (Tel.: 0533 695679)

National Sprint Association, P. Williams, 51 Hale Street, Warrington, Cheshire WA2 7PH

New Era M.C.C., Mrs S. Brockwell, 'Stepheila', Billing Road, Lower End, Brafield on the Green, Northampton (Tel.: 0604 891592)

Pennine Drag Racing Club, J. Revill, 48 Broadacres, Durkar, Wakefield WF4 3BE (Tel.: 0924 252942)

Racing 50 M.C.C., Jean Maslin, 172 Tower Road, Ware, Herts (Tel.: 0920 5559)

R.A.F. Motor Sports Association, Sqn Ldr Underwood, MoD, M.O.V. 6A (RAF), Room 9228, Main Building, Whitehall, London SW1 2HB (Tel.: 01 218 7053)

The 50cc/80cc Road Racing Club, J. Rees, 24 Glevering Street, Llanelli, Dyfed

Triumph Owners M.C.C., Mrs E. Page, 101 Great Knightly, Basildon, Essex

Vincent H.R.D. Owners Club, W. Hancock, 39 Dawson Avenue, Beech Hill, Wigan, Lancs.

Vintage M.C.C., K. Hallworth, 26 Shigley Road North, nr Poynton, Stockport, Cheshire SK12 1TE

Welsh Trail Riders Association, P. R. J. Herbert, 20 Glasllwch View, Glasllwch Lane, Newport, Gwent (Tel.: Newport 894573)

MOTORCYCLE MANUFACTURERS AND CONCESSIONAIRES

BENELLI (Italy)

Benelli Concessionaires (G.B.) Ltd, 361–365 Chiswick High Road, London W4 4HS

BMW(G.B.) LTD (W. Germany)

B.M.W. (G.B.) Ltd, 21 Ellesfield Avenue, Bracknell, Berks. (Tel.: 0344 26565)

BULTACO (Spain)

Comerfords Ltd, Portsmouth Road, Thames Ditton, Surrey KT7 OXQ

CAGIVA (Italy)

Mick Walker (Cagiva) Ltd, 236 Norwich Road, Wisbech, Cambs.

C.Z. (Czechoslovakia)

Jawa–CZ, Skoda (Great Britain) Ltd, Bergen Way, North Lynn Industrial Estate, Kings Lynn, Norfolk PE30 2JH

DUCATI (Italy)

See CAGIVA.

FANTIC (Italy)

Barron Eurotrade Ltd, Fantic House, High Street, Hornchurch RM11 1TP

HARLEY-DAVIDSON (U.S.A.)

Harley–Davidson Concessionaires Ltd, 53–61 Park Street, Luton, Beds.

HONDA (U.K.) (Japan)

Honda (U.K.), Power Road, Chiswick, London (Tel.: 01 995 9381)

The Honda Information Centre, 61 Berners Street, London W1P 3AE (Tel.: 01 580 4853)

KAWASAKI MOTORS

Kawasaki Motors (U.K.) Ltd, 748 Deal Avenue, Trading Estate, Slough, Berks. (Tel.: 0753 38255)

Kawasaki Information Service, 28a High Street, Leighton Buzzard, Beds. LU7 7AE (Tel.: 0525 376422)

K.T.M. (Austria)

K.T.M. Motorcycles Ltd, Oxford House, Portsmouth Road, Thames Ditton, Surrey KT7 OXQ

LAVERDA (Italy)

Slater Bros., Collington, nr Bromyard, Herts.

MITSUI MACHINERY

Mitsui Machinery, Sales (U.K.) Ltd (Yamaha), Oakcroft Road, Chessington, Surrey (Tel.: 01 397 5111)

MONTESA (Spain)

Tim Sandiford (Imports) Ltd, 30/38 Walmersley Road, Bury, Lancs. BL9 6DP

MOTO GUZZI (Italy)

Moto Guzzi U.K. Ltd, 53–61 Park Street, Luton Beds.

NEVAL (U.S.S.R.)

Neval Motorcycles, Chapel Works, Barrow Road, New Holland, S. Humberside

SUZUKI (Japan)

Suzuki G.B., Heron Trading, 46 Gatwick Road, Crawley, W. Sussex (Tel.: 0293 51800)

YOUR BIKE'S SPECIFICATIONS

MAKE———————————————————— MODEL—————

PLUG GAP ————————————————— MM. (————INS.)

POINTS GAP ———————————————— MM. (————INS.)

TYRE PRESSURES: FRONT ——————————————— P.S.I.

REAR ——————————————— P.S.I.

OIL CAPACITIES: ENGINE/GEARBOX ———————— LITRES

(ON TWO-STROKES) TWO-STROKE OIL ———————— LITRES

CHAIN OIL TANK (if fitted)————————————— LITRES

FINAL-DRIVE OIL (shaft drive only)————————— C.C.

FRONT-FORK LEGS ——————————————— C.C.

LUBRICANT TYPES: ENGINE/GEARBOX OIL ————————

FRONT-FORK OIL ————————

GREASE POINTS————————————

HYDRAULIC BRAKES ————————

LUBRICANT POINTS————————

CHAIN OIL ————————————

COOLANT CAPACITIES: OVERALL ————————— LITRES

RESERVE (if fitted) ———————— LITRES

VALVE CLEARANCES: INLET ——————— INS.(————MM.)

EXHAUST ——————— INS.(————MM.)

FUSES: ————————————————————

BULB SIZES: INDICATOR————————————————

HEADLAMP————————————

TAILLAMP ————————————

STOPLAMP————————————

YOUR BIKE'S SPECIFICATIONS

MAKE——————————————————————— MODEL—————————

PLUG GAP ————————————————————— MM. (—————INS.)

POINTS GAP ———————————————————— MM. (—————INS.)

TYRE PRESSURES: FRONT ———————————————————— P.S.I.

REAR ————————————————————— P.S.I.

OIL CAPACITIES: ENGINE/GEARBOX ————————————— LITRES

(ON TWO-STROKES) TWO-STROKE OIL ————————— LITRES

CHAIN OIL TANK (if fitted)————————————————————— LITRES

FINAL-DRIVE OIL (shaft drive only)—————————————— C.C.

FRONT-FORK LEGS ——————————————————— C.C.

LUBRICANT TYPES: ENGINE/GEARBOX OIL ———————————

FRONT-FORK OIL ————————————

GREASE POINTS————————————————

HYDRAULIC BRAKES —————————————

LUBRICANT POINTS ————————————

CHAIN OIL ————————————————

COOLANT CAPACITIES: OVERALL ———————————— LITRES

RESERVE (if fitted) ————————— LITRES

VALVE CLEARANCES: INLET ————————— INS.(————MM.)

EXHAUST ————————— INS.(————MM.)

FUSES: ——————————————————————————

BULB SIZES: INDICATOR————————————————————

HEADLAMP————————————————————

TAILLAMP ————————————————————

STOPLAMP————————————————————

YOUR BIKE'S SPECIFICATIONS

MAKE——————————————————————— MODEL—————————

PLUG GAP ——————————————————— MM. (————————INS.)

POINTS GAP ————————————————— MM. (————————INS.)

TYRE PRESSURES: FRONT ———————————————————— P.S.I.

REAR ———————————————————————— P.S.I.

OIL CAPACITIES: ENGINE/GEARBOX ————————————— LITRES

(ON TWO-STROKES) TWO-STROKE OIL ——————— LITRES

CHAIN OIL TANK (if fitted)————————————————————— LITRES

FINAL-DRIVE OIL (shaft drive only)————————————————— C.C.

FRONT-FORK LEGS ——————————————————————— C.C.

LUBRICANT TYPES: ENGINE/GEARBOX OIL ——————————

FRONT-FORK OIL ——————————————

GREASE POINTS————————————————

HYDRAULIC BRAKES ————————————

LUBRICANT POINTS————————————

CHAIN OIL ————————————————————

COOLANT CAPACITIES: OVERALL ——————————————— LITRES

RESERVE (if fitted) ———————————— LITRES

VALVE CLEARANCES: INLET ————————————— INS.(————MM.)

EXHAUST ———————————— INS.(————MM.)

FUSES: ——————————————————————————————

BULB SIZES: INDICATOR———————————————————————

HEADLAMP————————————————————

TAILLAMP —————————————————————

STOPLAMP——————————————————————

YOUR BIKE'S SPECIFICATIONS

MAKE——————————————————— MODEL—————

PLUG GAP ————————————————— MM. (————INS.)

POINTS GAP ———————————————— MM. (————INS.)

TYRE PRESSURES: FRONT ——————————————— P.S.I.

REAR ———————————————— P.S.I.

OIL CAPACITIES: ENGINE/GEARBOX ———————— LITRES

(ON TWO-STROKES) TWO-STROKE OIL ———— LITRES

CHAIN OIL TANK (if fitted)—————————————— LITRES

FINAL-DRIVE OIL (shaft drive only) ————————— C.C.

FRONT-FORK LEGS ——————————————— C.C.

LUBRICANT TYPES: ENGINE/GEARBOX OIL —————————

FRONT-FORK OIL —————————————

GREASE POINTS—————————————

HYDRAULIC BRAKES ————————————

LUBRICANT POINTS—————————————

CHAIN OIL ————————————————

COOLANT CAPACITIES: OVERALL ————————— LITRES

RESERVE (if fitted) ———————— LITRES

VALVE CLEARANCES: INLET ——————————— INS.(————MM.)

EXHAUST ————————— INS.(————MM.)

FUSES: ————————————————————

BULB SIZES: INDICATOR—————————————

HEADLAMP—————————————

TAILLAMP ——————————————

STOPLAMP ——————————————

INDEX

Air filter:
  Condition, 66, 178
  Foam filters, 67
  Metal and cloth filters,
    67
  Paper filters, 67
  Replacing paper filters,
    83
Air forks:
  Air pressure, 52
Air intake:
  Restricted, 107, 148,
    162, 169, 172
Auto-lube pump:
  Air locks, 231
  Incorrectly adjusted, 175
Auto-lube tank:
  Empty, 175

Battery:
  Casing damaged, 227
  Charging system, 214
  Condition, 38, 120, 199
  Defective, 124, 225
  Electrical charge, 38,
    214, 225, 227
  Insufficient charge,
    122–4
  Terminals, 38, 124
Bottom dead centre, 12
Brake fluid:
  Changing, 78–9
Brake line:
  Hydraulic, 52
Brakes:
  Adjustment
    disc, 49
    drum, 50, 77
    front, 50
    twin-leading shoes, 51
  Binding, 174
  Bleeding, 233
  Excessive lever/pedal
    travel, 231
  Fluid, 78
  Grabbing, 232
  Lights, 207
  Loss of stopping power,
    233

Pad/shoe wear, 48, 49
  Pedal position, 78
  Squeal, 232
  Sticking, 232
Bulbs: 204
  Air leaks, 206
  Broken filament, 204
  Cheap bulbs, 234
  Defective, 216
  Earth, 234
  Filament unbroken, 207
  Loose, 213
  Old age, 204
  Overheating, 206
  Using wrong one, 207
Bump-starting, 234

Camshaft chain
    adjustment, 67
Carburettor:
  Cleaning, 72
  Dirt or water inside,
    104–7, 153, 161, 251
  Float level too high, 171
  Flooding, 171
  Mixture screw, 156
  Petrol leakage, 251
  Pilot jet, 156
  Security, 250
  Slide needle defective,
    153
  Slide needle worn, 164
  Synchronization, 74–5
  Top loose, 165
  Tuning, 72–4, 104, 173
Carburettor manifold:
  Loose or cracked, 106,
    154, 164, 166, 178
Chain: see Final-drive
    chain
Charging system:
  Defective, 225
Checks:
  Daily, 25, 27–30
  Monthly, 26, 41–52
  Off-road riding, 27, 85–6
  Six-monthly, 26, 68–77
  Three-monthly, 26,
    52–68

Two-yearly, 27, 84–5
  Weekly, 26, 30–41
  Yearly, 27, 77–84
Choke:
  Position and operation,
    103–4, 155, 171
Circuit test lamp, 235
Circuit tester, 201
Cleaning your motorcycle,
    235
Clutch:
  Adjustment, 42, 194
  Broken lever, 237
  Cable is dry, 192, 195
  Drum/plate drive tangs
    worn, 193
  Friction plates worn, 194
  Lever/cable adjustment,
    189, 196
  Operation stiff, 196
  Push-rod bent, 196
  Slip, 194
  Spring tension, 195
Coil: see Ignition coil
Combustion:
  Abnormal, 251–2
  Normal, 11, 251
Combustion stroke, 16
Compression:
  Gauge, 132
  Instrument checks, 132
  Lack of, 132
  Manual checks, 132
  Ratio, 14
Compression stroke, 15,
    18
Condenser defective, 117
Contact breakers:
  Condition, 60–61
  Faulty, 113–16
  Gap, 61–2, 150, 157,
    252
  Mechanism lubrication,
    62
Control cable:
  Condition and
    lubrication, 42, 196
Cooling fins:
  Blocked, 181

Crankcase breather tubes, 68
Crankcase joints leaking, 40, 140, 166, 178
Cut-out switch position, 100
C.V. carburettor:
 Cracked or split diaphragm, 154
Cyclinder bore:
 Worn, 168, 174
Cylinder configurations, 11, 20
Cylinder head gasket:
 Blown, 133

Decarbonize: 63
 Cylinder, 65–6
 Exhaust system, 63–5
Decompressor fouled or poorly adjusted, 135
Disc brakes, 77
Drum-brakes, 77
Dust cap, 37

Earth:
 Poor, 219, 221
Electrical continuity, 200
Electrical system:
 Basic components, 199–201
Electrical wires:
 Broken, 128
Electrolyte:
 Boiling, 227
 Level, 38
Engine:
 Differences, 11–20
 Differing characteristics, 21
 Differing sounds, 21
 Improve efficiency, 252
 Mounting bolts, 68
 Seizure, 252–5
Engine-mounting bolts:
 Loose, 165
Exhaust baffle:
 Blocked, 162
 Removal, 244
Exhaust fumes:
 Four-strokes, 255
 Two-strokes, 256
Exhaust port blocked, 154
Exhaust stroke, 16

Exhaust system:
 Blocked, 149
 External condition, 63, 158
 Security, 63

Final-drive chain:
 Adjustment, 30
 Cleaning, 54
 Condition and tension, 30, 35, 54
 Links, 235
 Lubrication, 34, 57
 Off rear sprockets, 194
 Old chains, 235
 Removal, 54
 Replacing, 58
 Snapped, 193
 Snatching, 191
 Too tight, 165, 174
 Wear, 30, 54–7
Flasher unit:
 Defective, 219, 222
Footrest security, 52
Forks:
 Bottoming out, 237
Four-strokes:
 Maintenance, 22
Frame condition, 76
Front brake:
 Adjustment, 48
Front-fork oil:
 Changing, 82
Fuel:
 Cap vent, 103
 Contaminated, 163
 Filter, 71, 102
 Insufficient in tank, 101
 Lines, 71, 102
 Stale, 107
 System, 71
 Tank, 71
 Tap, 71, 101, 257
Fuel/oil ratio incorrect, 136
Funnels, 267
Fuses and fuse box: 83
 Blown, 125, 209, 211, 220
 Continually blowing, 223

Gear lever:
 Bent, 190
 Changing difficulties, 237

Lost lever, 237
 Return spring, 190
Gearbox oil:
 Insufficient, 189
 Wrong grade, 189
Generator, 199
Generator rotor, 238
Glass fibre: 238
 Repairing holes, 238
 Repairing splits or cracks, 238
 Surface damage, 238

Handlebar controls, 27
Handlebar grips:
 Loose, 151, 239
 Refitting, 239
 Removal, 238
Handlebar movement, 27
Head-gaskets:
 Copper, 237
Headlamp, 29
Horn: 29, 172
 Faulty, 218
 Incorrectly adjusted, 218
 Push-button defective, 217
H.T. coil: see Ignition coil

Ignition:
 A.C. flywheel/magneto system, 121
 D.C. coil/generator system, 120
 Transistorized, 258
Ignition coil:
 Defective, 116, 119
Ignition switch:
 Defective, 130
 Position, 100
Ignition system:
 Breaks in cables and wires, 128
 Damp inside, 125–6
 Wiring defects, 160
Ignition timing: 62
 Advanced, 150
 Incorrect, 119, 150
 Retarded, 150, 179
 Static, 63
 Strobe, 62
Indicators: 30
 Four lamps lighting but not flashing, 221

Four lamps not lighting, 219
One lamp not lighting, 218
Switch defective, 219, 221
Two lamps on one side not lighting, 219
Inlet stroke, 14
Instability, 258
Insulation, 240

Jump-starting, 240

Kickstart:
Lever and splines loose or worn, 197
Lever bent, 198
Ratchet assembly worn, 197
Return spring, 197
Slip, 197

Lean mixture, 177
Lights:
Additional, 234
Excessive, 226
Failure, 215
Flicker, 212
Improvements, 216
Servicing, 29
Liquid-cooling system:
Blocked, 179
Changing coolant, 84
Draining, 84
Flushing, 84
Servicing, 76
Top up, 39, 179
Underheating, 176
Loose or fractured connectors, 128
Lubrication:
Four-stroke, 16
Two-stroke, 21

Main jet:
Blocked by water or dirt, 153
Incorrect, 177
Loose, 172
Maintenance:
Do it cool, 244
Why do it, 22
Miles per gallon:

Measuring, 28
Misfires, 182–9

Noises, 261
Nuts, bolts and screws, 241–4

Off-road riding:
Tips, 267–9
Ohmmeter, 201
Oil:
Additives, 241
Changes, 52
Grades of, 240
In four-strokes, 39
In two-strokes, 39
Its purpose, 240
Leaks, 170
Levels, 39, 136, 167, 176, 180
Mobile supply, 241
Quantity used, 174
Using the incorrect type, 139, 240
Warning light, 227
Oil filter:
Change, 53, 69
Clean, 52
Oil lines:
Cracked, broken or blocked, 138, 142, 175
Oil pump:
Adjustment, 58, 170
Cable broken, 137
Failure, 140, 142
Setting incorrect, 138
Strainer, 84, 142
Overheating, 176
Owner's handbook, 24

Petroil:
Incorrect proportions, 137, 170
Petrol:
Grade, 28
Leaks, 173
Tips on saving, 263
Pilot jet:
Blocked, 156
Loose, 172
Piston:
Damaged, 133
Rings, 133

Piston rings:
Seized or broken, 252
Plastic parts:
Removing scuffs, 244
Points: *see* Contact breakers
Ports:
Exhaust, 18
Inlet, 18, 20
Transfer, 18
Power stroke, 18, 20
Problem-solving: 87–8
When to start checking, 88–9

Rearlamp, 29
Rearview mirror, 27
Rectifier: 199
Defective, 225

Screw tappet adjustment, 70
Seat, 41
Seat covers, 244
Security locks, 27
Selector forks:
Bent, 190, 192
Service intervals, 23
Service manual, 24
Shaft drive:
Lubrication, 83
Oil change, 84
Oil level, 83
Regreasing, 84
Shim tappet adjustment, 71
Short circuit: 127, 223
Tracking down, 224
Sidecar:
And the law, 269
Driving, 269
Maintenance, 269
Slide needle:
Defective, 15
Worn, 164
Spark plug:
Carbon-fouled tip, 144
Cleaning, 47
Cold, 265
Condition, 44, 107–9
Defective, 110
Dimensions, 265
Heat gauges, 264
Hot, 265

Spark plug—*contd*.
  Loose, 159
  Lubrication, 267
  Operating conditions, 264
  Removing, 44
  Replacing, 48
  Setting the gap, 47, 107–9
  Shorting out, 118
  Test for a spark, 109–10
  Using incorrect grade, 177
  Wet or otherwise fouled, 152
Spark plug cap defective, 112
Spark plug condition:
  Burned electrodes, 48
  Carbon-fouled, 46
  Lead-fouled, 46
  Melted electrodes, 46
  Normal, 44
  Oil-fouled, 45
  Whiskering, 163
  Worn out, 46
Spark too weak, 117
Speedometer, 27
Split pins:
  Replacement, 245
Spoke tension, 37
Sprockets:
  Wear, 30
Stale fuel, 107
Stands:
  Centre and side, 41
Starter motor:
  Defective, 131
  Sluggish, 227
  Worn brushes, 228
Starting:
  Electric, 122
  Kick, 122

Static ignition timing, 62
Steering lock, 52
Steering-head bearings: 79
  Adjustment, 79–80
Stoplamp, 30
Storing motorcycles, 267
Strobe timing, 62
Stroke, 12
Suppressors:
  Metal shields, 267
Suspension:
  Rear units, 75
Swinging-arm movement, 76
Switches:
  Dirty, corroded or damp, 209
  Incorrectly adjusted, 210

Tappets:
  Screw-type, 70
  Shim-type, 71
Test lamp, 200
Thermostat defective, 176
Throttle cable:
  Adjustment, 41
  Broken, 151, 248
  Replacement, 245
Throttle stop screw:
  Adjustment, 165
Tools: 24, 270
  For day to day riding, 270
  For home, 270
  For long distance trips, 270
  Tips, 271
Top dead centre, 12
Twin-leading brake shoes, 51
Tyres:
  Condition, 37

How to get more miles, 250
  Pressure, 35
  Refitting, 246
  Removal, 245
  Repairing punctures, 249
  Tubeless, 248

Underheating, 176

Valve guide oil seal:
  Worn, 168
Valve mechanism:
  Worn, 174
Valves:
  Adjustment, 20
  Clearances, 157
  Exhaust, 14, 16
  Inlet, 14
  Operation, 16
  Overlap, 16
  Sliding, 18
  Sticking, 134
Vibrations:
  Excessive, 205
Visors:
  Misty, 271
  Scratched, 271
Voltage regulator, 200
Voltage surge, 207
Voltmeter, 200

Washers, 250
What to wear, 272
Wheels:
  Alignment, 34
  Balance, 81–2
  Bearings worn, 80
  Rims, 249
  Spindle condition, 80
Workshop manuals, 24